P9-DXI-195

This is the last page.

In keeping with the original Japanese comic format, this book reads from right to left—so action, sound effects, and word balloons are completely reversed. This preserves the orientation of the original artwork—plus, it's fun! Check out the diagram shown here to get the hang of things, and then turn to the other side of the book to get started!

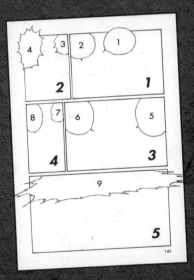

library wars

Volume 1
Shojo Beat Edition

Story & Art by **Kiiro Yumi**
Original Concept by **Hiro Arikawa**

ENGLISH TRANSLATION & ADAPTATION Kinami Watabe
TOUCH-UP ART & LETTERING Sean McCoy
DESIGN Courtney Utt
EDITOR Pancha Diaz

Toshokan Sensou LOVE&WAR by Kiiro Yumi and Hiro Arikawa
© Kiiro Yumi 2008
© 2008 Hiro Arikawa
Licensed by KADOKAWA CORPORATION ASCII MEDIA WORKS
All rights reserved.
First published in Japan in 2008 by HAKUSENSHA, Inc., Tokyo.
English language translation rights arranged with HAKUSENSHA,
Inc., Tokyo.

Printed in the U.S.A.

Published by VIZ Media, LLC
P.O. Box 77010
San Francisco, CA 94107

10 9 8 7
First printing, June 2010
Seventh printing, July 2018

www.shojobeat.com   www.viz.com

library wars

Love & War

1

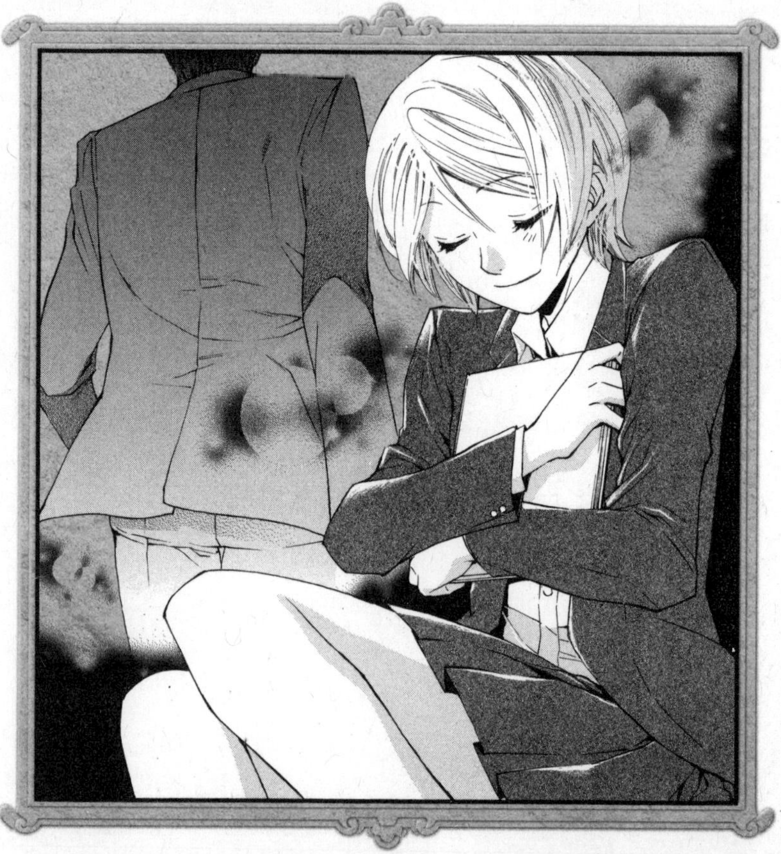

STORY & ART BY Kiiro Yumi ORIGINAL CONCEPT BY Hiro Arikawa

library wars

Love & War

Contents

The Library Freedom Act

Libraries have the freedom to acquire their collections.

Libraries have the freedom to circulate
materials in their collections.

Libraries guarantee the privacy of their patrons.

Libraries oppose any type of censorship.

When libraries are imperiled,
librarians will join together
to secure their freedom.

library wars

Love & War

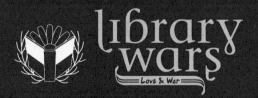

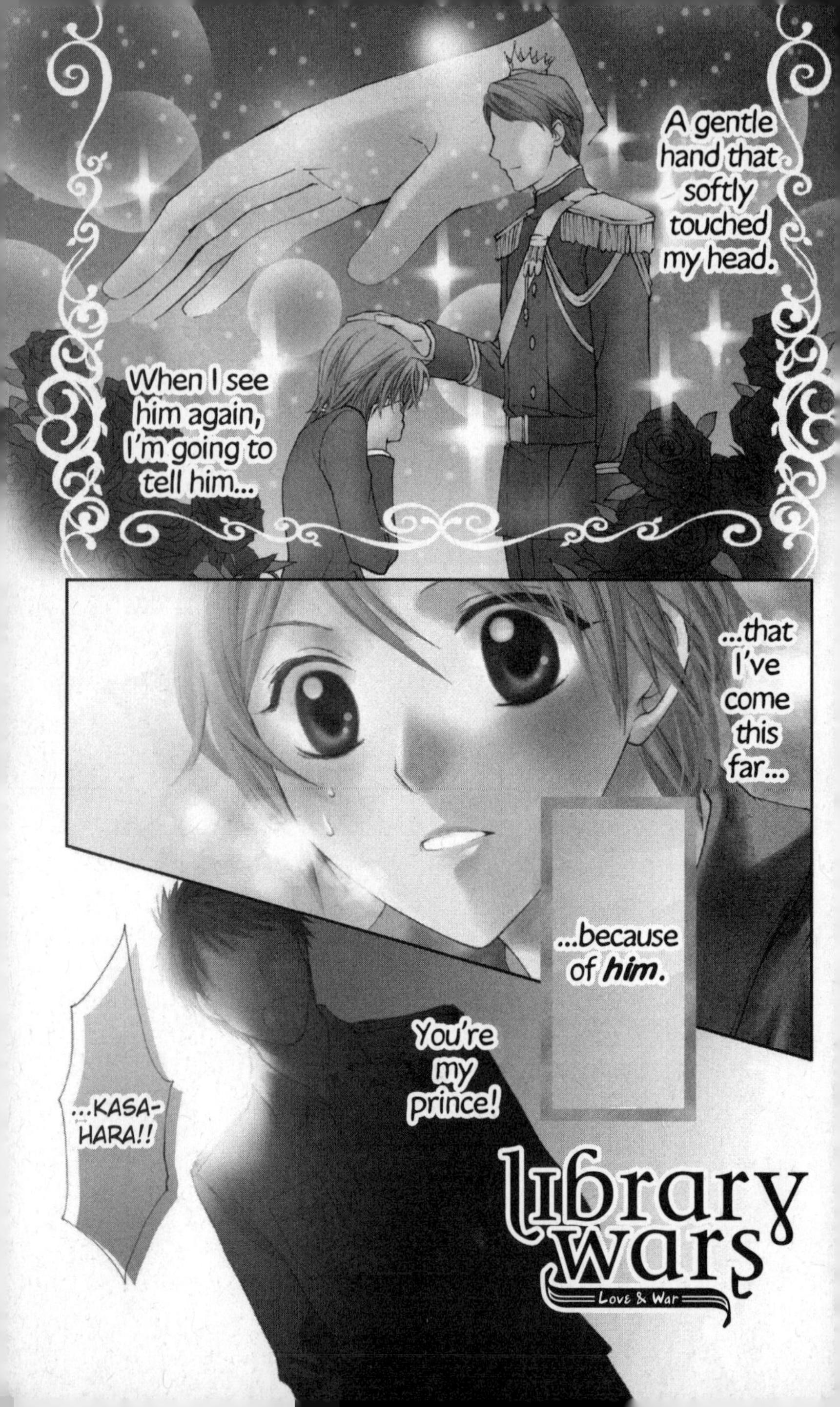
A gentle hand that softly touched my head.
When I see him again, I'm going to tell him...
...that I've come this far...
...because of *him*.
You're my prince!
...KASA-HARA!!
library wars
Love & War

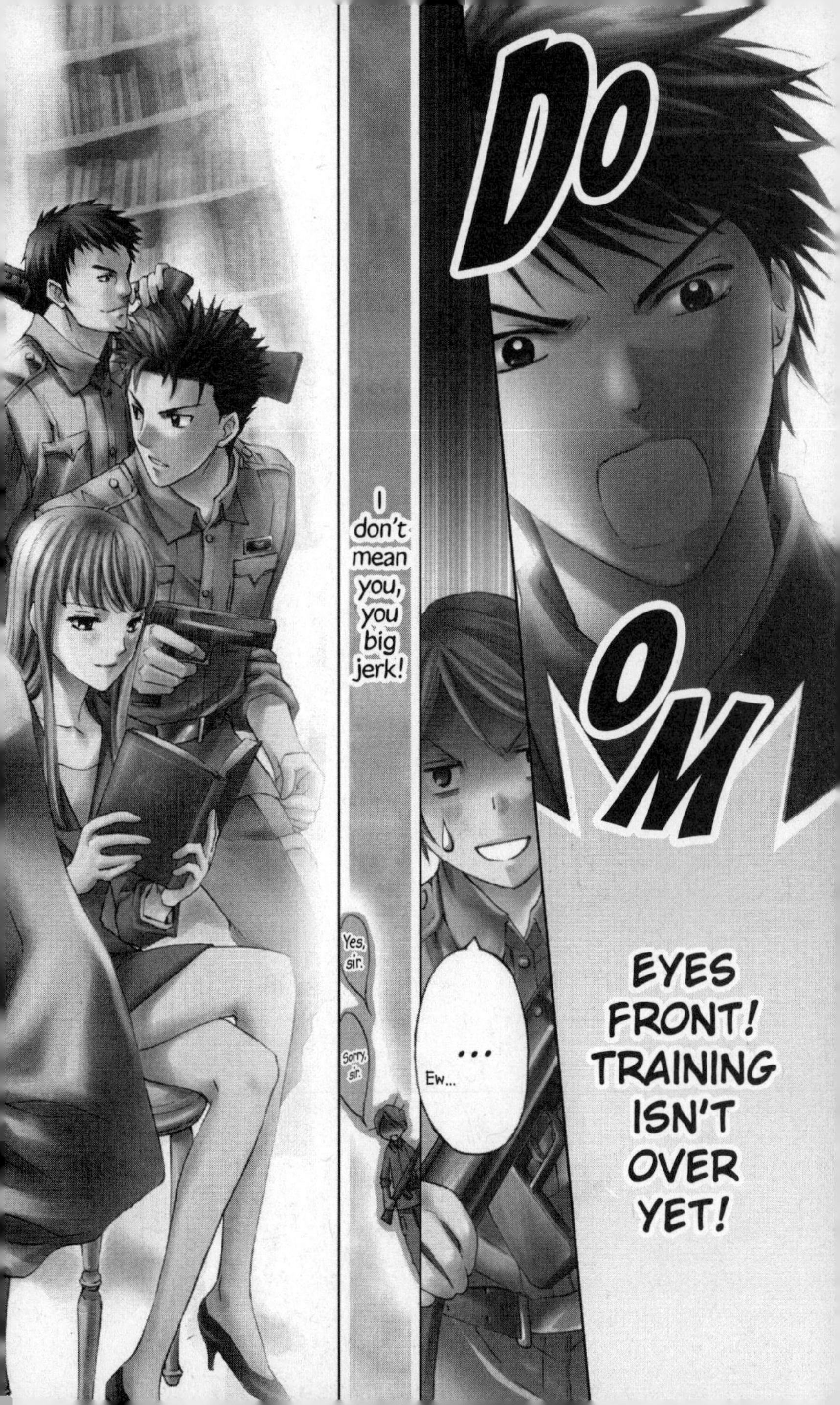
DOOM
EYES FRONT! TRAINING ISN'T OVER YET!
...
Ew...
I don't mean you, you big jerk!
Yes, sir.
Sorry, sir.

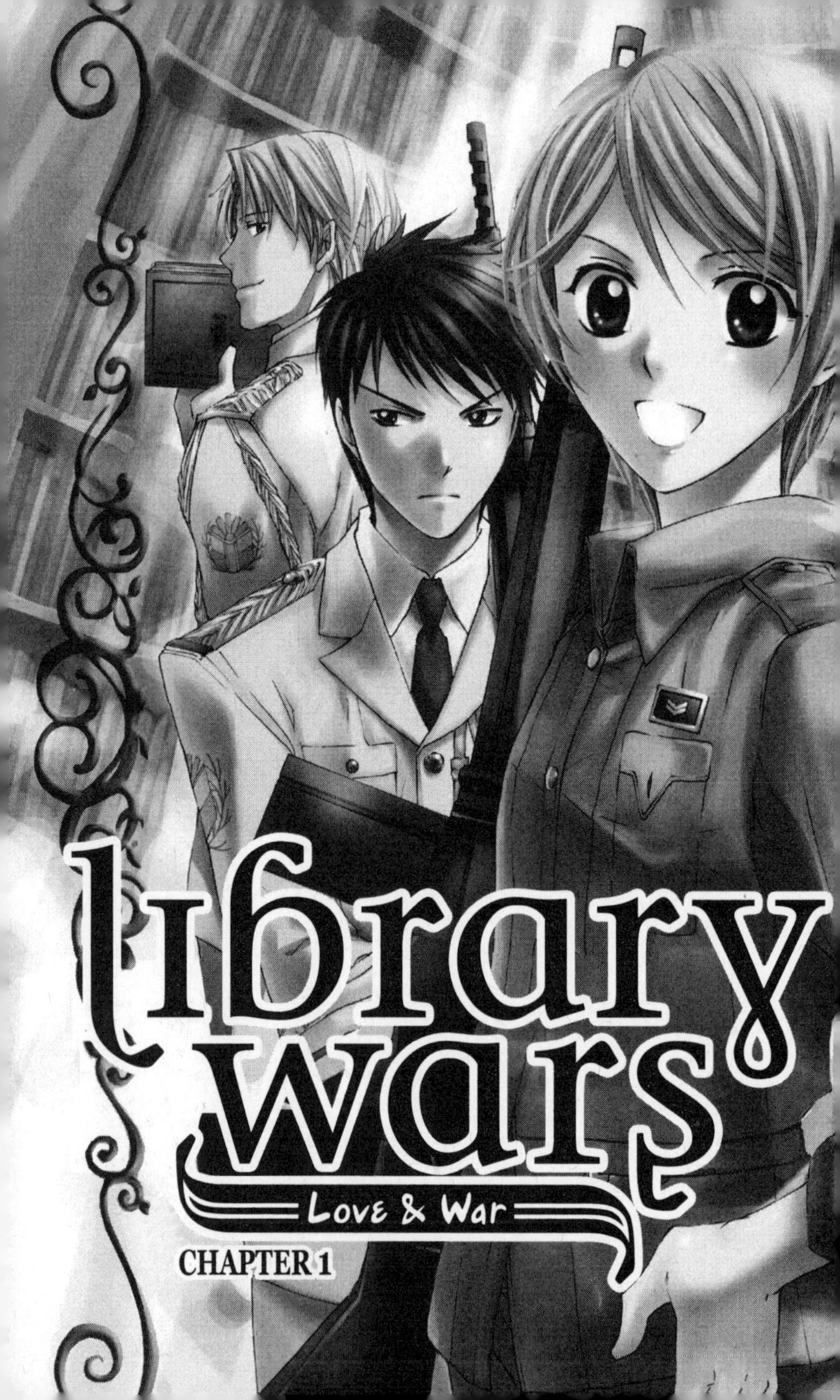
library wars
Love & War
CHAPTER 1

Library Wars LOVE&WAR Vol.1

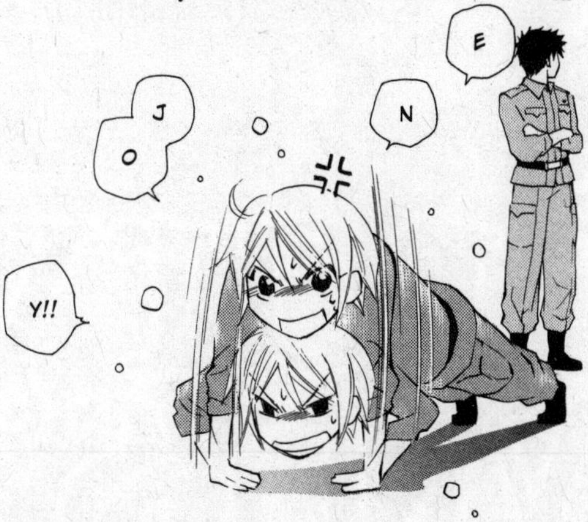

E
N
J
O
Y!!

Hope you enjoy the story!

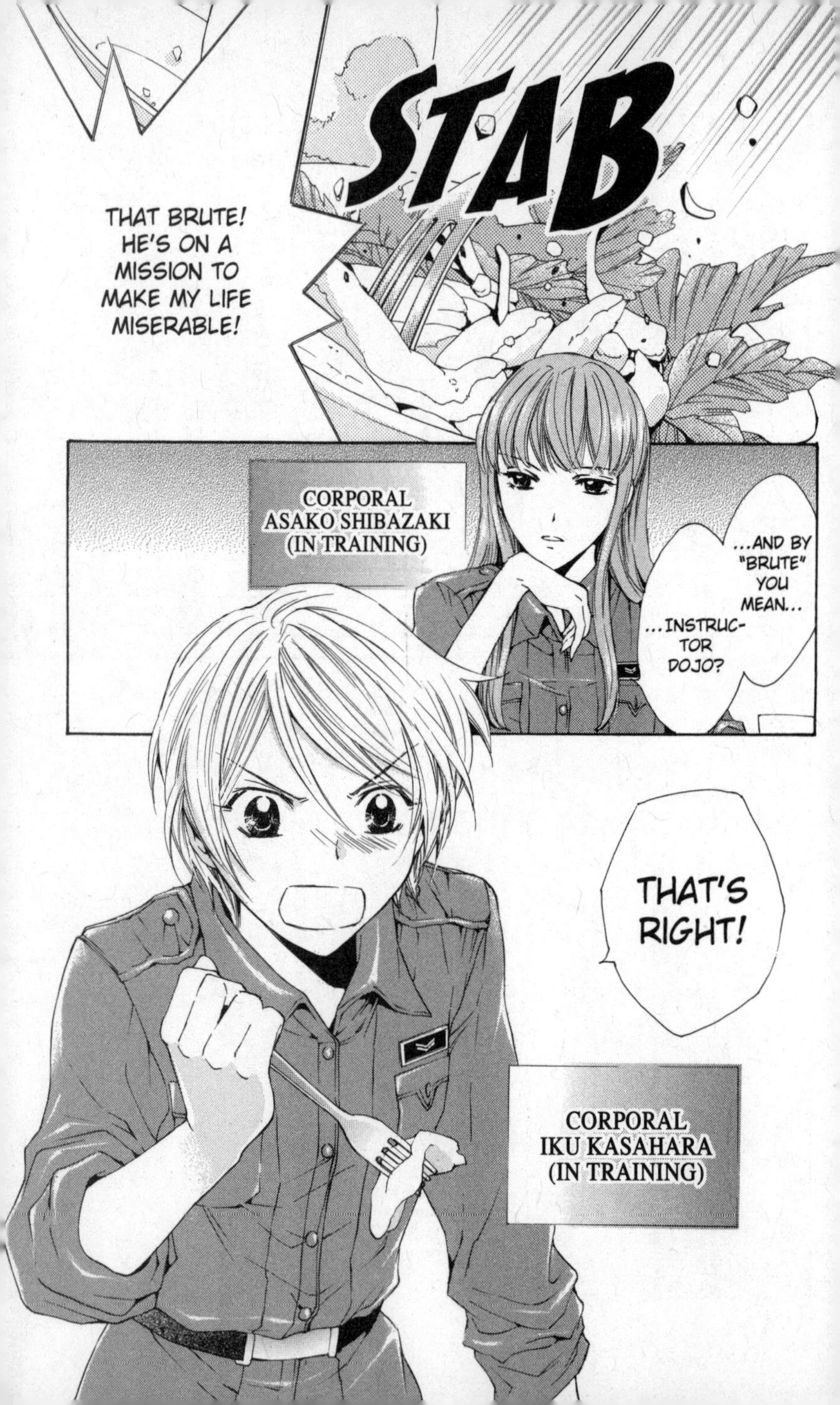
STAB
THAT BRUTE! HE'S ON A MISSION TO MAKE MY LIFE MISERABLE!
...AND BY "BRUTE" YOU MEAN... ...INSTRUC-TOR DOJO?
CORPORAL ASAKO SHIBAZAKI (IN TRAINING)
THAT'S RIGHT!
CORPORAL IKU KASAHARA (IN TRAINING)

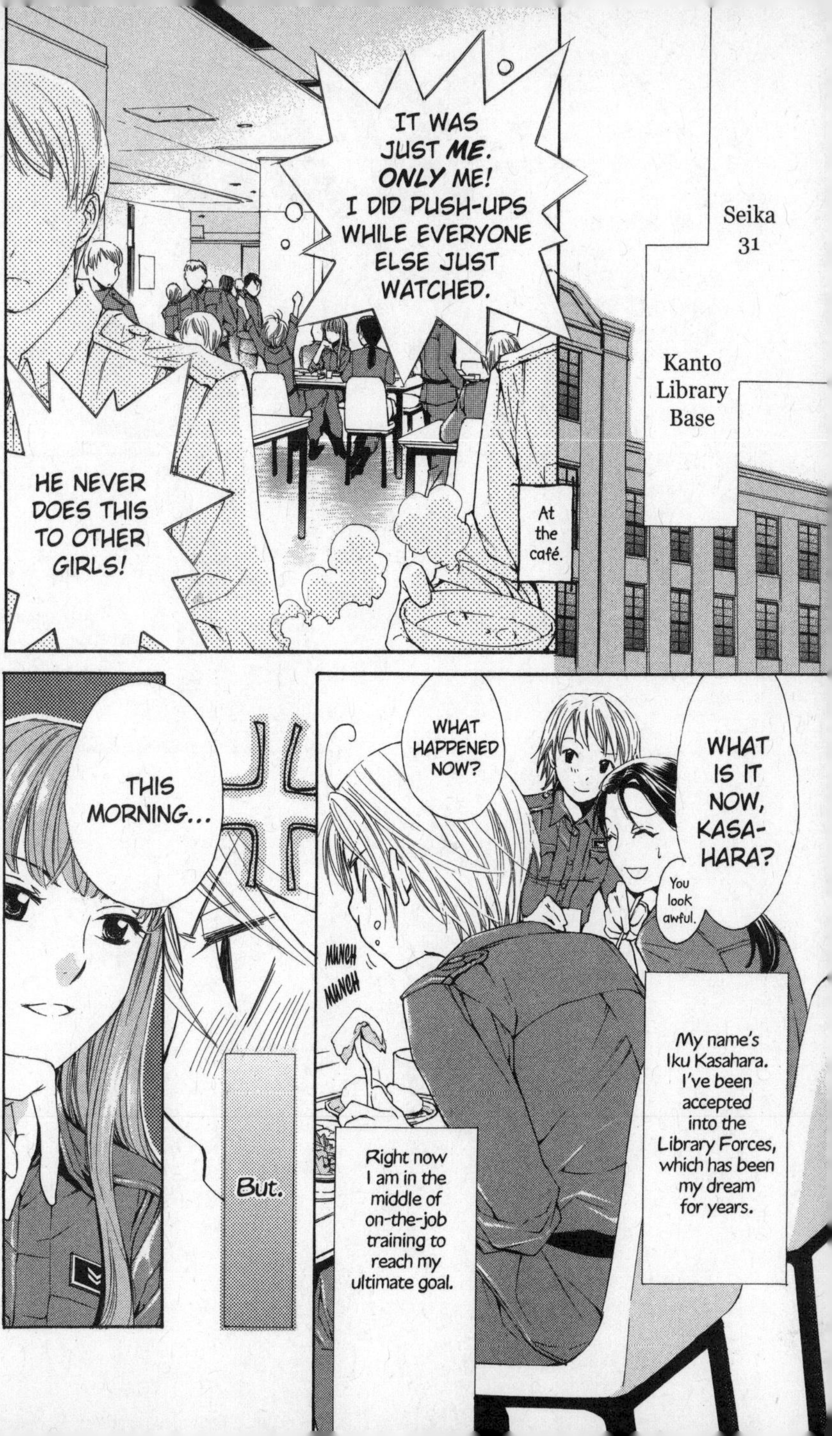
Seika 31
Kanto Library Base
At the café.
IT WAS JUST *ME*. *ONLY* ME! I DID PUSH-UPS WHILE EVERYONE ELSE JUST WATCHED.
HE NEVER DOES THIS TO OTHER GIRLS!
WHAT IS IT NOW, KASAHARA?
You look awful.
WHAT HAPPENED NOW?
MUNCH MUNCH
My name's Iku Kasahara. I've been accepted into the Library Forces, which has been my dream for years.
Right now I am in the middle of on-the-job training to reach my ultimate goal.
THIS MORNING...
But.

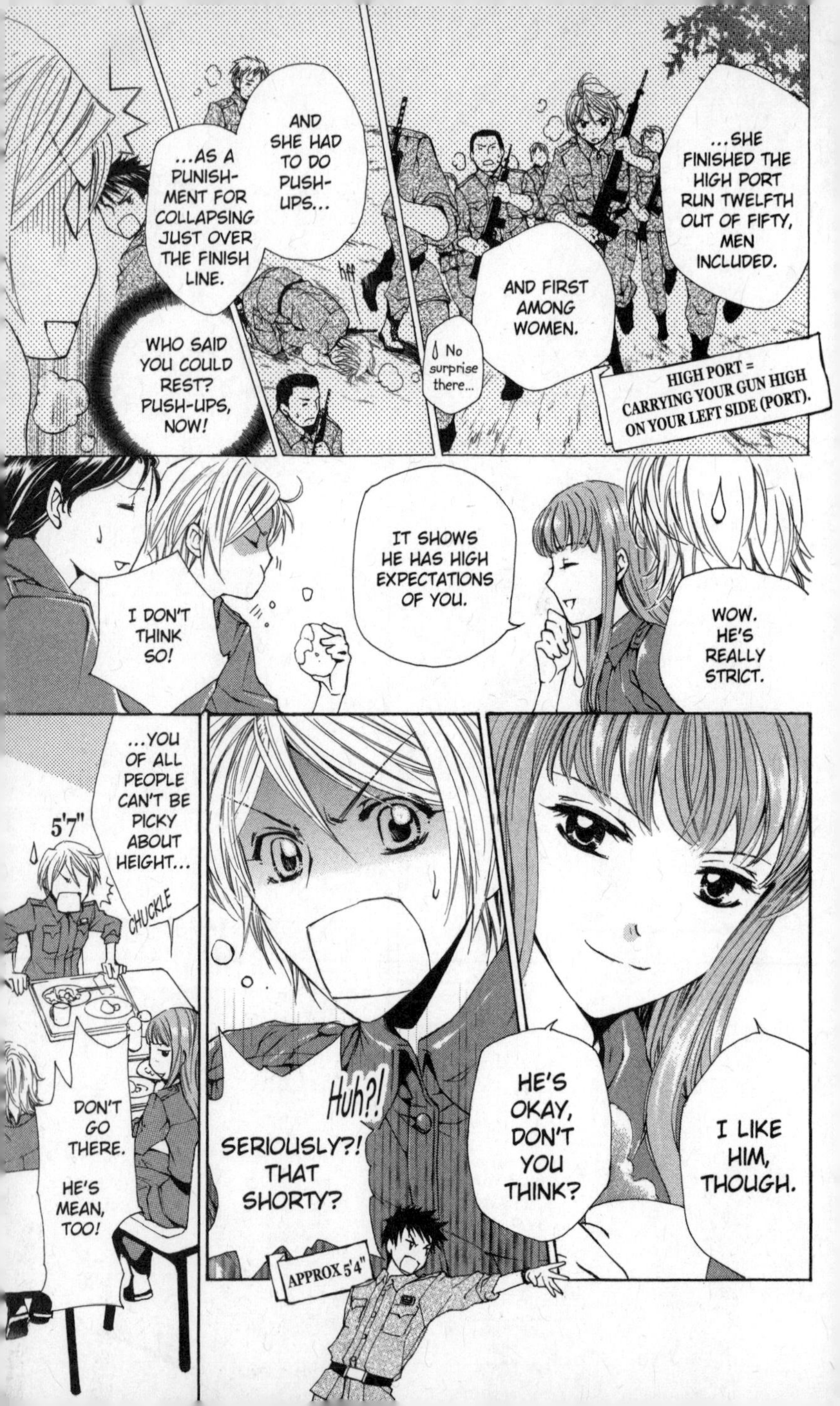
...SHE FINISHED THE HIGH PORT RUN TWELFTH OUT OF FIFTY, MEN INCLUDED.
AND FIRST AMONG WOMEN.
HIGH PORT = CARRYING YOUR GUN HIGH ON YOUR LEFT SIDE (PORT).
No surprise there...
AND SHE HAD TO DO PUSH-UPS...
...AS A PUNISH-MENT FOR COLLAPSING JUST OVER THE FINISH LINE.
hff
WHO SAID YOU COULD REST? PUSH-UPS, NOW!
WOW. HE'S REALLY STRICT.
IT SHOWS HE HAS HIGH EXPECTATIONS OF YOU.
I DON'T THINK SO!
I LIKE HIM, THOUGH.
HE'S OKAY, DON'T YOU THINK?
Huh?!
SERIOUSLY?! THAT SHORTY?
APPROX 5'4"
...YOU OF ALL PEOPLE CAN'T BE PICKY ABOUT HEIGHT...
5'7"
CHUCKLE
DON'T GO THERE.
HE'S MEAN, TOO!

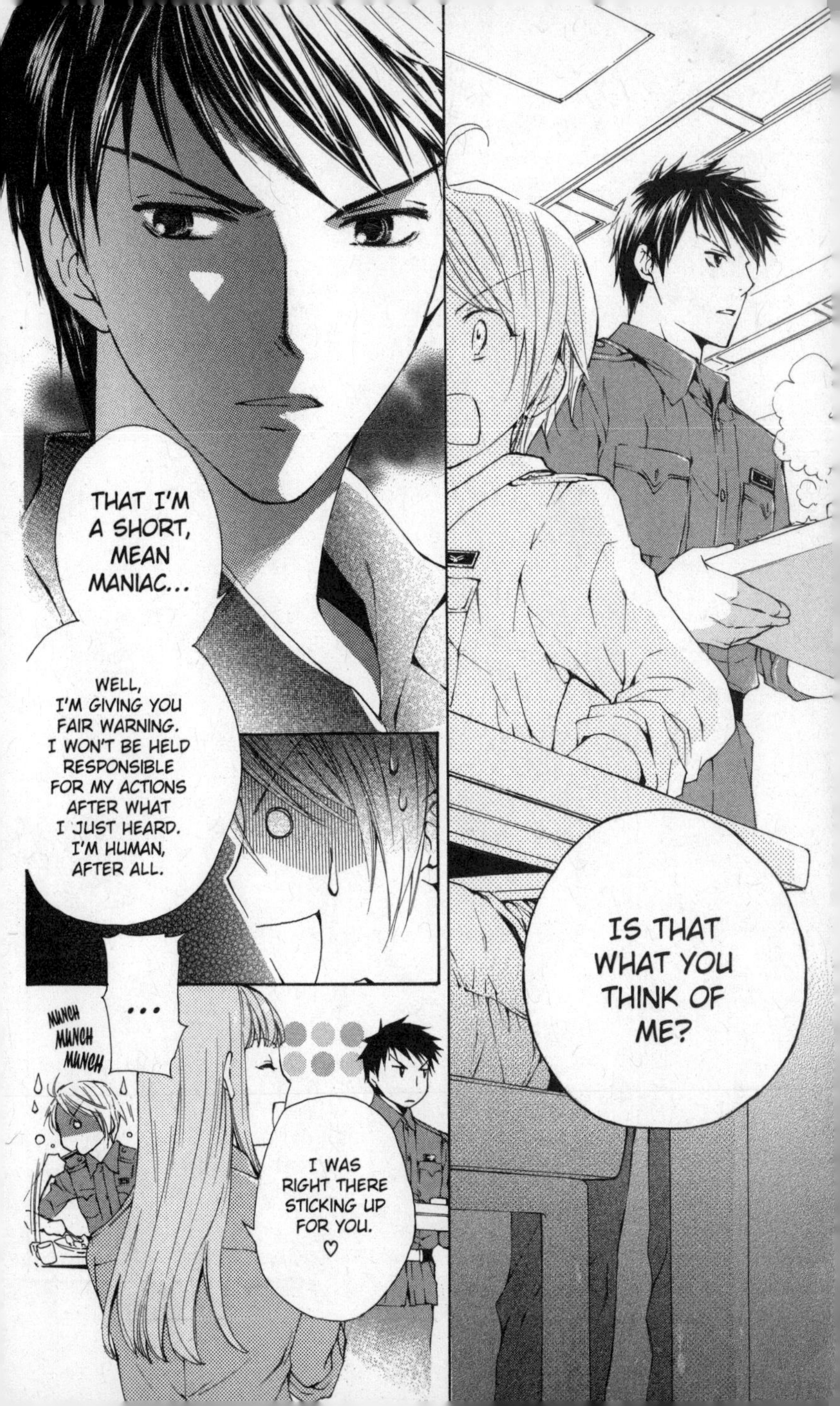
IS THAT WHAT YOU THINK OF ME?
THAT I'M A SHORT, MEAN MANIAC...
WELL, I'M GIVING YOU FAIR WARNING. I WON'T BE HELD RESPONSIBLE FOR MY ACTIONS AFTER WHAT I JUST HEARD. I'M HUMAN, AFTER ALL.
...
I WAS RIGHT THERE STICKING UP FOR YOU. ♡
MUNCH MUNCH MUNCH

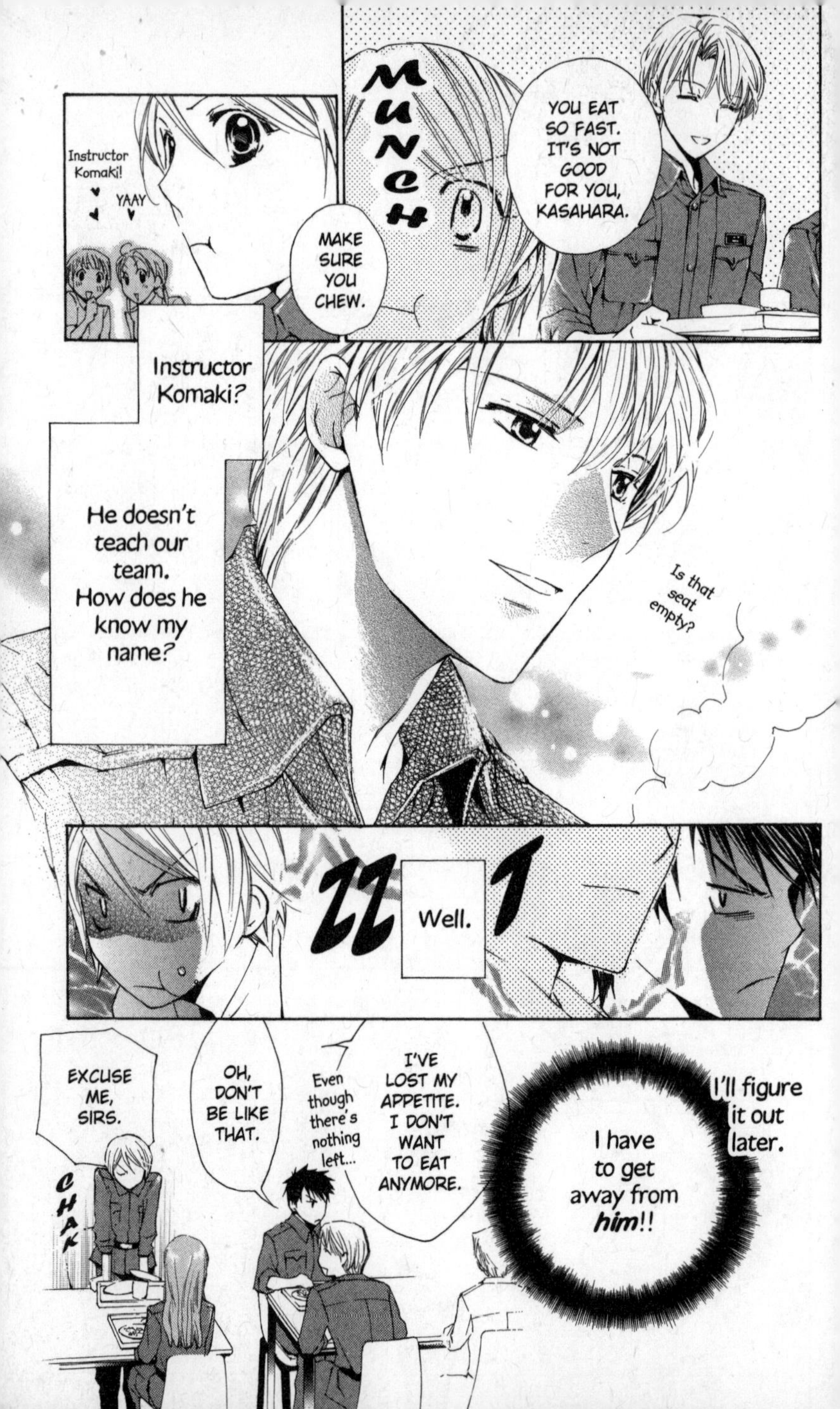
YOU EAT SO FAST. IT'S NOT GOOD FOR YOU, KASAHARA.
MUNCH
MAKE SURE YOU CHEW.
Instructor Komaki!
YAAY
Instructor Komaki?
Is that seat empty?
He doesn't teach our team. How does he know my name?
Well.
I'll figure it out later.
I have to get away from *him*!!
I'VE LOST MY APPETITE. I DON'T WANT TO EAT ANYMORE.
Even though there's nothing left...
OH, DON'T BE LIKE THAT.
EXCUSE ME, SIRS.
CHAK

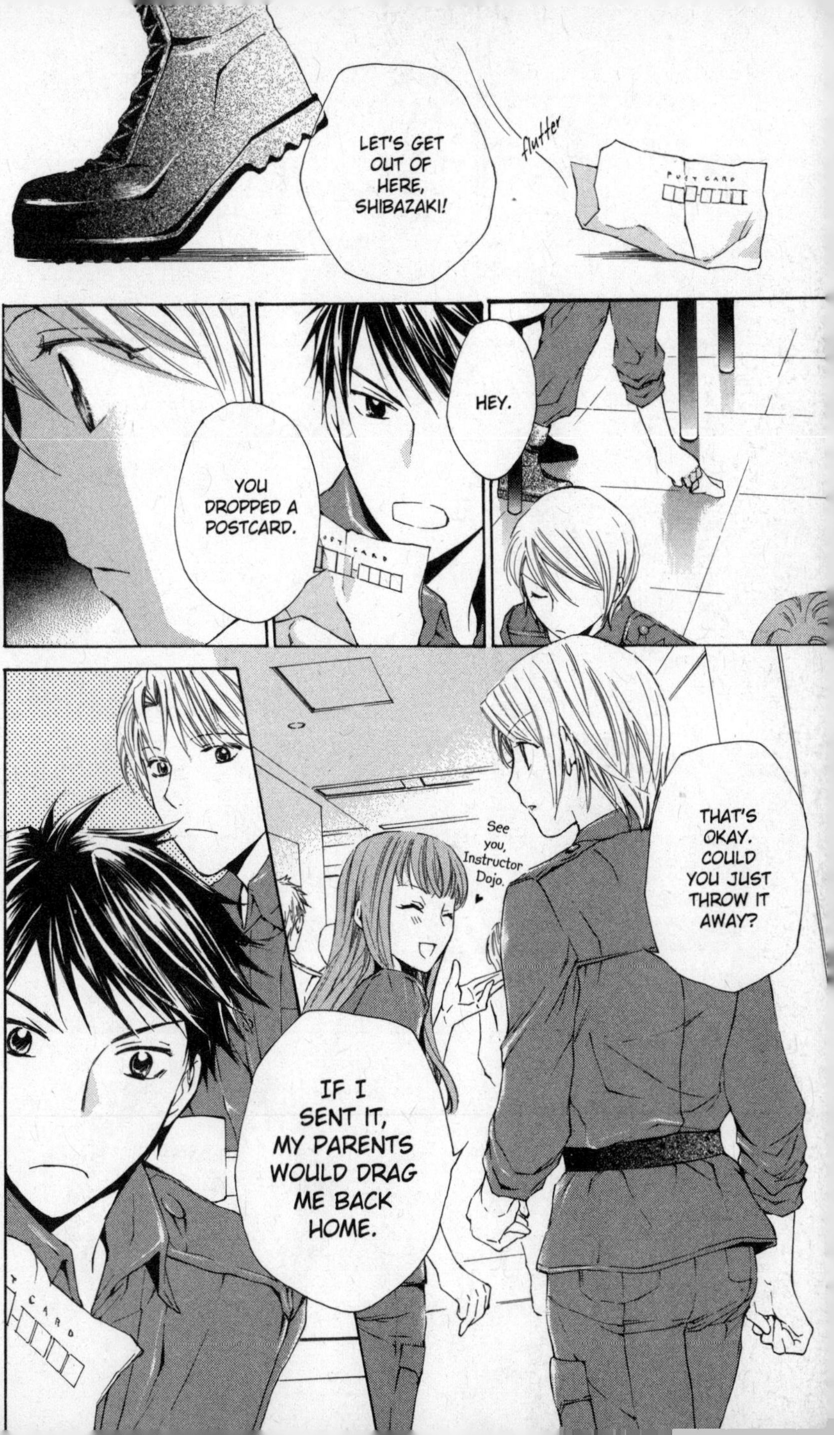
flutter
LET'S GET OUT OF HERE, SHIBAZAKI!
HEY.
YOU DROPPED A POSTCARD.
THAT'S OKAY. COULD YOU JUST THROW IT AWAY?
See you, Instructor Dojo.
IF I SENT IT, MY PARENTS WOULD DRAG ME BACK HOME.

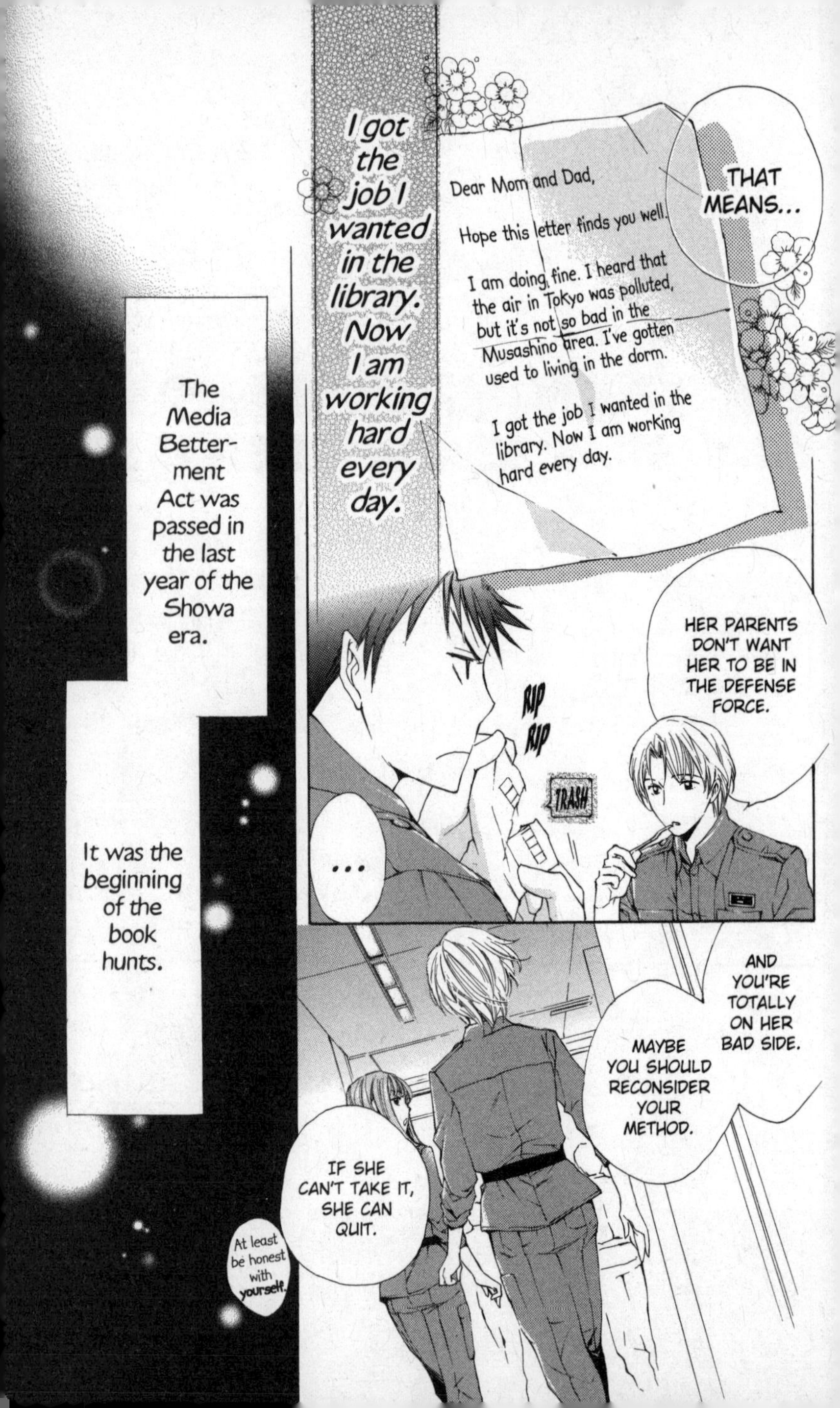
Dear Mom and Dad,
Hope this letter finds you well.
I am doing fine. I heard that the air in Tokyo was polluted, but it's not so bad in the Musashino area. I've gotten used to living in the dorm.
I got the job I wanted in the library. Now I am working hard every day.
I got the job I wanted in the library. Now I am working hard every day.
THAT MEANS...
HER PARENTS DON'T WANT HER TO BE IN THE DEFENSE FORCE.
RIP RIP
TRASH
...
AND YOU'RE TOTALLY ON HER BAD SIDE.
MAYBE YOU SHOULD RECONSIDER YOUR METHOD.
IF SHE CAN'T TAKE IT, SHE CAN QUIT.
At least be honest with yourself.
The Media Betterment Act was passed in the last year of the Showa era.
It was the beginning of the book hunts.

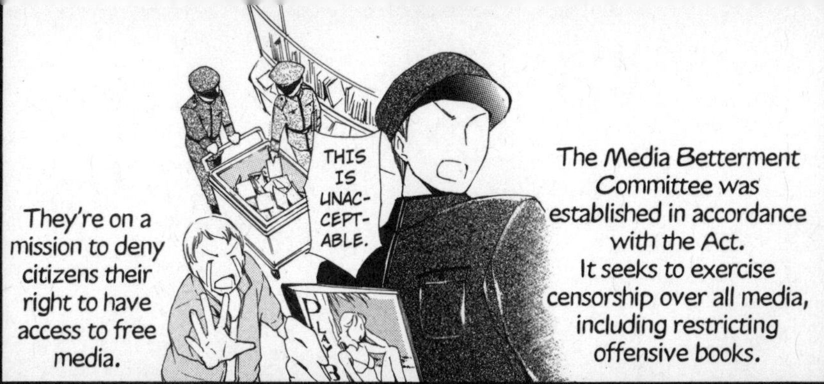
The Media Betterment Committee was established in accordance with the Act.
It seeks to exercise censorship over all media, including restricting offensive books.
THIS IS UNACCEPTABLE.
They're on a mission to deny citizens their right to have access to free media.

Libraries are the only institution that can oppose their censorship.

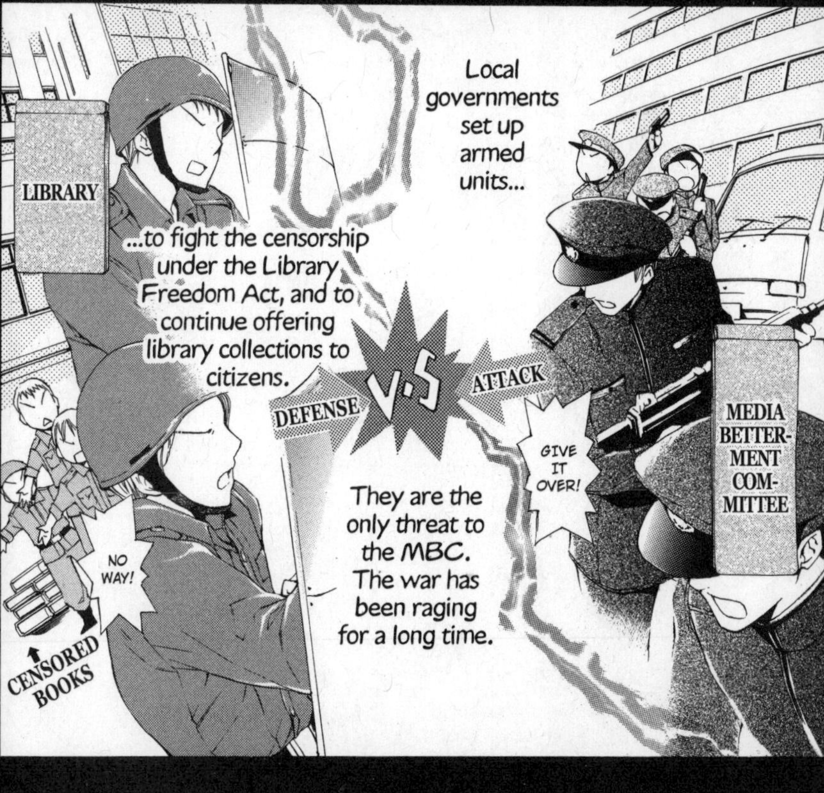
Local governments set up armed units...
MEDIA BETTERMENT COMMITTEE
ATTACK
GIVE IT OVER!
V.S
DEFENSE
...to fight the censorship under the Library Freedom Act, and to continue offering library collections to citizens.
LIBRARY
They are the only threat to the MBC. The war has been raging for a long time.
NO WAY!
CENSORED BOOKS

The Library Forces were formed in Seika 16

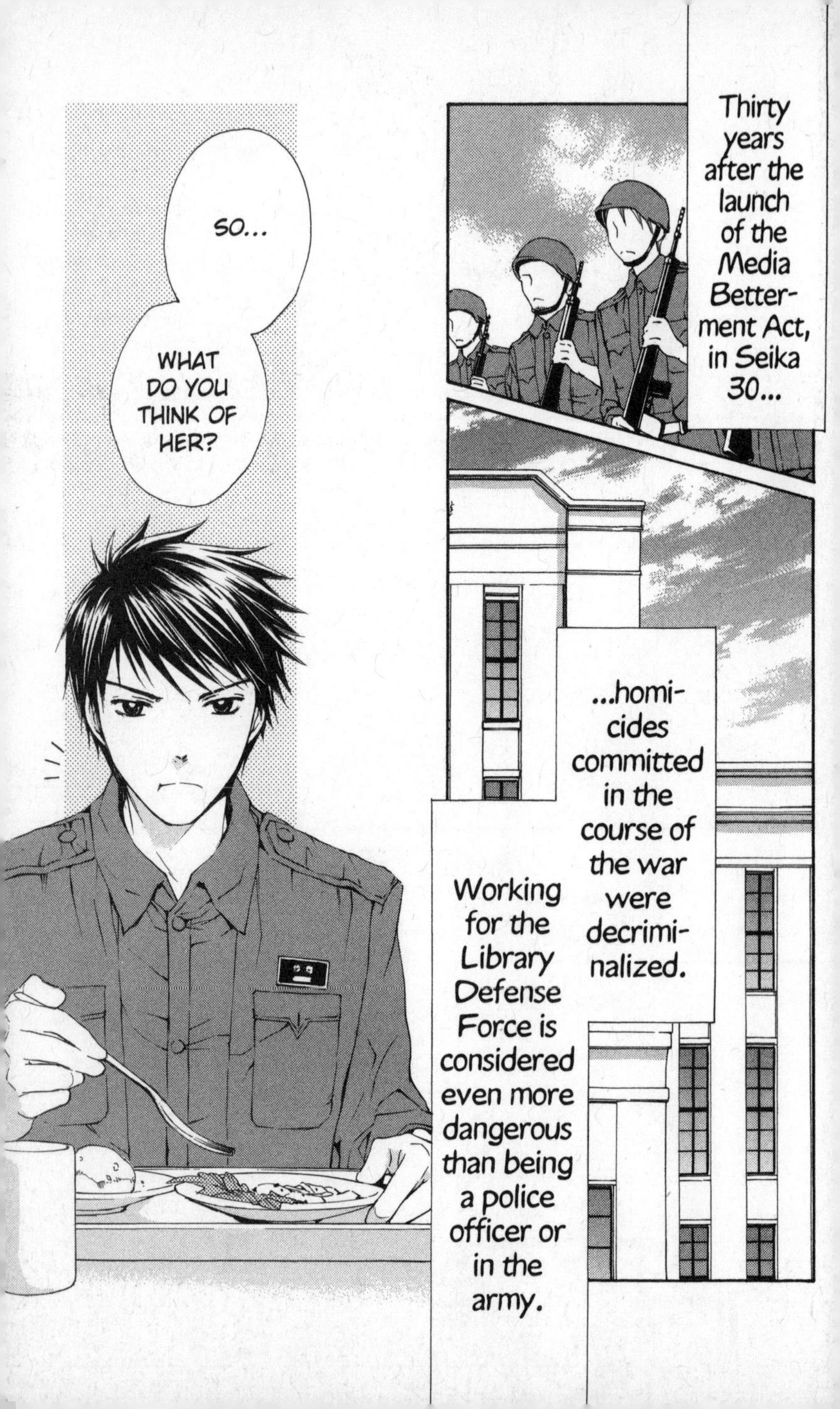
Thirty years after the launch of the Media Betterment Act, in Seika 30...
...homicides committed in the course of the war were decriminalized.
Working for the Library Defense Force is considered even more dangerous than being a police officer or in the army.
SO...
WHAT DO YOU THINK OF HER?

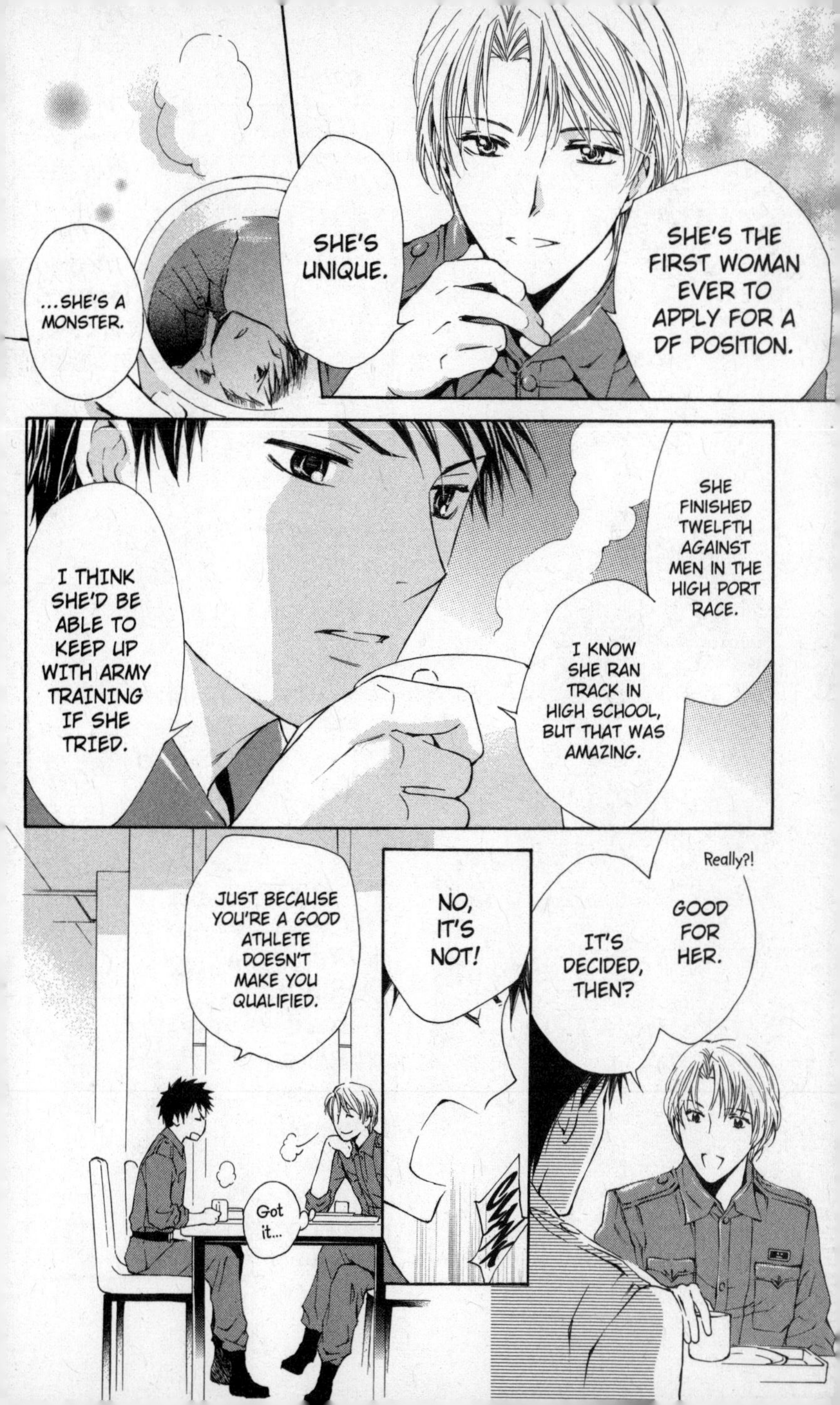
SHE'S THE FIRST WOMAN EVER TO APPLY FOR A DF POSITION.
SHE'S UNIQUE.
...SHE'S A MONSTER.
SHE FINISHED TWELFTH AGAINST MEN IN THE HIGH PORT RACE.
I KNOW SHE RAN TRACK IN HIGH SCHOOL, BUT THAT WAS AMAZING.
I THINK SHE'D BE ABLE TO KEEP UP WITH ARMY TRAINING IF SHE TRIED.
Really?!
GOOD FOR HER.
IT'S DECIDED, THEN?
NO, IT'S NOT!
JUST BECAUSE YOU'RE A GOOD ATHLETE DOESN'T MAKE YOU QUALIFIED.
Got it...

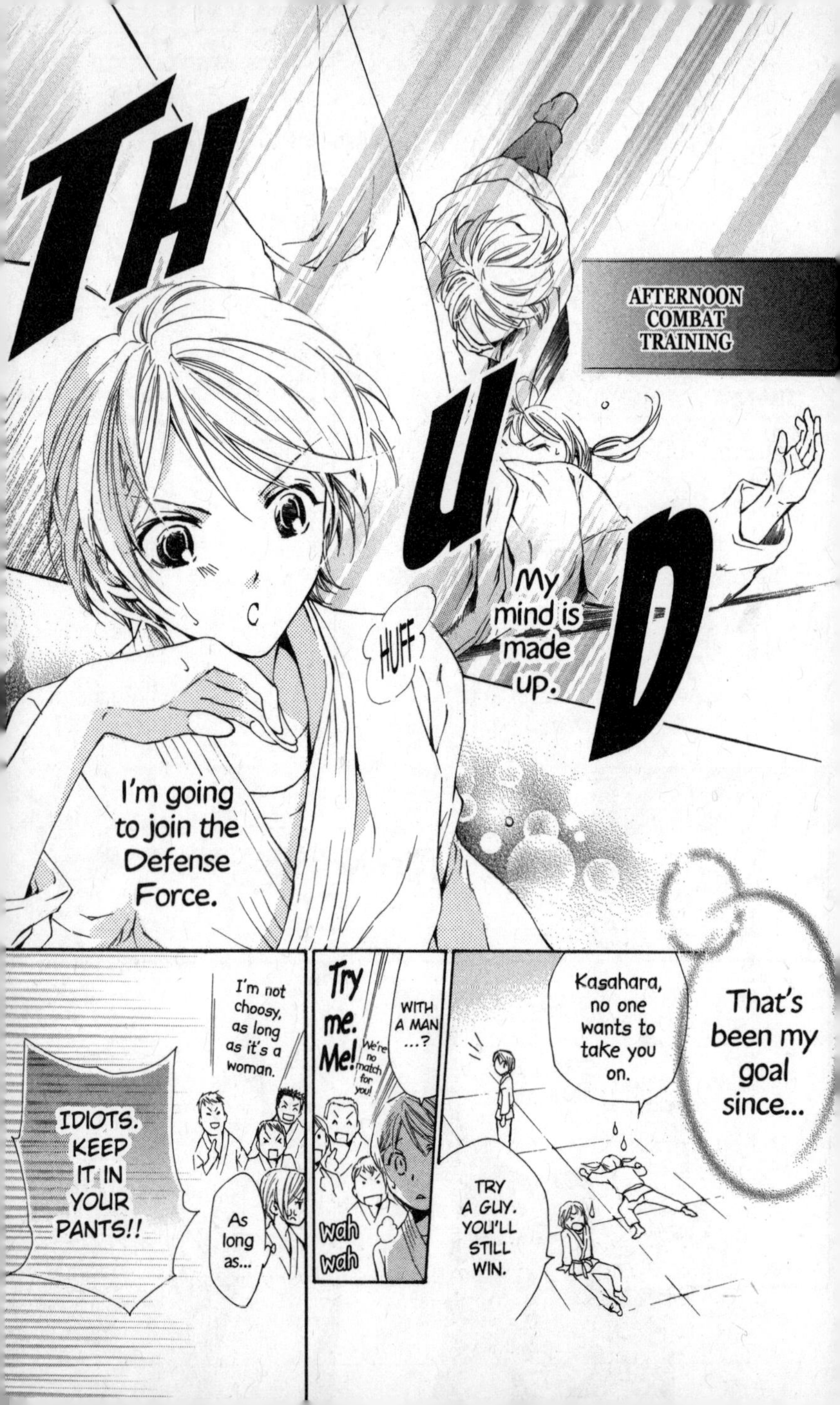
AFTERNOON COMBAT TRAINING
THUD
My mind is made up.
HUFF
I'm going to join the Defense Force.
That's been my goal since...
Kasahara, no one wants to take you on.
TRY A GUY. YOU'LL STILL WIN.
WITH A MAN ...?
Try me. Me!
We're no match for you!
wah wah
I'm not choosy, as long as it's a woman.
As long as...
IDIOTS. KEEP IT IN YOUR PANTS!!

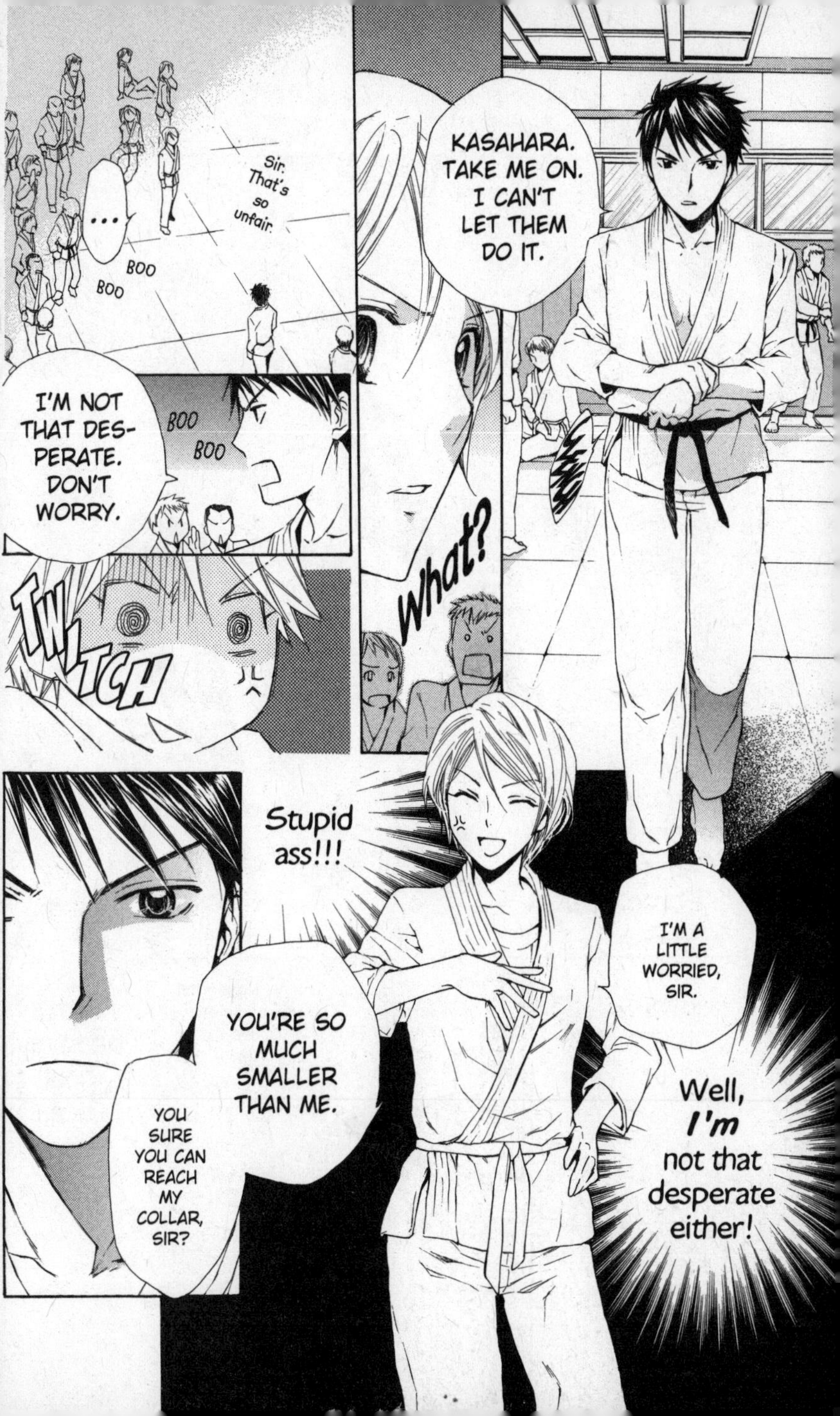
KASAHARA. TAKE ME ON. I CAN'T LET THEM DO IT.
What?
Sir. That's so unfair.
...
BOO BOO
BOO BOO
I'M NOT THAT DES-PERATE. DON'T WORRY.
TWITCH
I'M A LITTLE WORRIED, SIR.
YOU'RE SO MUCH SMALLER THAN ME.
YOU SURE YOU CAN REACH MY COLLAR, SIR?
Stupid ass!!!
Well, *I'm* not that desperate either!

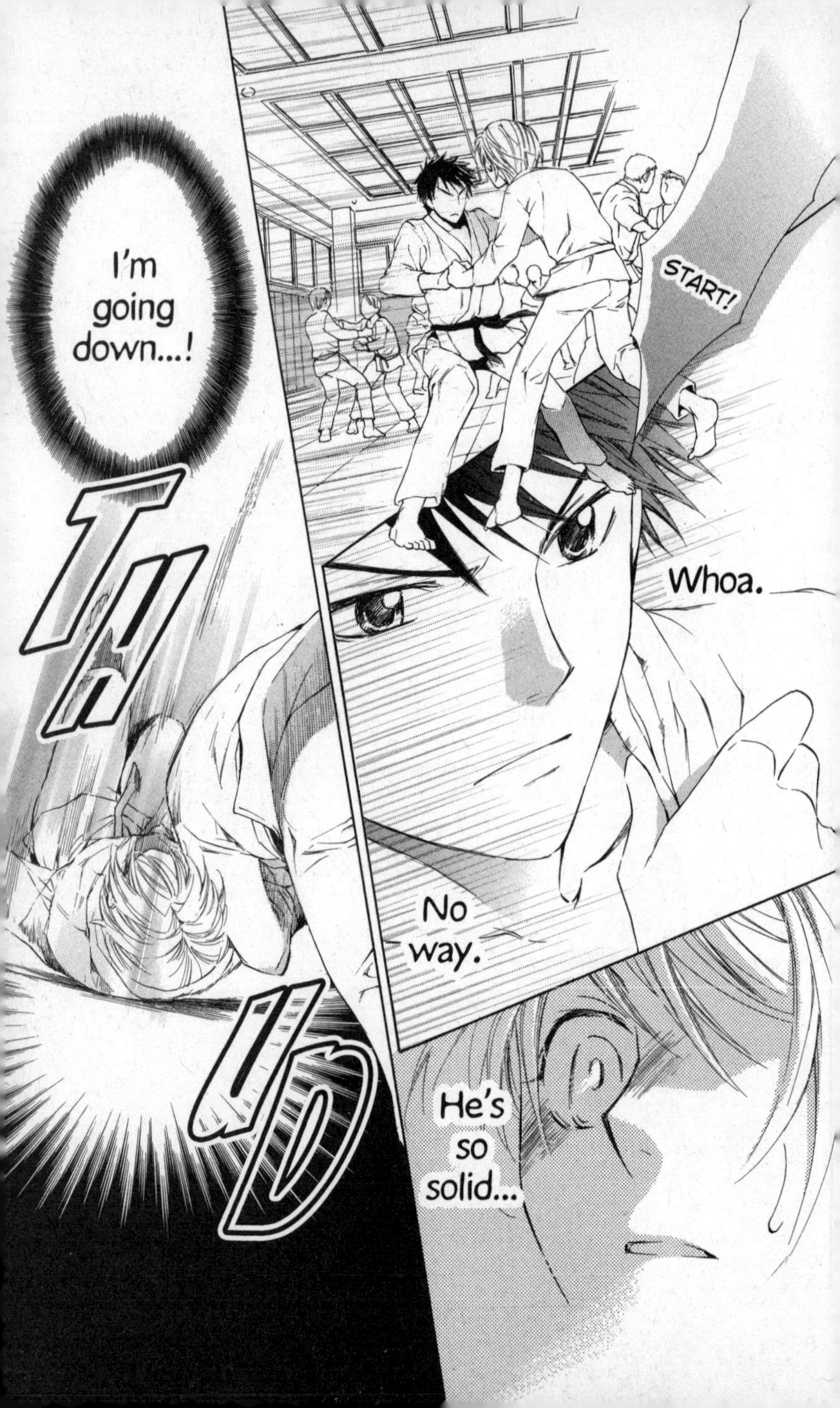
START!
Whoa.
No way.
He's so solid...
I'm going down...!
THUD

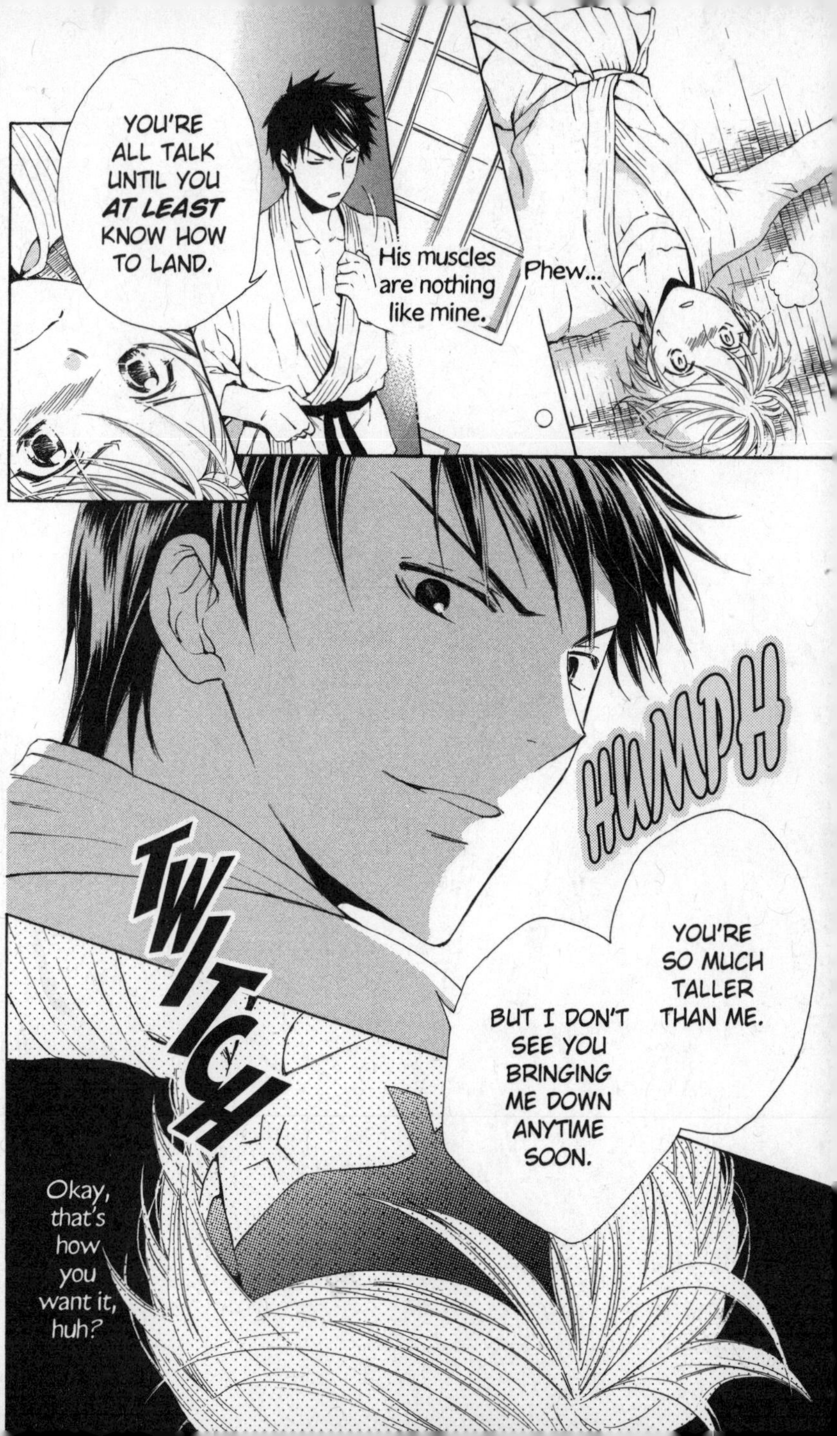
Phew...
YOU'RE ALL TALK UNTIL YOU AT LEAST KNOW HOW TO LAND.
His muscles are nothing like mine.
HUMPH
YOU'RE SO MUCH TALLER THAN ME.
BUT I DON'T SEE YOU BRINGING ME DOWN ANYTIME SOON.
TWITCH
Okay, that's how you want it, huh?

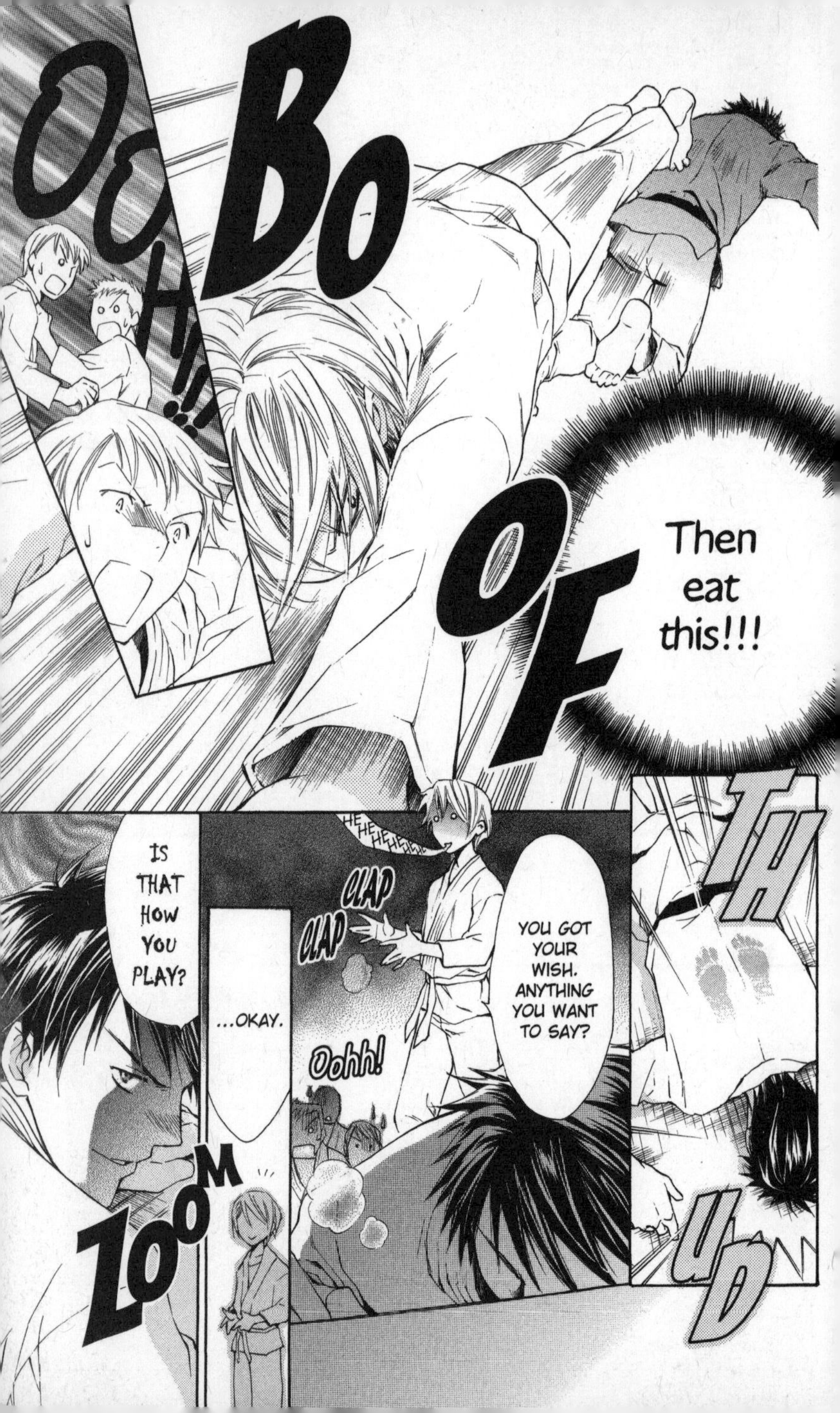
Then eat this!!!
BOOF
OOOH!!!
THUD
HEHEHEHE
YOU GOT YOUR WISH. ANYTHING YOU WANT TO SAY?
CLAP CLAP
Oohh!
IS THAT HOW YOU PLAY?
...OKAY.
ZOOM

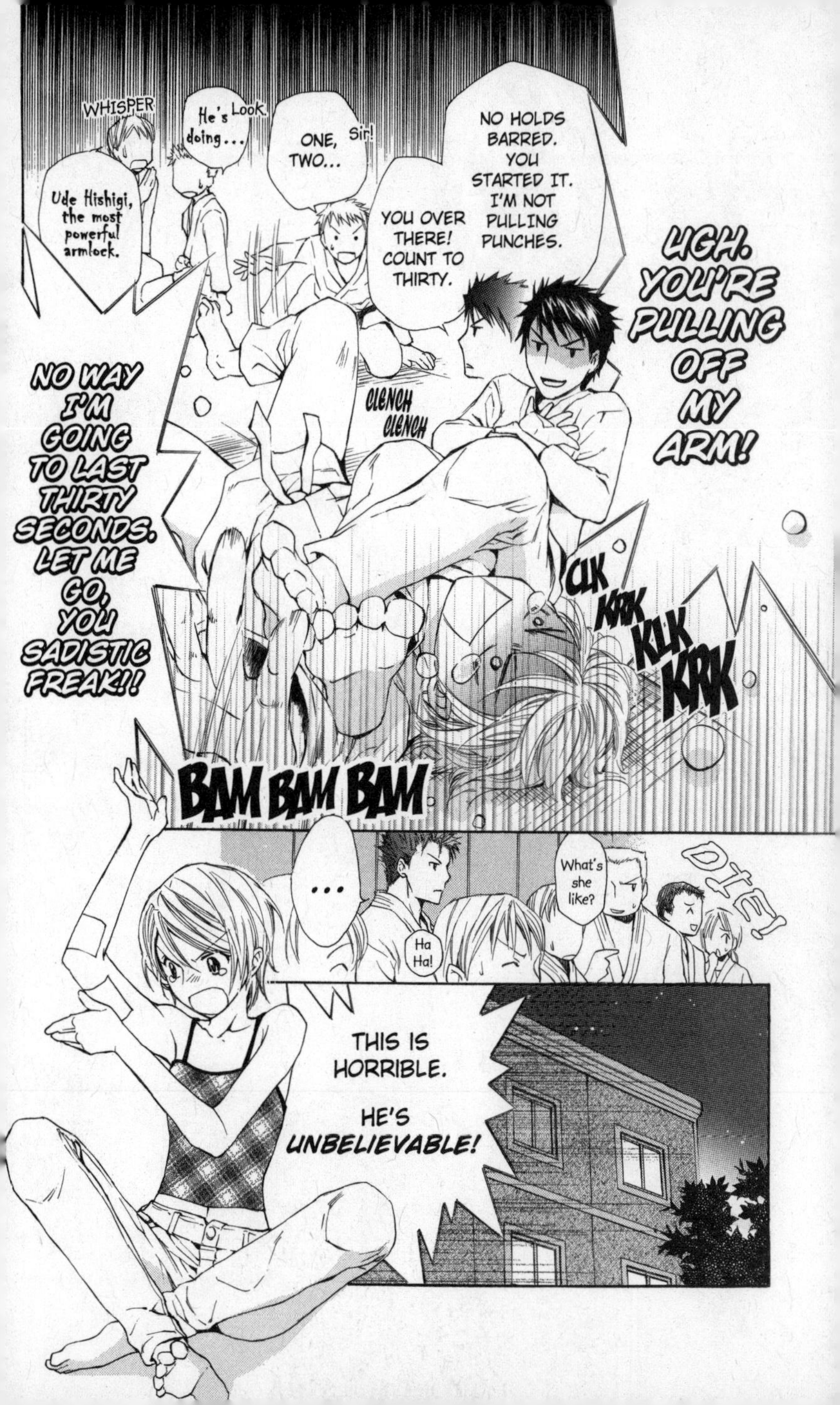
NO HOLDS BARRED. YOU STARTED IT. I'M NOT PULLING PUNCHES.
UGH. YOU'RE PULLING OFF MY ARM!
YOU OVER THERE! COUNT TO THIRTY.
Sir!
ONE, TWO...
Look.
He's doing...
WHISPER
Ude Hishigi, the most powerful armlock.
CLENCH CLENCH
CLK KRK KLK KRK
NO WAY I'M GOING TO LAST THIRTY SECONDS. LET ME GO, YOU SADISTIC FREAK!!
BAM BAM BAM
DIE!
What's she like?
Ha Ha!
...
THIS IS HORRIBLE.
HE'S *UNBELIEVABLE!*

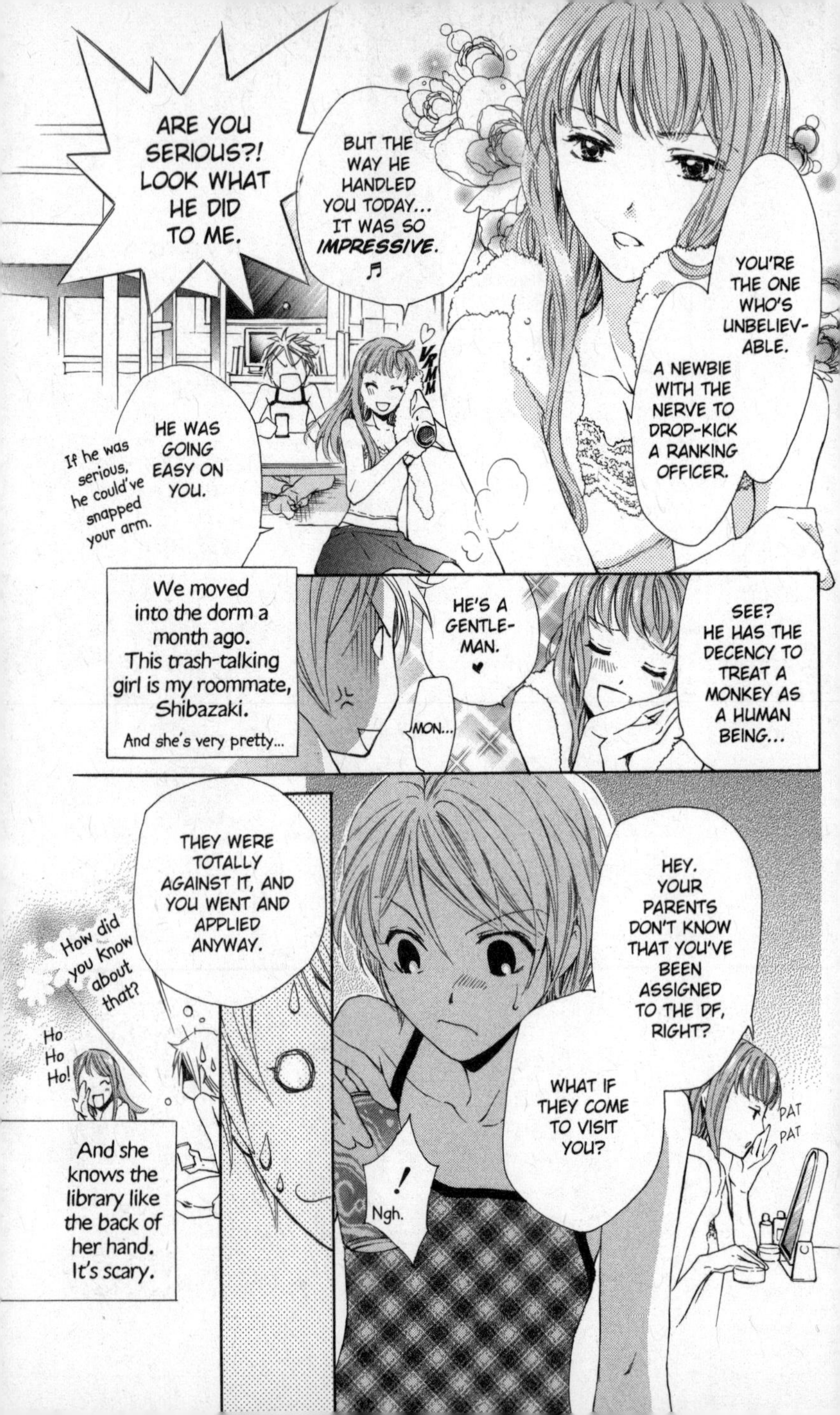
BUT THE WAY HE HANDLED YOU TODAY... IT WAS SO *IMPRESSIVE*. ♬
ARE YOU SERIOUS?! LOOK WHAT HE DID TO ME.
YOU'RE THE ONE WHO'S UNBELIEV-ABLE. A NEWBIE WITH THE NERVE TO DROP-KICK A RANKING OFFICER.
VRMM
HE WAS GOING EASY ON YOU.
If he was serious, he could've snapped your arm.
SEE? HE HAS THE DECENCY TO TREAT A MONKEY AS A HUMAN BEING...
HE'S A GENTLE-MAN. ♥
MON...
We moved into the dorm a month ago. This trash-talking girl is my roommate, Shibazaki.
And she's very pretty...
HEY. YOUR PARENTS DON'T KNOW THAT YOU'VE BEEN ASSIGNED TO THE DF, RIGHT?
WHAT IF THEY COME TO VISIT YOU?
PAT PAT
!
Ngh.
THEY WERE TOTALLY AGAINST IT, AND YOU WENT AND APPLIED ANYWAY.
How did you know about that?
Ho Ho Ho!
And she knows the library like the back of her hand. It's scary.

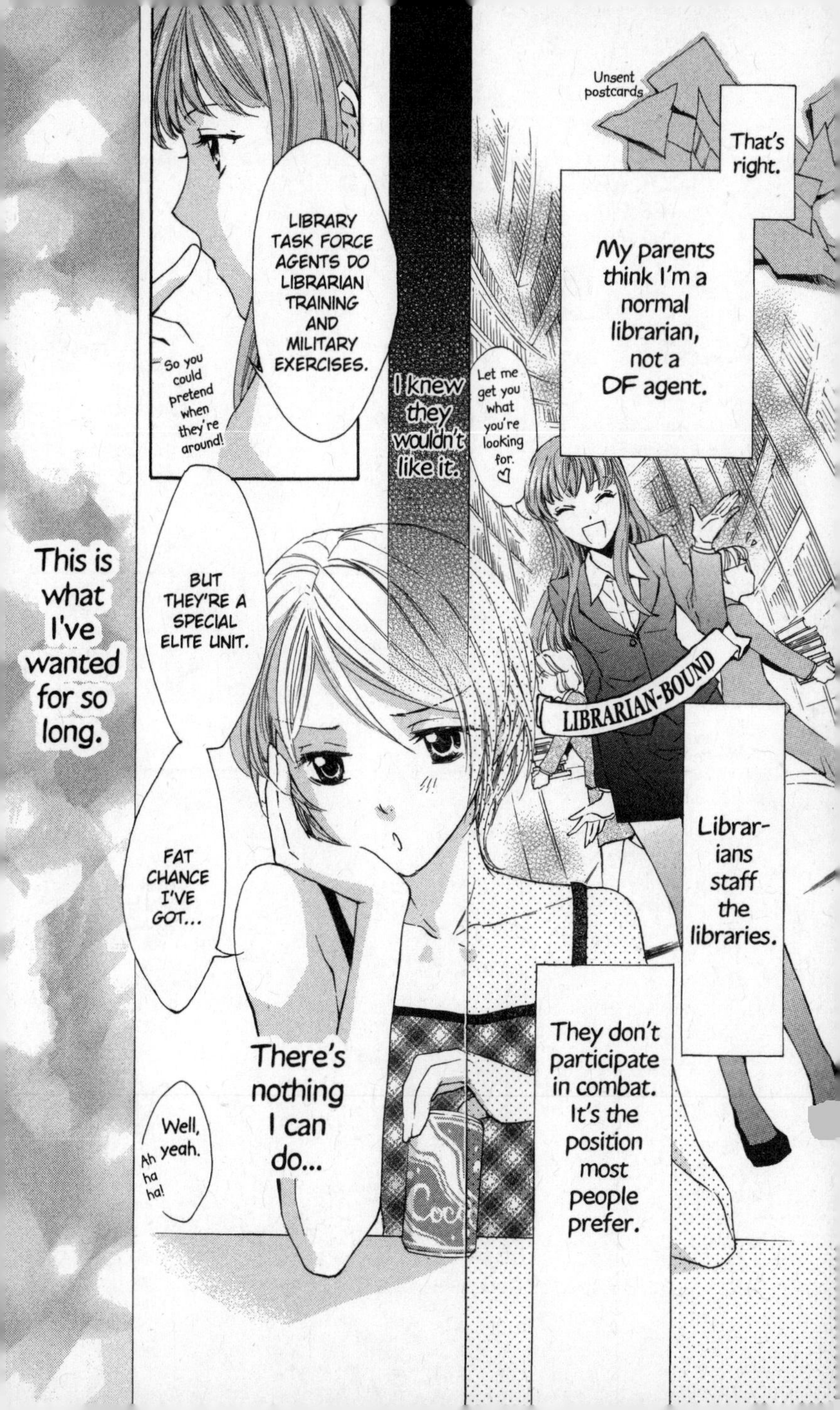

Unsent postcards
That's right.
My parents think I'm a normal librarian, not a DF agent.
Let me get you what you're looking for. ♡
LIBRARIAN-BOUND
Librar-ians staff the libraries.
They don't participate in combat. It's the position most people prefer.
I knew they wouldn't like it.
LIBRARY TASK FORCE AGENTS DO LIBRARIAN TRAINING AND MILITARY EXERCISES.
So you could pretend when they're around!
BUT THEY'RE A SPECIAL ELITE UNIT.
FAT CHANCE I'VE GOT...
There's nothing I can do...
Well, yeah.
Ah ha ha!
This is what I've wanted for so long.

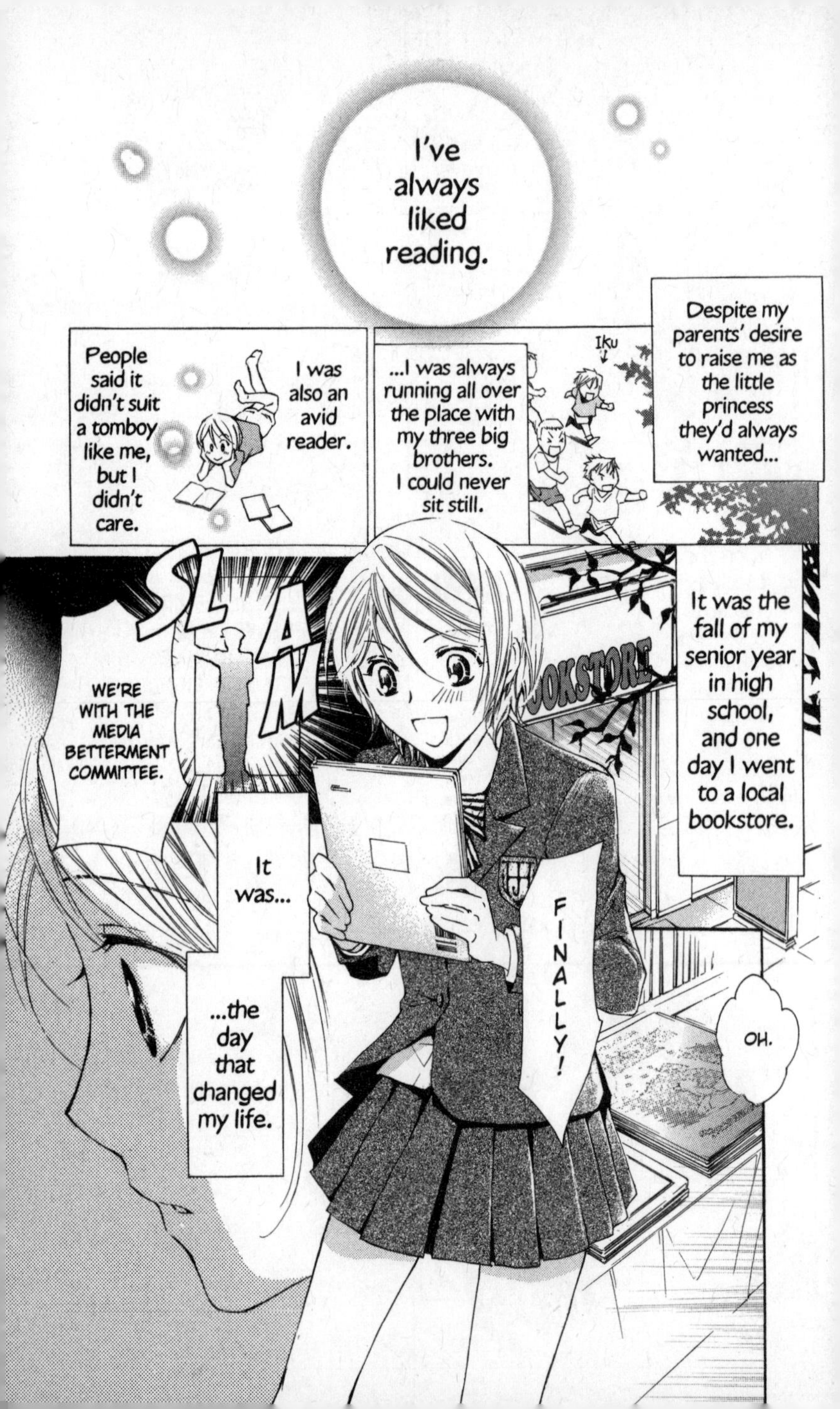

I've always liked reading.
Despite my parents' desire to raise me as the little princess they'd always wanted...
Iku
...I was always running all over the place with my three big brothers. I could never sit still.
I was also an avid reader.
People said it didn't suit a tomboy like me, but I didn't care.
It was the fall of my senior year in high school, and one day I went to a local bookstore.
OH.
FINALLY!
It was...
SLAM
WE'RE WITH THE MEDIA BETTERMENT COMMITTEE.
...the day that changed my life.

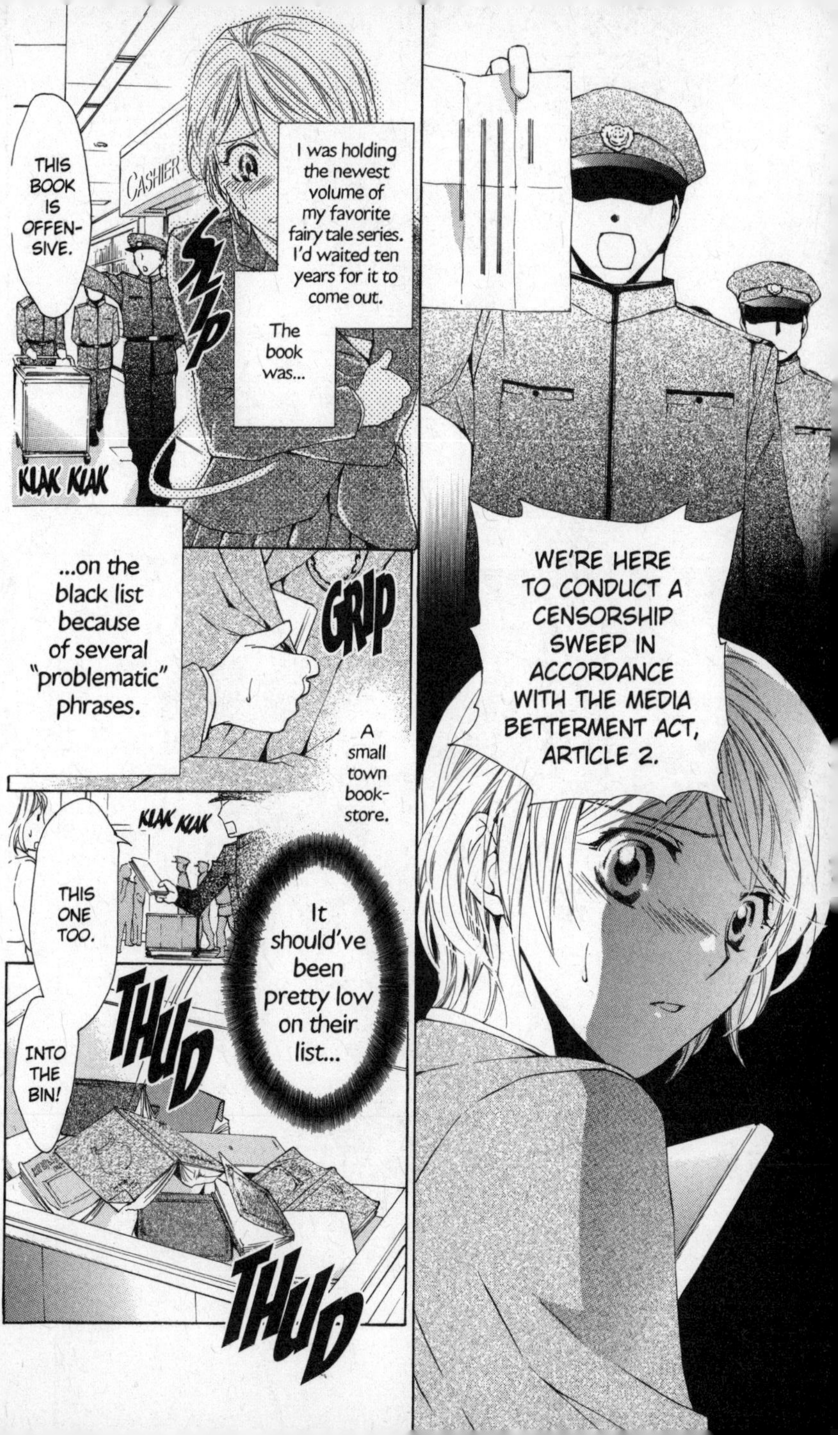

WE'RE HERE TO CONDUCT A CENSORSHIP SWEEP IN ACCORDANCE WITH THE MEDIA BETTERMENT ACT, ARTICLE 2.
I was holding the newest volume of my favorite fairy tale series. I'd waited ten years for it to come out.
The book was...
SLIP
THIS BOOK IS OFFEN-SIVE.
CASHIER
KLAK KLAK
GRIP
...on the black list because of several "problematic" phrases.
A small town book-store.
It should've been pretty low on their list...
KLAK KLAK
THIS ONE TOO.
THUD
INTO THE BIN!
THUD

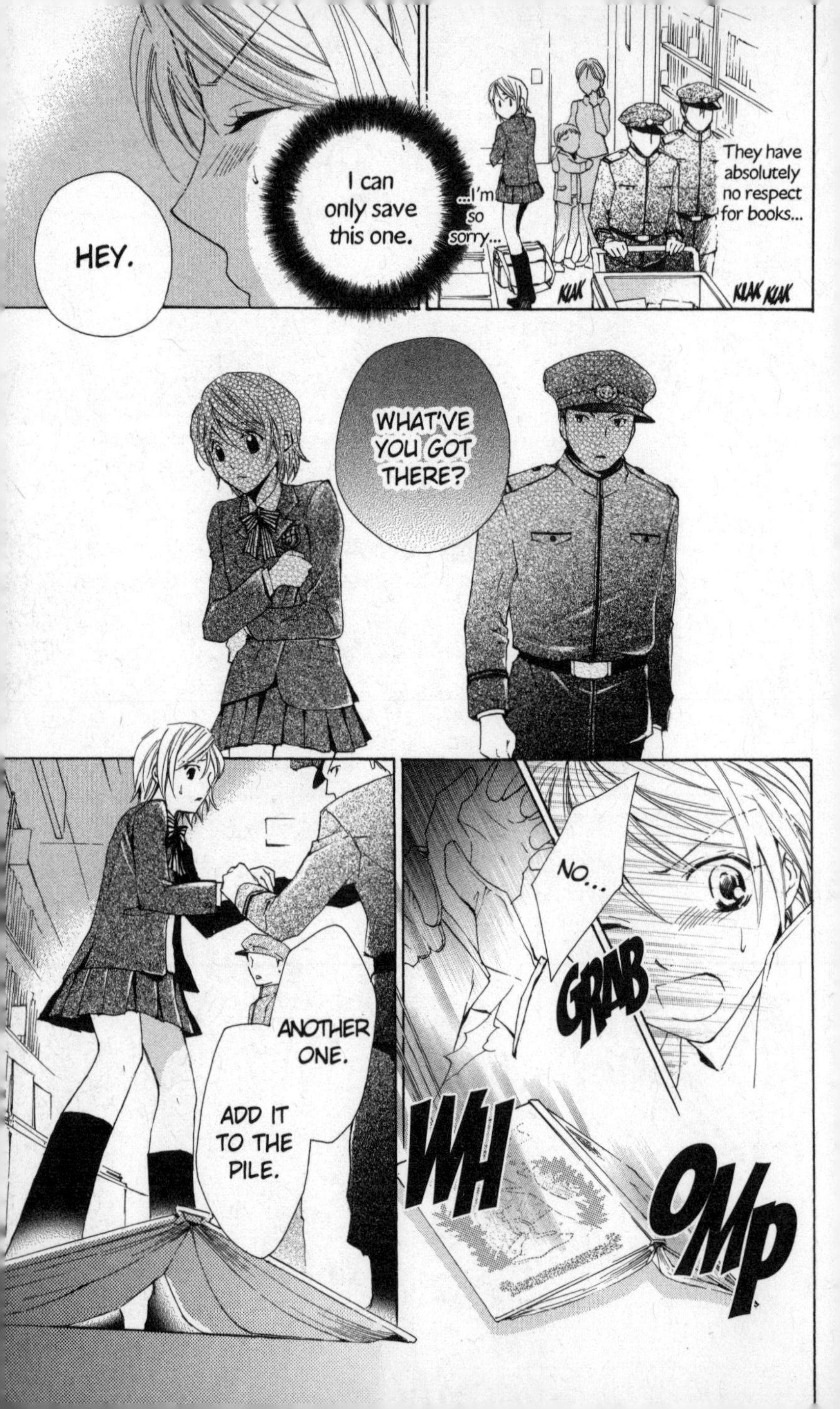
They have absolutely no respect for books...
KLAK KLAK
KLAK
...I'm so sorry...
I can only save this one.
HEY.
WHAT'VE YOU GOT THERE?
NO...
GRAB
WHOMP
ANOTHER ONE.
ADD IT TO THE PILE.

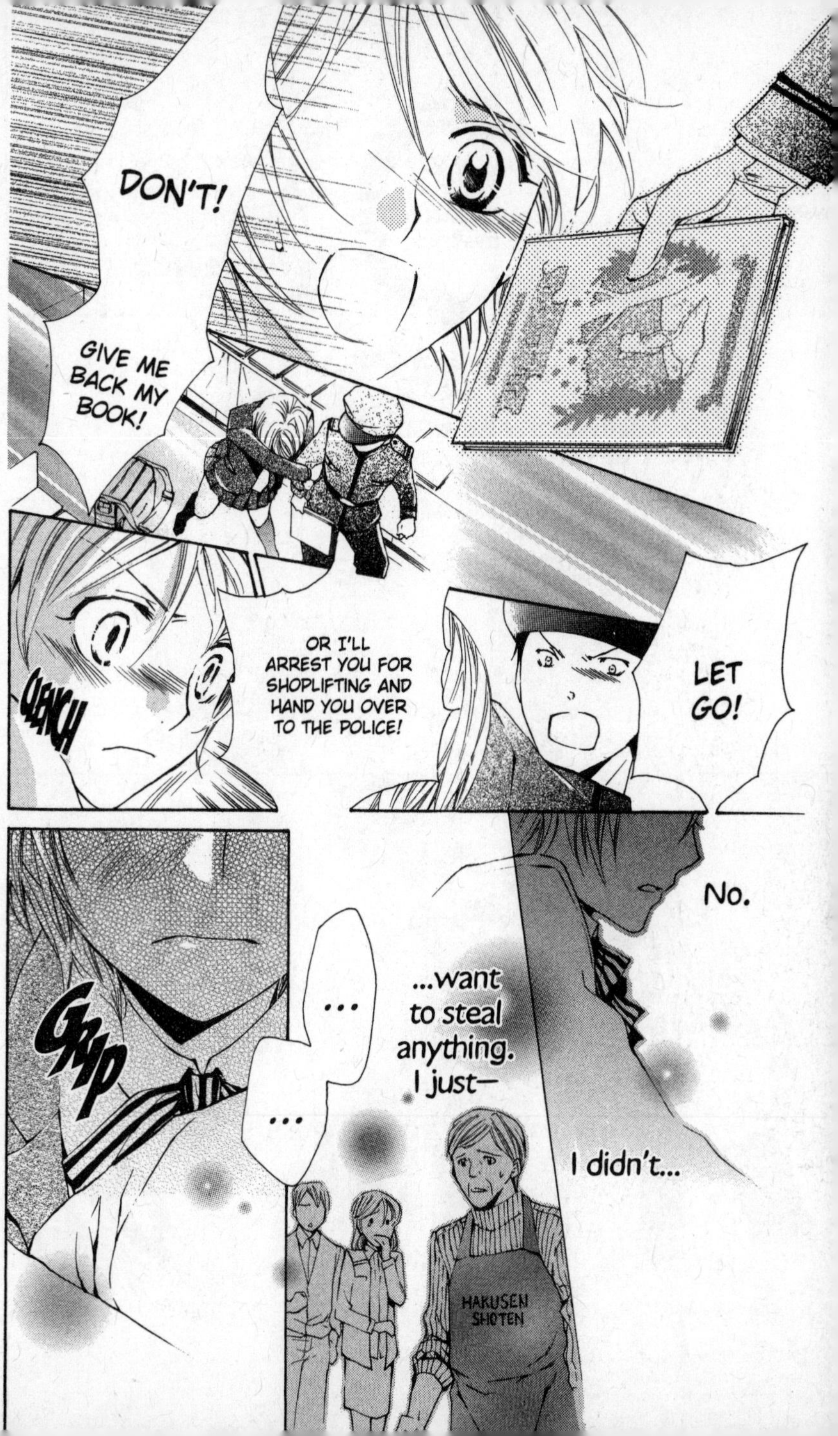
DON'T!
GIVE ME BACK MY BOOK!
LET GO!
OR I'LL ARREST YOU FOR SHOPLIFTING AND HAND YOU OVER TO THE POLICE!
CLENCH
No.
I didn't...
...want to steal anything. I just—
HAKUSEN SHOTEN
...
...
GRIP

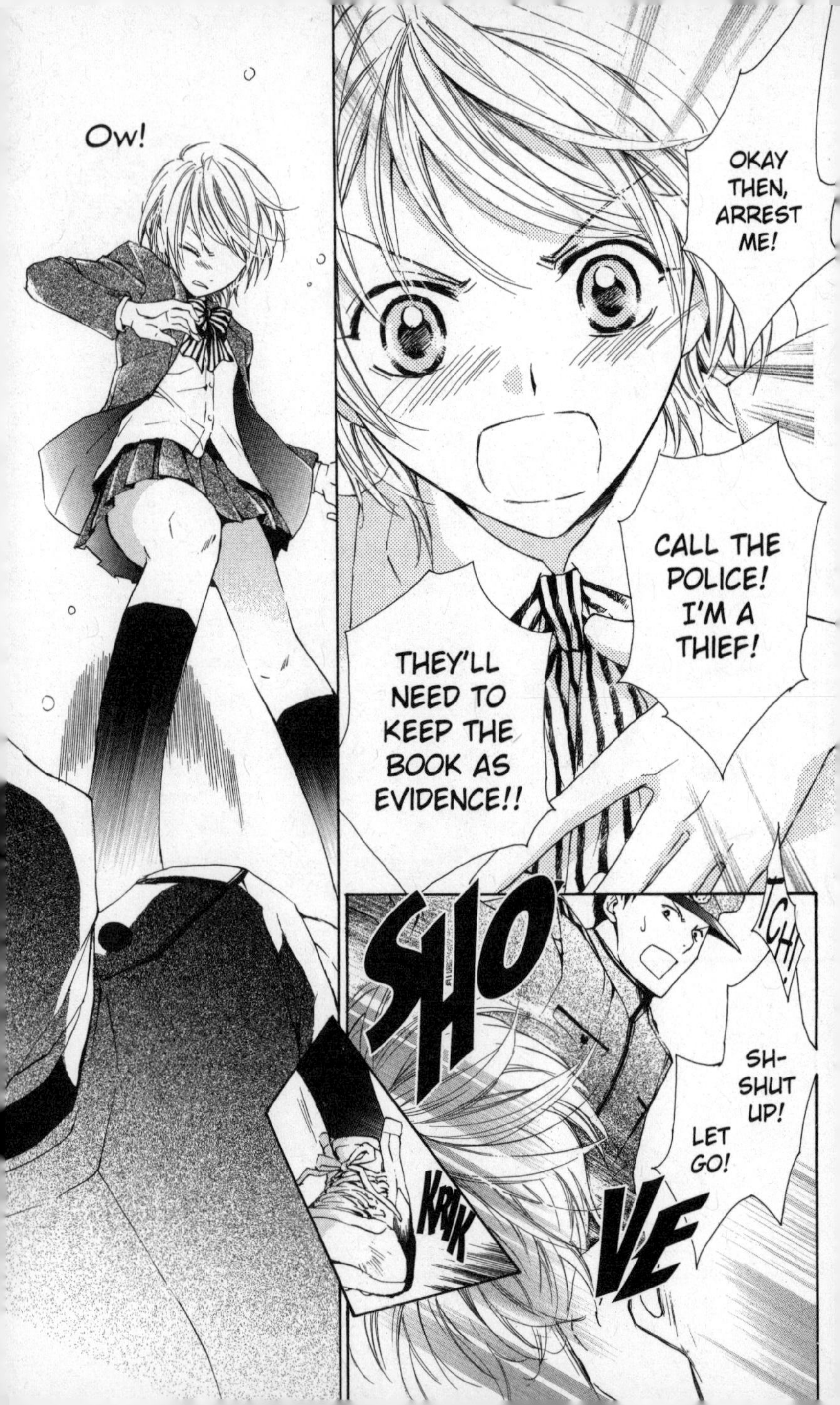
OKAY THEN, ARREST ME!
CALL THE POLICE! I'M A THIEF!
THEY'LL NEED TO KEEP THE BOOK AS EVIDENCE!!
TCH!
SHOVE
SH-SHUT UP!
LET GO!
KRIK
Ow!

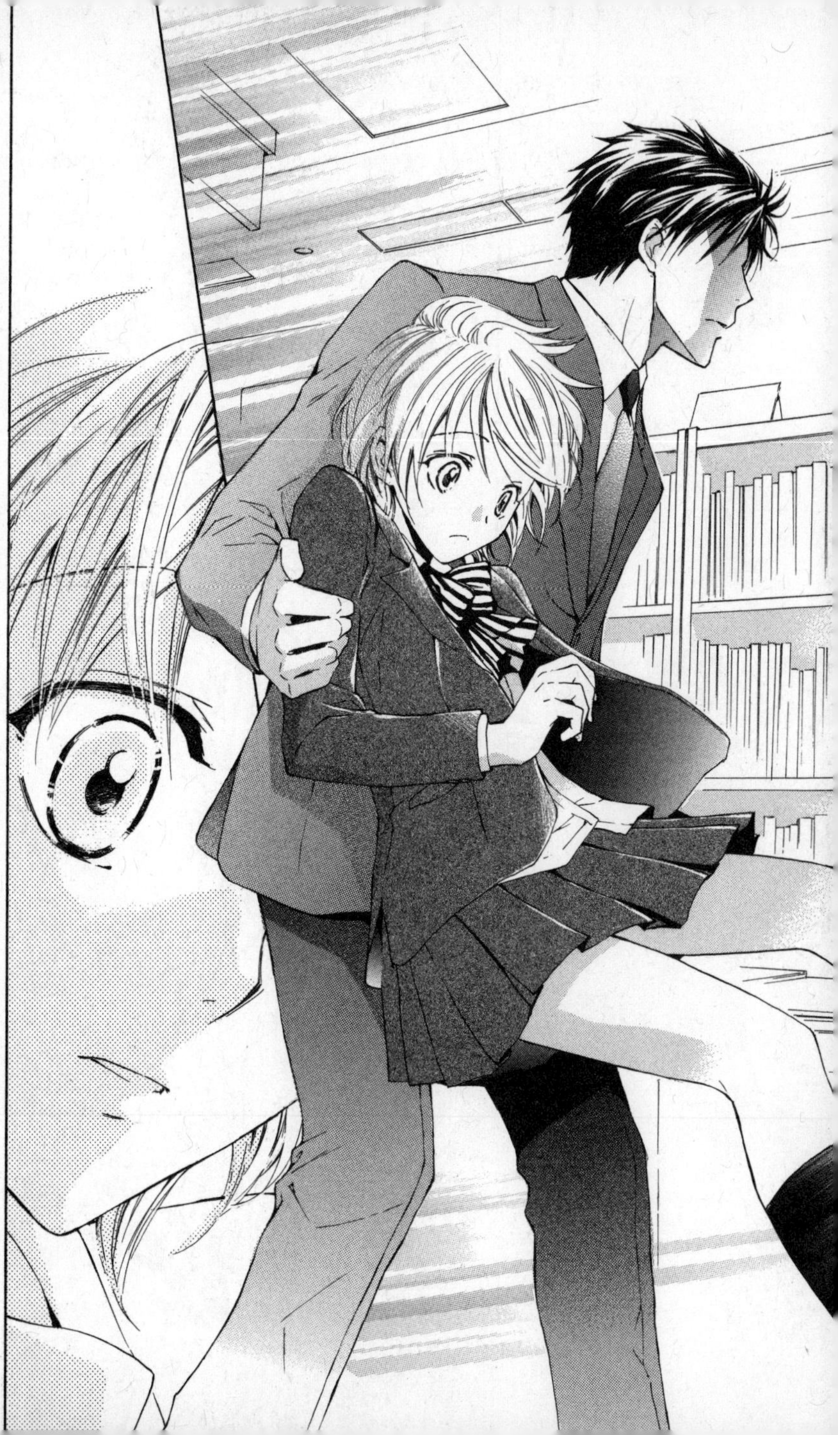

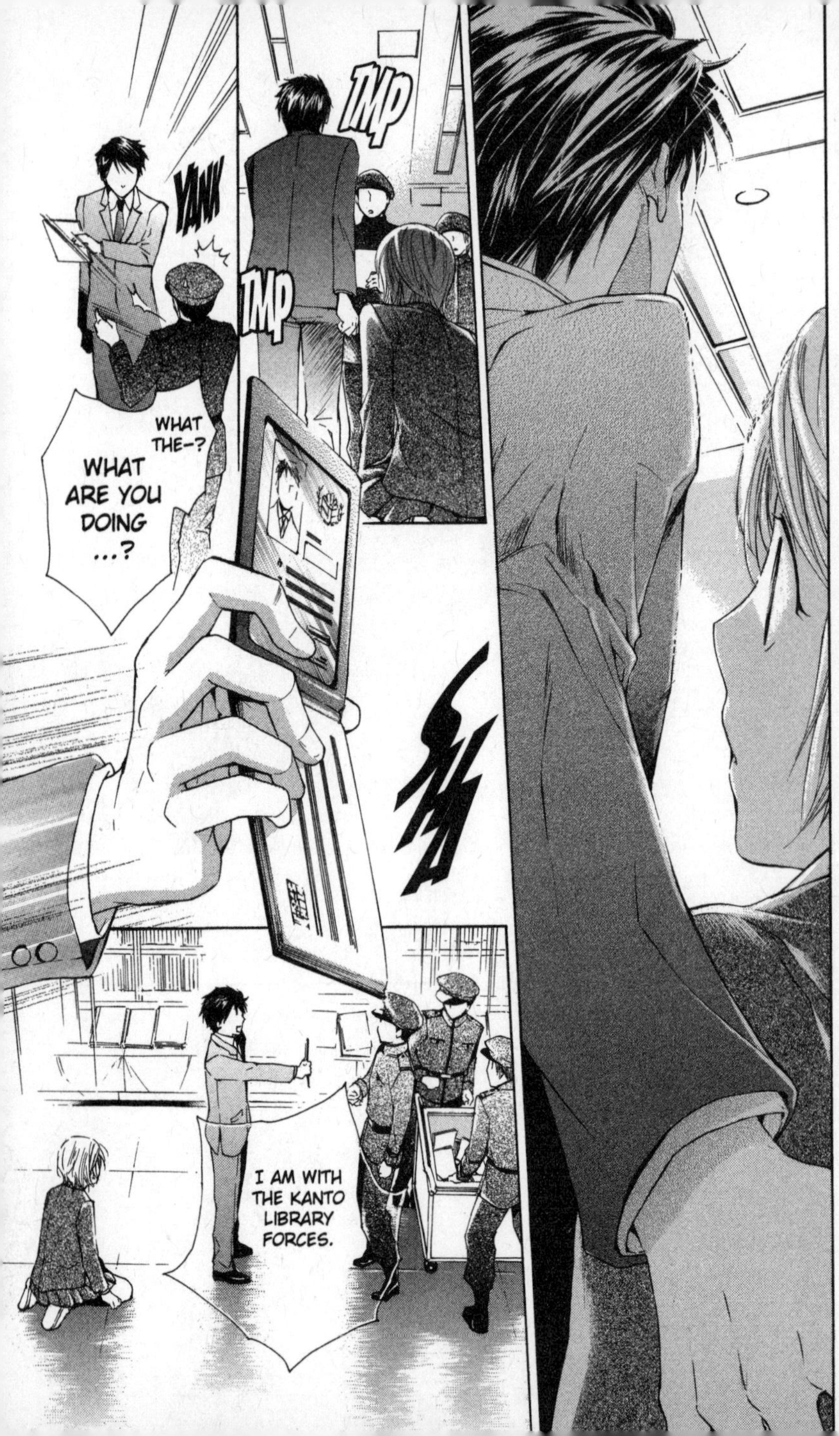
TMP
TMP
YANK
WHAT THE-?
WHAT ARE YOU DOING ...?
I AM WITH THE KANTO LIBRARY FORCES.

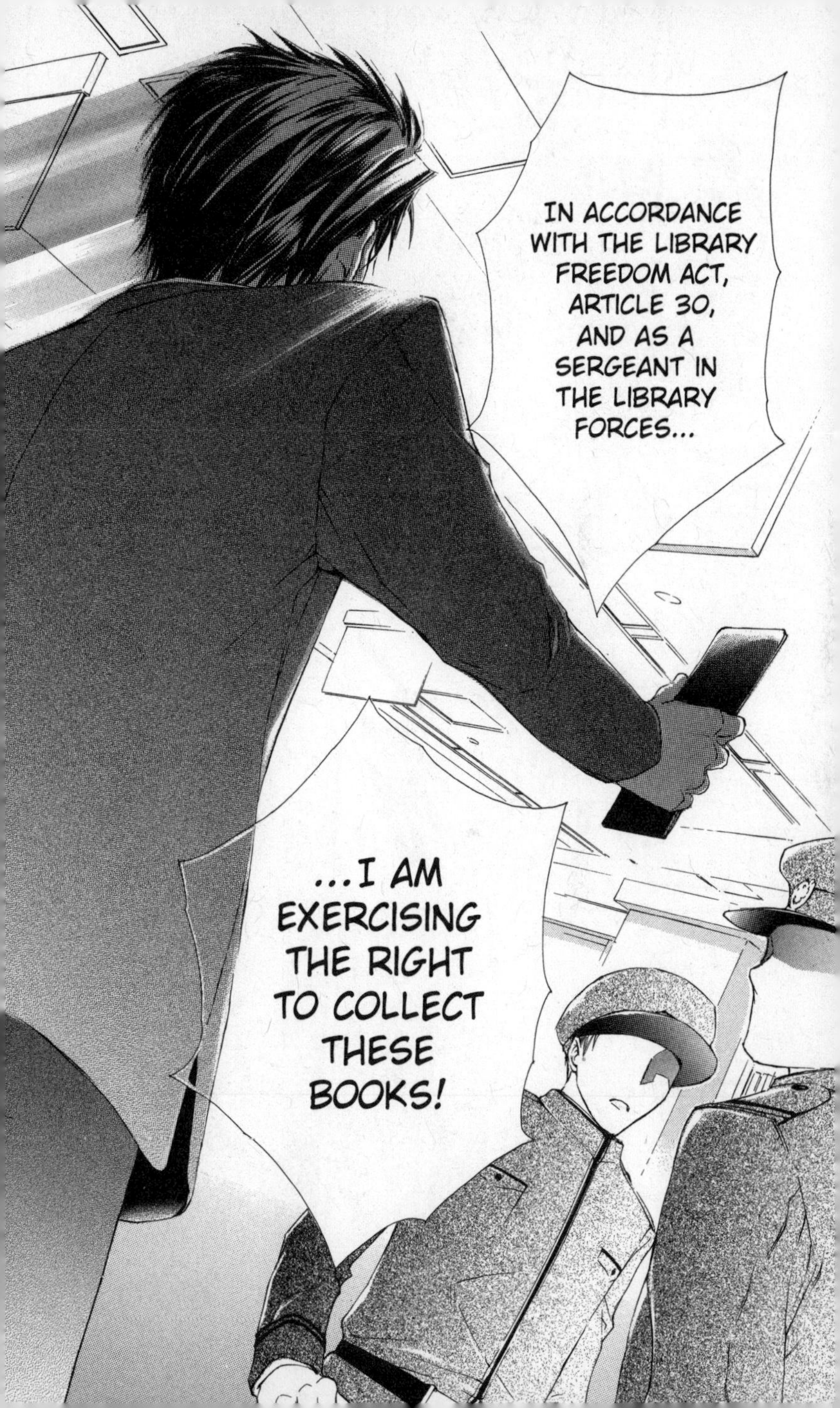
IN ACCORDANCE WITH THE LIBRARY FREEDOM ACT, ARTICLE 30, AND AS A SERGEANT IN THE LIBRARY FORCES...
...I AM EXERCISING THE RIGHT TO COLLECT THESE BOOKS!

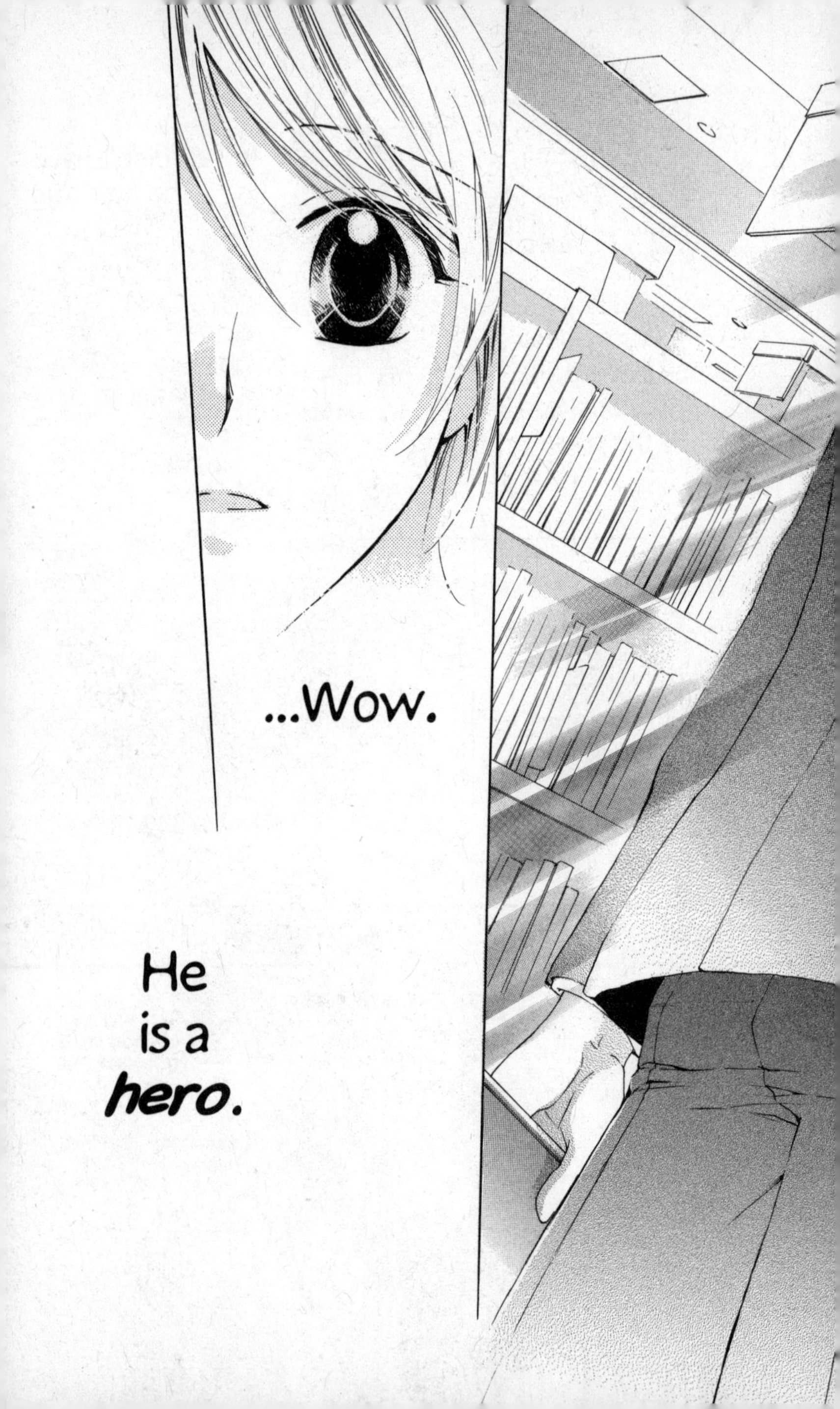
...Wow.
He is a *hero*.

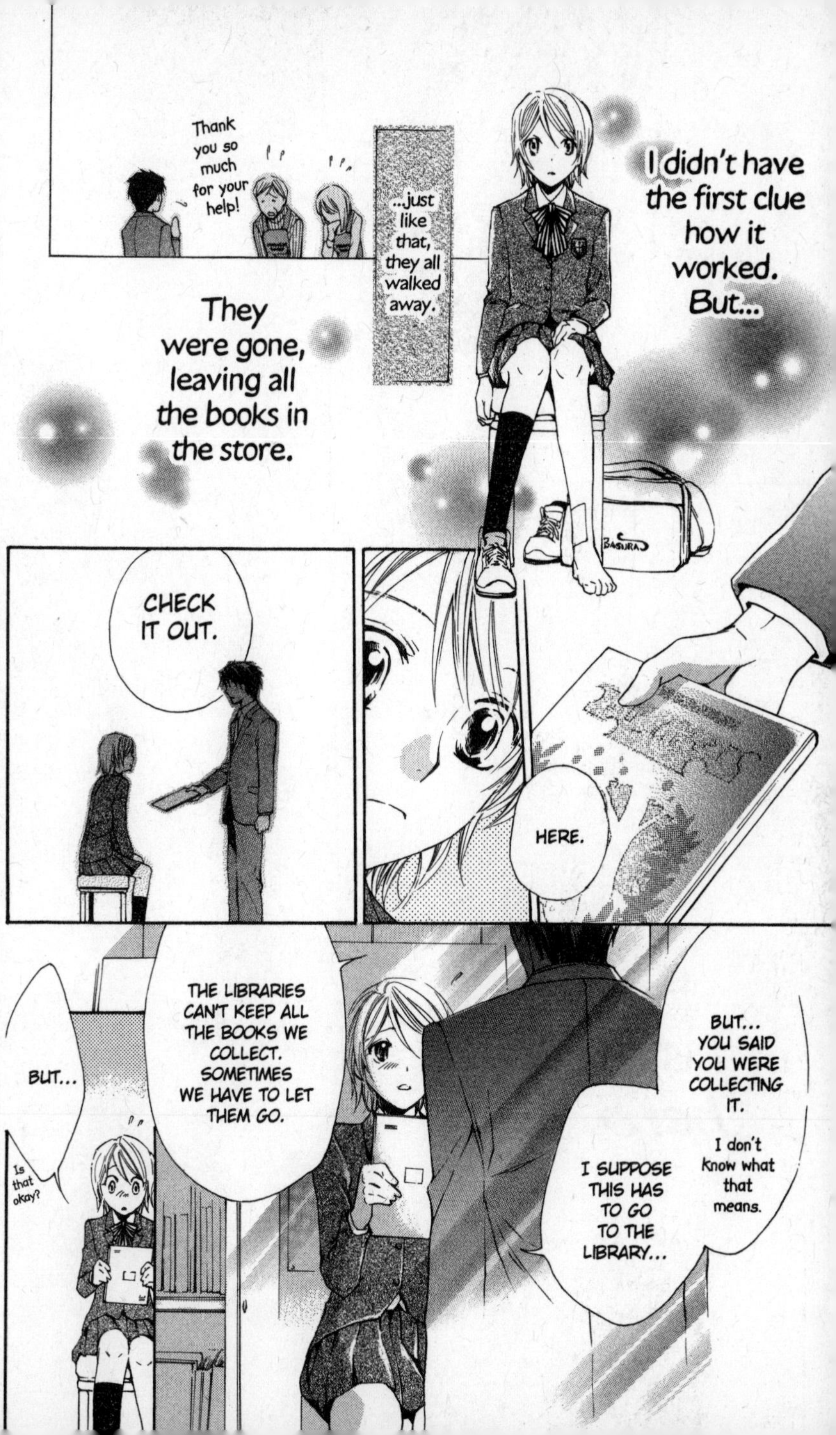
I didn't have the first clue how it worked. But...
Thank you so much for your help!
...just like that, they all walked away.
They were gone, leaving all the books in the store.
HERE.
CHECK IT OUT.
BUT... YOU SAID YOU WERE COLLECTING IT.
I don't know what that means.
I SUPPOSE THIS HAS TO GO TO THE LIBRARY...
THE LIBRARIES CAN'T KEEP ALL THE BOOKS WE COLLECT. SOMETIMES WE HAVE TO LET THEM GO.
BUT...
Is that okay?
BASURA

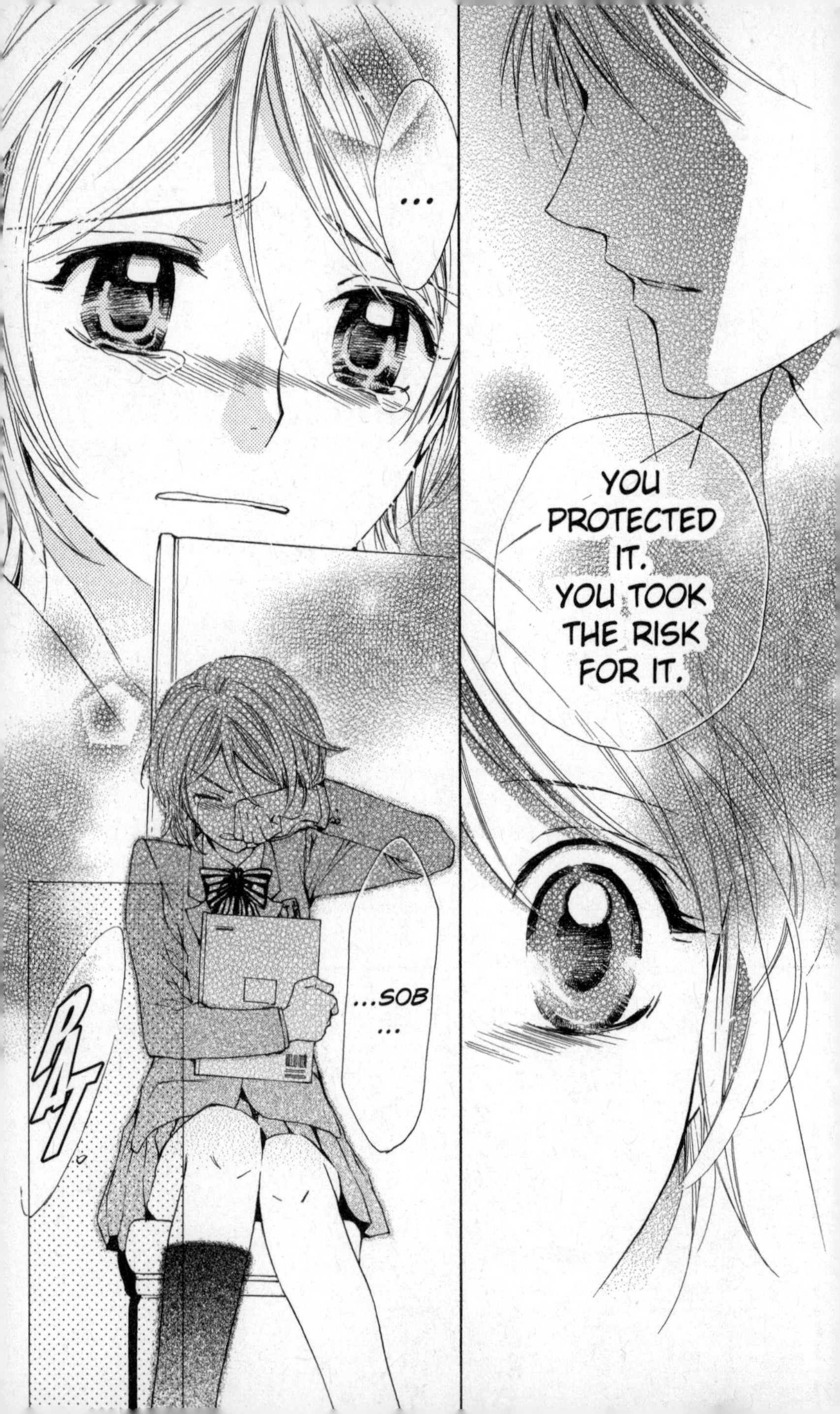

YOU PROTECTED IT. YOU TOOK THE RISK FOR IT.
...
...SOB ...
PAT

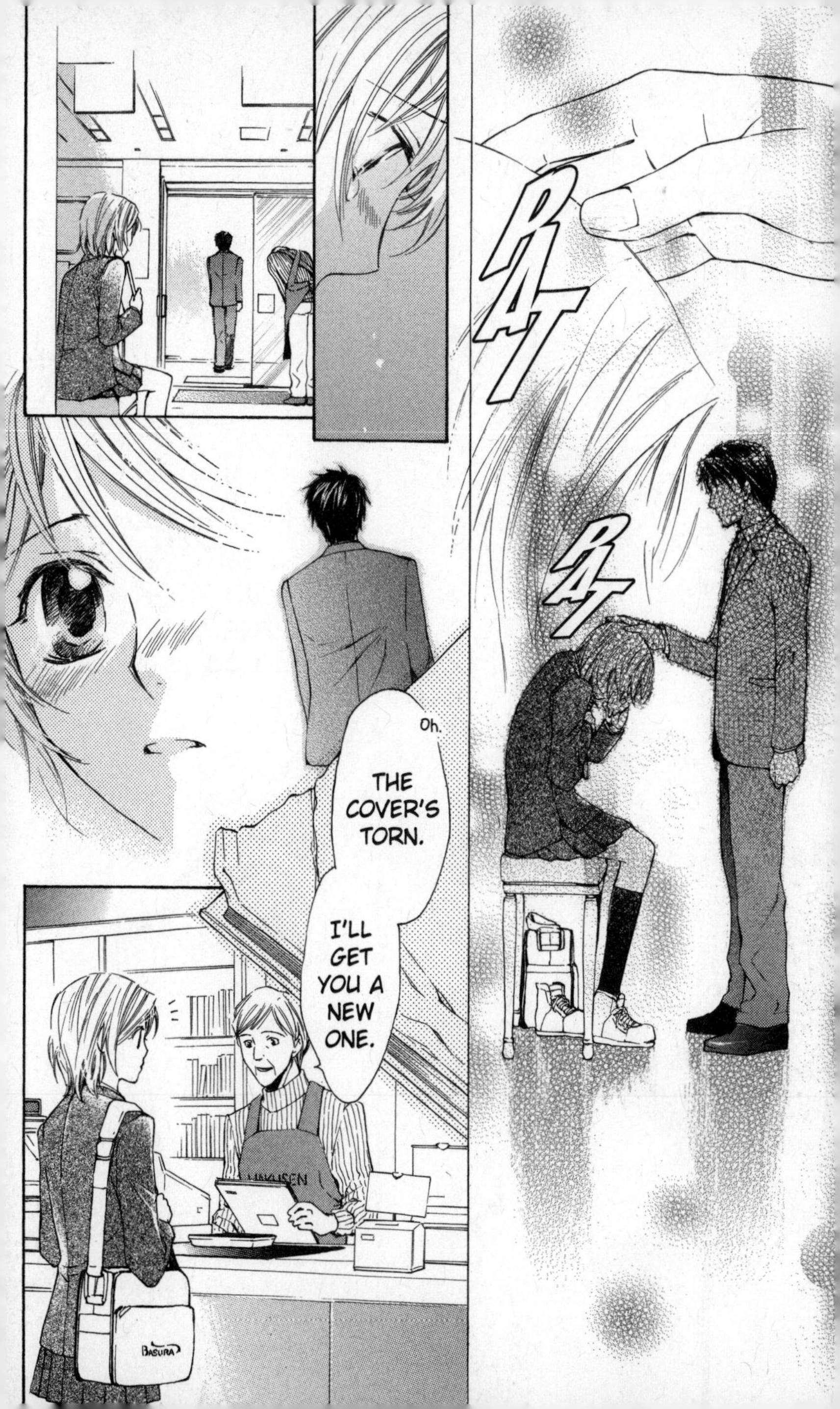
RAT
RAT
Oh.
THE COVER'S TORN.
I'LL GET YOU A NEW ONE.
BASURA

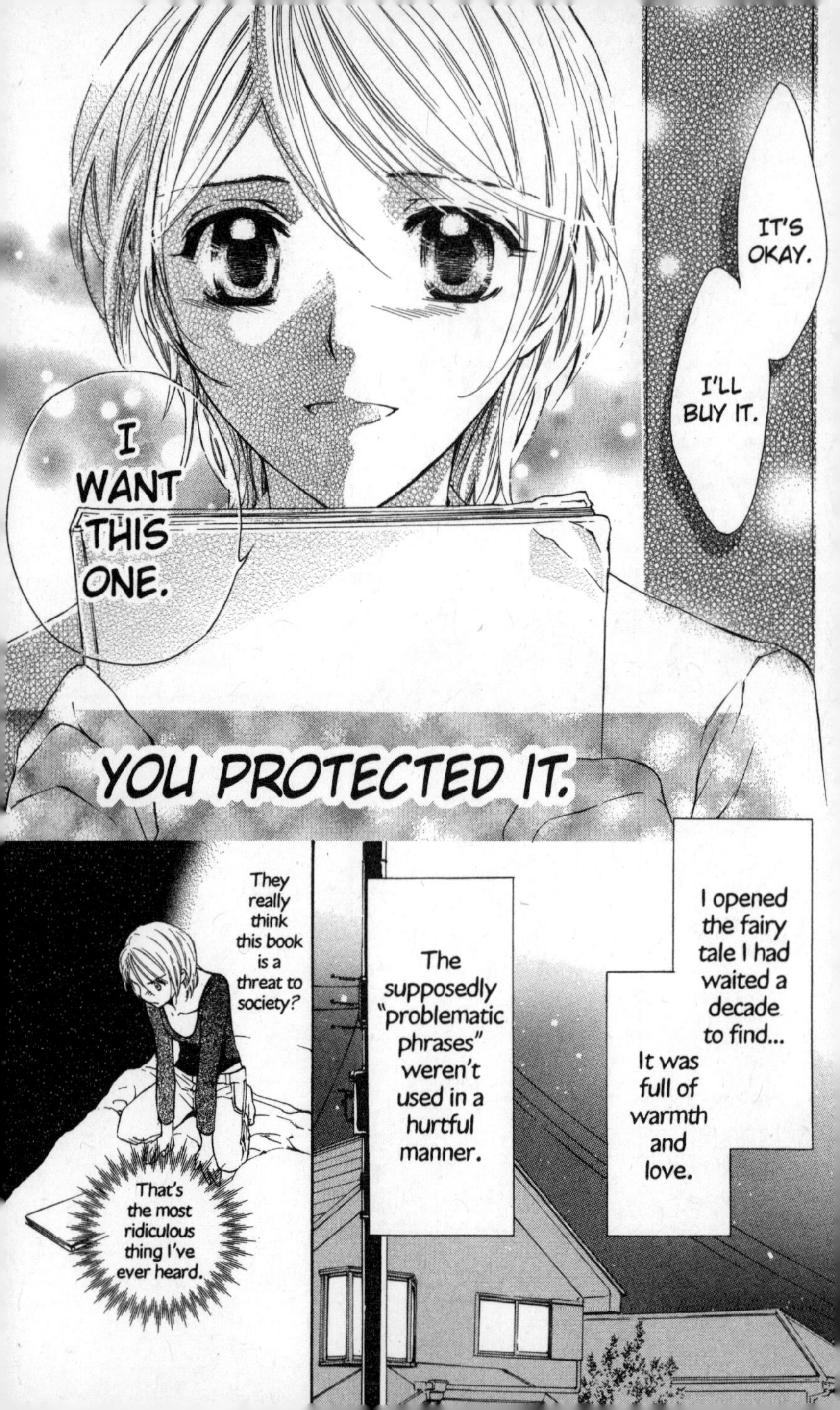
IT'S OKAY.
I'LL BUY IT.
I WANT THIS ONE.
YOU PROTECTED IT.
I opened the fairy tale I had waited a decade to find...
It was full of warmth and love.
The supposedly "problematic phrases" weren't used in a hurtful manner.
They really think this book is a threat to society?
That's the most ridiculous thing I've ever heard.

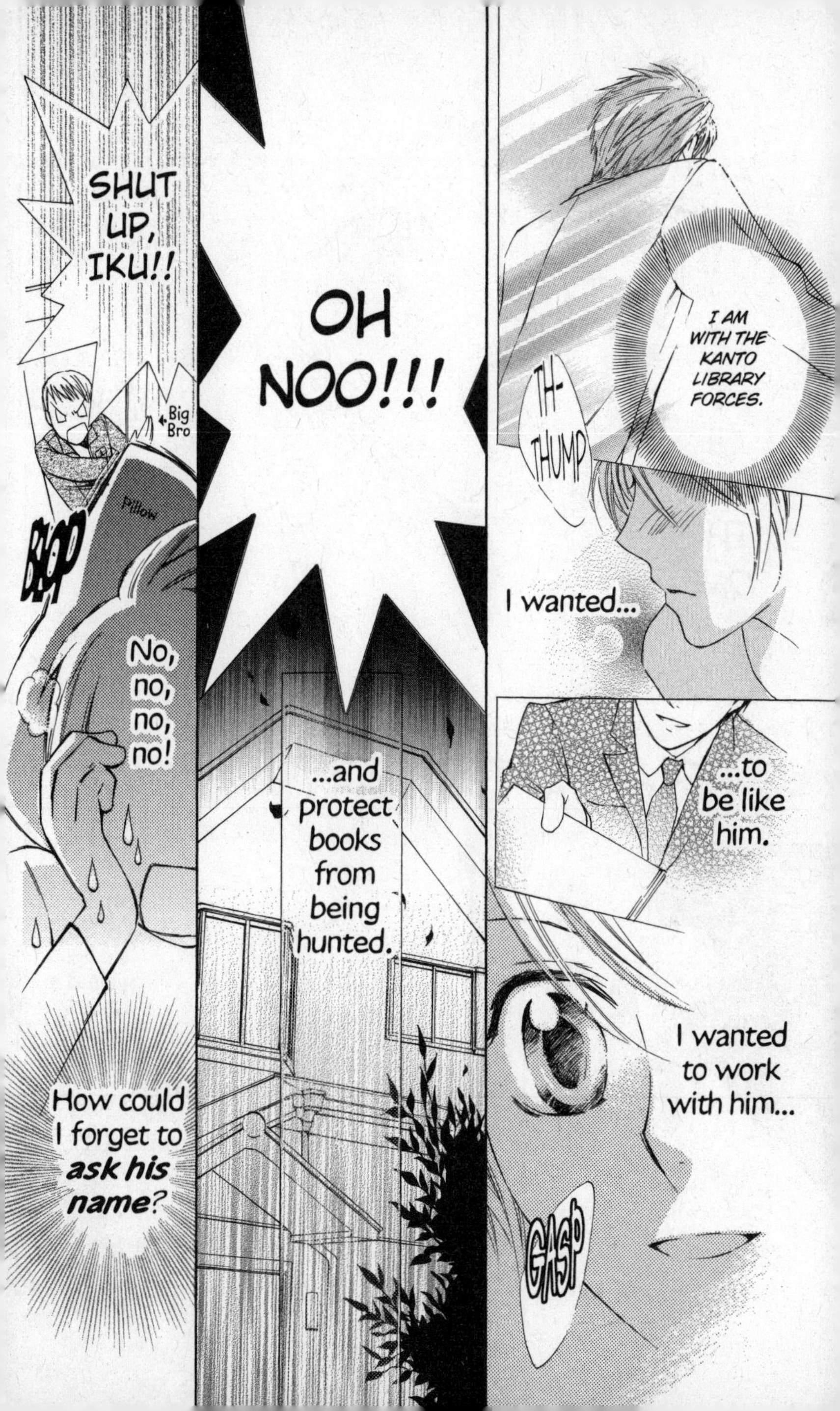
I AM WITH THE KANTO LIBRARY FORCES.
TH-THUMP
I wanted...
...to be like him.
I wanted to work with him...
GASP
OH NOO!!!
...and protect books from being hunted.
SHUT UP, IKU!!
Big Bro
Pillow
No, no, no, no!
How could I forget to ***ask his name***?

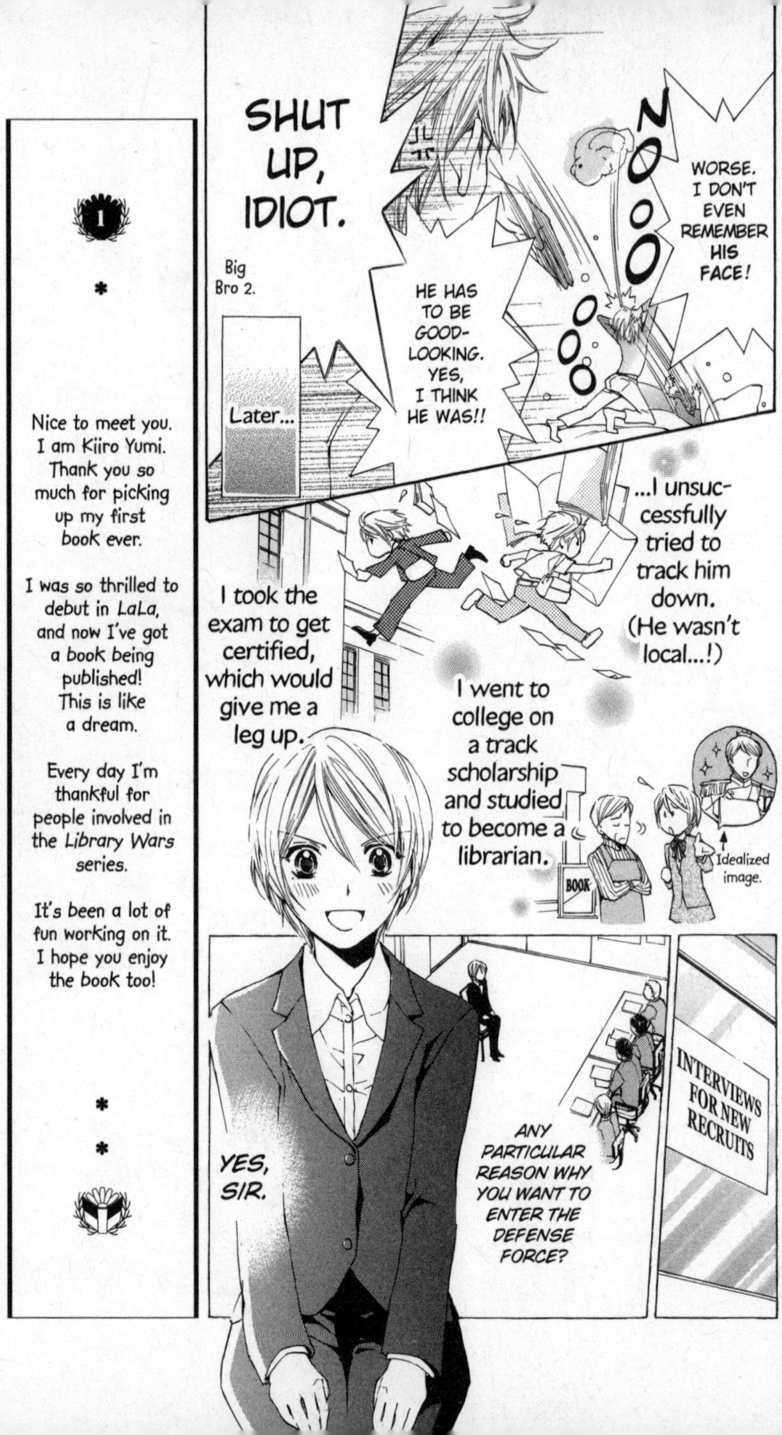
WORSE. I DON'T EVEN REMEMBER HIS FACE!
NOOOOOOOO
HE HAS TO BE GOOD-LOOKING. YES, I THINK HE WAS!!
SHUT UP, IDIOT.
Big Bro 2.
Later...
...I unsuccessfully tried to track him down. (He wasn't local...!)
I took the exam to get certified, which would give me a leg up.
Idealized image.
BOOK
I went to college on a track scholarship and studied to become a librarian.
INTERVIEWS FOR NEW RECRUITS
ANY PARTICULAR REASON WHY YOU WANT TO ENTER THE DEFENSE FORCE?
YES, SIR.

1

*

Nice to meet you. I am Kiiro Yumi. Thank you so much for picking up my first book ever.

I was so thrilled to debut in *LaLa*, and now I've got a book being published! This is like a dream.

Every day I'm thankful for people involved in the *Library Wars* series.

It's been a lot of fun working on it. I hope you enjoy the book too!

*

*

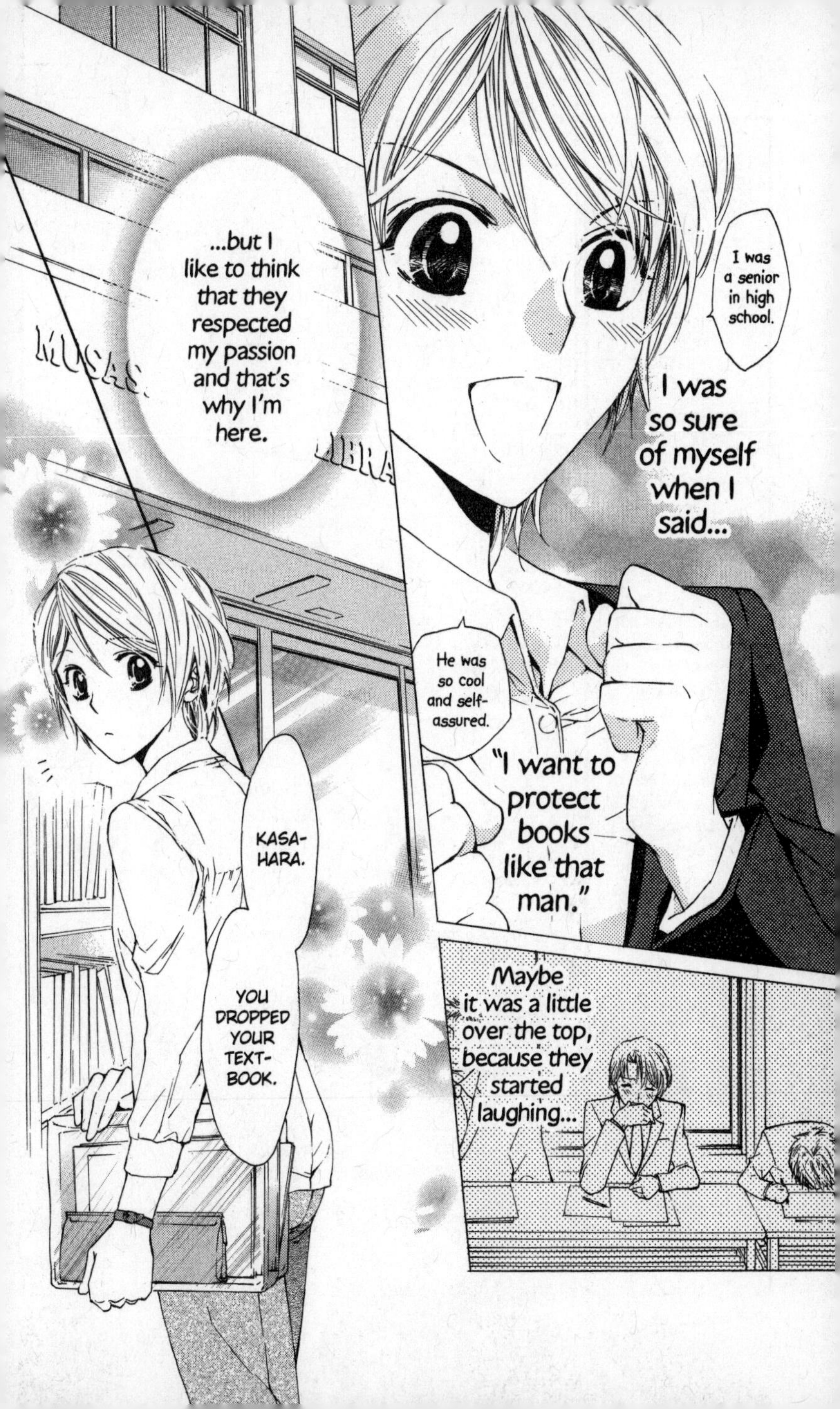
I was a senior in high school.
I was so sure of myself when I said...
He was so cool and self-assured.
"I want to protect books like that man."
Maybe it was a little over the top, because they started laughing...
...but I like to think that they respected my passion and that's why I'm here.
KASA-HARA.
YOU DROPPED YOUR TEXT-BOOK.

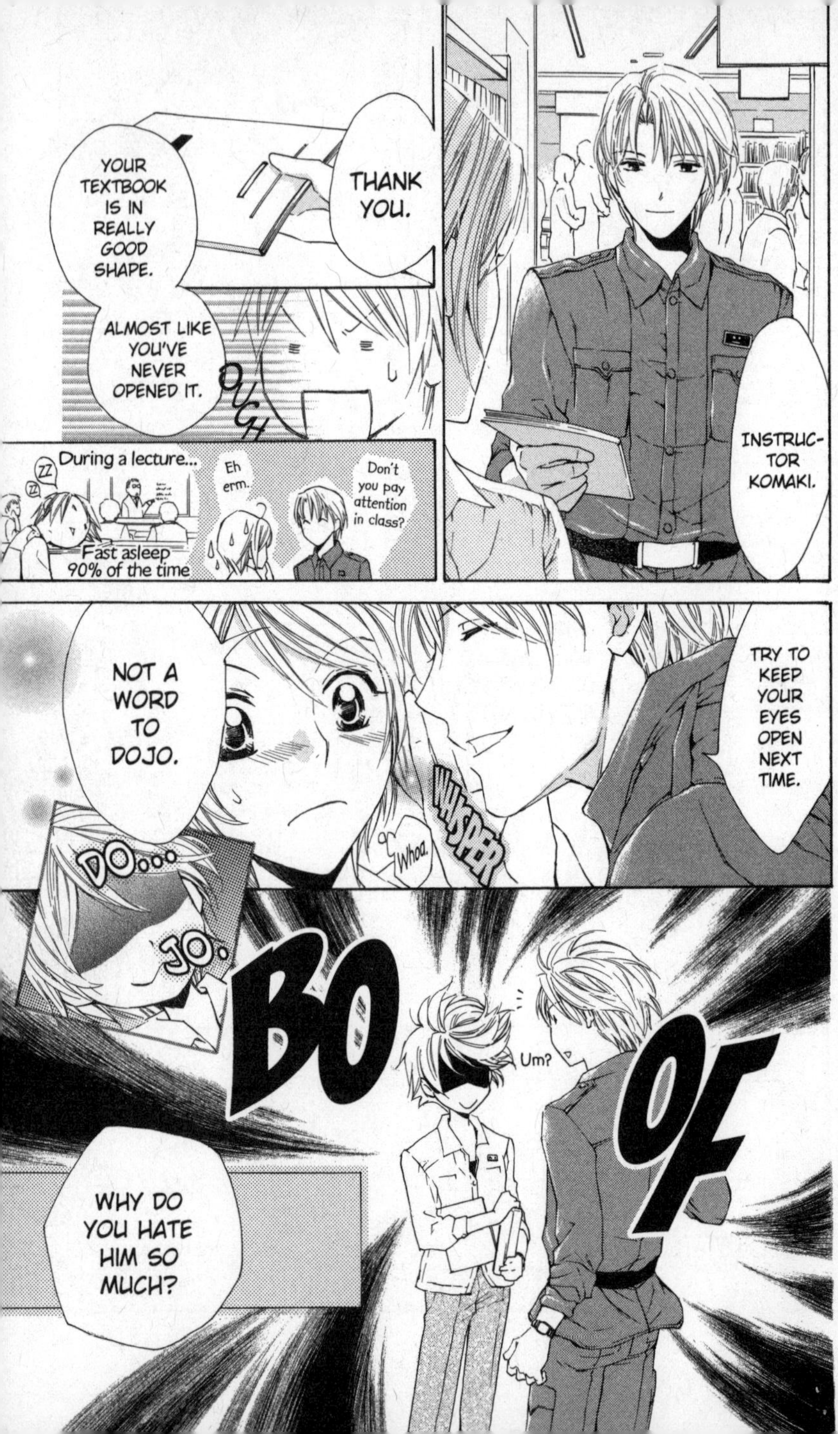

INSTRUCTOR KOMAKI.
THANK YOU.
YOUR TEXTBOOK IS IN REALLY GOOD SHAPE.
ALMOST LIKE YOU'VE NEVER OPENED IT.
OUCH
Don't you pay attention in class?
Eh erm.
During a lecture...
ZZ
ZZ
Fast asleep 90% of the time
TRY TO KEEP YOUR EYES OPEN NEXT TIME.
WHISPER
Whoa.
NOT A WORD TO DOJO.
DO...
JO.
BO OF
Um?
WHY DO YOU HATE HIM SO MUCH?

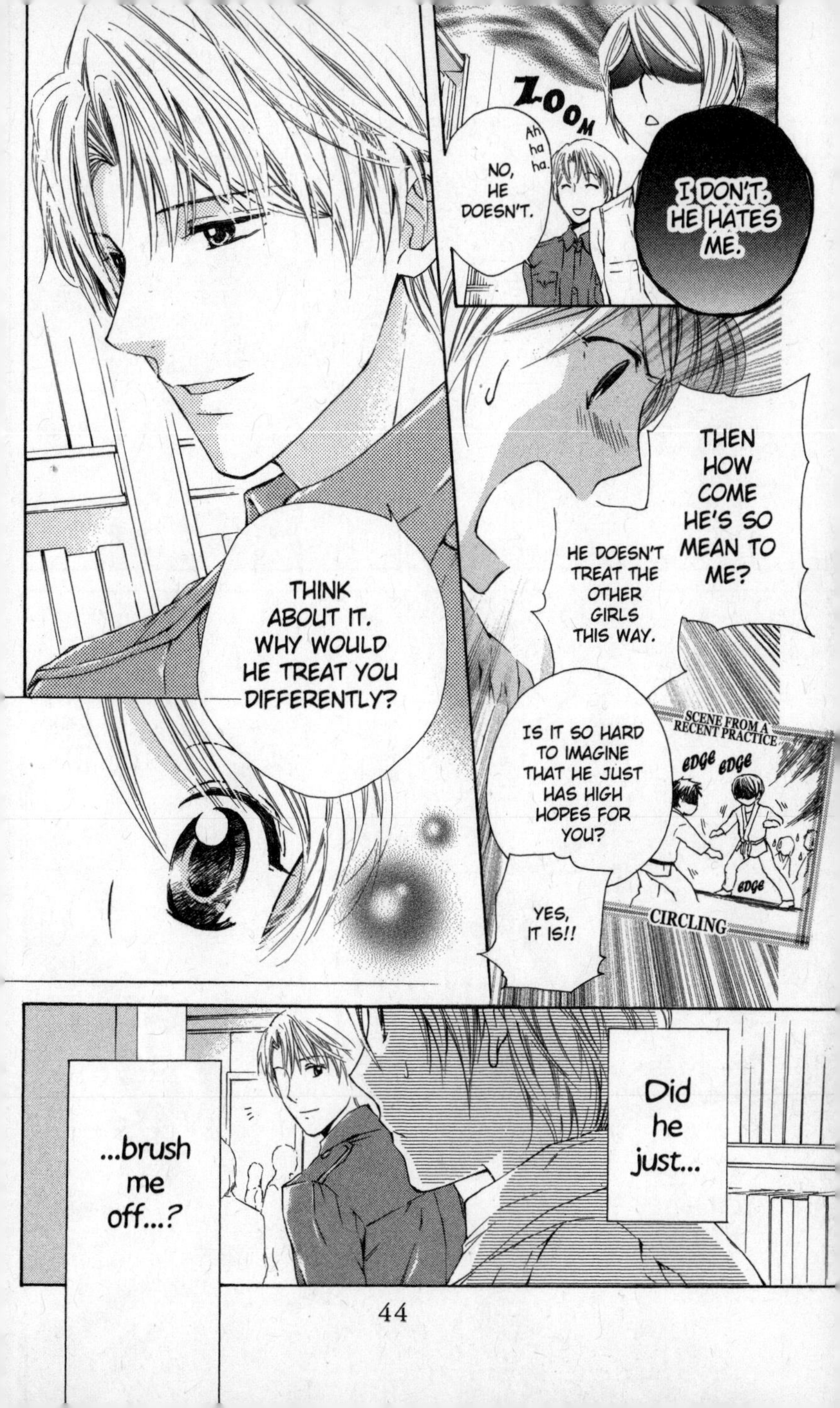
ZOOM
I DON'T. HE HATES ME.
Ah ha ha.
NO, HE DOESN'T.
THEN HOW COME HE'S SO MEAN TO ME?
HE DOESN'T TREAT THE OTHER GIRLS THIS WAY.
IS IT SO HARD TO IMAGINE THAT HE JUST HAS HIGH HOPES FOR YOU?
SCENE FROM A RECENT PRACTICE
eDGe eDGe eDGe
CIRCLING
YES, IT IS!!
THINK ABOUT IT. WHY WOULD HE TREAT YOU DIFFERENTLY?
Did he just...
...brush me off...?

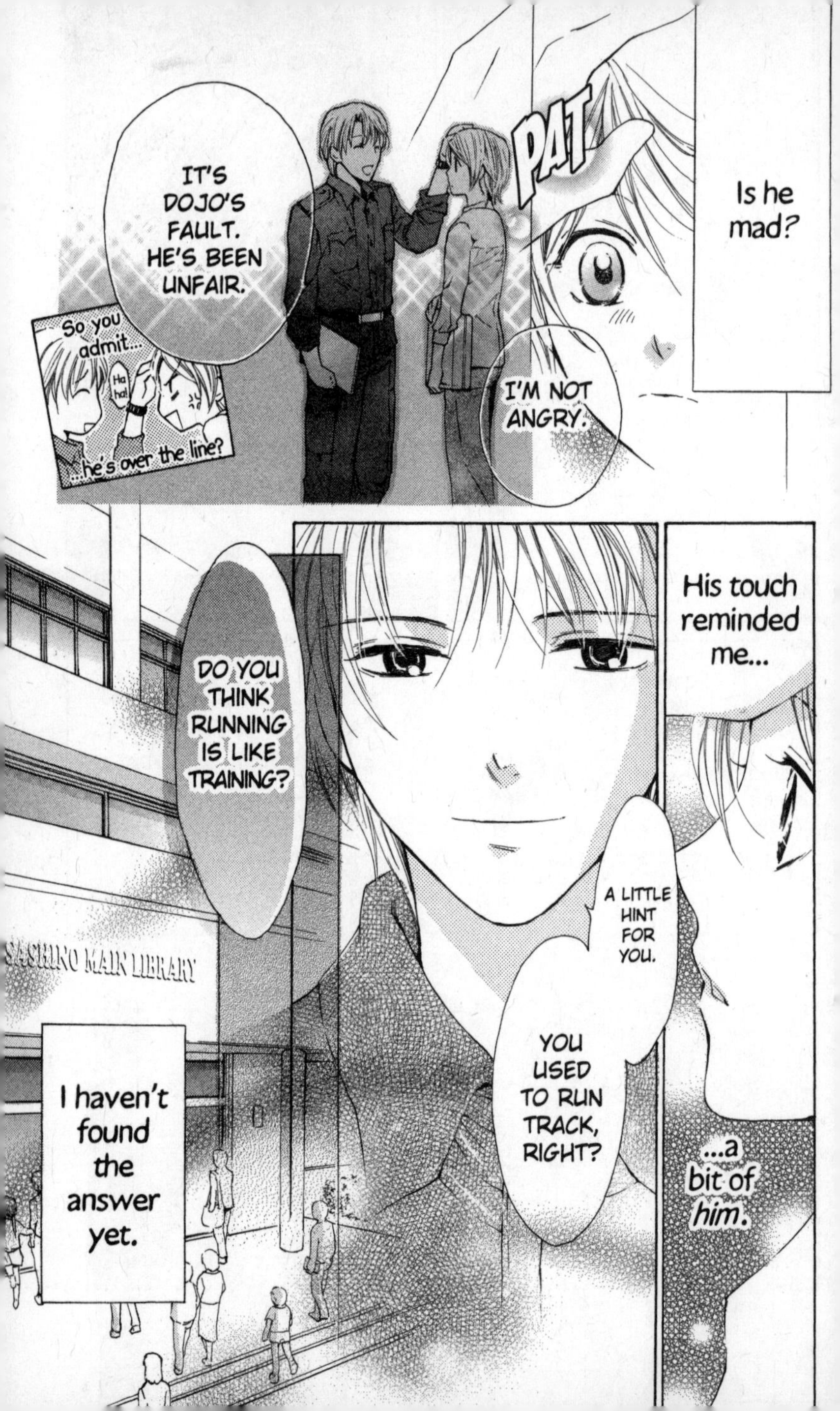

Is he mad?
PAT
I'M NOT ANGRY.
IT'S DOJO'S FAULT. HE'S BEEN UNFAIR.
So you admit...
Ha ha!
...he's over the line?
His touch reminded me...
...a bit of *him*.
A LITTLE HINT FOR YOU.
YOU USED TO RUN TRACK, RIGHT?
DO YOU THINK RUNNING IS LIKE TRAINING?
SASHINO MAIN LIBRARY
I haven't found the answer yet.

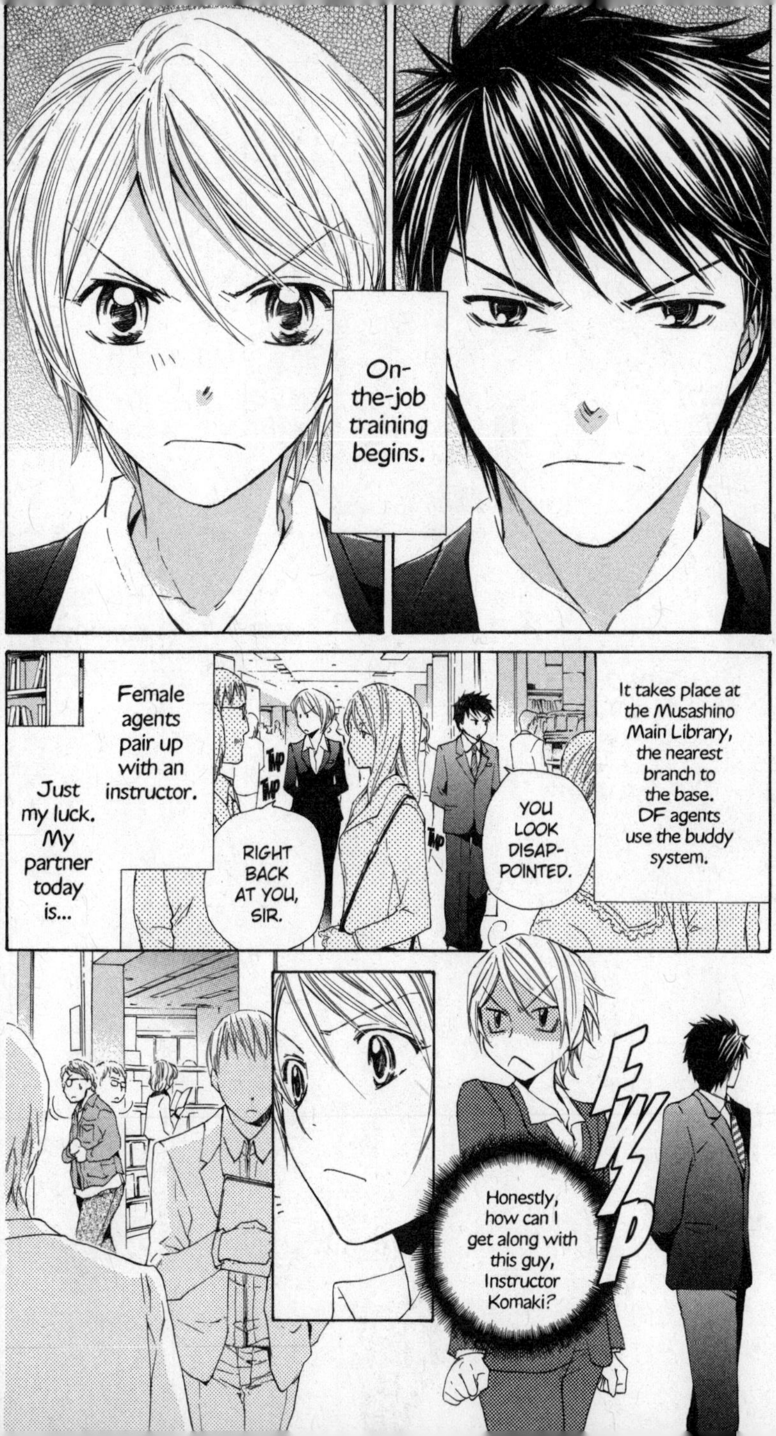

On-the-job training begins.
It takes place at the Musashino Main Library, the nearest branch to the base. DF agents use the buddy system.
YOU LOOK DISAPPOINTED.
RIGHT BACK AT YOU, SIR.
TMP
TMP
TMP
Female agents pair up with an instructor.
Just my luck. My partner today is...
FWSP
Honestly, how can I get along with this guy, Instructor Komaki?

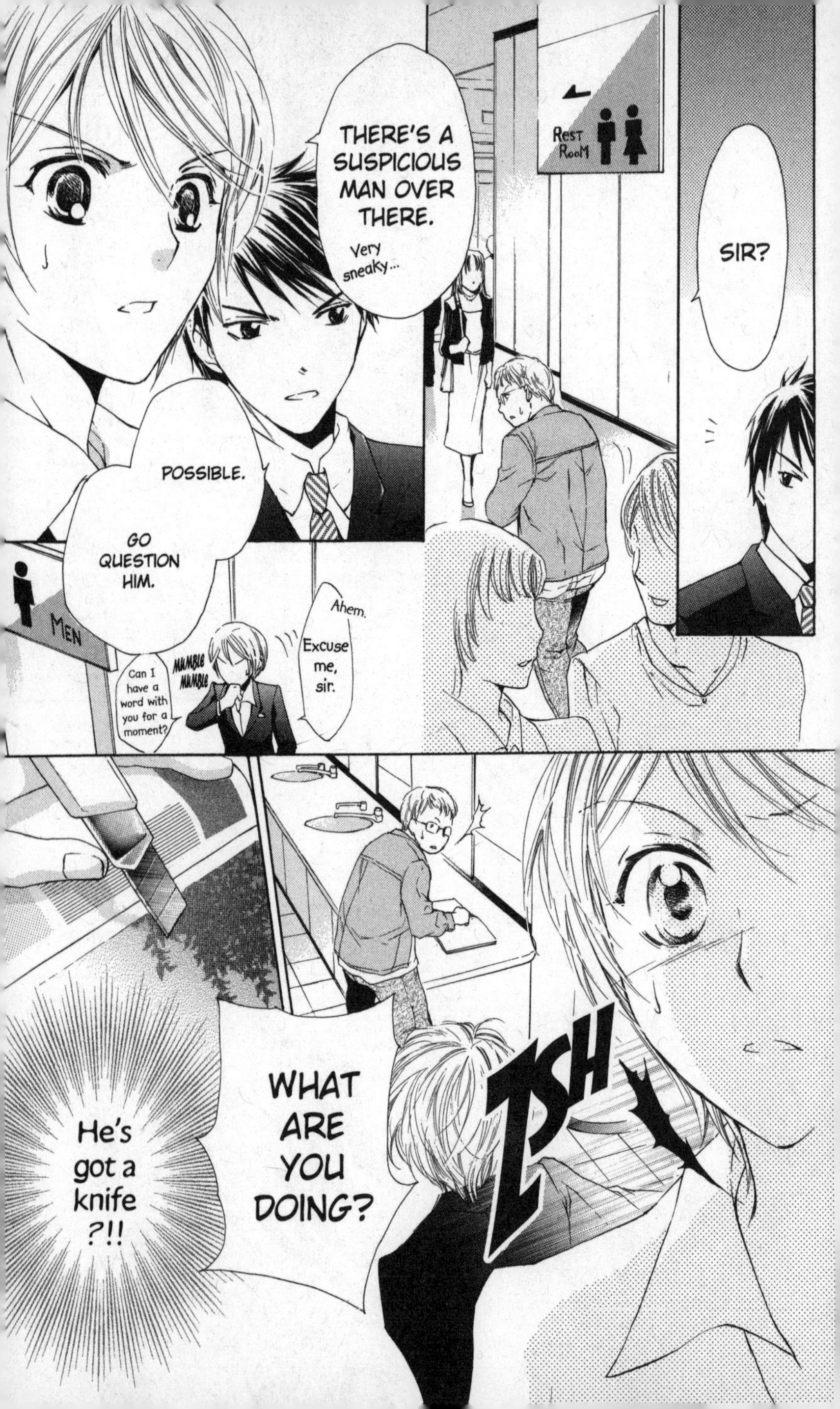
SIR?
REST ROOM
THERE'S A SUSPICIOUS MAN OVER THERE.
Very sneaky...
POSSIBLE.
GO QUESTION HIM.
MEN
Ahem.
Excuse me, sir.
MUMBLE MUMBLE
Can I have a word with you for a moment?
ZSH
WHAT ARE YOU DOING?
He's got a knife?!!

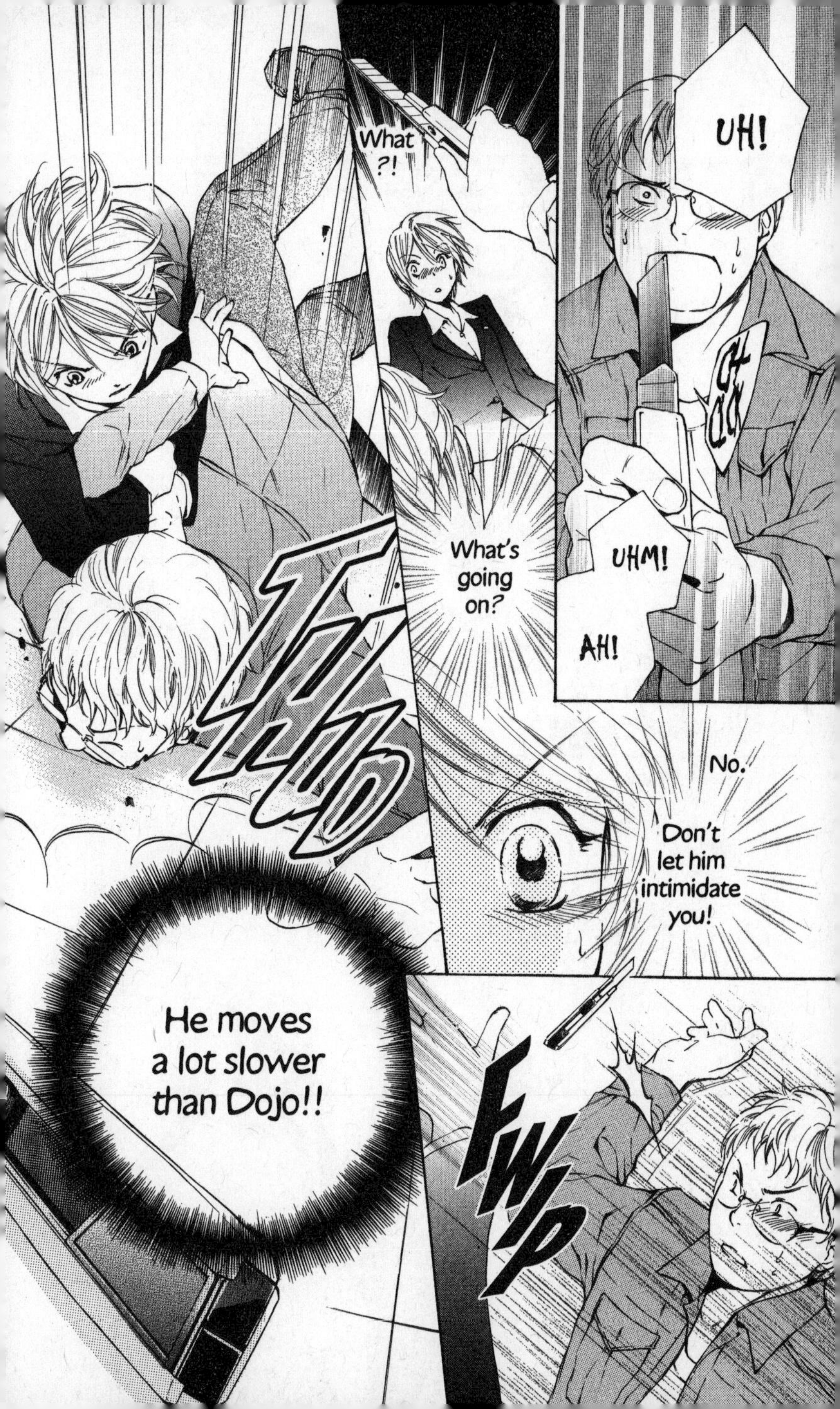
UH!
UHM!
AH!
What ?!
What's going on?
THUD
No.
Don't let him intimidate you!
FWIP
He moves a lot slower than Dojo!!

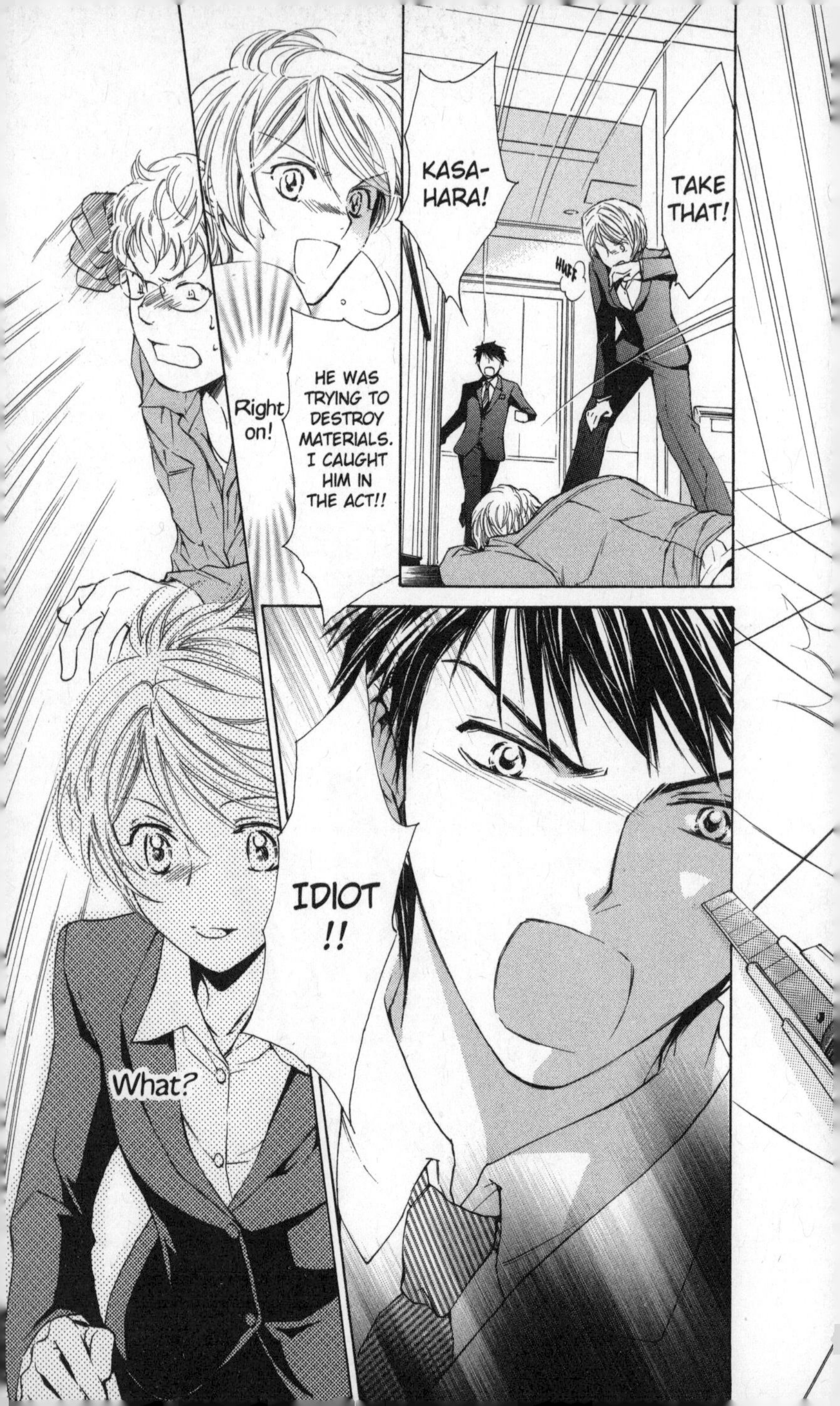
TAKE THAT!
HUFF
KASA-HARA!
HE WAS TRYING TO DESTROY MATERIALS. I CAUGHT HIM IN THE ACT!!
Right on!
IDIOT !!
What?

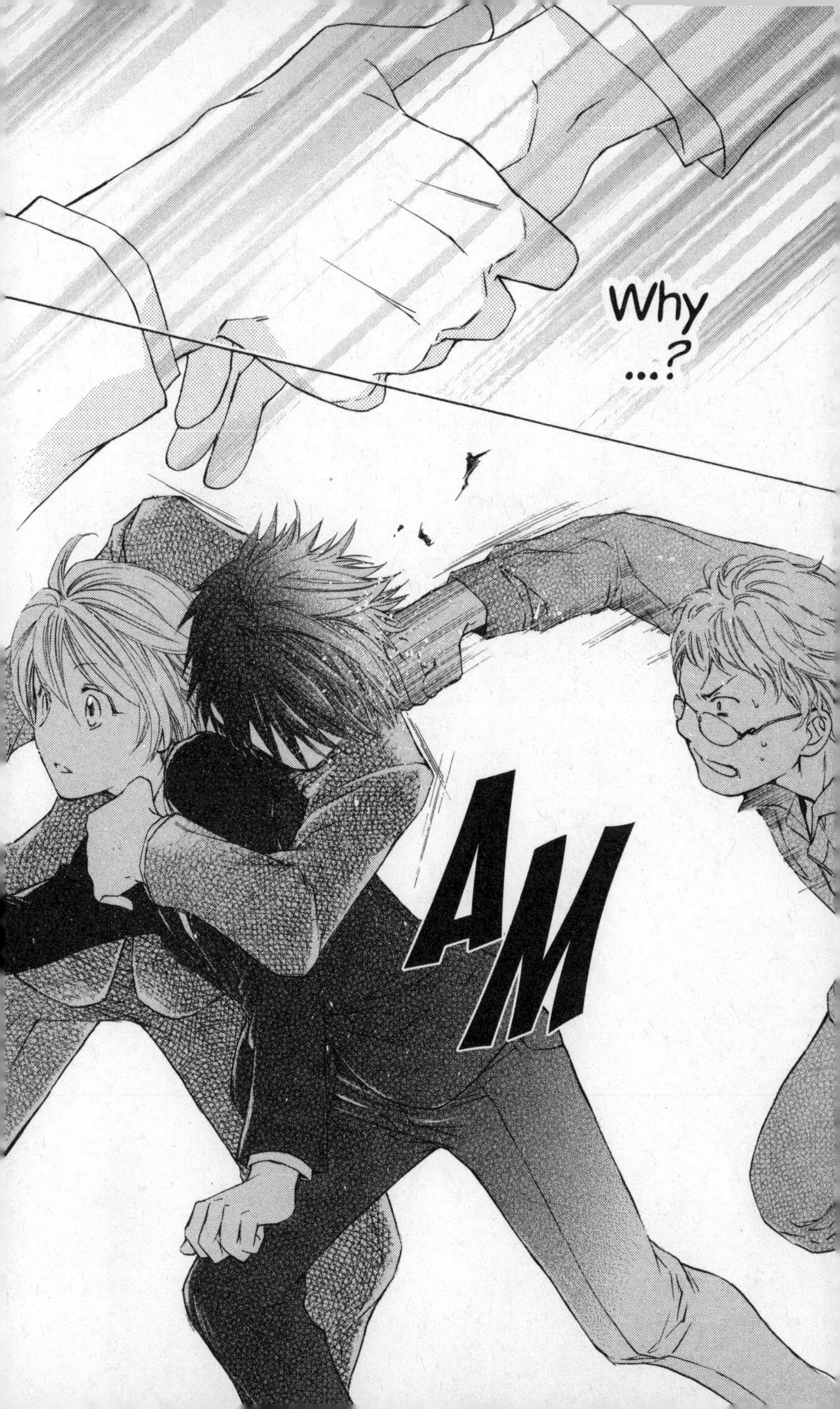
Why ...?
AM

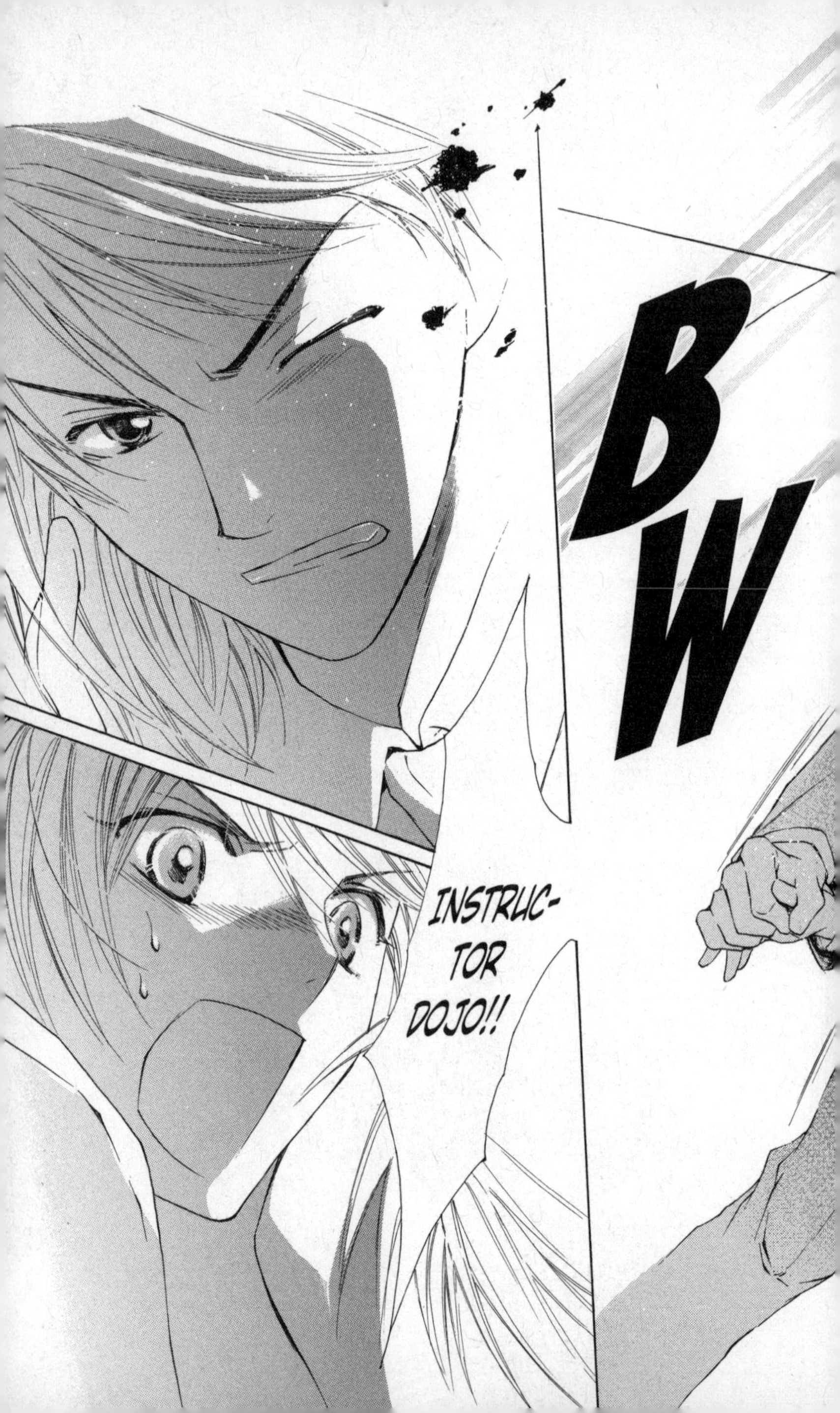
BW
INSTRUCTOR DOJO!!

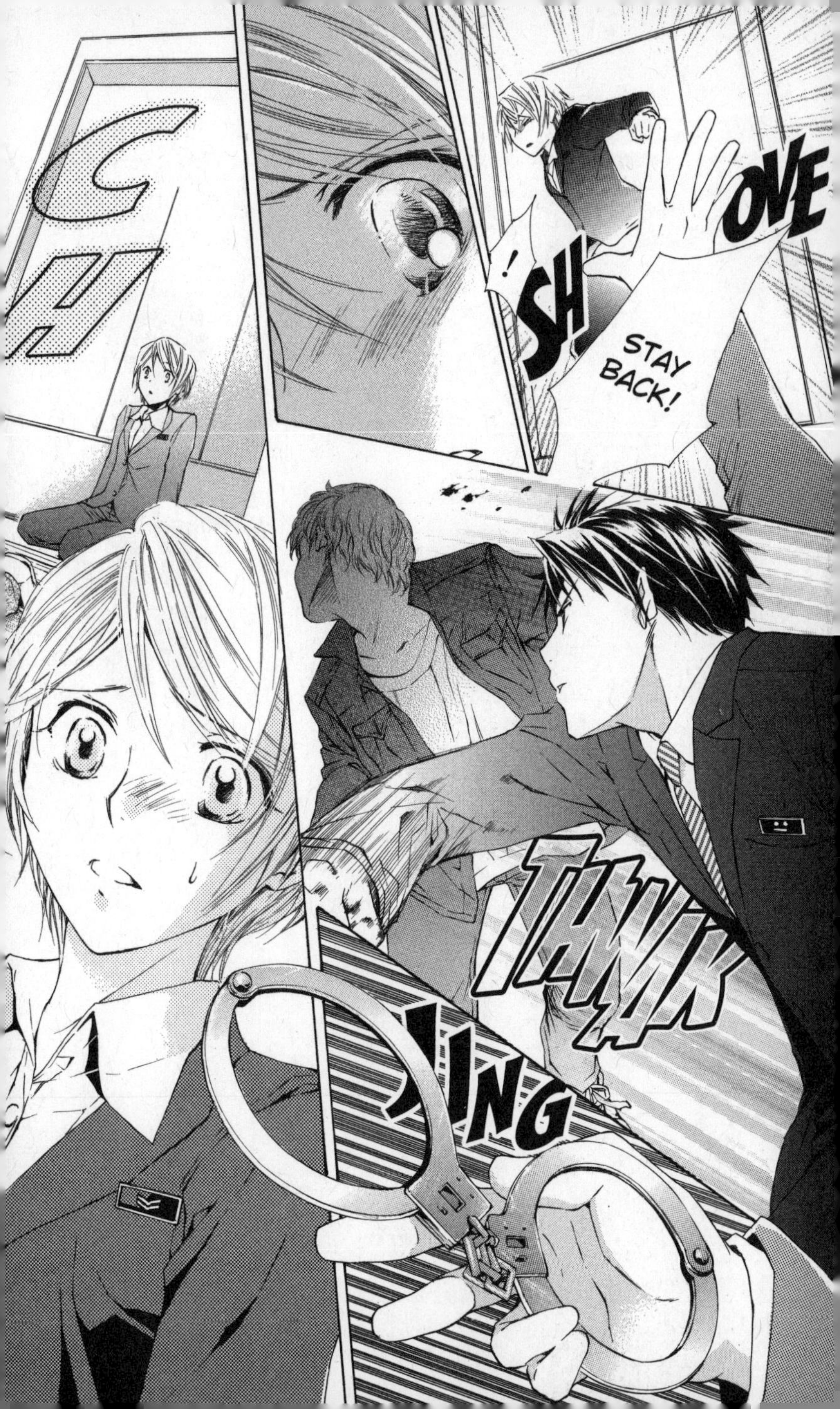

!
SHOVE
STAY BACK!
CH
THWK
ING

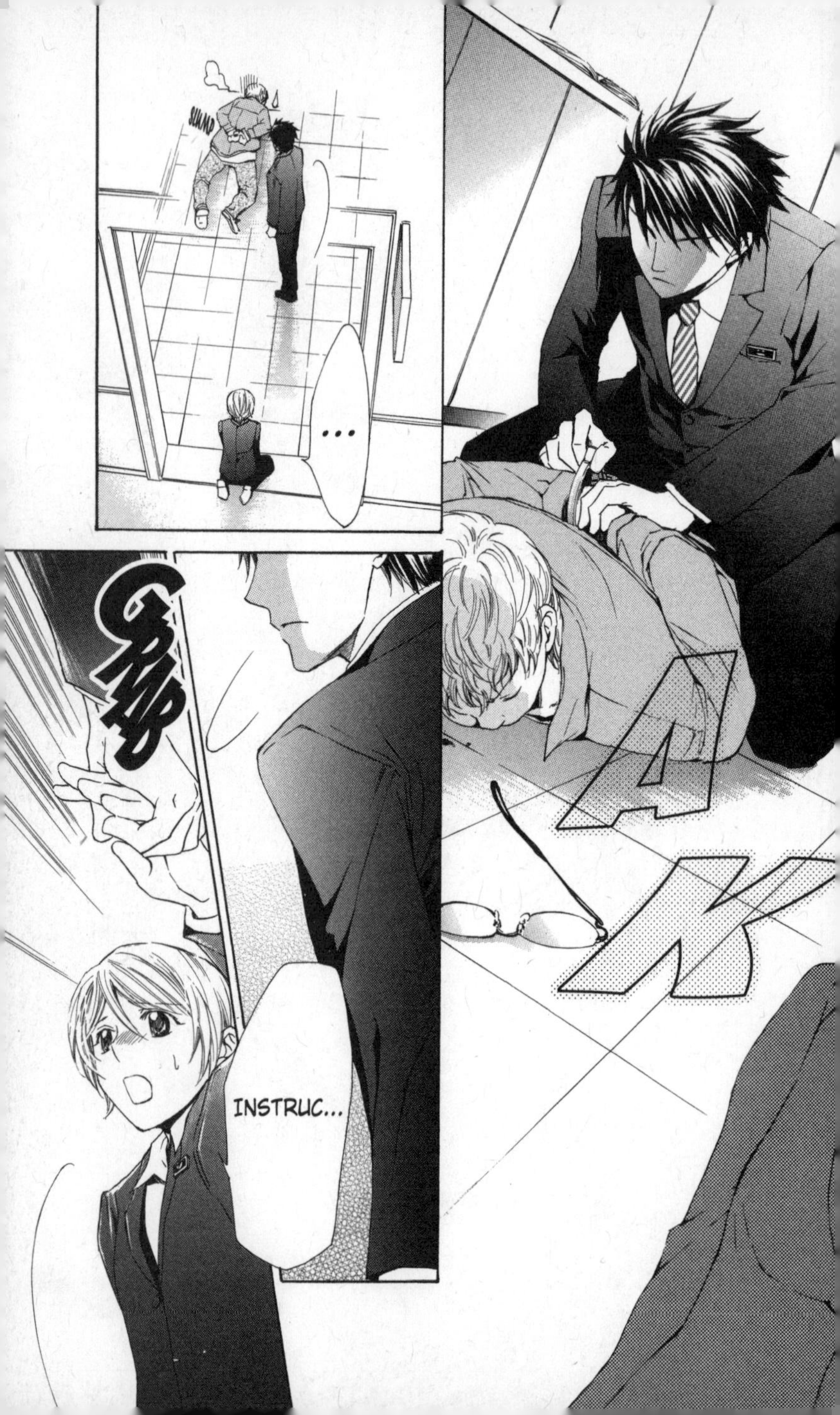
AK
SLUMP
...
GRAB
INSTRUC...

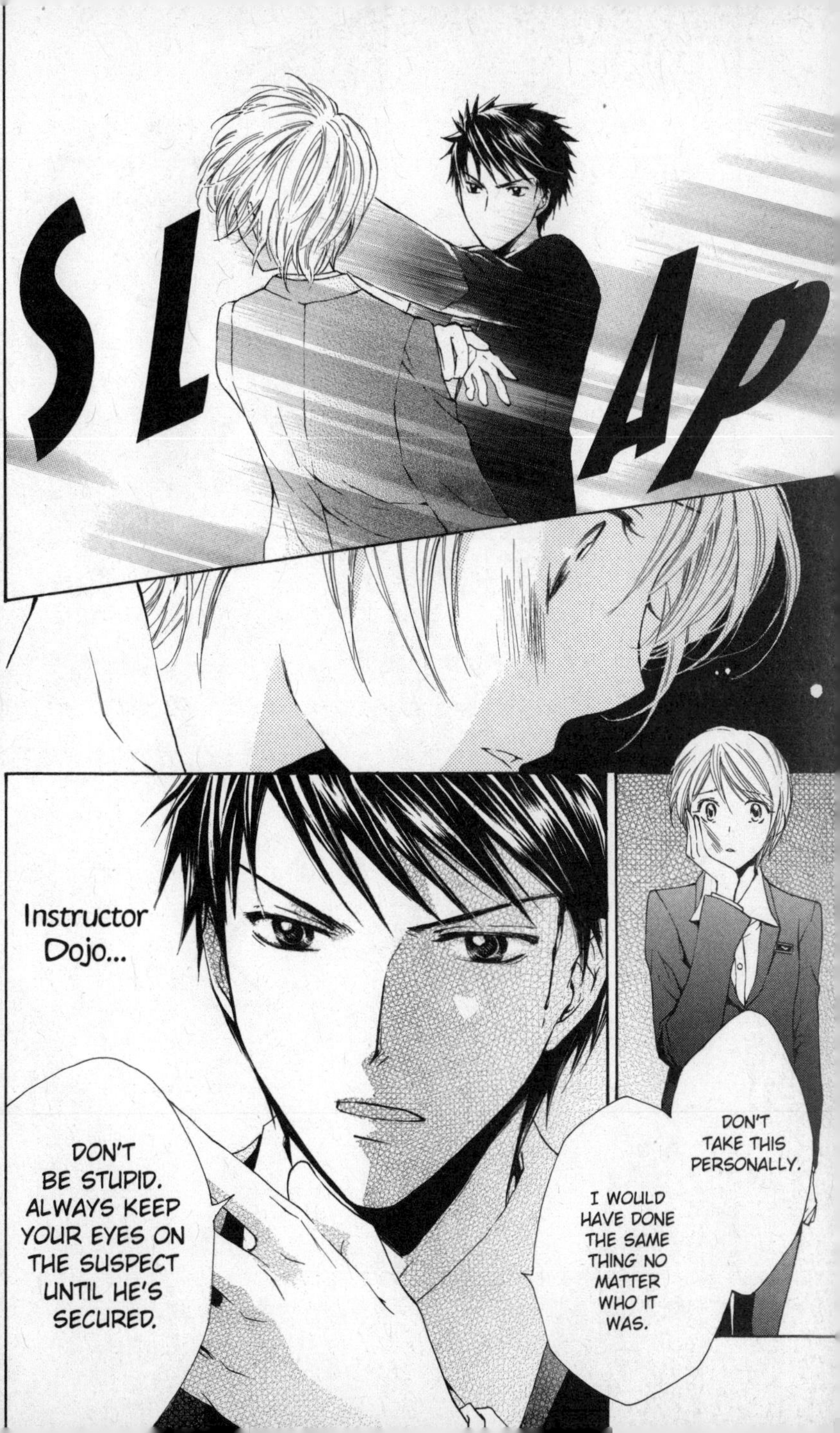
SLAP
..
Instructor Dojo...
DON'T BE STUPID. ALWAYS KEEP YOUR EYES ON THE SUSPECT UNTIL HE'S SECURED.
DON'T TAKE THIS PERSONALLY.
I WOULD HAVE DONE THE SAME THING NO MATTER WHO IT WAS.

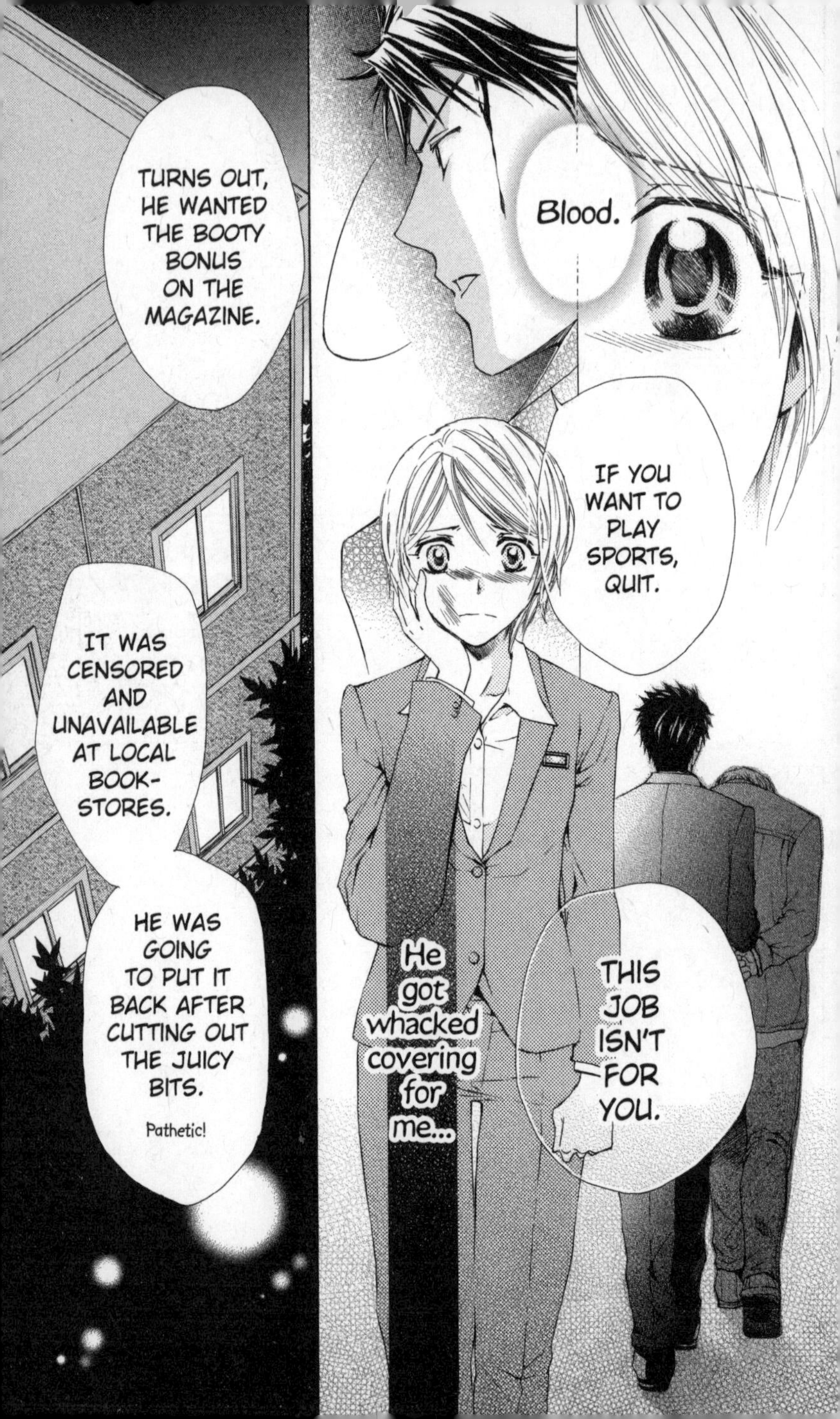
Blood.
IF YOU WANT TO PLAY SPORTS, QUIT.
THIS JOB ISN'T FOR YOU.
He got whacked covering for me...
TURNS OUT, HE WANTED THE BOOTY BONUS ON THE MAGAZINE.
IT WAS CENSORED AND UNAVAILABLE AT LOCAL BOOK-STORES.
HE WAS GOING TO PUT IT BACK AFTER CUTTING OUT THE JUICY BITS.
Pathetic!

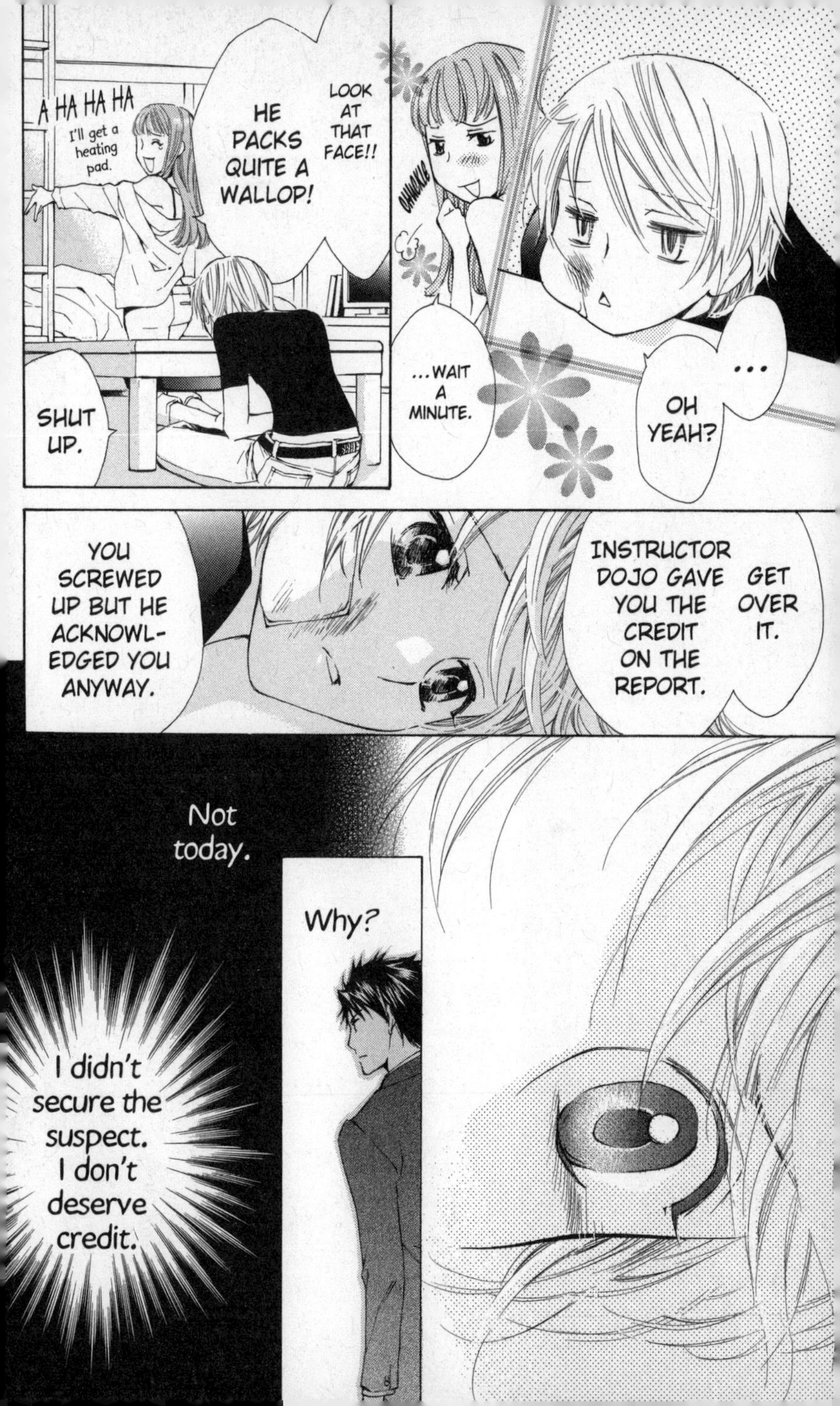
...
OH YEAH?
CHUCKLE
...WAIT A MINUTE.
LOOK AT THAT FACE!!
HE PACKS QUITE A WALLOP!
A HA HA HA
I'll get a heating pad.
SHUT UP.
GET OVER IT.
INSTRUCTOR DOJO GAVE YOU THE CREDIT ON THE REPORT.
YOU SCREWED UP BUT HE ACKNOWL-EDGED YOU ANYWAY.
Not today.
Why?
I didn't secure the suspect. I don't deserve credit.

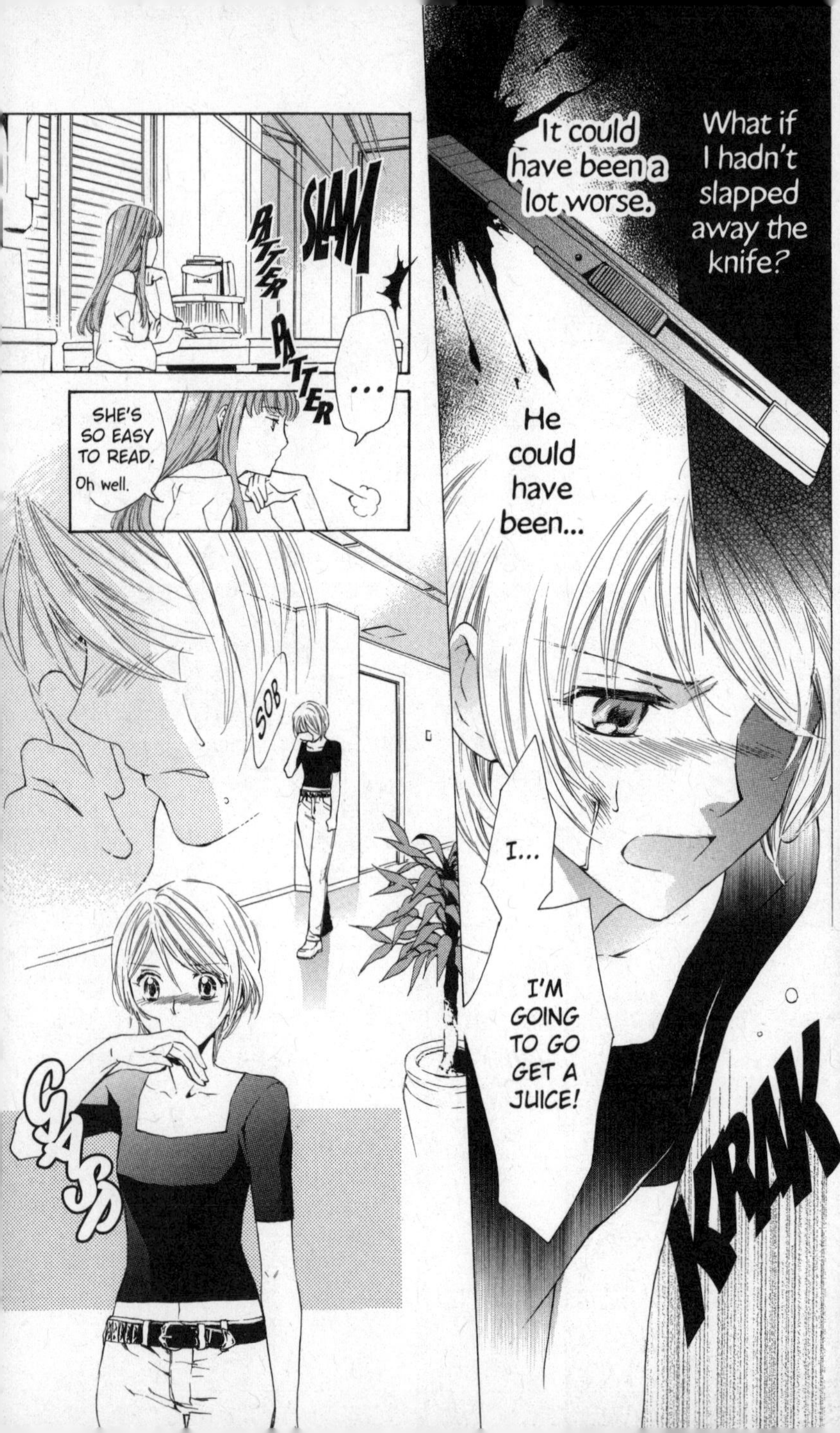
What if I hadn't slapped away the knife?
It could have been a lot worse.
He could have been...
I...
I'M GOING TO GO GET A JUICE!
KRAK
SLAM
PATTER PATTER
...
SHE'S SO EASY TO READ.
Oh well.
SOB
GASP

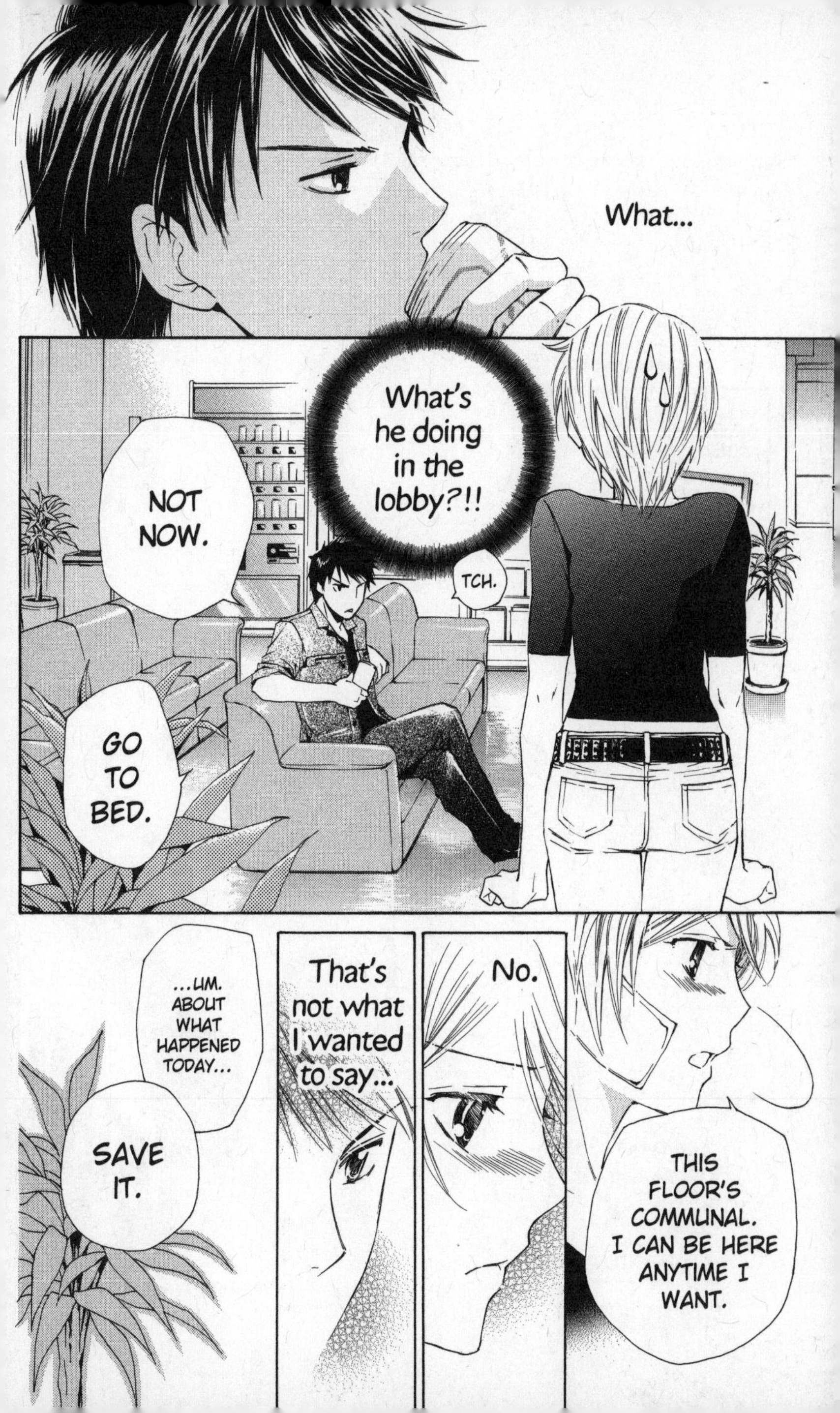

What...
What's he doing in the lobby?!!
NOT NOW.
TCH.
GO TO BED.
THIS FLOOR'S COMMUNAL. I CAN BE HERE ANYTIME I WANT.
No.
That's not what I wanted to say...
...UM. ABOUT WHAT HAPPENED TODAY...
SAVE IT.

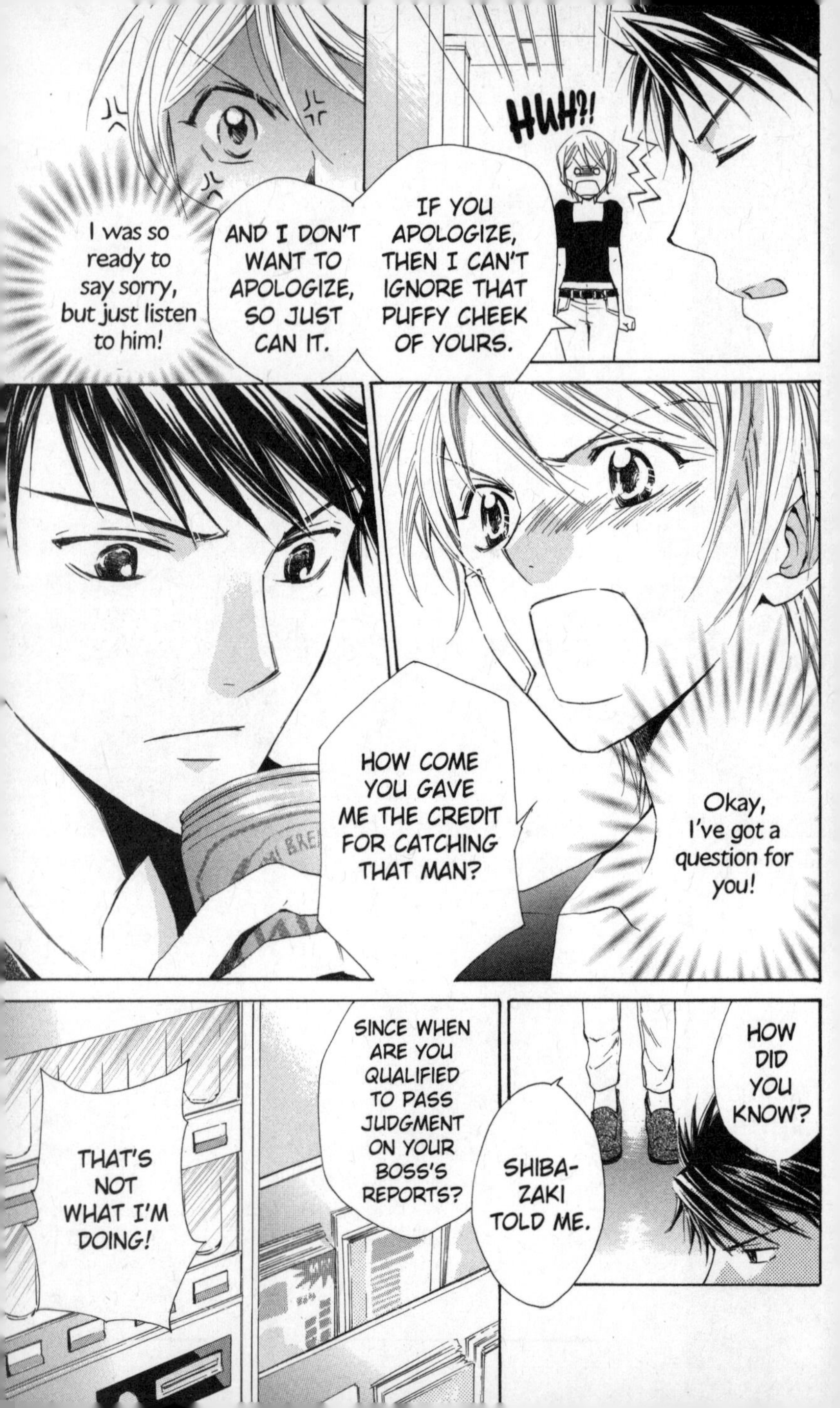
HUH?!
IF YOU APOLOGIZE, THEN I CAN'T IGNORE THAT PUFFY CHEEK OF YOURS.
AND I DON'T WANT TO APOLOGIZE, SO JUST CAN IT.
I was so ready to say sorry, but just listen to him!
Okay, I've got a question for you!
HOW COME YOU GAVE ME THE CREDIT FOR CATCHING THAT MAN?
HOW DID YOU KNOW?
SHIBA-ZAKI TOLD ME.
SINCE WHEN ARE YOU QUALIFIED TO PASS JUDGMENT ON YOUR BOSS'S REPORTS?
THAT'S NOT WHAT I'M DOING!

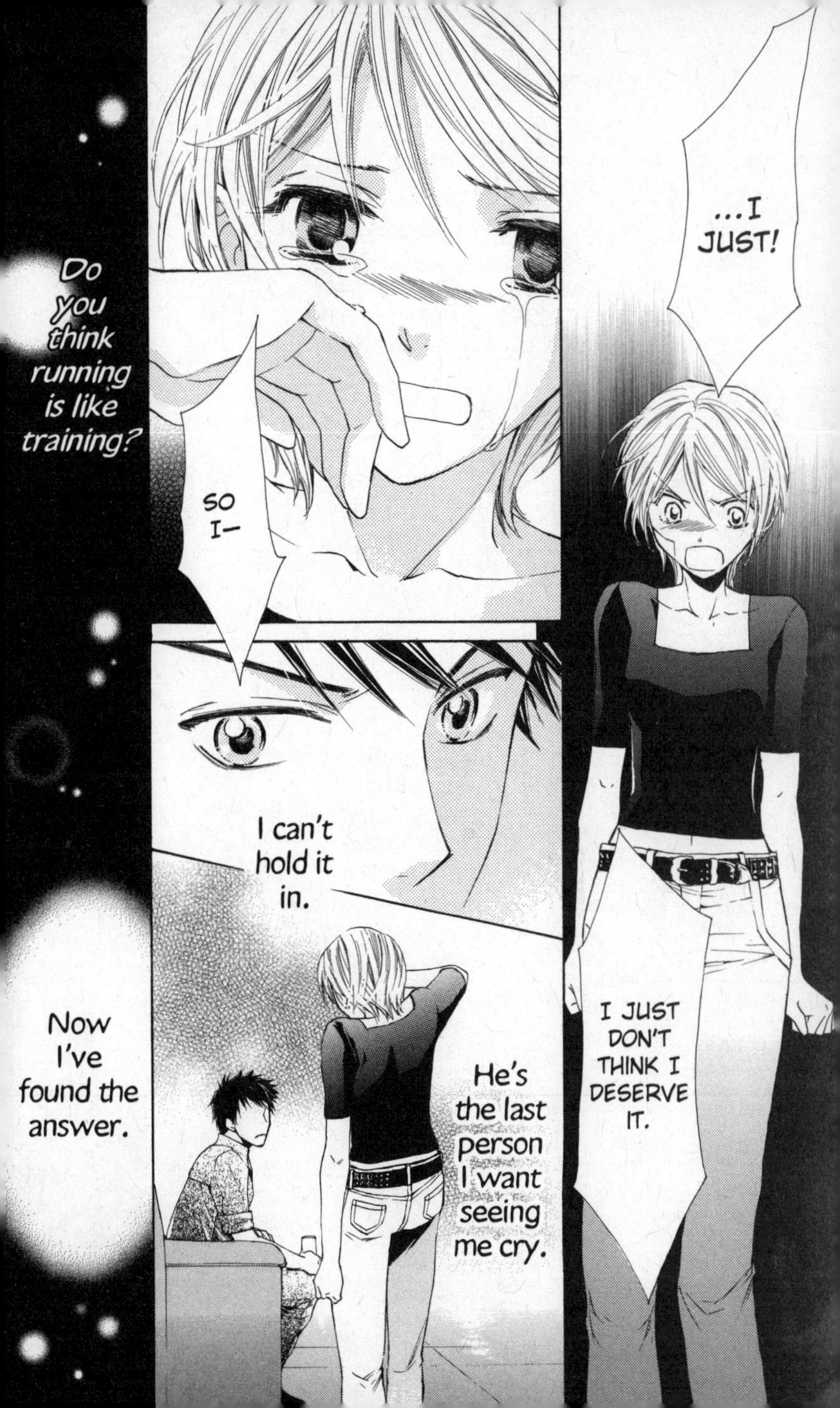
...I JUST!
I JUST DON'T THINK I DESERVE IT.
SO I–
I can't hold it in.
He's the last person I want seeing me cry.
Do you think running is like training?
Now I've found the answer.

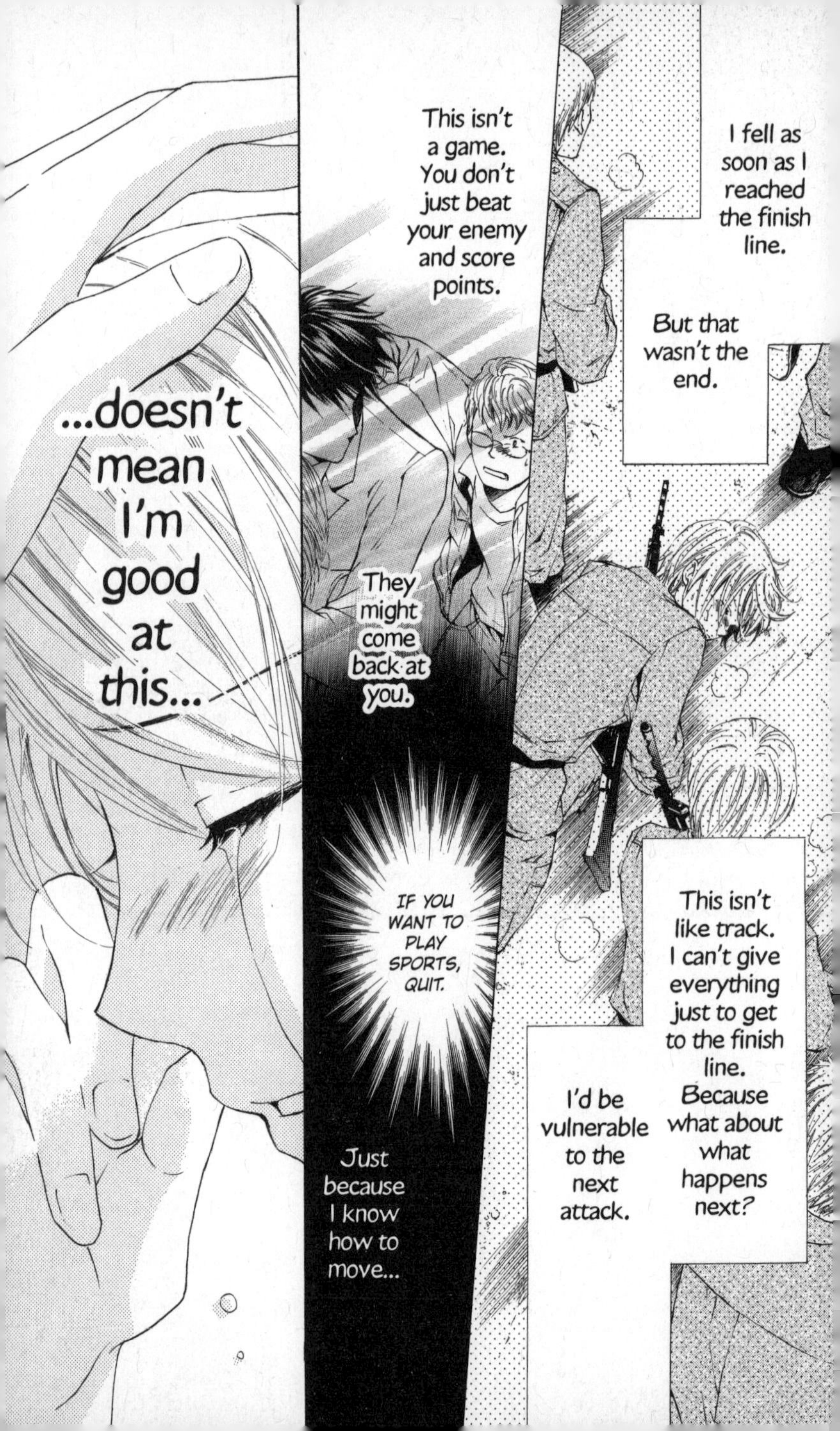
I fell as soon as I reached the finish line.
But that wasn't the end.
This isn't like track. I can't give everything just to get to the finish line. Because what about what happens next?
I'd be vulnerable to the next attack.
This isn't a game. You don't just beat your enemy and score points.
They might come back at you.
IF YOU WANT TO PLAY SPORTS, QUIT.
Just because I know how to move...
...doesn't mean I'm good at this...

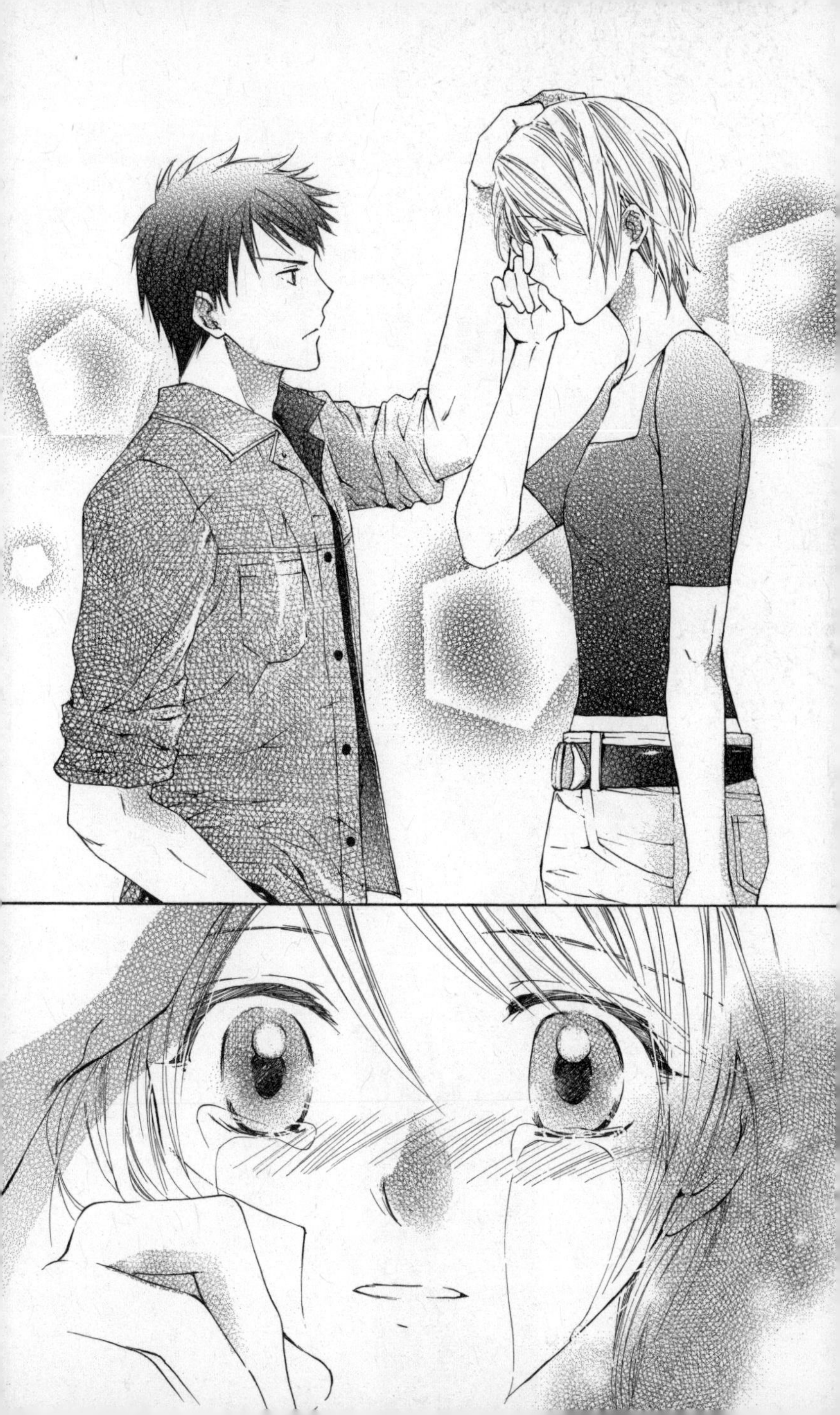

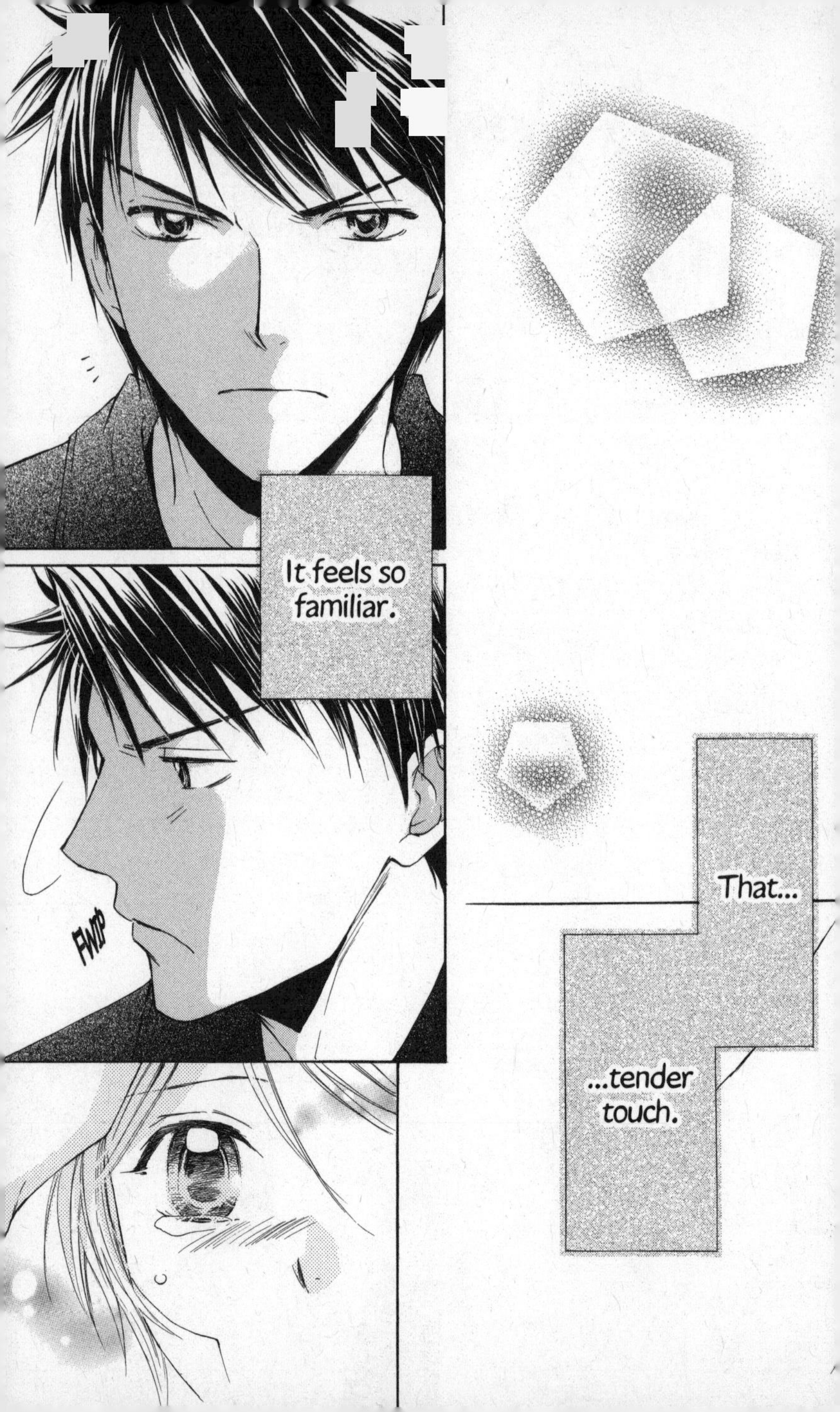
That...
...tender touch.
It feels so familiar.
FWIP

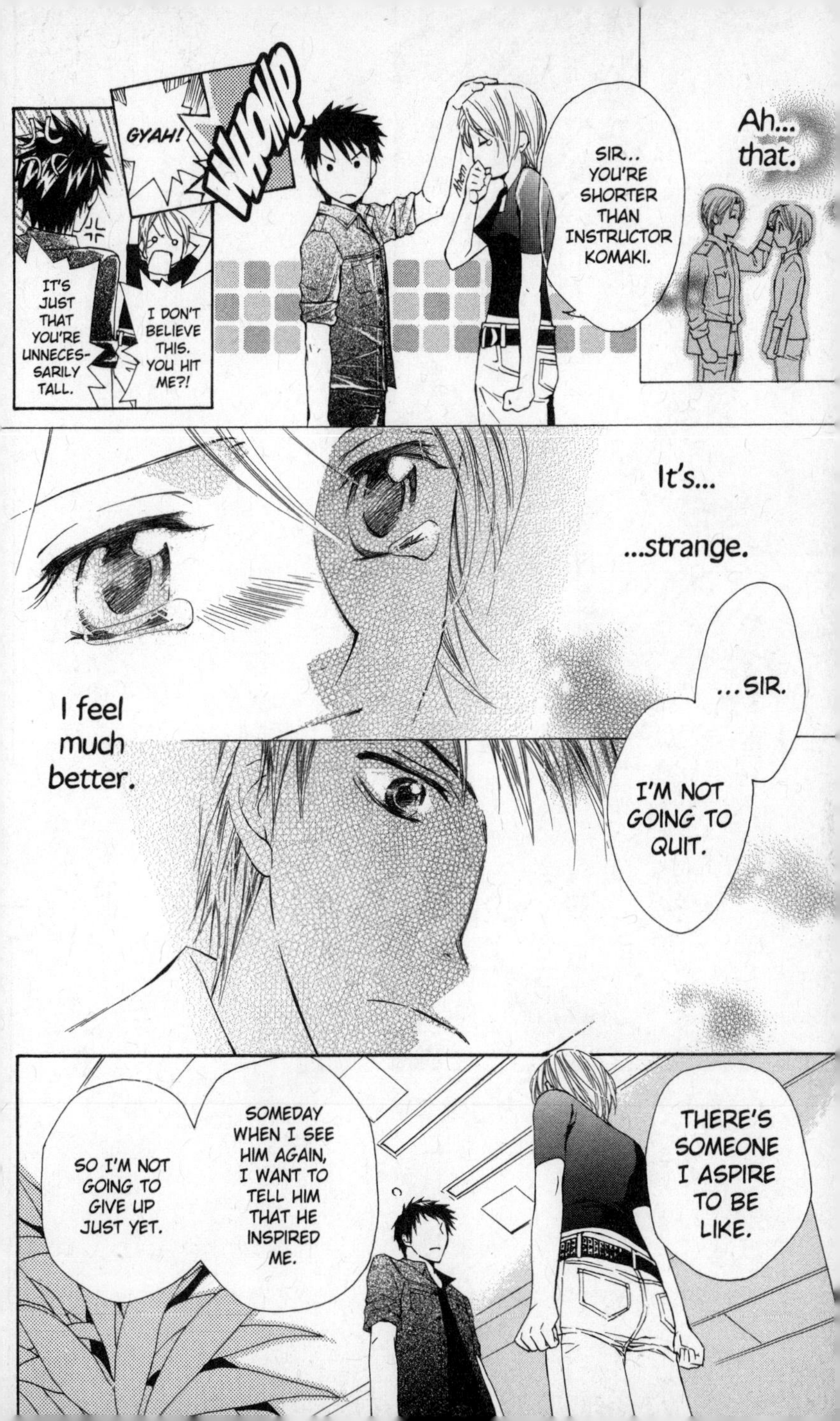
Ah... that.
SIR... YOU'RE SHORTER THAN INSTRUCTOR KOMAKI.
Ahem
WHOMP
GYAH!
I DON'T BELIEVE THIS. YOU HIT ME?!
IT'S JUST THAT YOU'RE UNNECES-SARILY TALL.
It's...
...strange.
...SIR.
I'M NOT GOING TO QUIT.
I feel much better.
THERE'S SOMEONE I ASPIRE TO BE LIKE.
SOMEDAY WHEN I SEE HIM AGAIN, I WANT TO TELL HIM THAT HE INSPIRED ME.
SO I'M NOT GOING TO GIVE UP JUST YET.

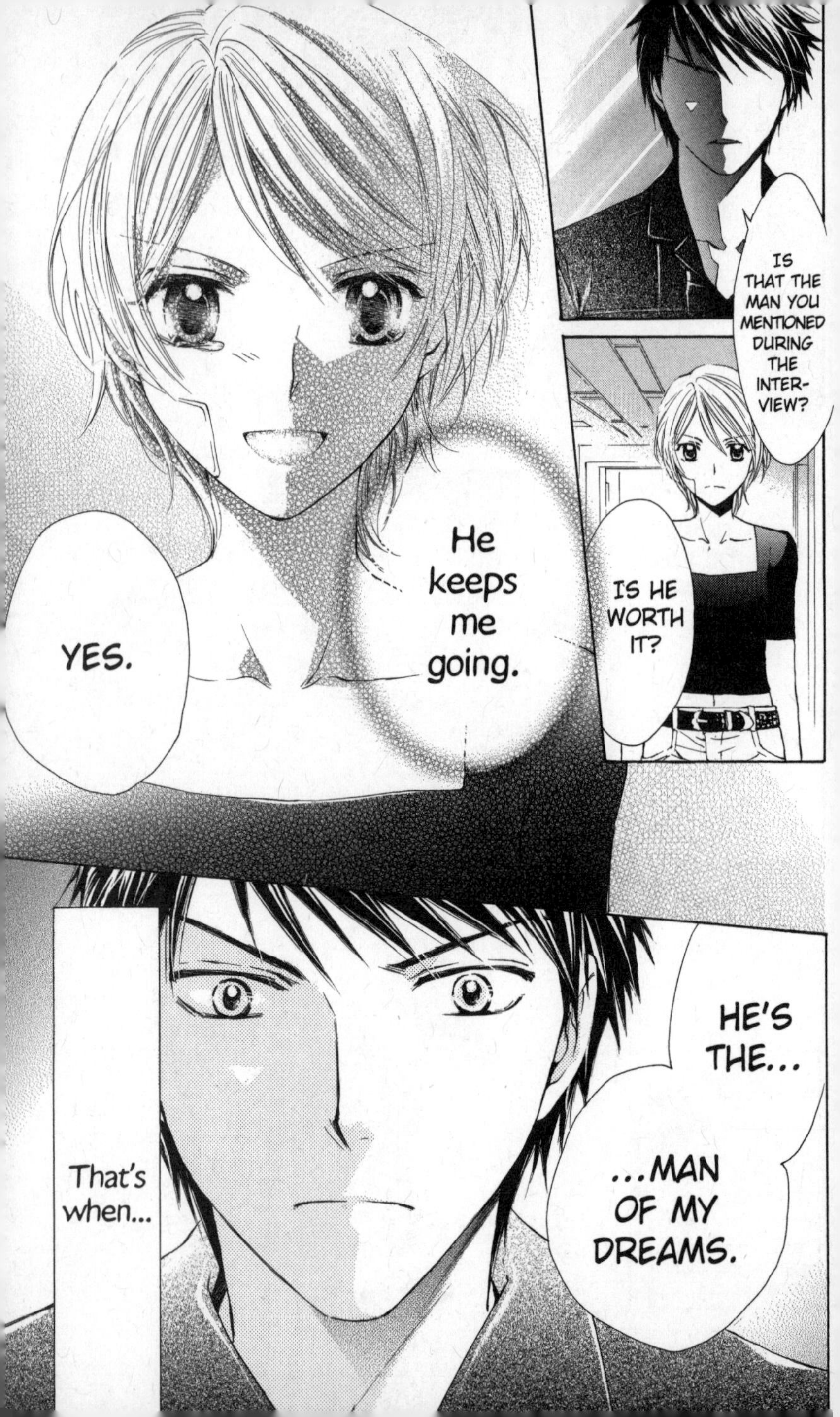
IS THAT THE MAN YOU MENTIONED DURING THE INTER-VIEW?
IS HE WORTH IT?
He keeps me going.
YES.
HE'S THE...
...MAN OF MY DREAMS.
That's when...

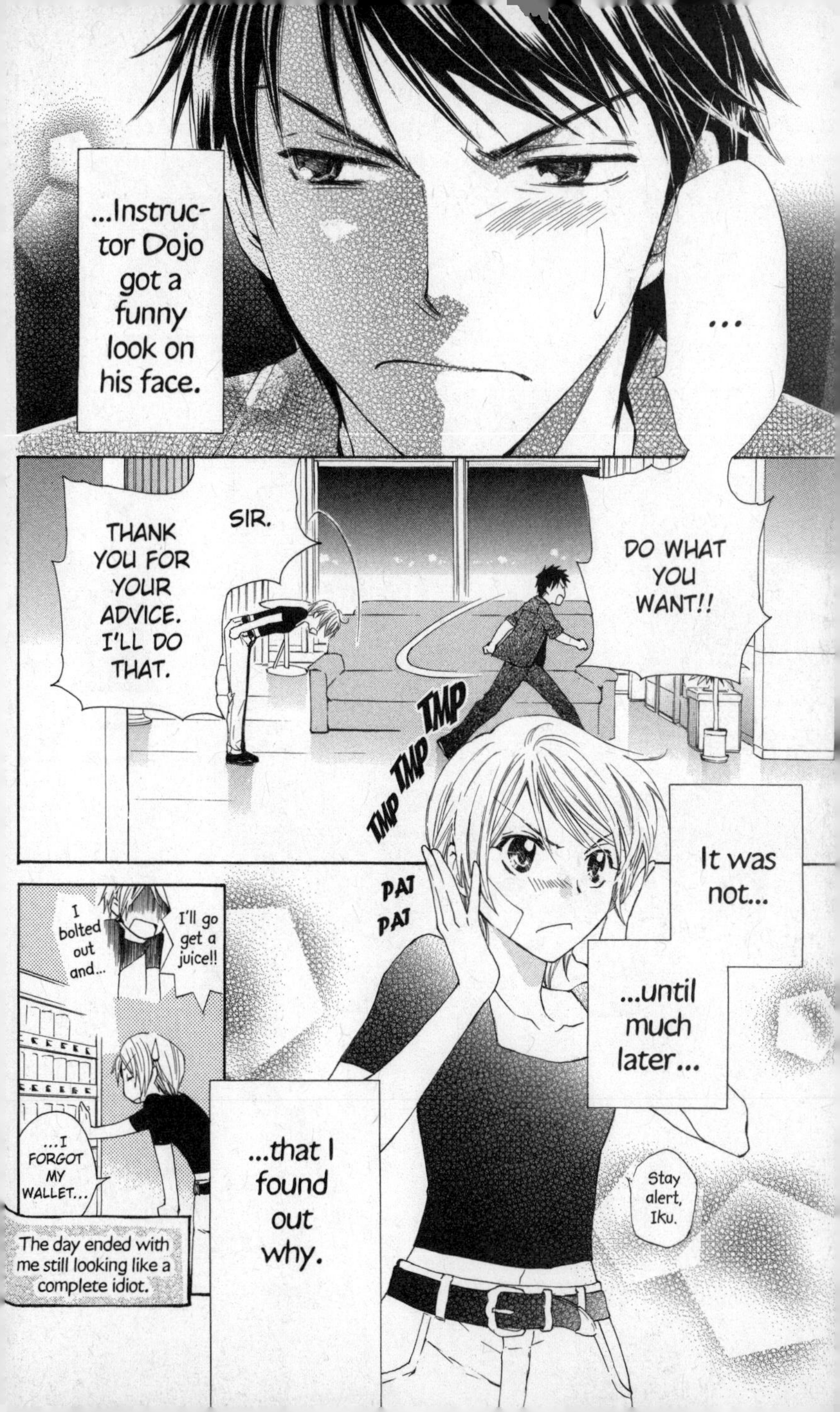

...
...Instructor Dojo got a funny look on his face.
DO WHAT YOU WANT!!
TMP TMP TMP
THANK YOU FOR YOUR ADVICE. I'LL DO THAT. SIR.
It was not...
...until much later...
PAT PAT
...that I found out why.
Stay alert, Iku.
I'll go get a juice!!
I bolted out and...
...I FORGOT MY WALLET...
The day ended with me still looking like a complete idiot.

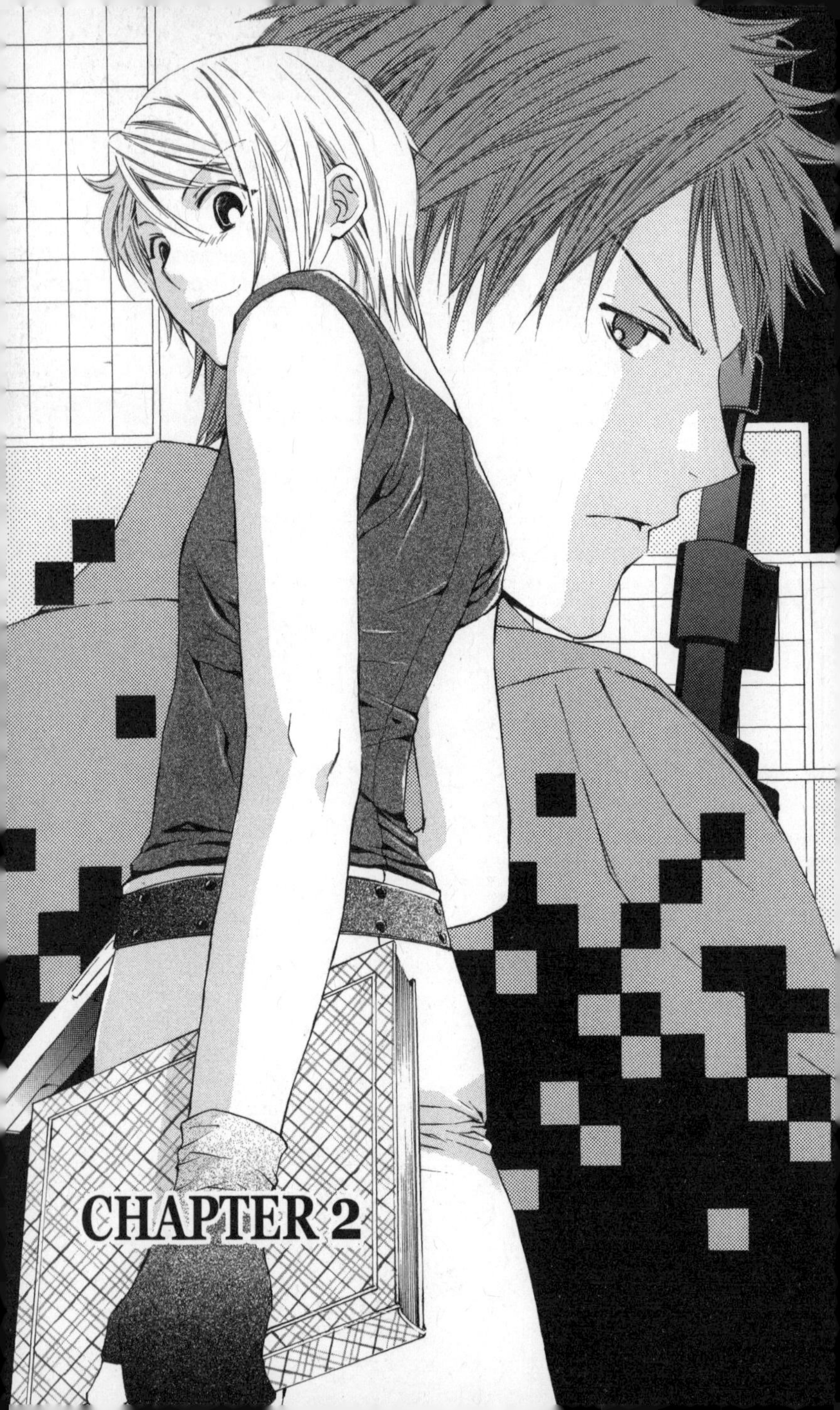
CHAPTER 2

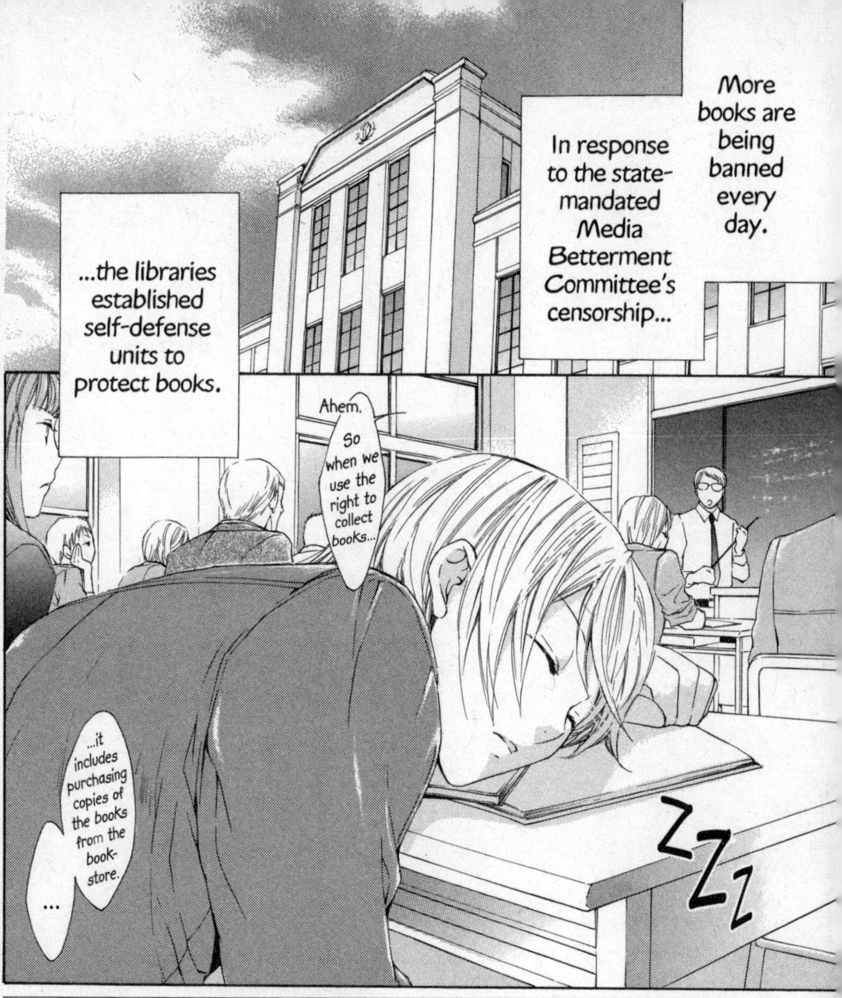
More books are being banned every day.
In response to the state-mandated Media Betterment Committee's censorship...
...the libraries established self-defense units to protect books.
Ahem.
So when we use the right to collect books...
...it includes purchasing copies of the books from the bookstore.
...
ZZZ

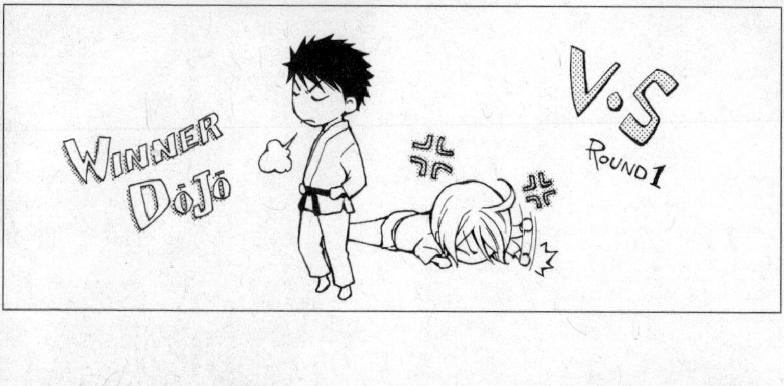
V.S
ROUND 1
WINNER
DŌJŌ

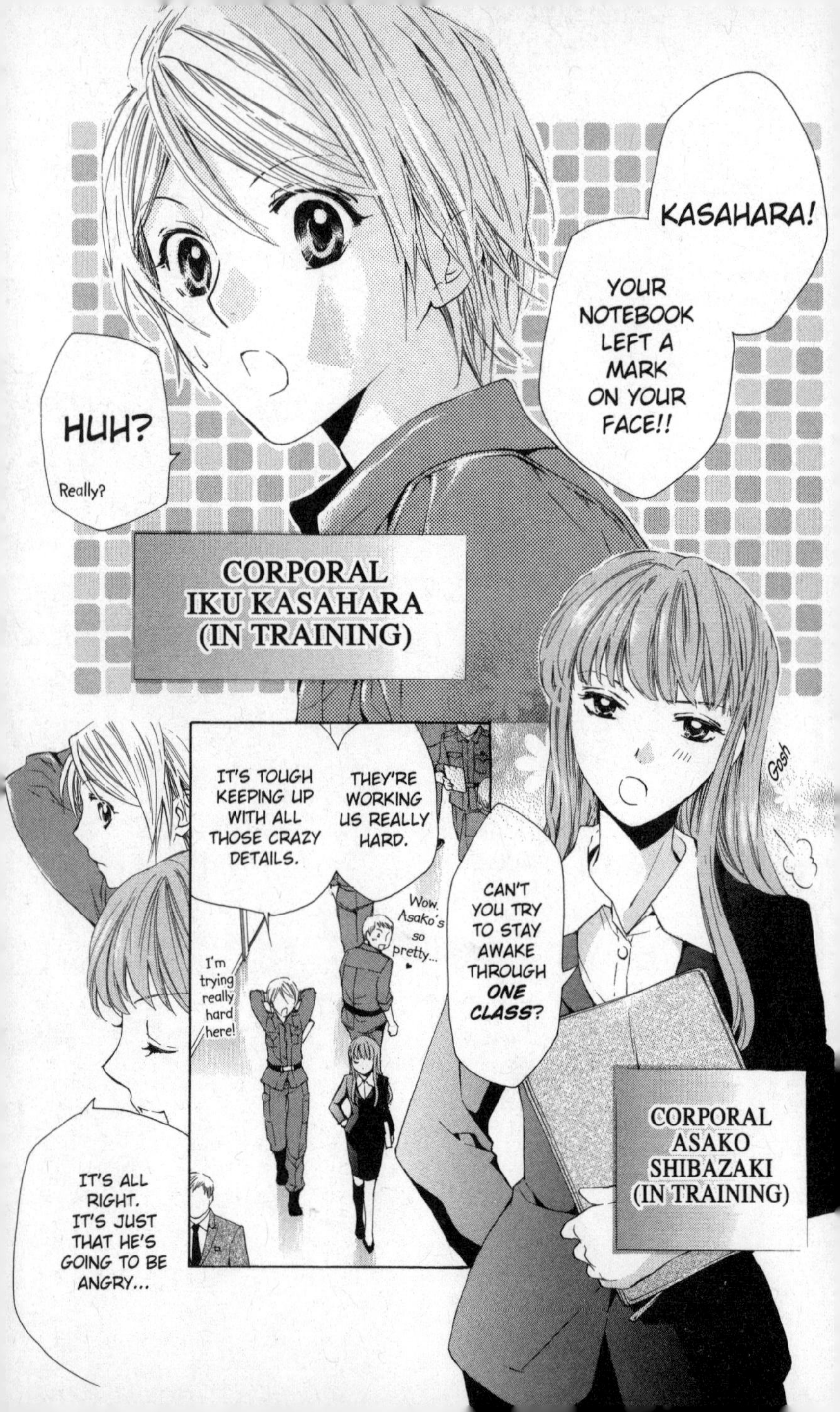
KASAHARA!
YOUR NOTEBOOK LEFT A MARK ON YOUR FACE!!
HUH?
Really?
CORPORAL IKU KASAHARA (IN TRAINING)
Gosh
CAN'T YOU TRY TO STAY AWAKE THROUGH ONE CLASS?
CORPORAL ASAKO SHIBAZAKI (IN TRAINING)
THEY'RE WORKING US REALLY HARD.
IT'S TOUGH KEEPING UP WITH ALL THOSE CRAZY DETAILS.
Wow. Asako's so pretty...
I'm trying really hard here!
IT'S ALL RIGHT. IT'S JUST THAT HE'S GOING TO BE ANGRY...

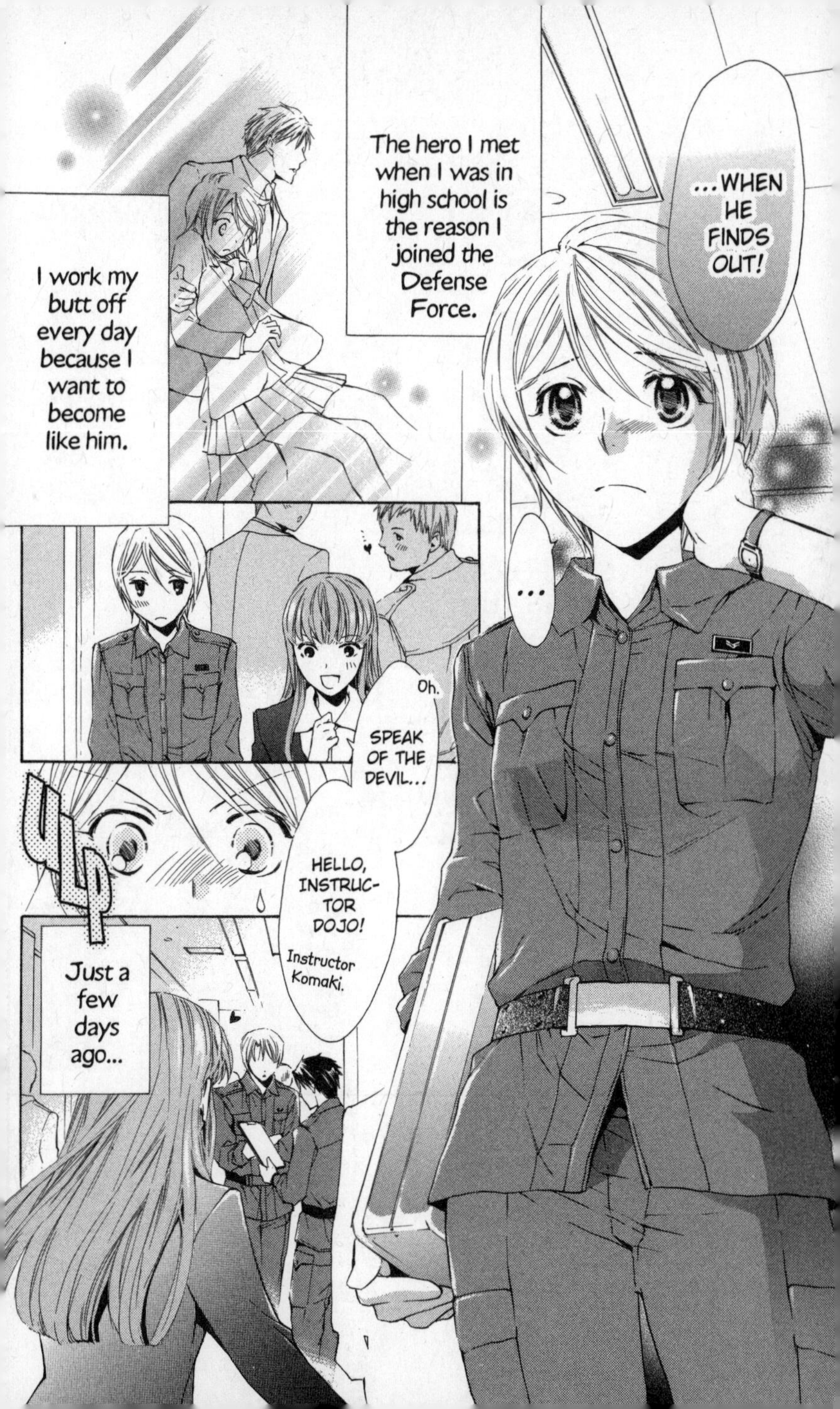
...WHEN HE FINDS OUT!
The hero I met when I was in high school is the reason I joined the Defense Force.
I work my butt off every day because I want to become like him.
...
Oh.
SPEAK OF THE DEVIL...
ULP
HELLO, INSTRUCTOR DOJO!
Instructor Komaki.
Just a few days ago...

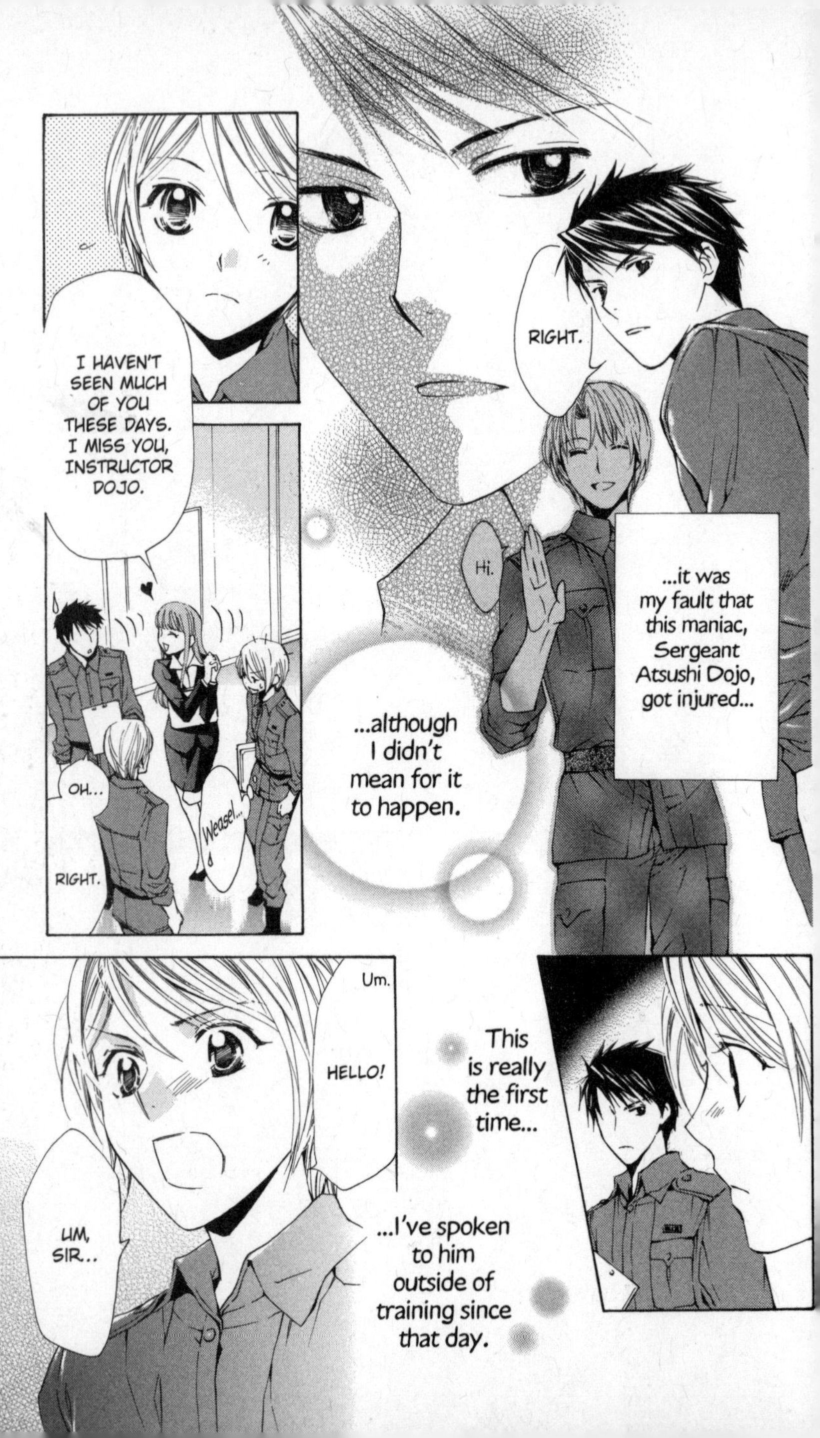

RIGHT.
Hi.
...it was my fault that this maniac, Sergeant Atsushi Dojo, got injured...
...although I didn't mean for it to happen.
I HAVEN'T SEEN MUCH OF YOU THESE DAYS. I MISS YOU, INSTRUCTOR DOJO.
OH...
Weasel...
RIGHT.
This is really the first time...
...I've spoken to him outside of training since that day.
Um.
HELLO!
UM, SIR...

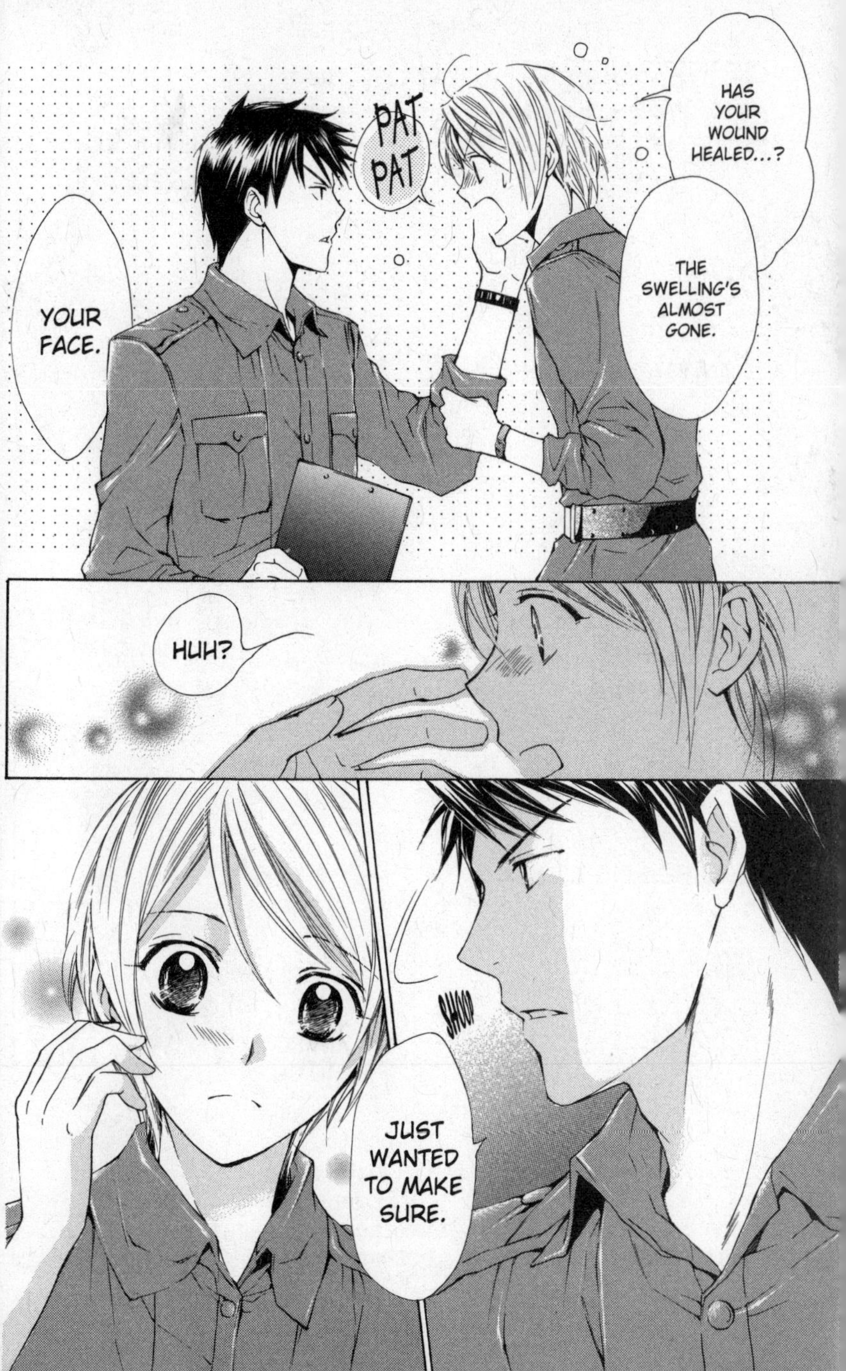
HAS YOUR WOUND HEALED...?
THE SWELLING'S ALMOST GONE.
PAT PAT
YOUR FACE.
HUH?
SHOOP
JUST WANTED TO MAKE SURE.

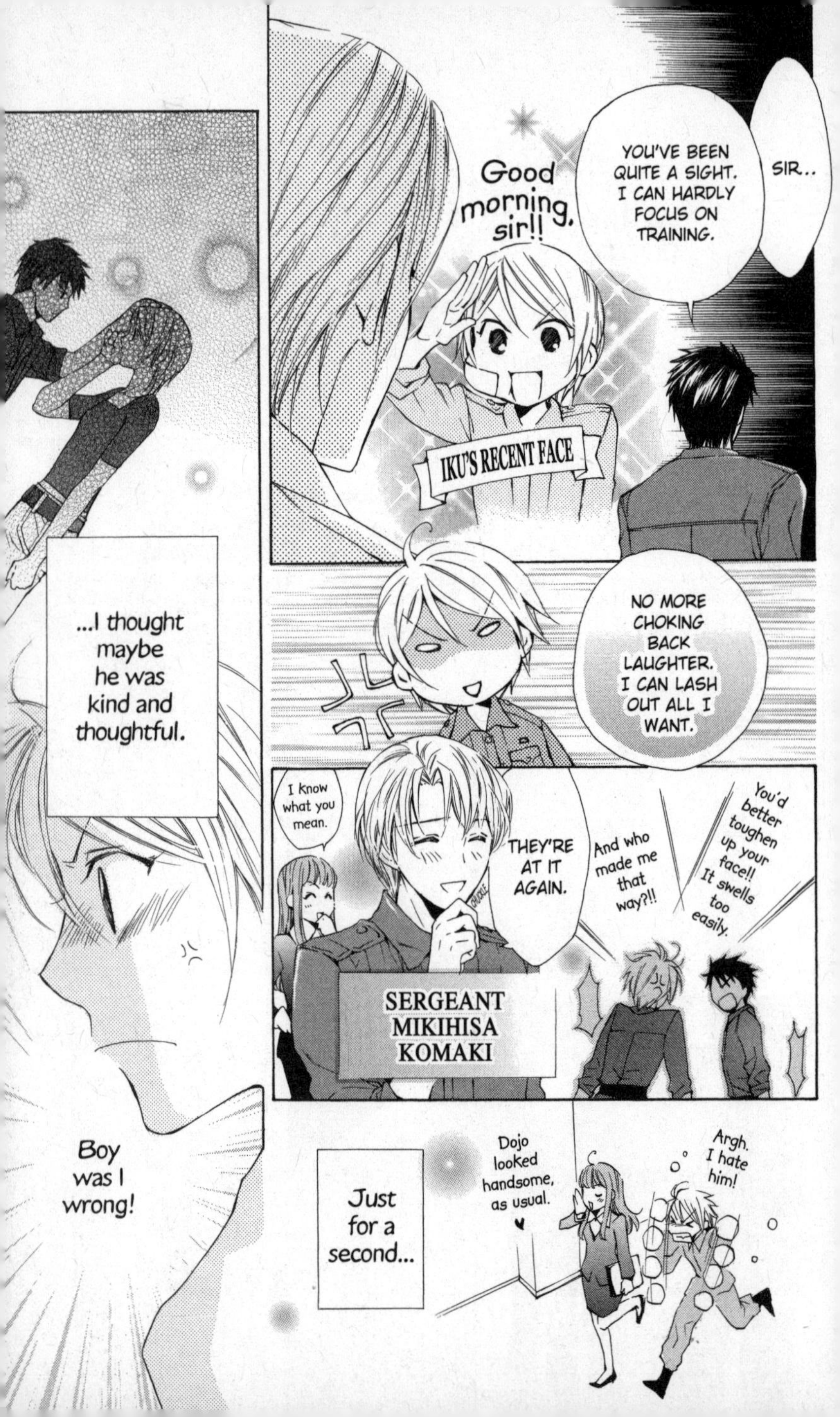

SIR...
YOU'VE BEEN QUITE A SIGHT. I CAN HARDLY FOCUS ON TRAINING.
Good morning, sir!!
IKU'S RECENT FACE
NO MORE CHOKING BACK LAUGHTER. I CAN LASH OUT ALL I WANT.
You'd better toughen up your face!! It swells too easily.
And who made me that way?!!
THEY'RE AT IT AGAIN.
CHUCKLE
I know what you mean.
SERGEANT MIKIHISA KOMAKI
Argh. I hate him!
Dojo looked handsome, as usual.
Just for a second...
...I thought maybe he was kind and thoughtful.
Boy was I wrong!

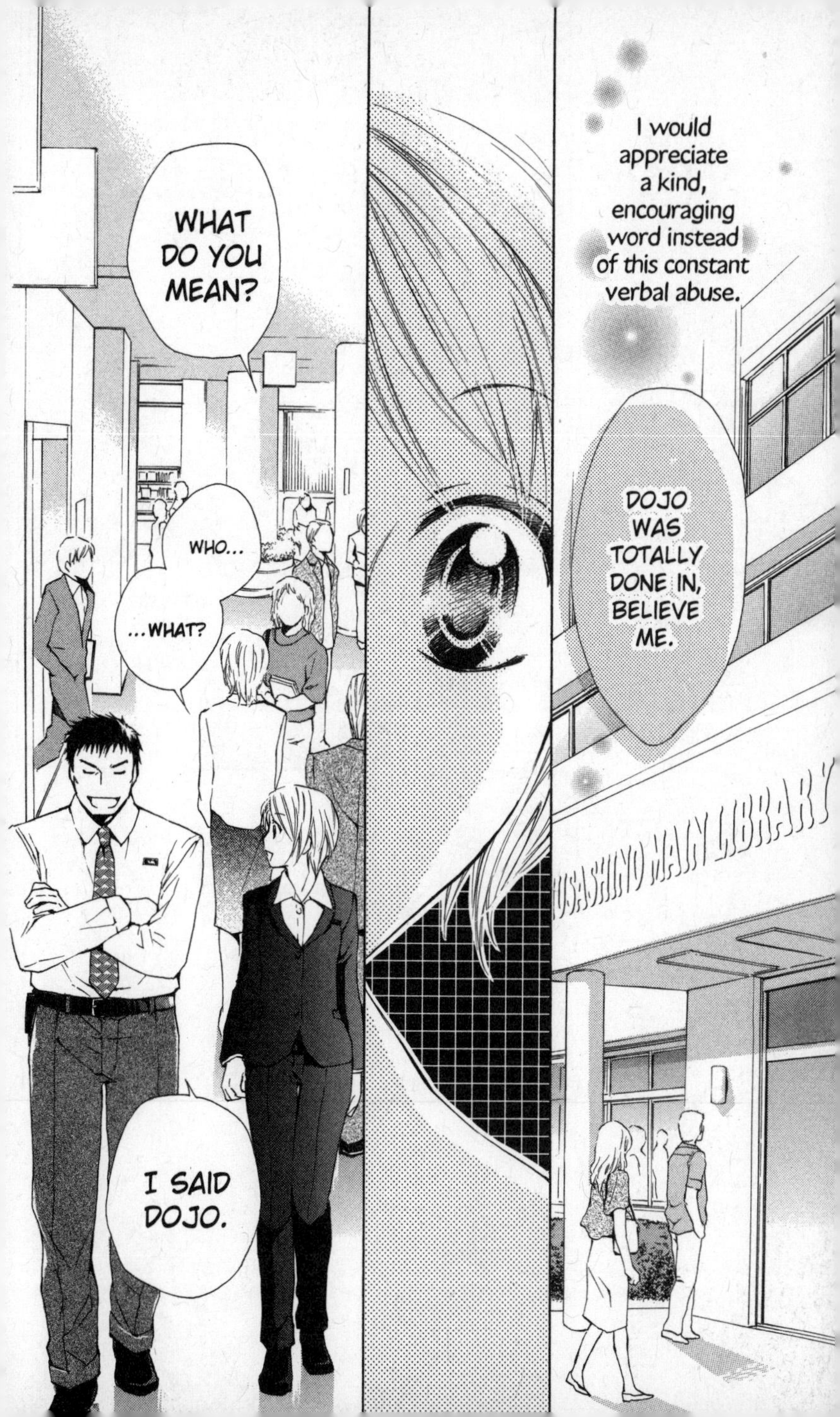
I would appreciate a kind, encouraging word instead of this constant verbal abuse.
DOJO WAS TOTALLY DONE IN, BELIEVE ME.
USASHINO MAIN LIBRARY
WHAT DO YOU MEAN?
WHO...
...WHAT?
I SAID DOJO.

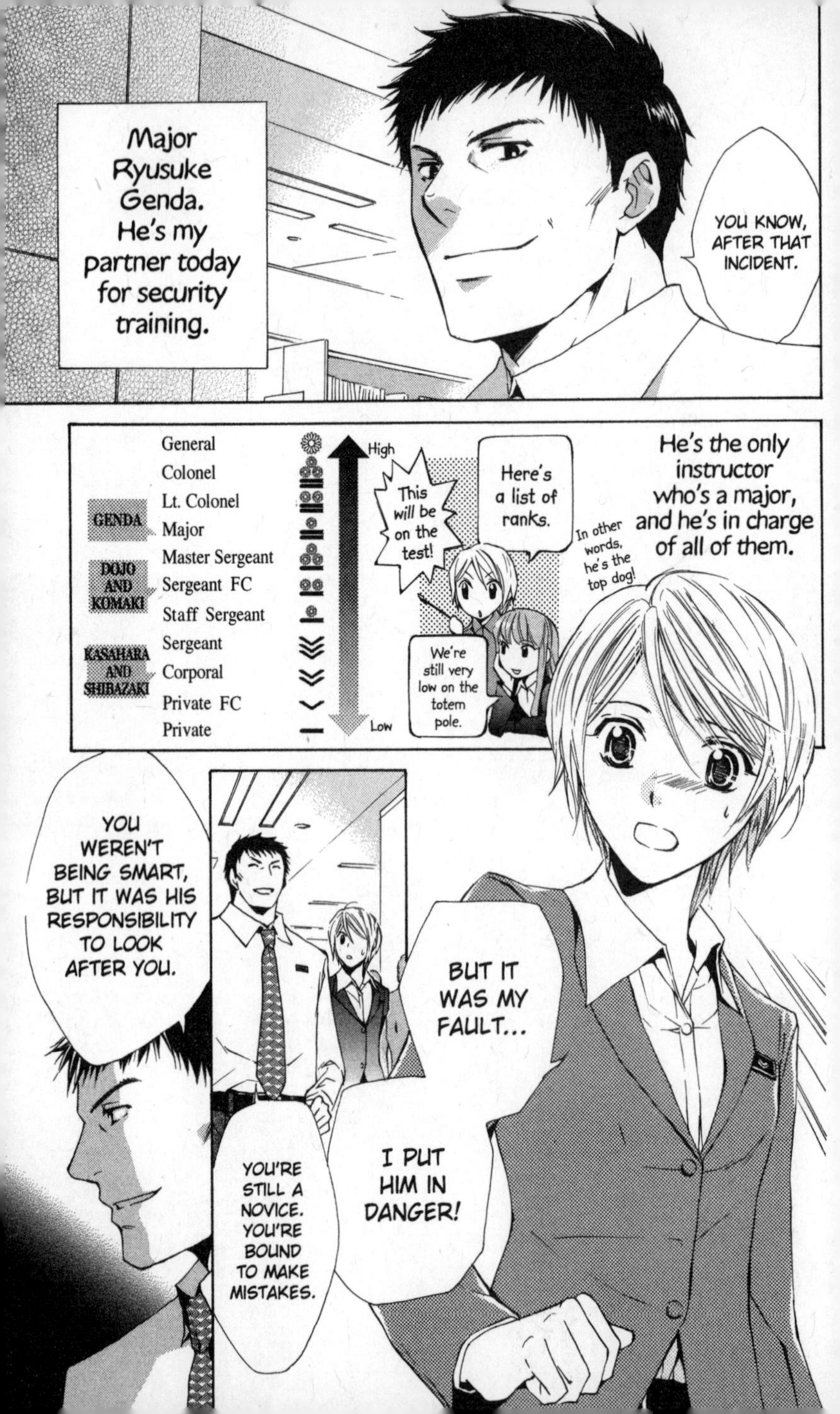
YOU KNOW, AFTER THAT INCIDENT.
Major Ryusuke Genda. He's my partner today for security training.
He's the only instructor who's a major, and he's in charge of all of them.
In other words, he's the top dog!
Here's a list of ranks.
This will be on the test!
We're still very low on the totem pole.
High
Low
General
Colonel
Lt. Colonel
GENDA
Major
Master Sergeant
DOJO AND KOMAKI
Sergeant FC
Staff Sergeant
Sergeant
KASAHARA AND SHIBAZAKI
Corporal
Private FC
Private
BUT IT WAS MY FAULT...
I PUT HIM IN DANGER!
YOU WEREN'T BEING SMART, BUT IT WAS HIS RESPONSIBILITY TO LOOK AFTER YOU.
YOU'RE STILL A NOVICE. YOU'RE BOUND TO MAKE MISTAKES.

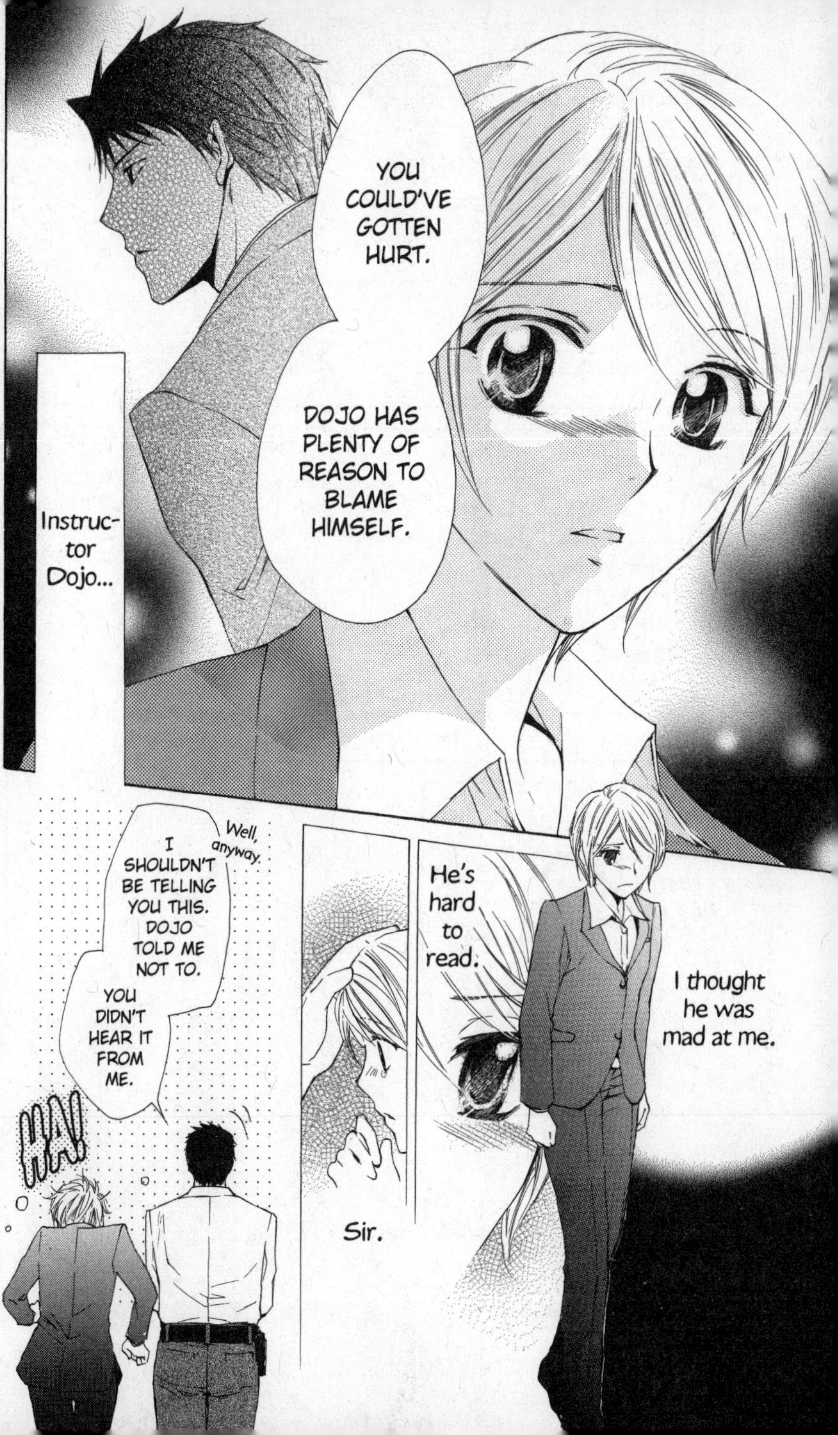
YOU COULD'VE GOTTEN HURT.
DOJO HAS PLENTY OF REASON TO BLAME HIMSELF.
Instructor Dojo...
I thought he was mad at me.
He's hard to read.
Sir.
Well, anyway.
I SHOULDN'T BE TELLING YOU THIS. DOJO TOLD ME NOT TO. YOU DIDN'T HEAR IT FROM ME.
HA!

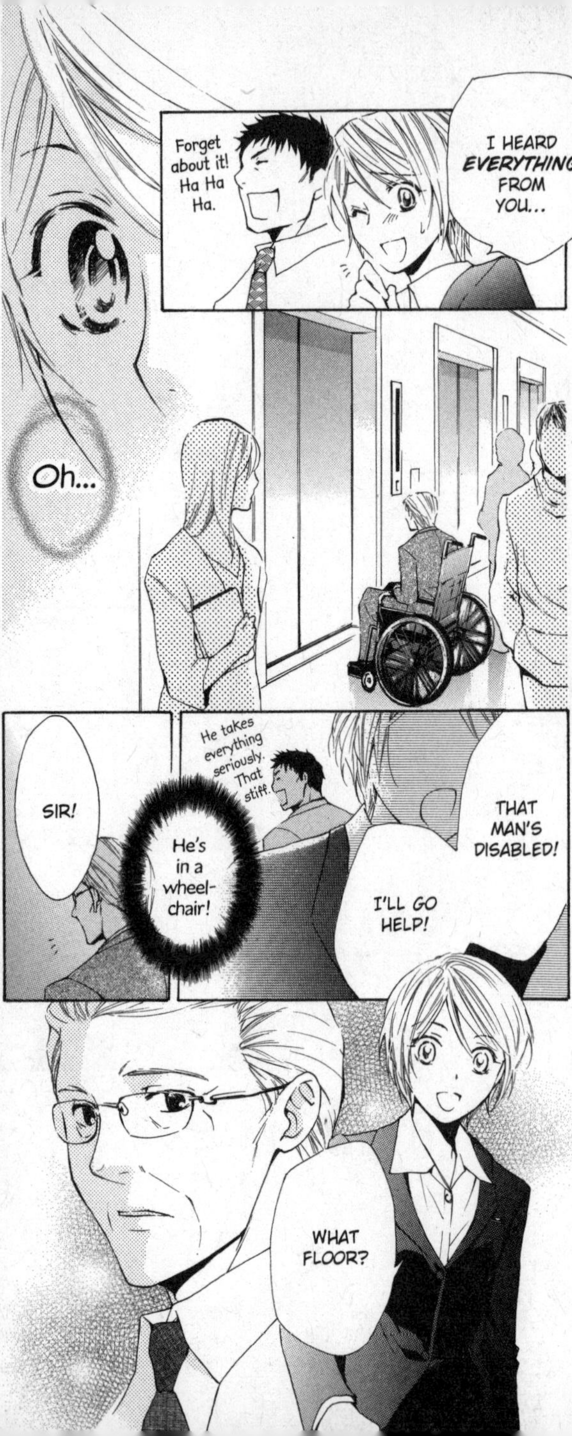

I HEARD *EVERYTHING* FROM YOU...
Forget about it! Ha Ha Ha.
Oh...
THAT MAN'S DISABLED!
He takes everything seriously. That stiff.
He's in a wheelchair!
SIR!
I'LL GO HELP!
WHAT FLOOR?

2

*

When I was asked about doing a manga of the *Library Wars* series, I was more frightened than pleased. I am such a chicken. I have been fighting this chicken heart of mine all my life. *Library Wars* is my favorite novel. I am so grateful for this opportunity. I was so engrossed in the story I actually had trouble breathing. I've never read anything like it before!

This has been really great. I hope I can turn it into a good manga without ruining my excitement...! It's a very hard and fun battle with myself.

*

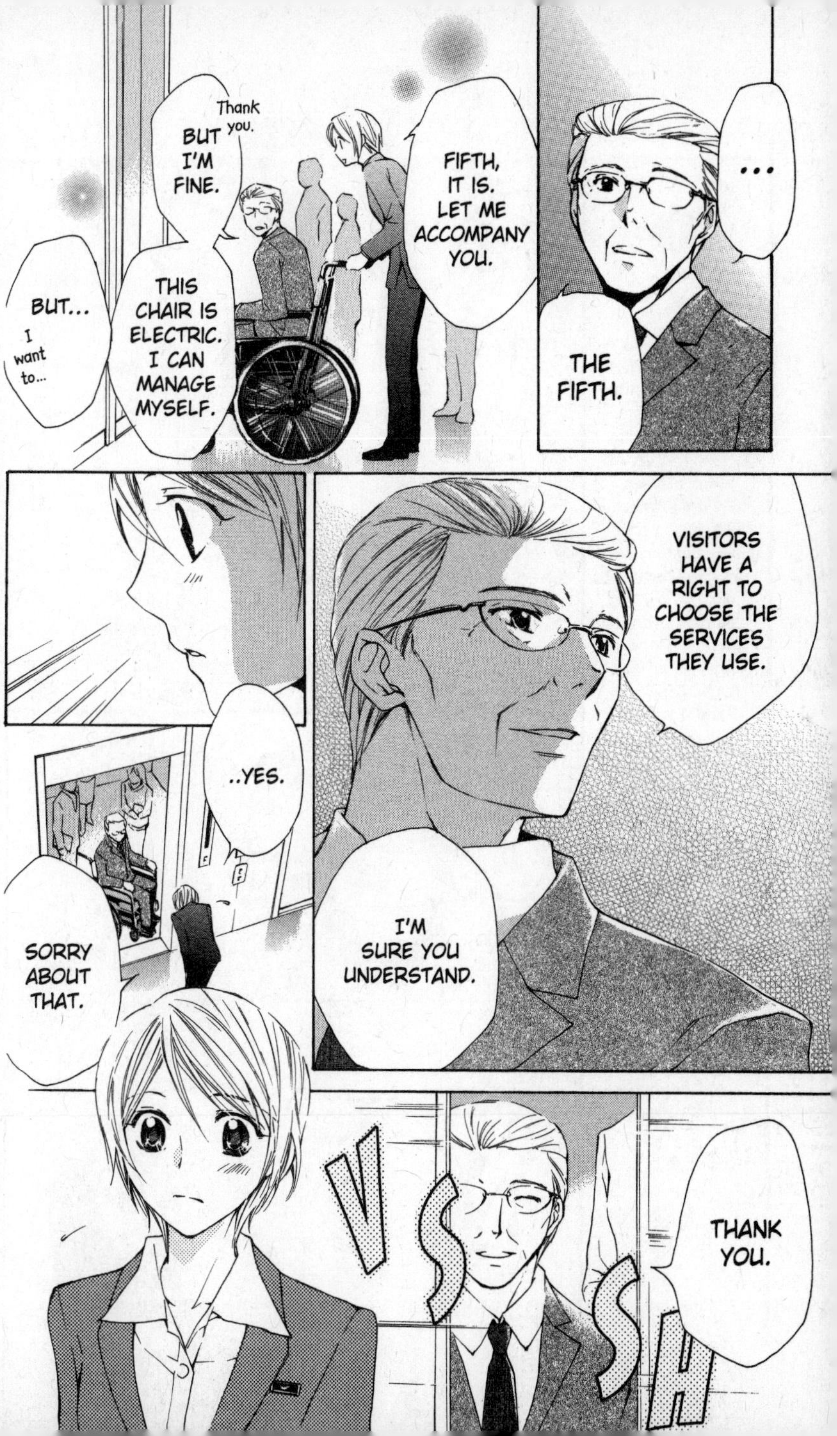
...
THE FIFTH.
FIFTH, IT IS. LET ME ACCOMPANY YOU.
Thank you.
BUT I'M FINE.
THIS CHAIR IS ELECTRIC. I CAN MANAGE MYSELF.
BUT...
I want to...
VISITORS HAVE A RIGHT TO CHOOSE THE SERVICES THEY USE.
I'M SURE YOU UNDERSTAND.
..YES.
SORRY ABOUT THAT.
THANK YOU.
VSSH

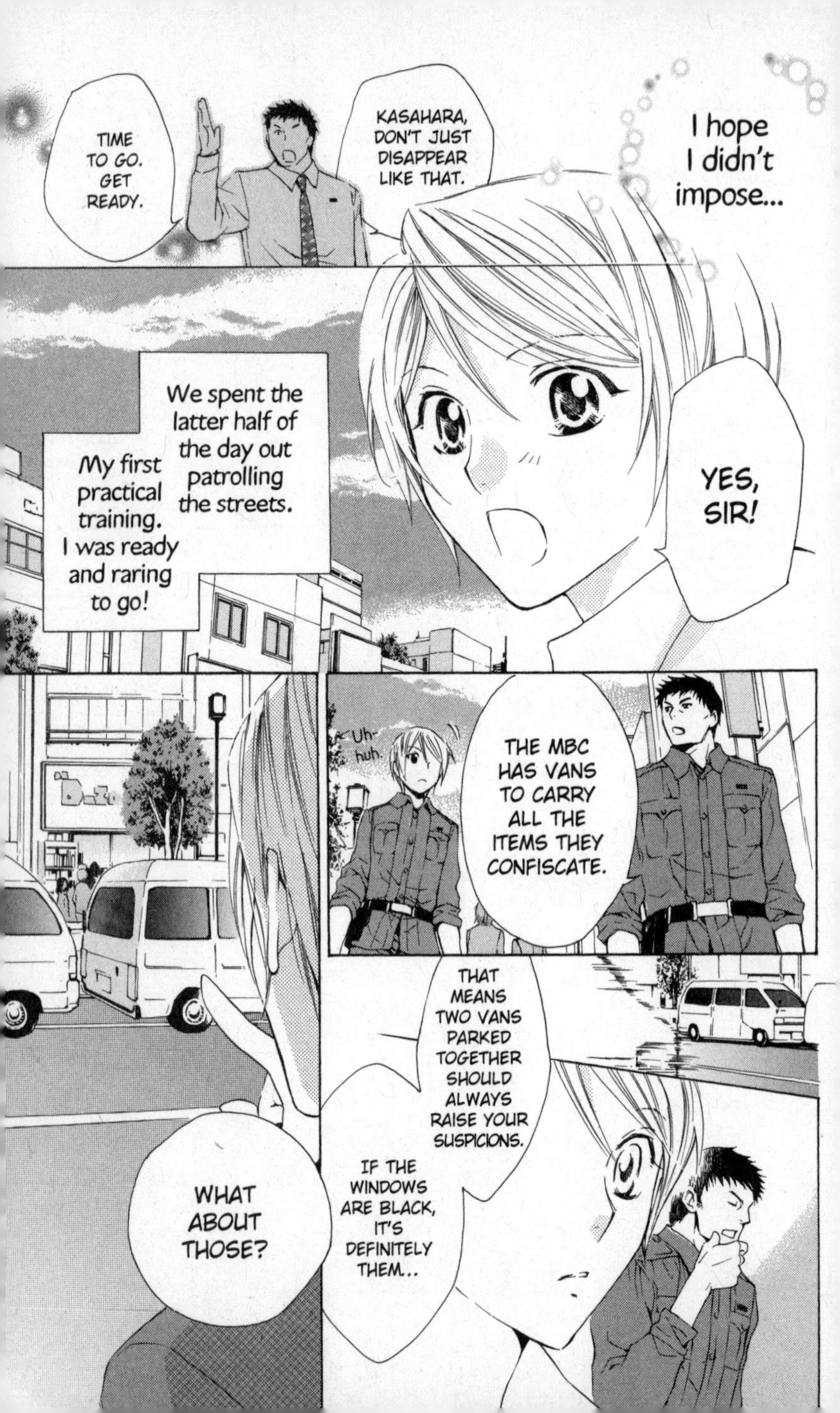
I hope I didn't impose...
KASAHARA, DON'T JUST DISAPPEAR LIKE THAT.
TIME TO GO. GET READY.
YES, SIR!
We spent the latter half of the day out patrolling the streets.
My first practical training. I was ready and raring to go!
THE MBC HAS VANS TO CARRY ALL THE ITEMS THEY CONFISCATE.
Uh-huh.
THAT MEANS TWO VANS PARKED TOGETHER SHOULD ALWAYS RAISE YOUR SUSPICIONS.
IF THE WINDOWS ARE BLACK, IT'S DEFINITELY THEM...
WHAT ABOUT THOSE?

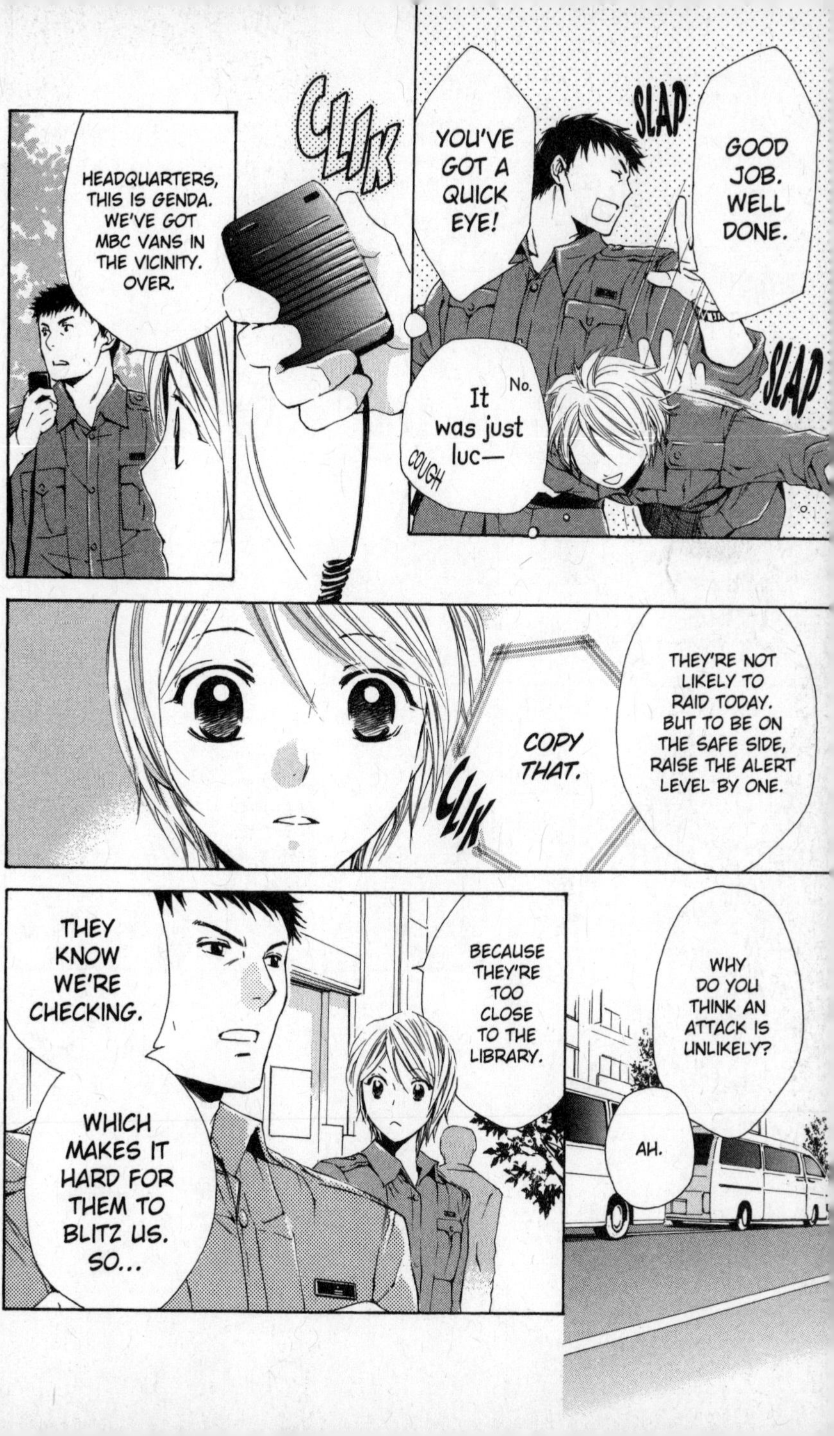
SLAP
GOOD JOB. WELL DONE.
YOU'VE GOT A QUICK EYE!
SLAP
No. It was just luc—
COUGH
CLIK
HEADQUARTERS, THIS IS GENDA. WE'VE GOT MBC VANS IN THE VICINITY. OVER.
THEY'RE NOT LIKELY TO RAID TODAY. BUT TO BE ON THE SAFE SIDE, RAISE THE ALERT LEVEL BY ONE.
COPY THAT.
CLIK
WHY DO YOU THINK AN ATTACK IS UNLIKELY?
AH.
BECAUSE THEY'RE TOO CLOSE TO THE LIBRARY.
THEY KNOW WE'RE CHECKING.
WHICH MAKES IT HARD FOR THEM TO BLITZ US. SO...

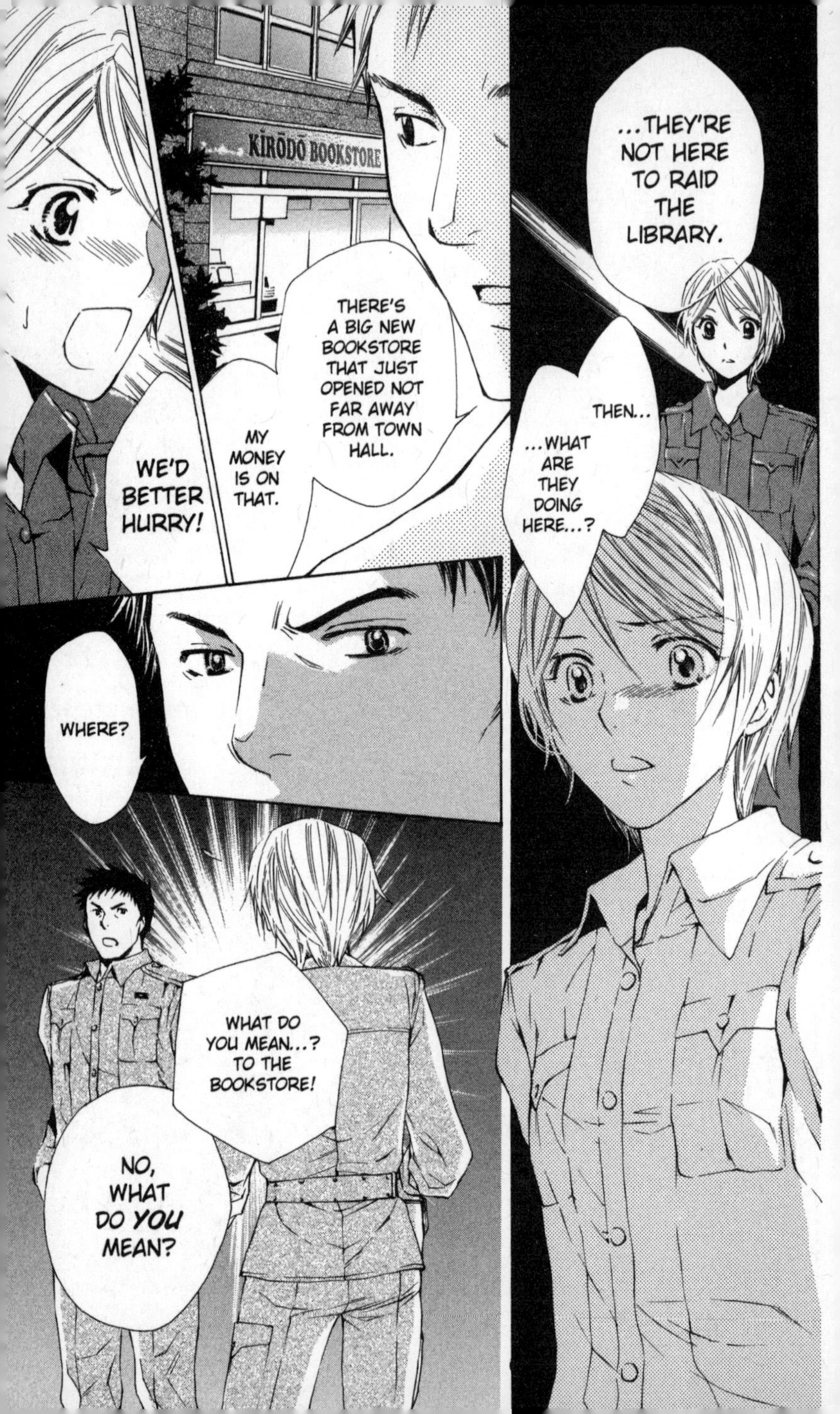
...THEY'RE NOT HERE TO RAID THE LIBRARY.
THEN...
...WHAT ARE THEY DOING HERE...?
KIRŌDŌ BOOKSTORE
THERE'S A BIG NEW BOOKSTORE THAT JUST OPENED NOT FAR AWAY FROM TOWN HALL.
MY MONEY IS ON THAT.
WE'D BETTER HURRY!
WHERE?
WHAT DO YOU MEAN...? TO THE BOOKSTORE!
NO, WHAT DO *YOU* MEAN?

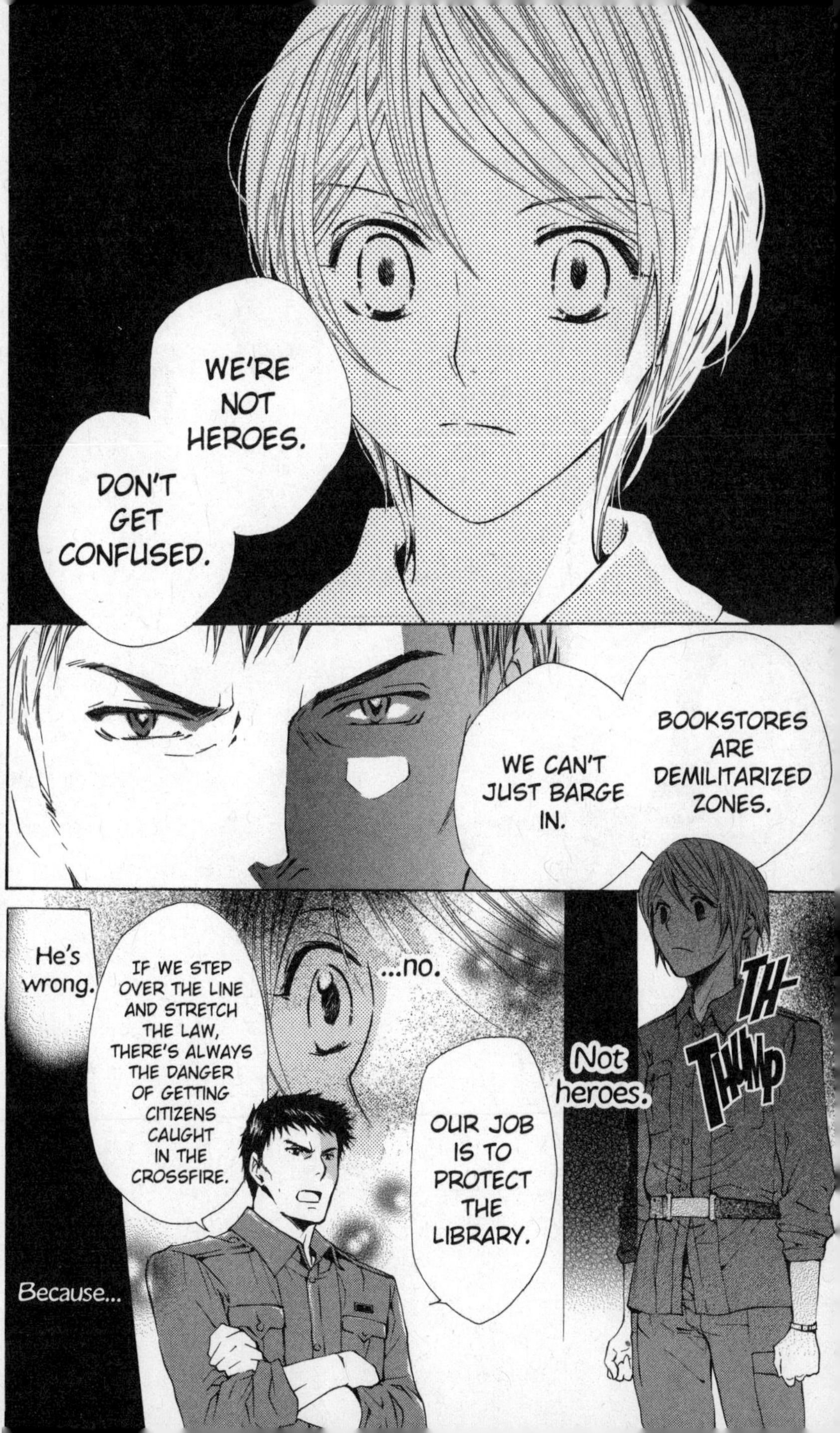
WE'RE NOT HEROES.
DON'T GET CONFUSED.
BOOKSTORES ARE DEMILITARIZED ZONES.
WE CAN'T JUST BARGE IN.
TH- THUMP
Not heroes.
...no.
OUR JOB IS TO PROTECT THE LIBRARY.
IF WE STEP OVER THE LINE AND STRETCH THE LAW, THERE'S ALWAYS THE DANGER OF GETTING CITIZENS CAUGHT IN THE CROSSFIRE.
He's wrong.
Because...

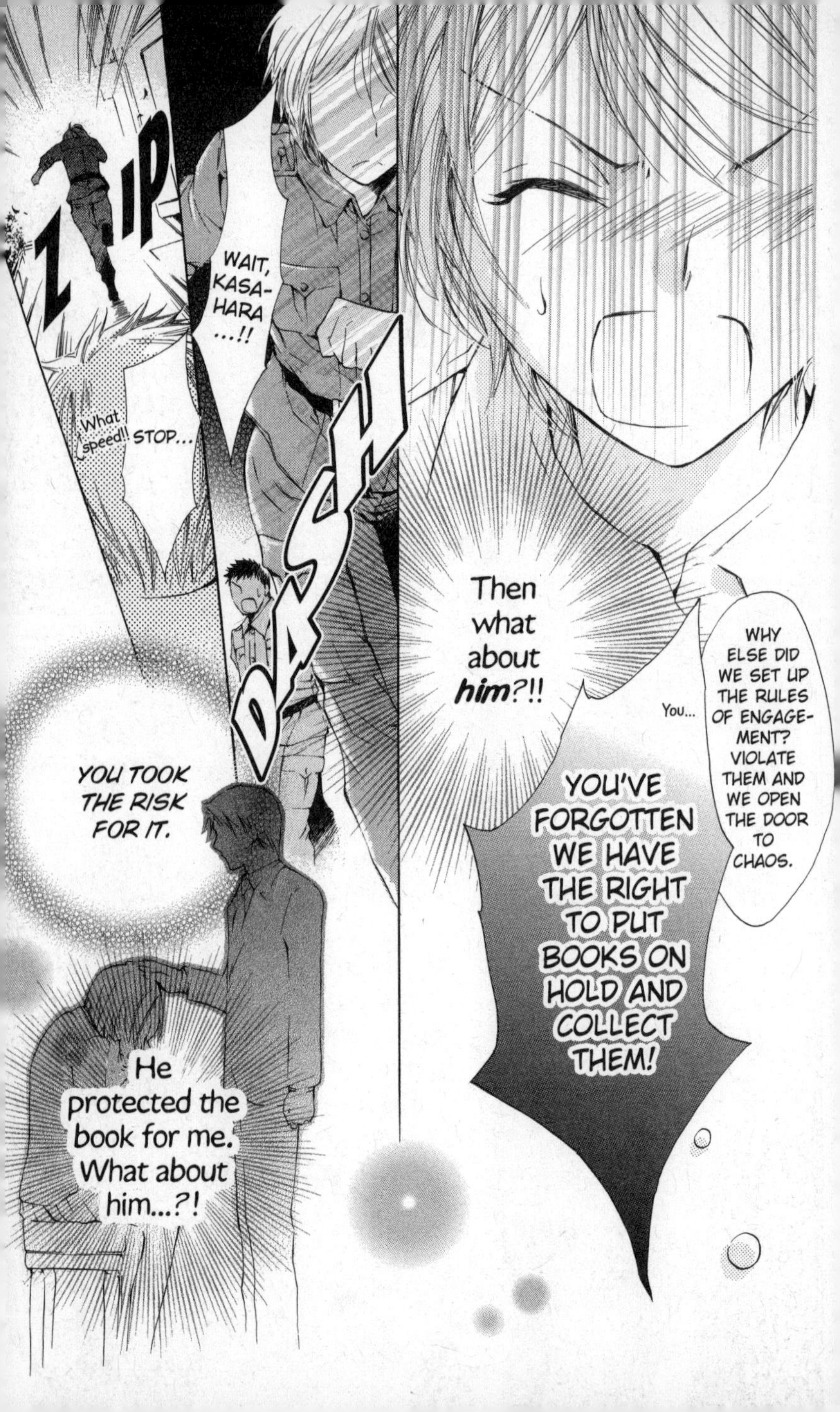
Then what about him?!!
You...
WHY ELSE DID WE SET UP THE RULES OF ENGAGEMENT? VIOLATE THEM AND WE OPEN THE DOOR TO CHAOS.
YOU'VE FORGOTTEN WE HAVE THE RIGHT TO PUT BOOKS ON HOLD AND COLLECT THEM!
WAIT, KASAHARA...!!
ZIP
DASH
What speed!!
STOP...
YOU TOOK THE RISK FOR IT.
He protected the book for me. What about him...?!

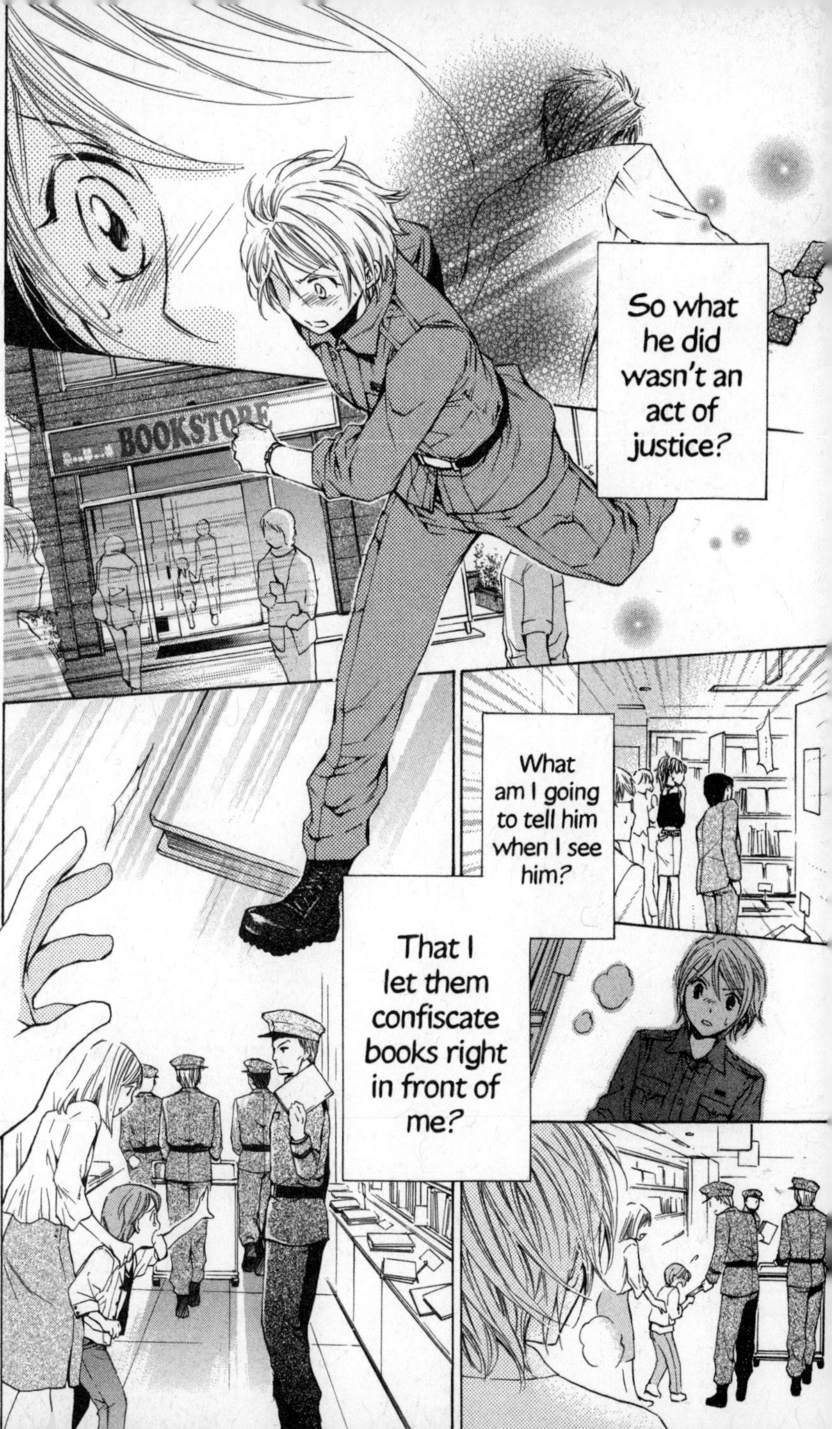
So what he did wasn't an act of justice?
BOOKSTORE
What am I going to tell him when I see him?
That I let them confiscate books right in front of me?

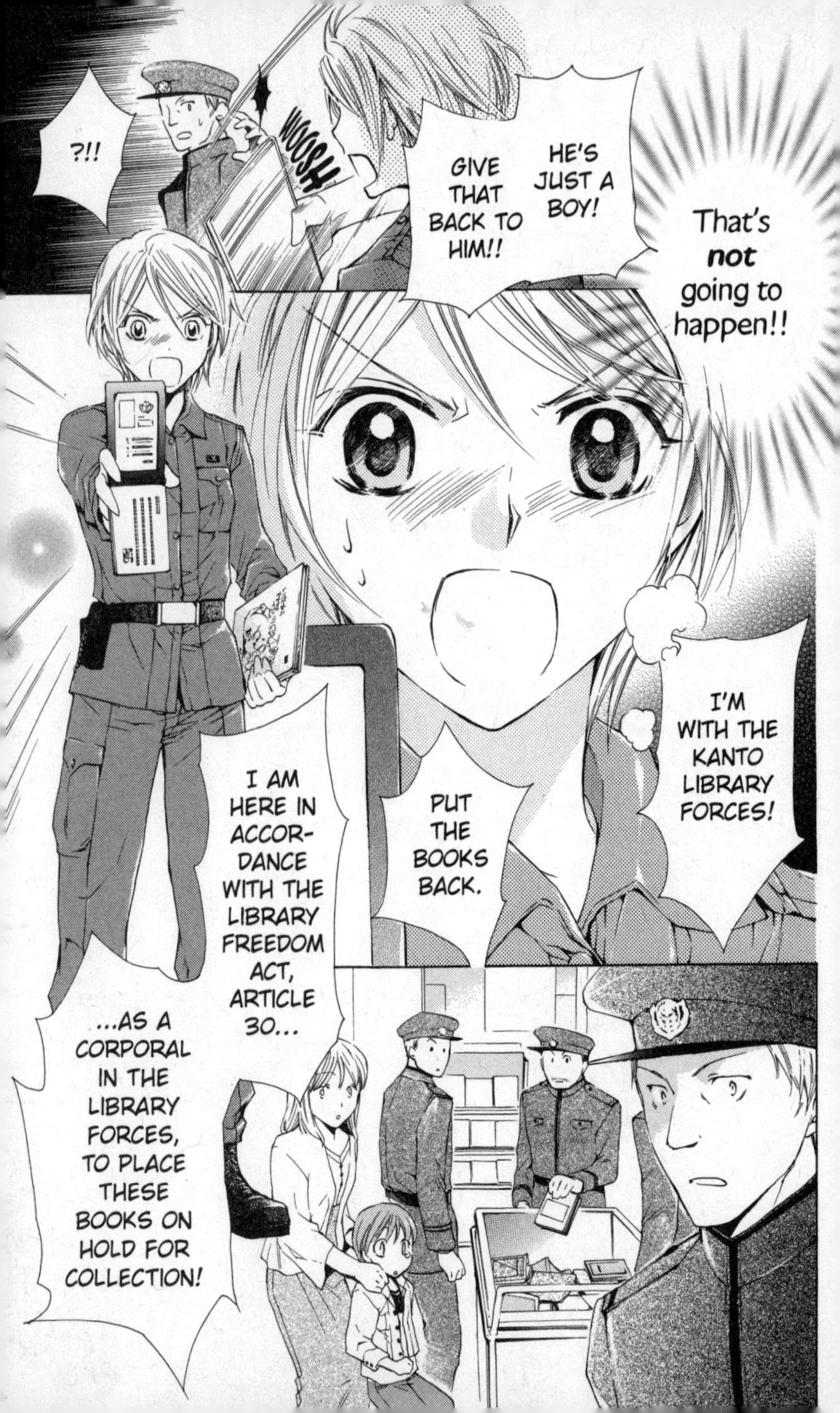
That's **not** going to happen!!
HE'S JUST A BOY! GIVE THAT BACK TO HIM!!
WOOSH
?!!
I'M WITH THE KANTO LIBRARY FORCES!
PUT THE BOOKS BACK.
I AM HERE IN ACCORDANCE WITH THE LIBRARY FREEDOM ACT, ARTICLE 30...
...AS A CORPORAL IN THE LIBRARY FORCES, TO PLACE THESE BOOKS ON HOLD FOR COLLECTION!

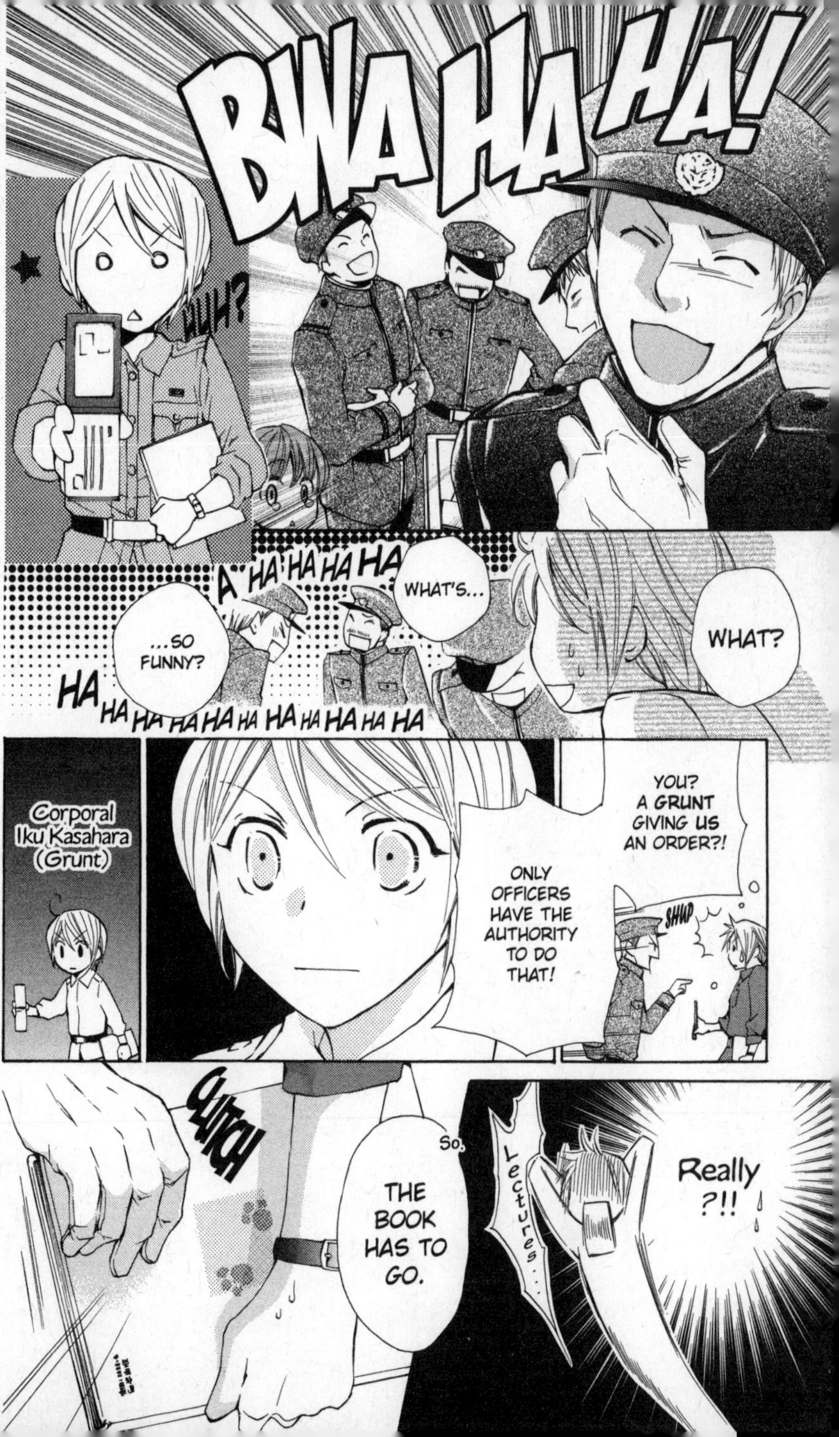
BWA HA HA!
HUH?
WHAT?
WHAT'S...
...SO FUNNY?
A HA HA HA HA
HA HA HA HA HA HA HA HA HA HA HA
YOU? A GRUNT GIVING US AN ORDER?!
ONLY OFFICERS HAVE THE AUTHORITY TO DO THAT!
SHUP
Corporal Iku Kasahara (Grunt)
Really ?!!
Lectures...
So.
THE BOOK HAS TO GO.
CLUTCH

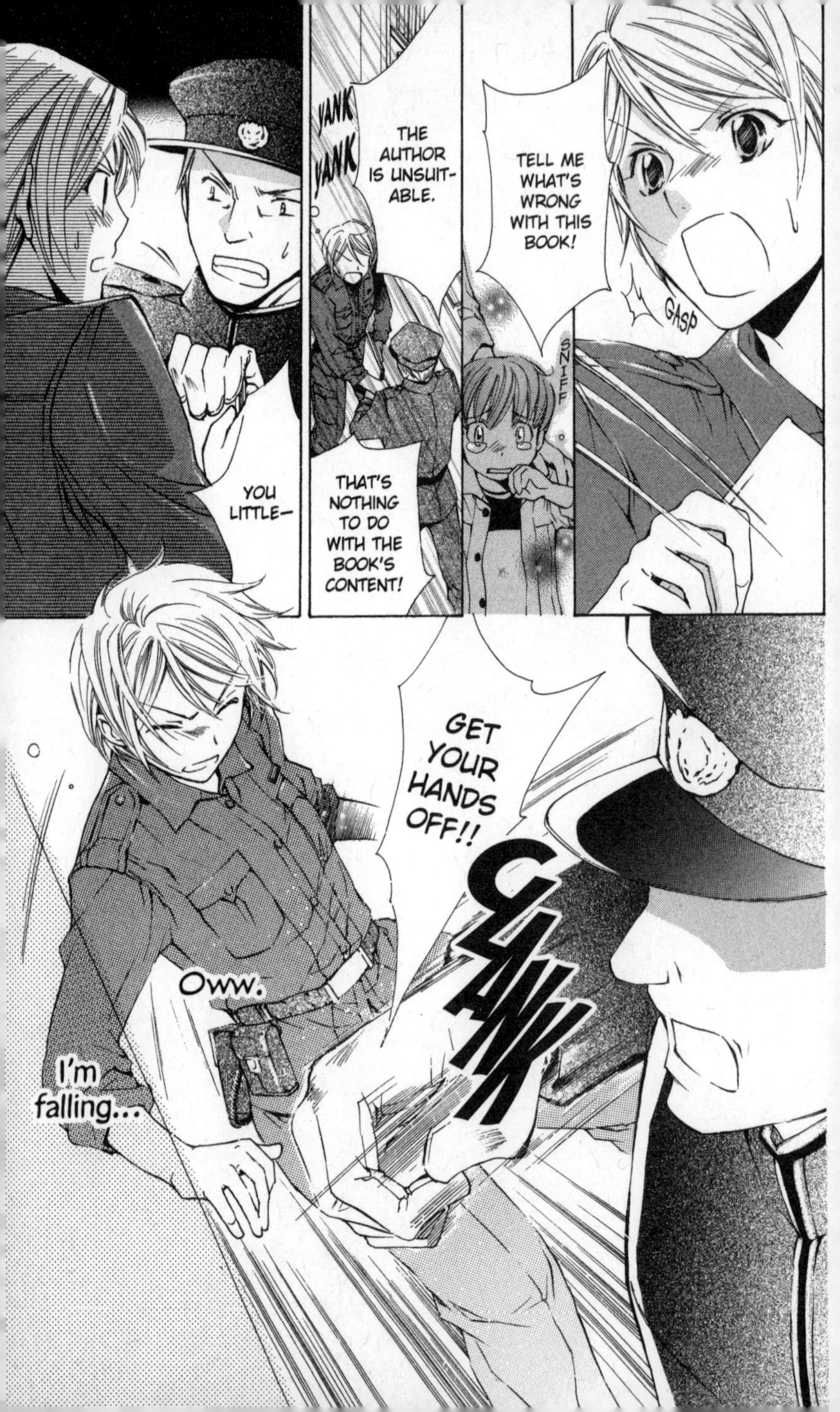

GASP
TELL ME WHAT'S WRONG WITH THIS BOOK!
SNIFF
YANK YANK
THE AUTHOR IS UNSUIT-ABLE.
THAT'S NOTHING TO DO WITH THE BOOK'S CONTENT!
YOU LITTLE—
GET YOUR HANDS OFF!!
CLANK
Oww.
I'm falling...

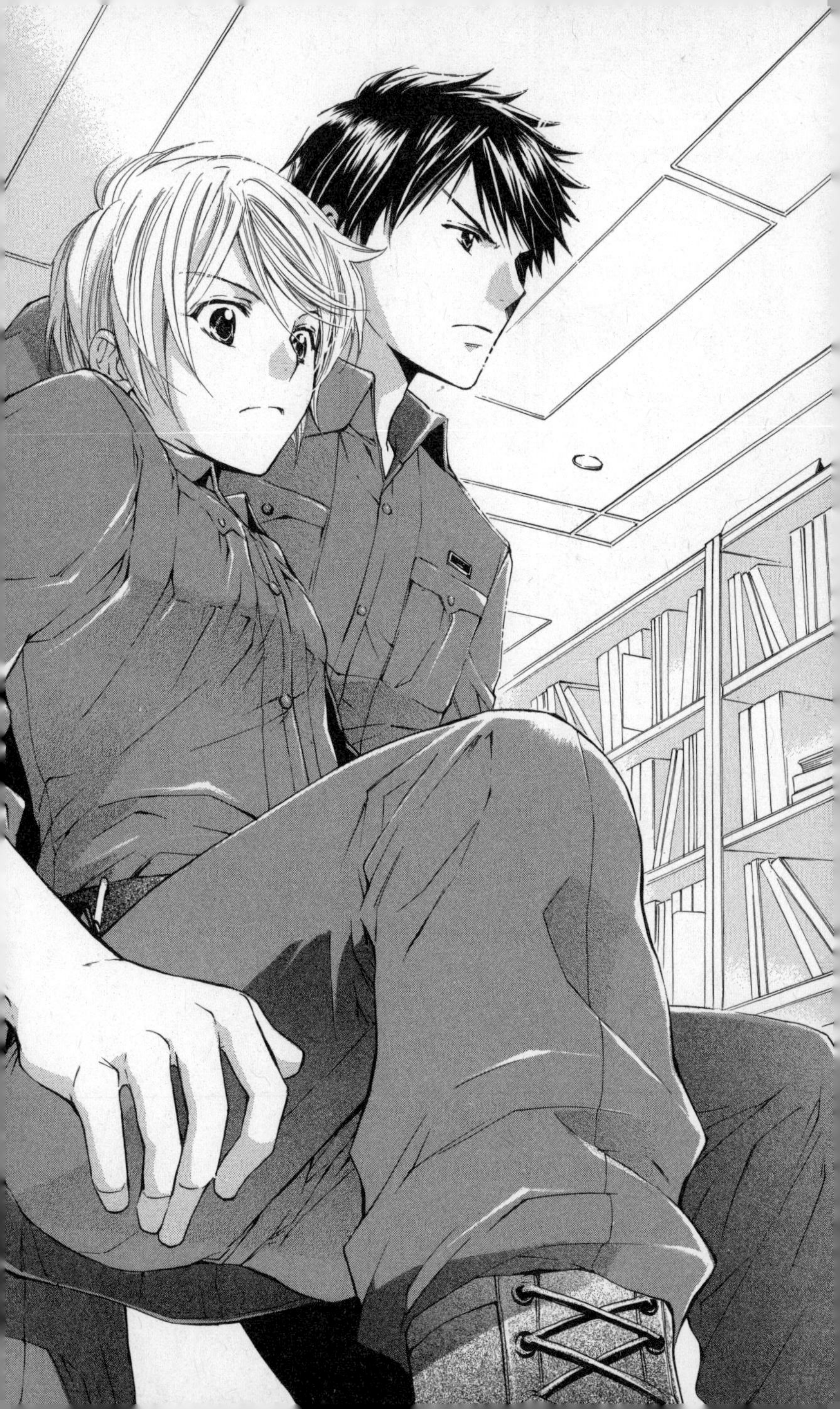

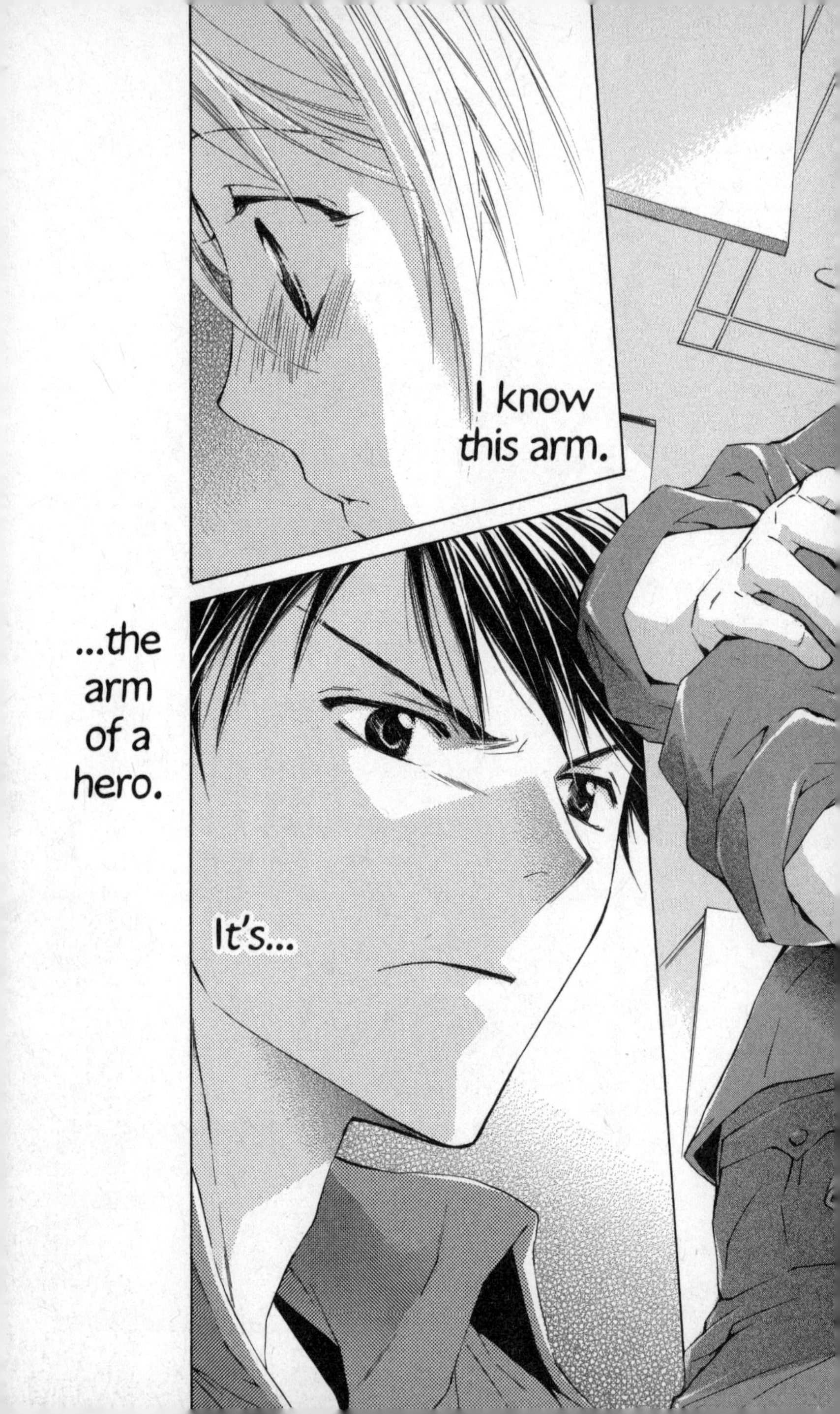
I know this arm.
It's...
...the arm of a hero.

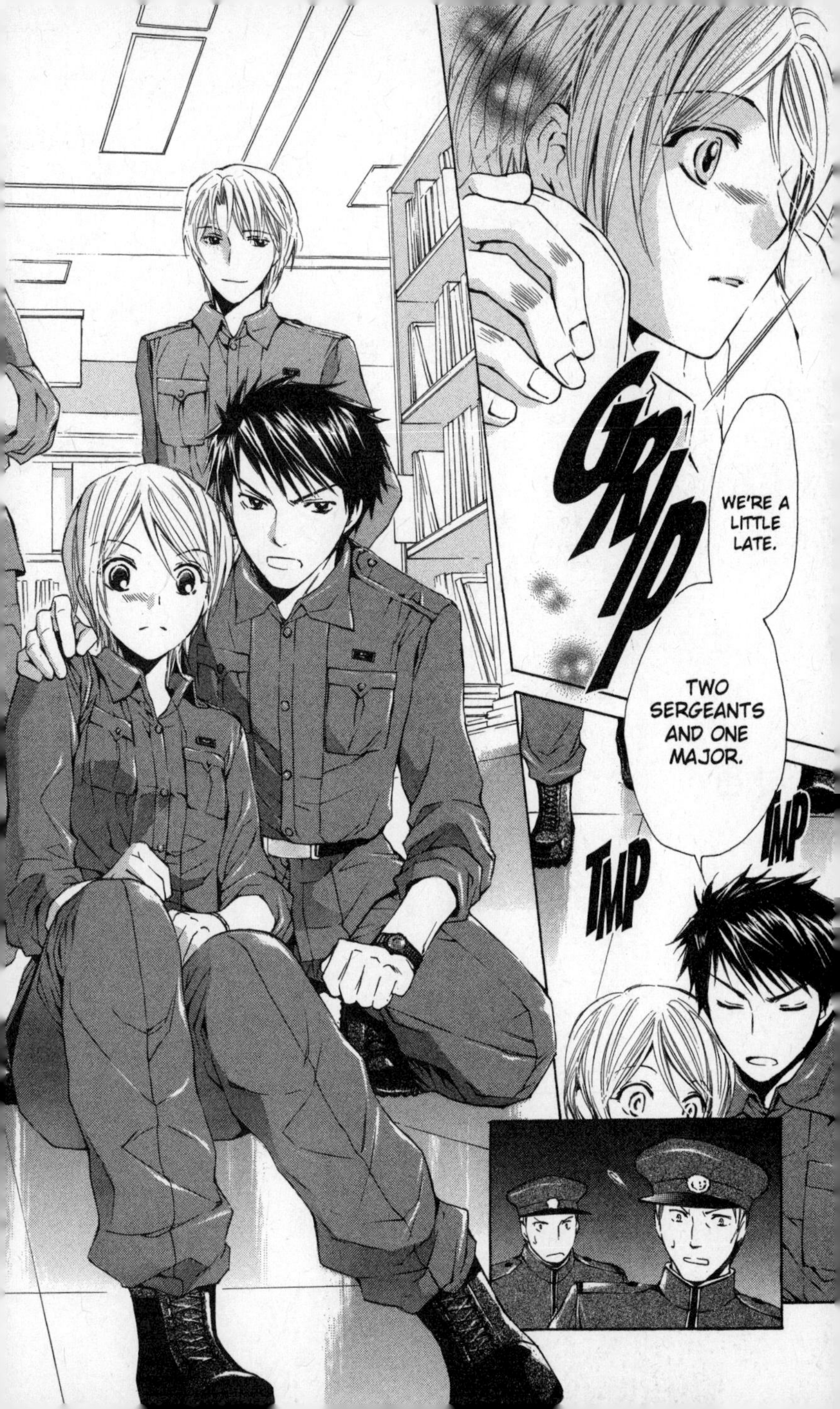
GRIP
WE'RE A LITTLE LATE.
TWO SERGEANTS AND ONE MAJOR.
TMP
TMP

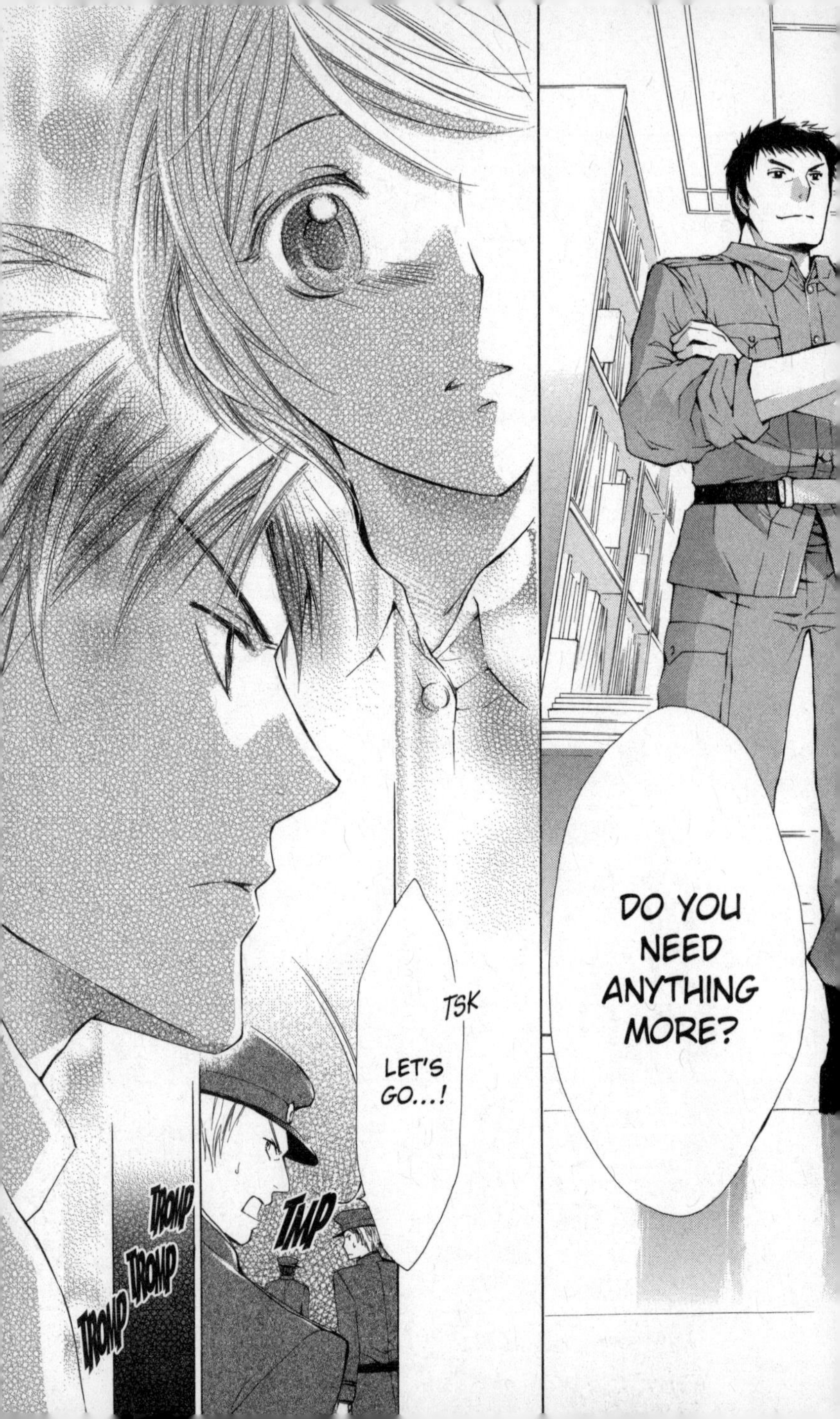
DO YOU NEED ANYTHING MORE?
TSK
LET'S GO...!
TMP
TROMP
TROMP
TROMP

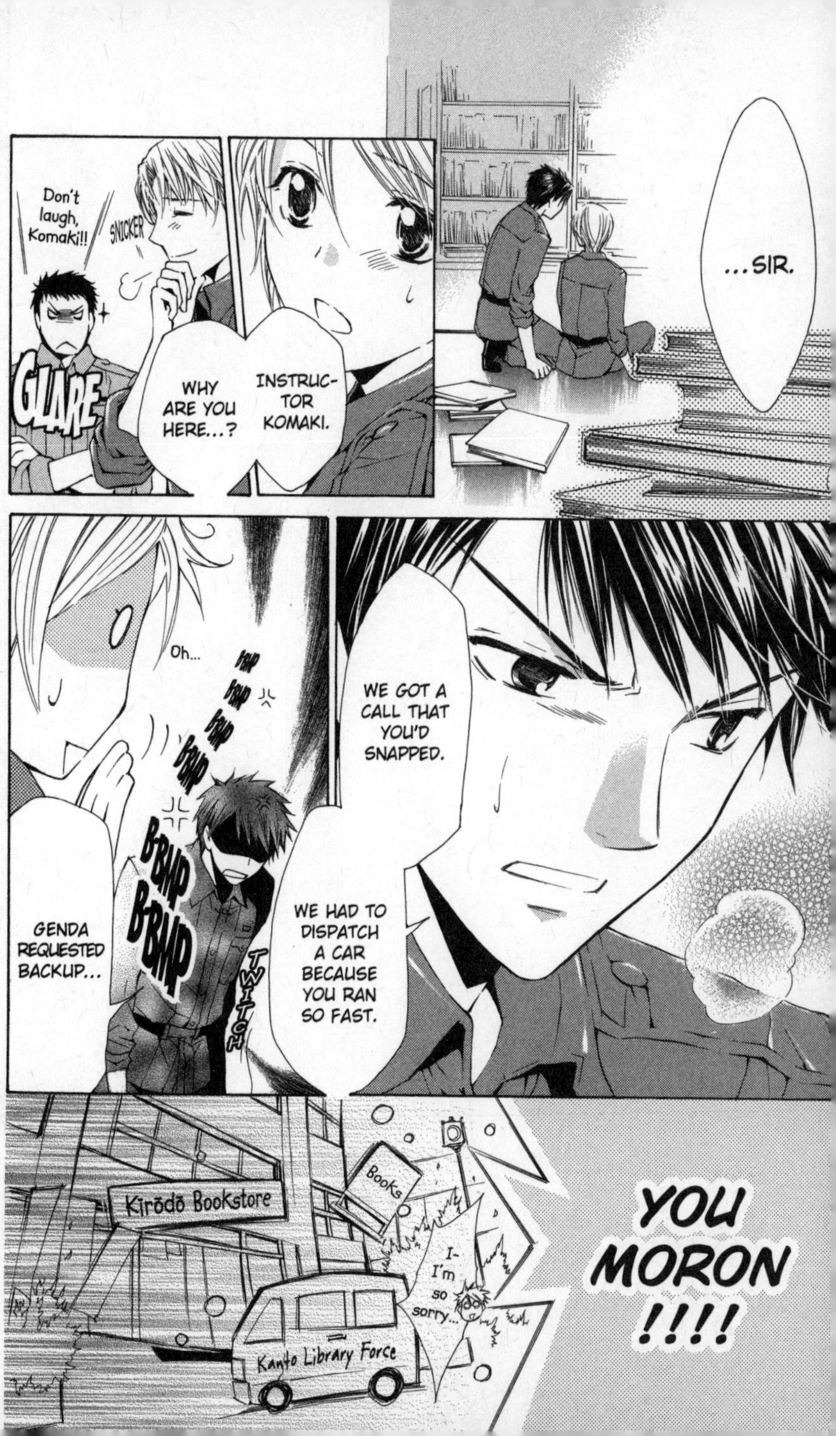
...SIR.
INSTRUC-
TOR
KOMAKI.
WHY
ARE YOU
HERE...?
SNICKER
Don't laugh, Komaki!!
GLARE
WE GOT A CALL THAT YOU'D SNAPPED.
WE HAD TO DISPATCH A CAR BECAUSE YOU RAN SO FAST.
Oh...
B-BMP B-BMP B-BMP B-BMP B-BMP B-BMP
TWITCH
GENDA REQUESTED BACKUP...
YOU MORON!!!!
Kirōdō Bookstore
Books
I-I'm so sorry...
Kanto Library Force

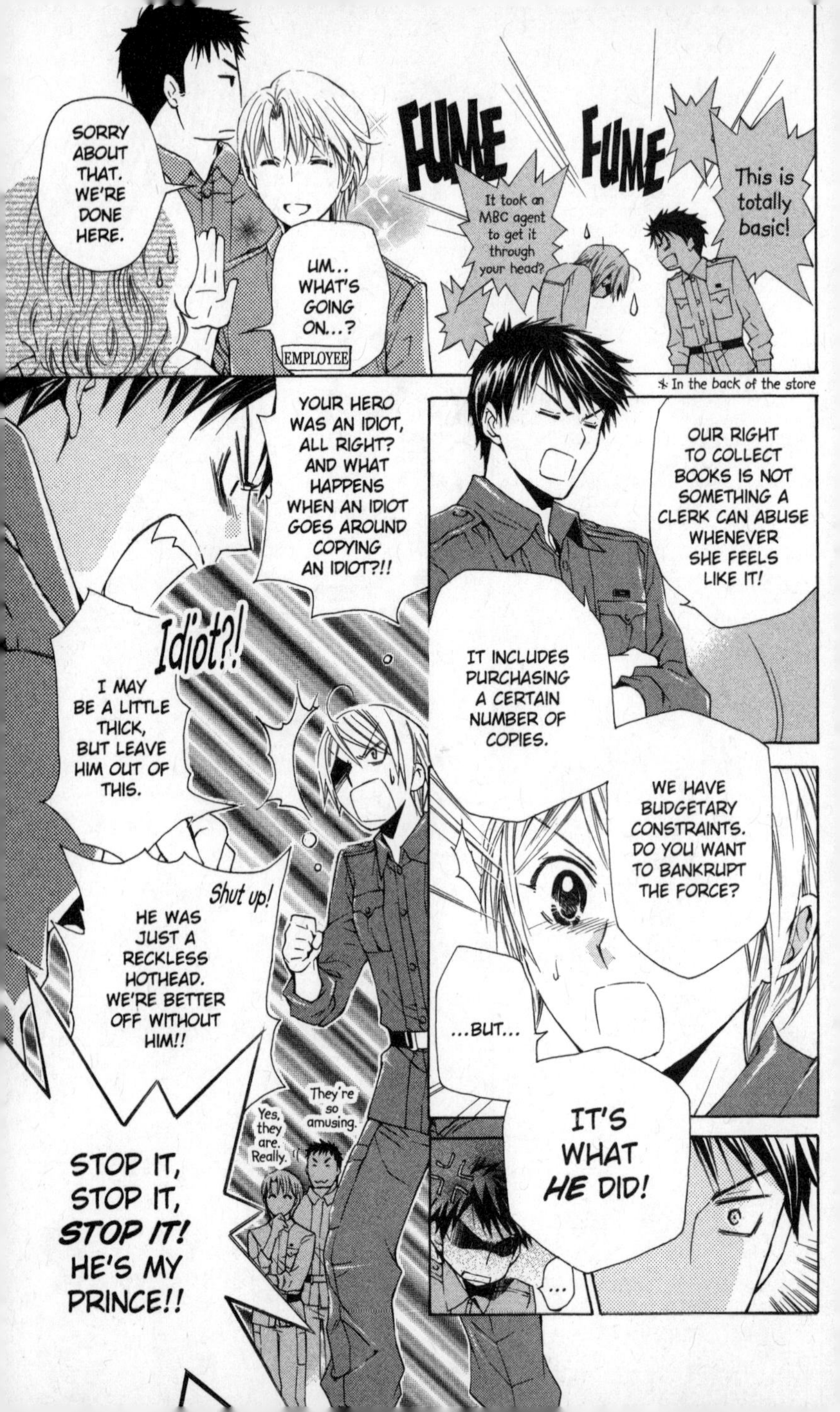

FUME FUME
This is totally basic!
It took an MBC agent to get it through your head?
* In the back of the store
SORRY ABOUT THAT. WE'RE DONE HERE.
UM... WHAT'S GOING ON...?
EMPLOYEE
OUR RIGHT TO COLLECT BOOKS IS NOT SOMETHING A CLERK CAN ABUSE WHENEVER SHE FEELS LIKE IT!
IT INCLUDES PURCHASING A CERTAIN NUMBER OF COPIES.
WE HAVE BUDGETARY CONSTRAINTS. DO YOU WANT TO BANKRUPT THE FORCE?
...BUT...
IT'S WHAT *HE* DID!
...
YOUR HERO WAS AN IDIOT, ALL RIGHT? AND WHAT HAPPENS WHEN AN IDIOT GOES AROUND COPYING AN IDIOT?!!
Idiot?!
I MAY BE A LITTLE THICK, BUT LEAVE HIM OUT OF THIS.
Shut up!
HE WAS JUST A RECKLESS HOTHEAD. WE'RE BETTER OFF WITHOUT HIM!!
They're so amusing.
Yes, they are. Really.
STOP IT, STOP IT, *STOP IT!* HE'S MY PRINCE!!

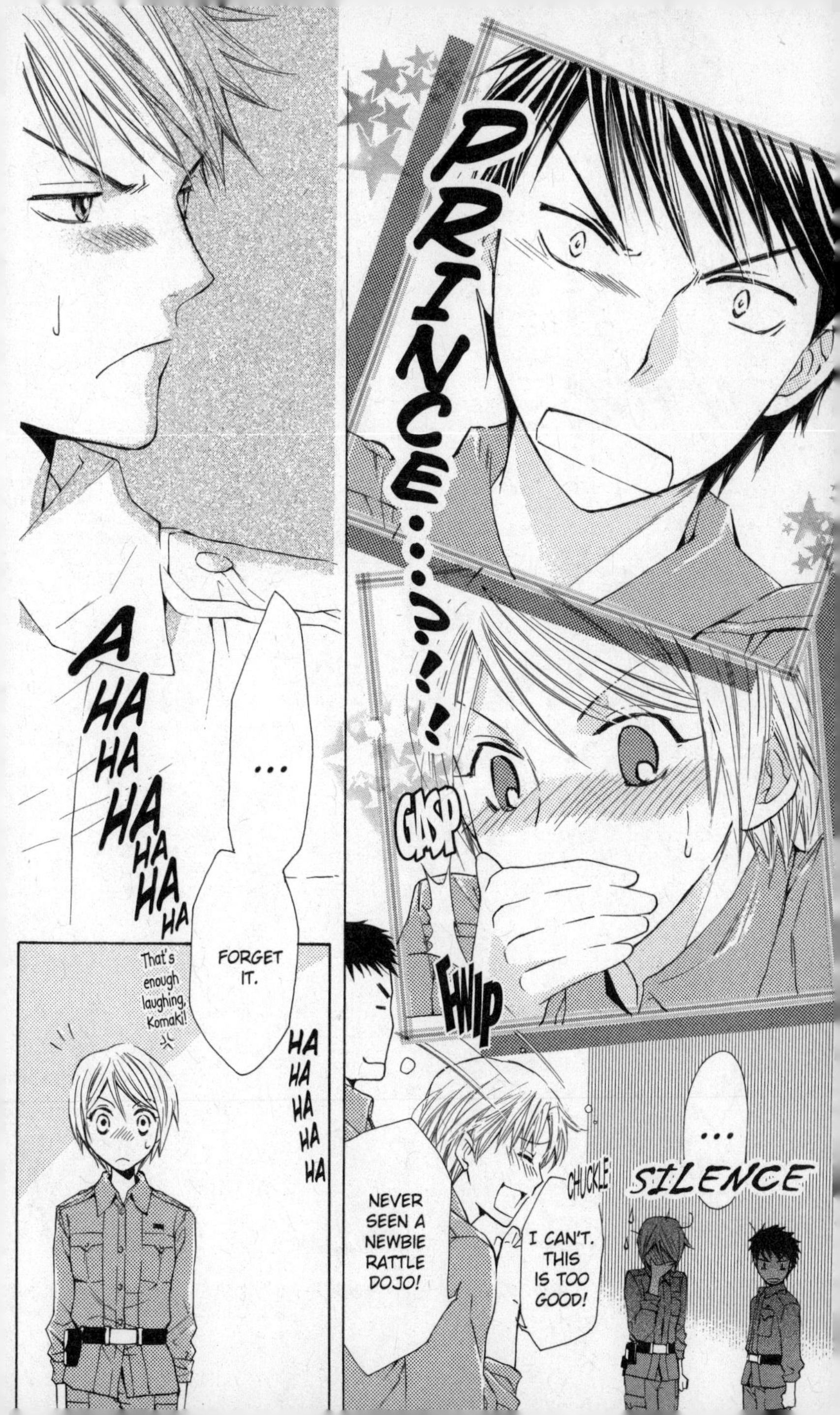
PRINCE...?!!
GASP
FWIP
...
SILENCE
CHUCKLE
I CAN'T. THIS IS TOO GOOD!
NEVER SEEN A NEWBIE RATTLE DOJO!
AHAHAHAHAHAHAHAHA
...
FORGET IT.
HAHAHAHAHAHA
That's enough laughing, Komaki!

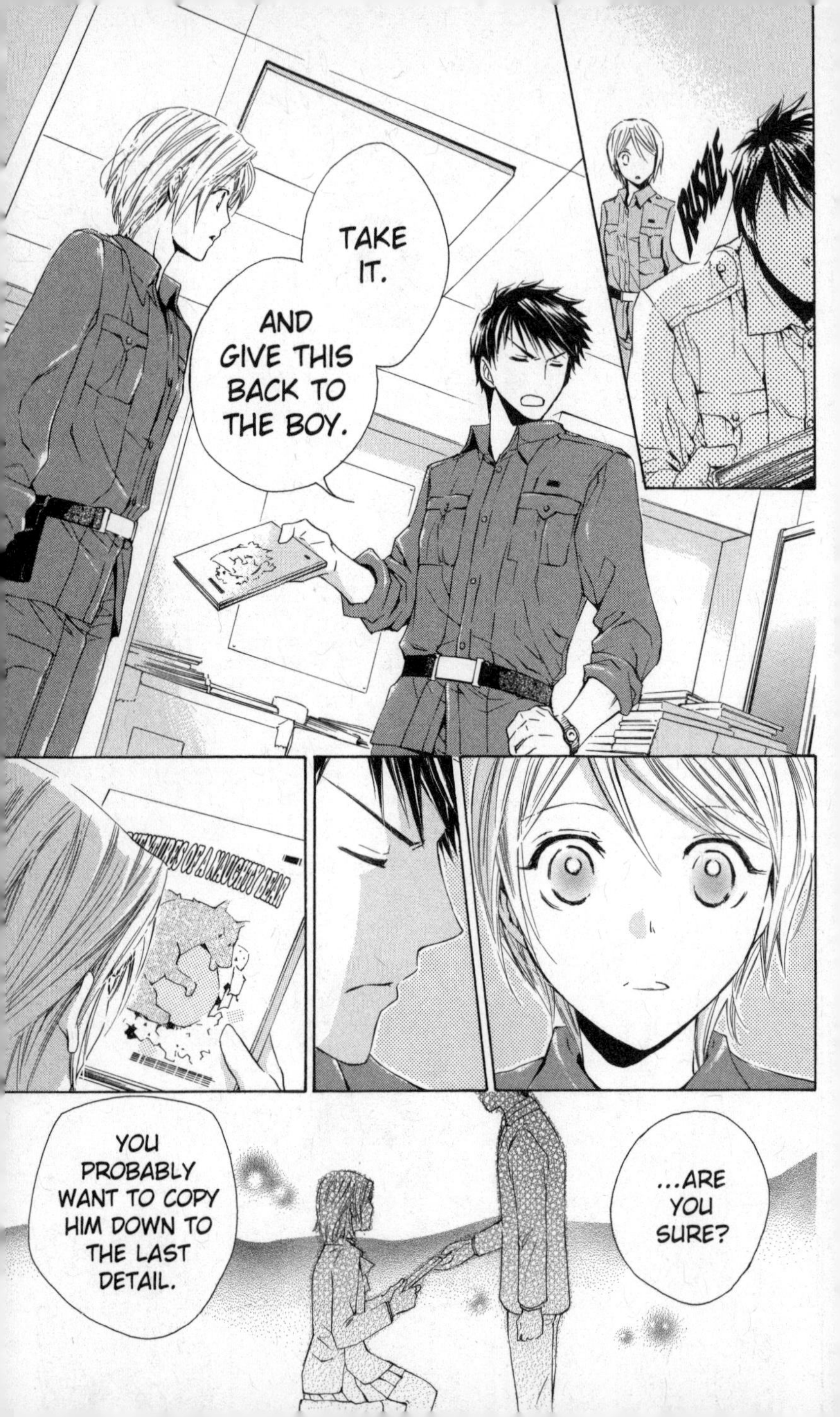
RUSTLE
TAKE IT.
AND GIVE THIS BACK TO THE BOY.
OF A NAUGHTY BEAR
...ARE YOU SURE?
YOU PROBABLY WANT TO COPY HIM DOWN TO THE LAST DETAIL.

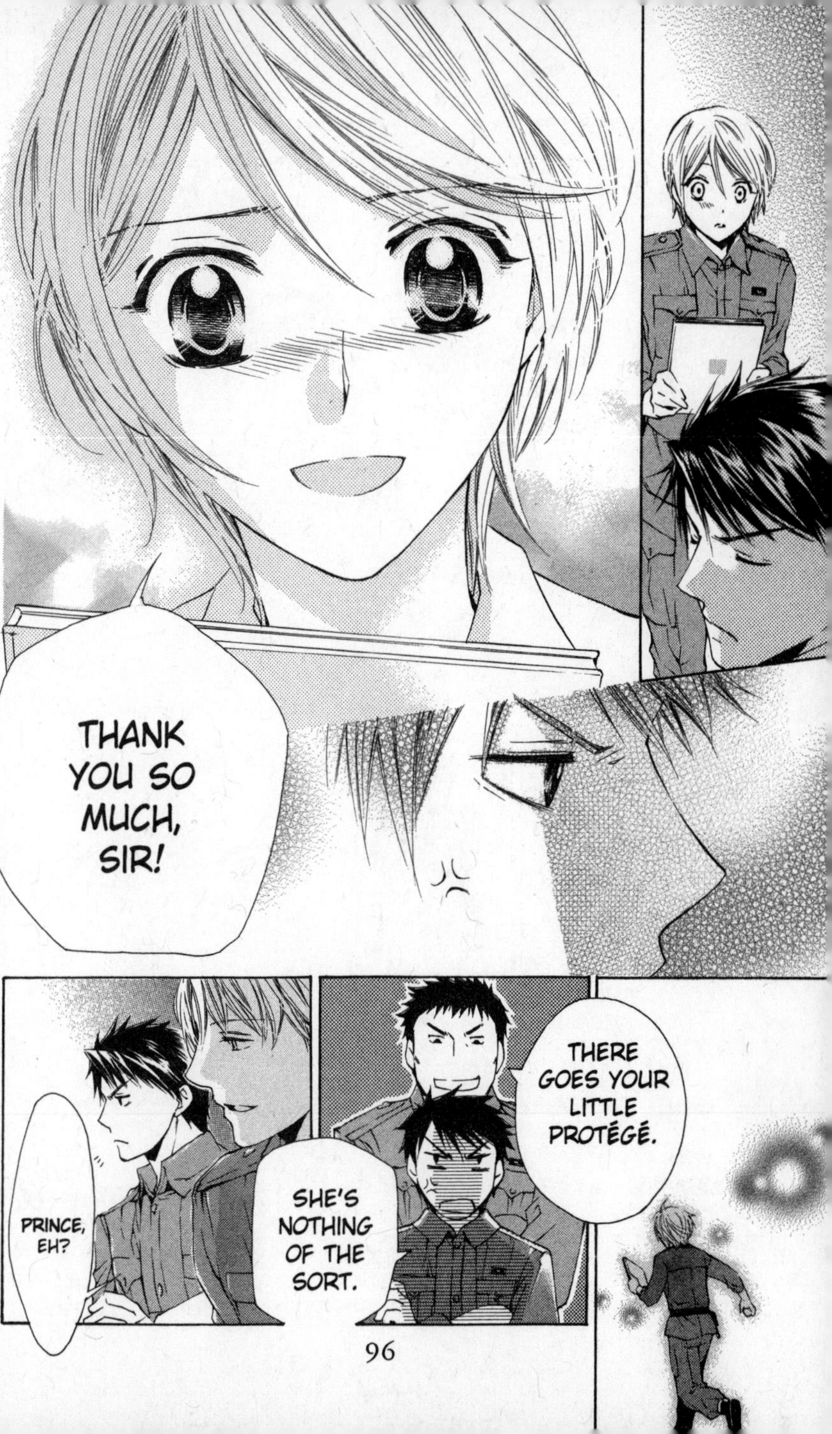

THANK YOU SO MUCH, SIR!
THERE GOES YOUR LITTLE PROTÉGÉ.
SHE'S NOTHING OF THE SORT.
PRINCE, EH?

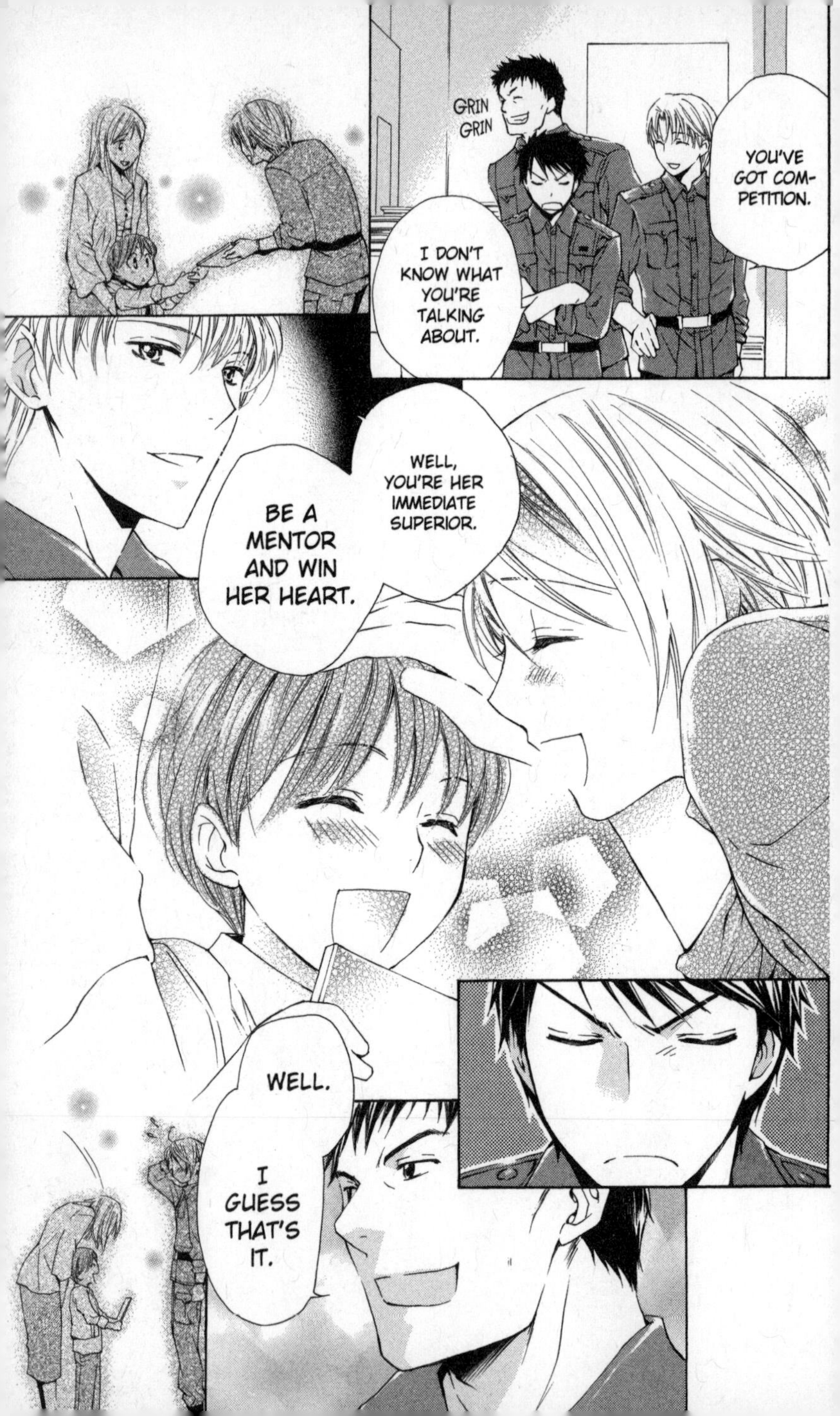
YOU'VE GOT COMPETITION.
GRIN GRIN
I DON'T KNOW WHAT YOU'RE TALKING ABOUT.
WELL, YOU'RE HER IMMEDIATE SUPERIOR.
BE A MENTOR AND WIN HER HEART.
WELL.
I GUESS THAT'S IT.

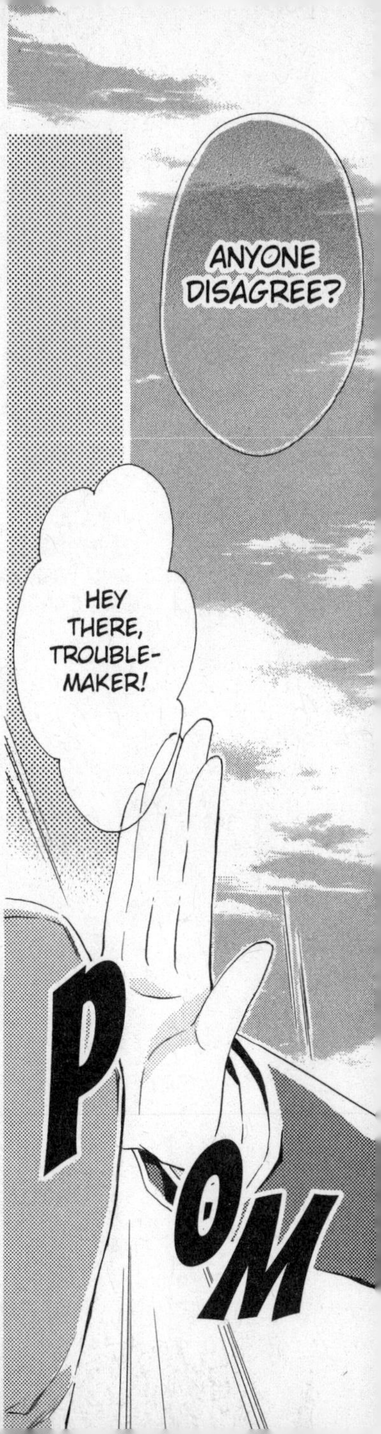
ANYONE DISAGREE?
HEY THERE, TROUBLE-MAKER!
POM

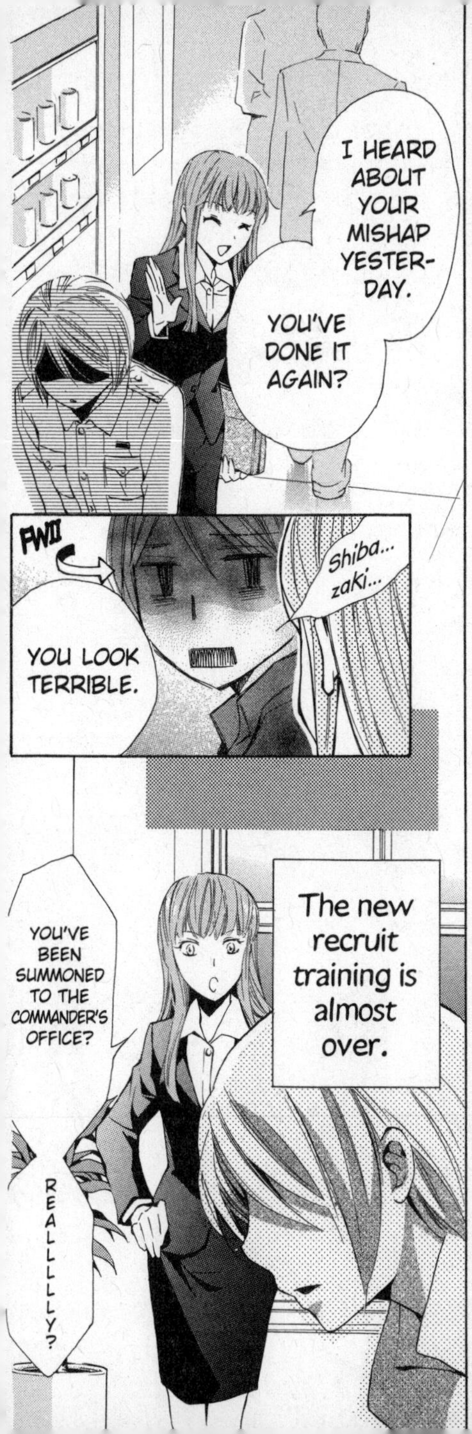
I HEARD ABOUT YOUR MISHAP YESTER-DAY.
YOU'VE DONE IT AGAIN?
Shiba... zaki...
FWII
YOU LOOK TERRIBLE.
The new recruit training is almost over.
YOU'VE BEEN SUMMONED TO THE COMMANDER'S OFFICE?
REALLLLLY?

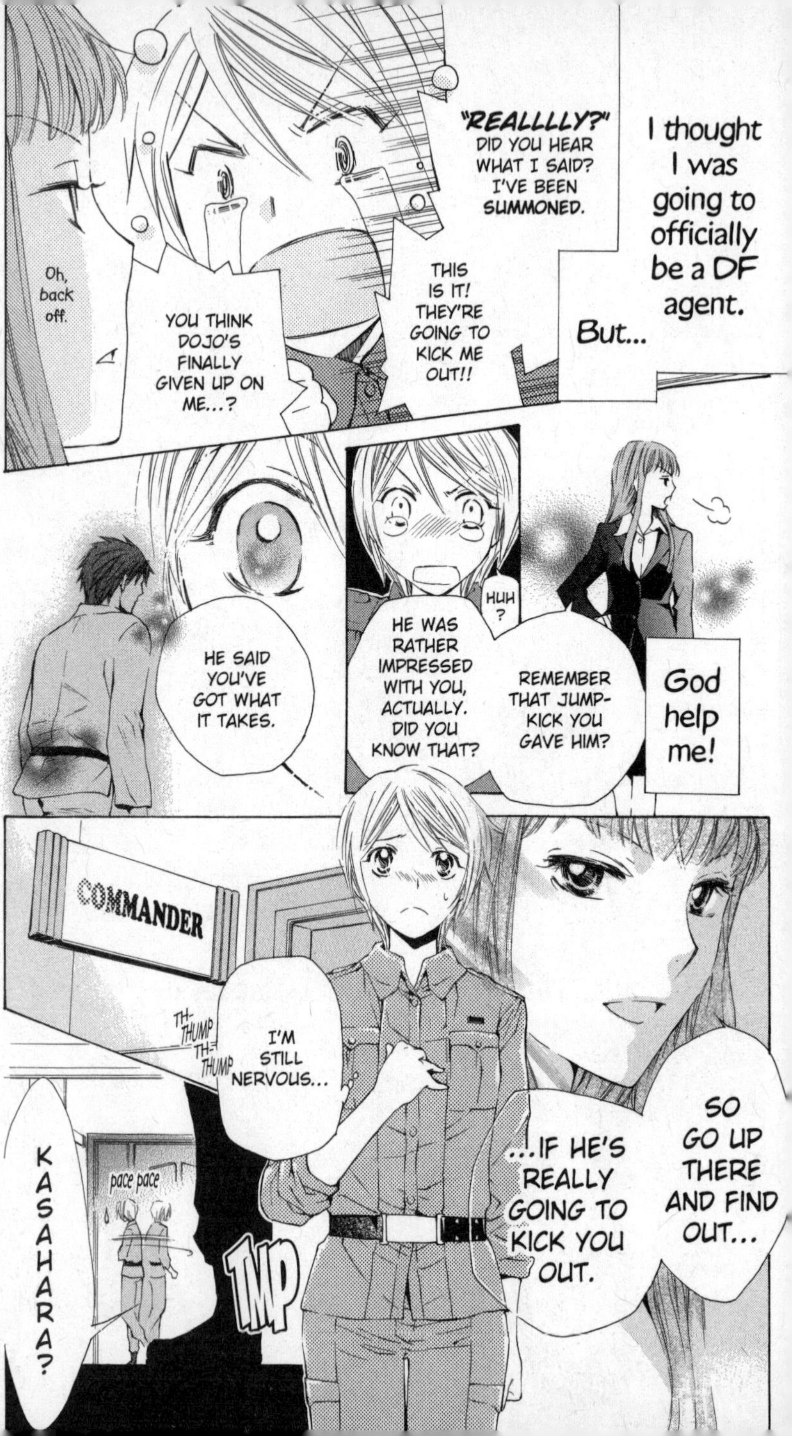
I thought I was going to officially be a DF agent.
But...
"REALLLLY?" DID YOU HEAR WHAT I SAID? I'VE BEEN SUMMONED.
THIS IS IT! THEY'RE GOING TO KICK ME OUT!!
YOU THINK DOJO'S FINALLY GIVEN UP ON ME...?
Oh, back off.
God help me!
REMEMBER THAT JUMP-KICK YOU GAVE HIM?
HE WAS RATHER IMPRESSED WITH YOU, ACTUALLY. DID YOU KNOW THAT?
HUH?
HE SAID YOU'VE GOT WHAT IT TAKES.
SO GO UP THERE AND FIND OUT...
...IF HE'S REALLY GOING TO KICK YOU OUT.
I'M STILL NERVOUS...
TH-THUMP TH-THUMP
COMMANDER
TMP
pace pace
KASAHARA?

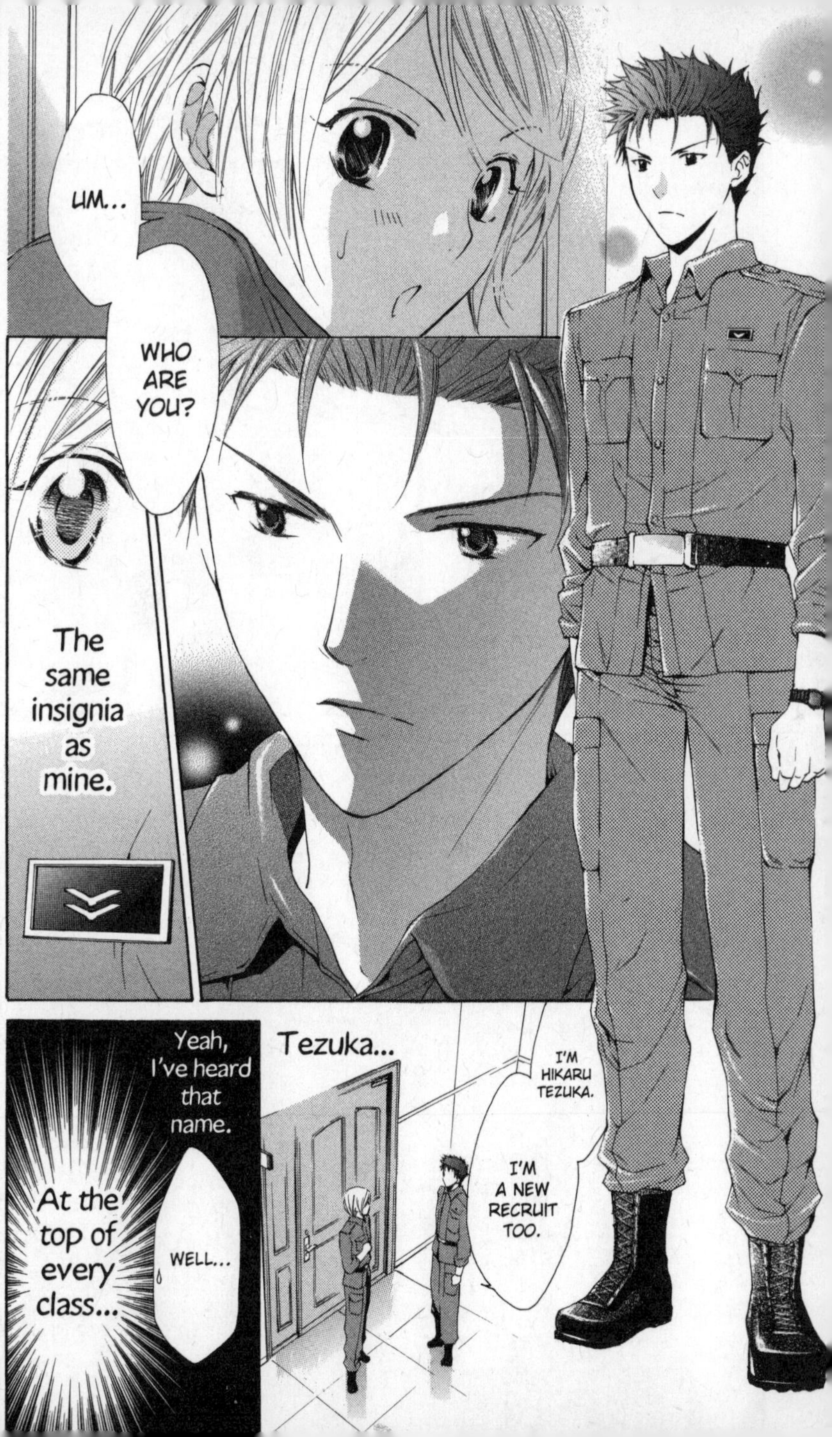
UM...
WHO ARE YOU?
The same insignia as mine.
I'M HIKARU TEZUKA.
I'M A NEW RECRUIT TOO.
Tezuka...
WELL...
Yeah, I've heard that name.
At the top of every class...

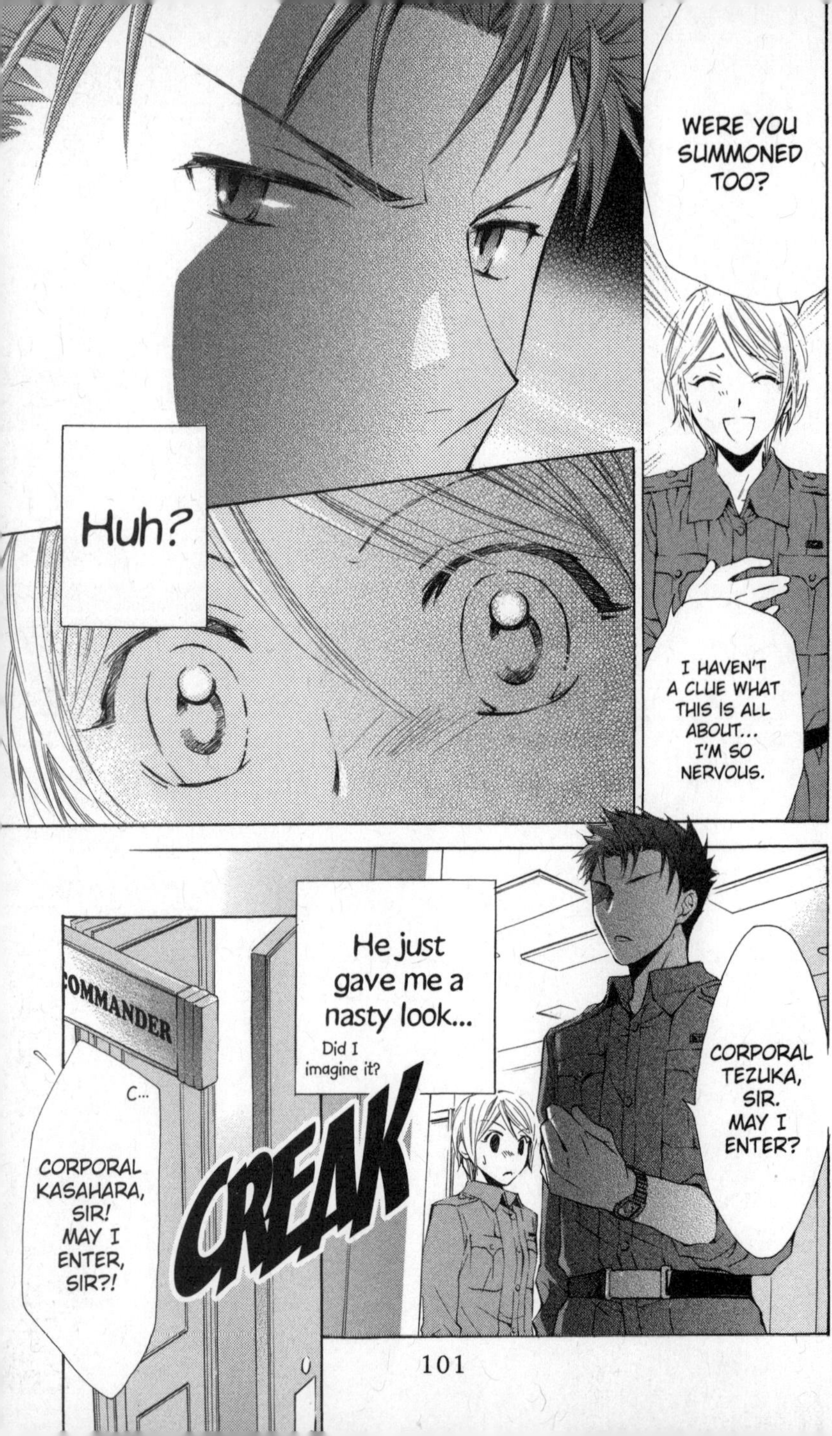
WERE YOU SUMMONED TOO?
I HAVEN'T A CLUE WHAT THIS IS ALL ABOUT... I'M SO NERVOUS.
Huh?
COMMANDER
CORPORAL TEZUKA, SIR. MAY I ENTER?
He just gave me a nasty look...
Did I imagine it?
CREAK
C...
CORPORAL KASAHARA, SIR! MAY I ENTER, SIR?!

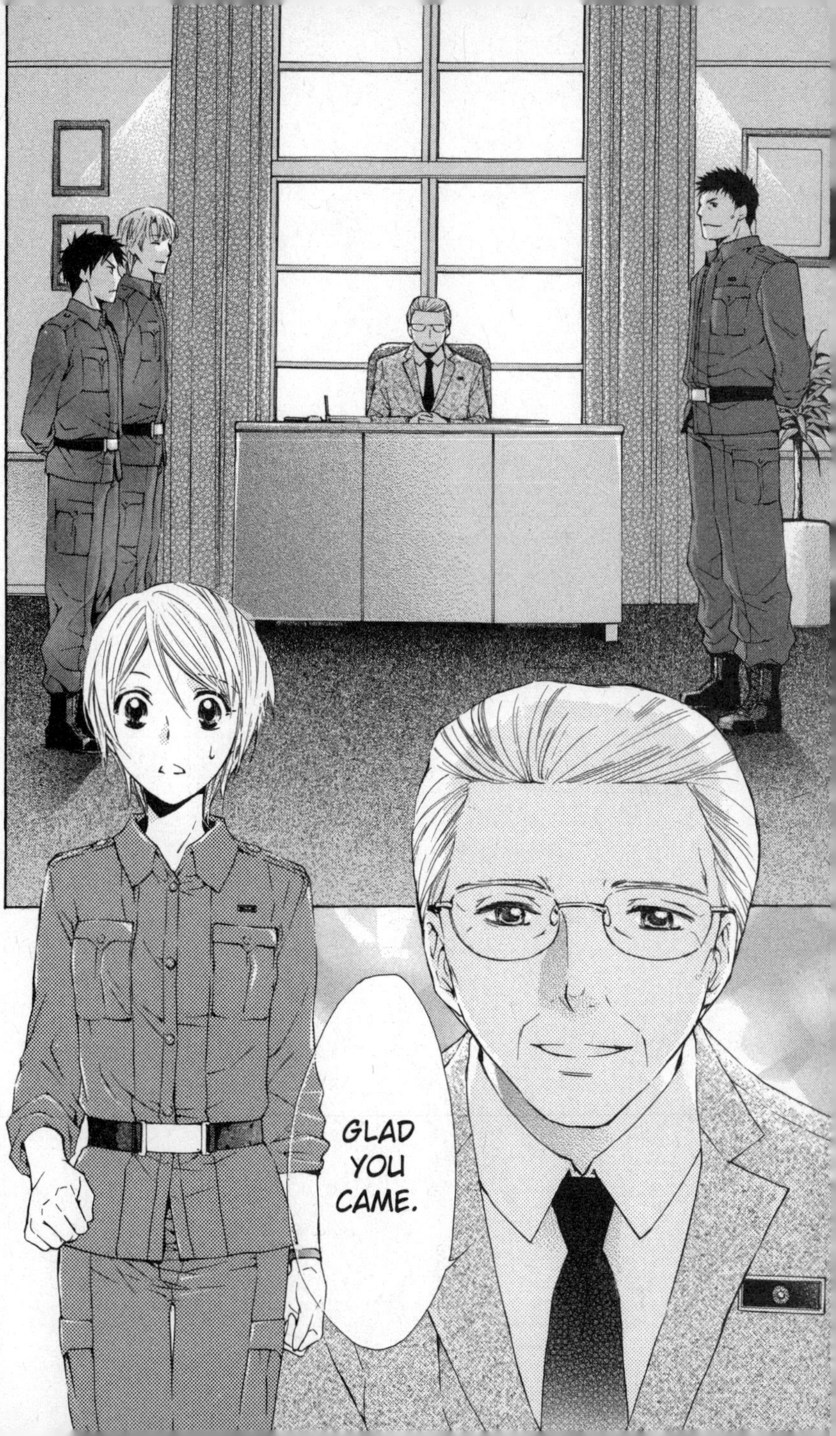
GLAD YOU CAME.

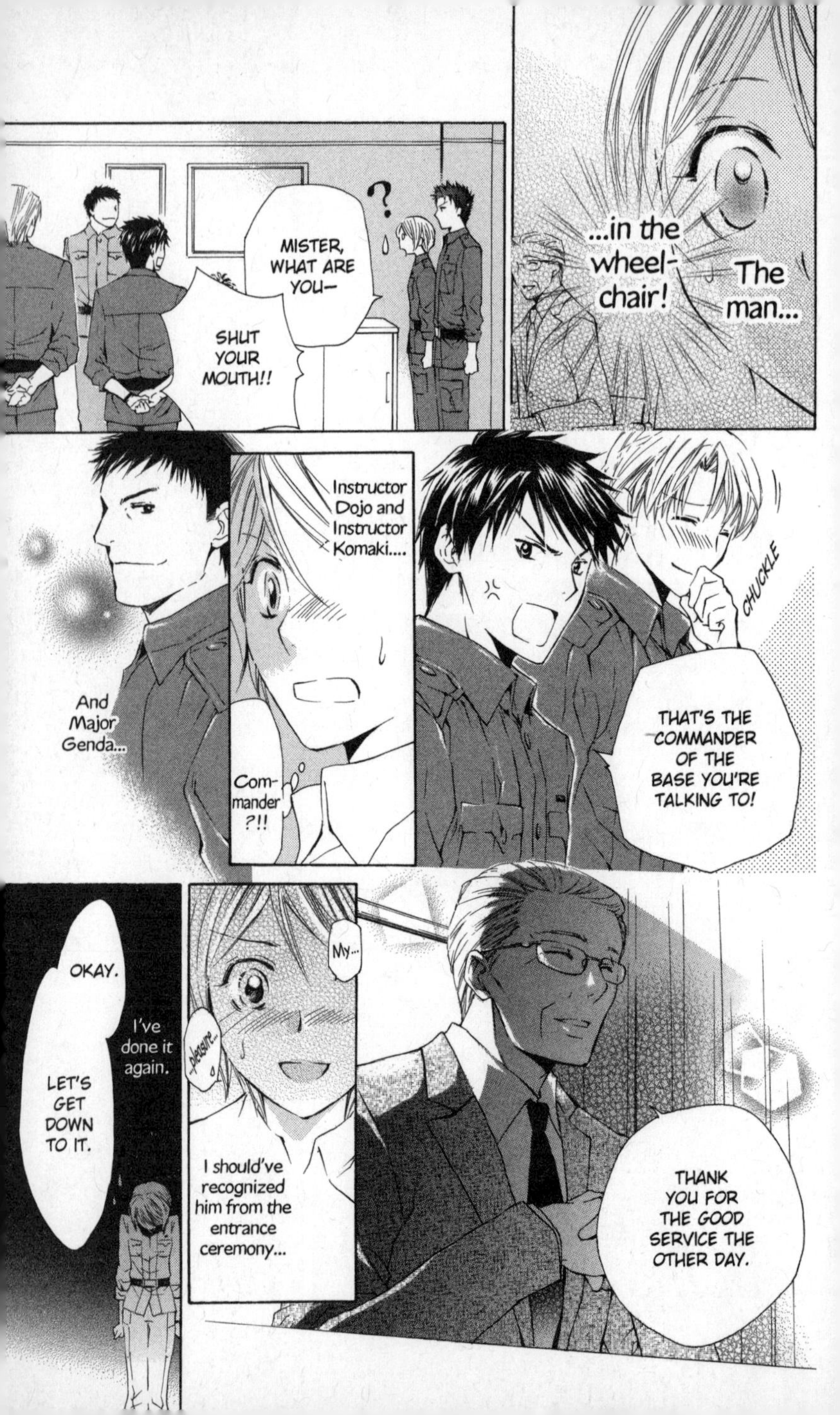
The man...
...in the wheel-chair!
MISTER, WHAT ARE YOU—
SHUT YOUR MOUTH!!
CHUCKLE
THAT'S THE COMMANDER OF THE BASE YOU'RE TALKING TO!
Instructor Dojo and Instructor Komaki....
Com-mander?!!
And Major Genda...
THANK YOU FOR THE GOOD SERVICE THE OTHER DAY.
My...
...pleasure...
I should've recognized him from the entrance ceremony...
I've done it again.
OKAY.
LET'S GET DOWN TO IT.

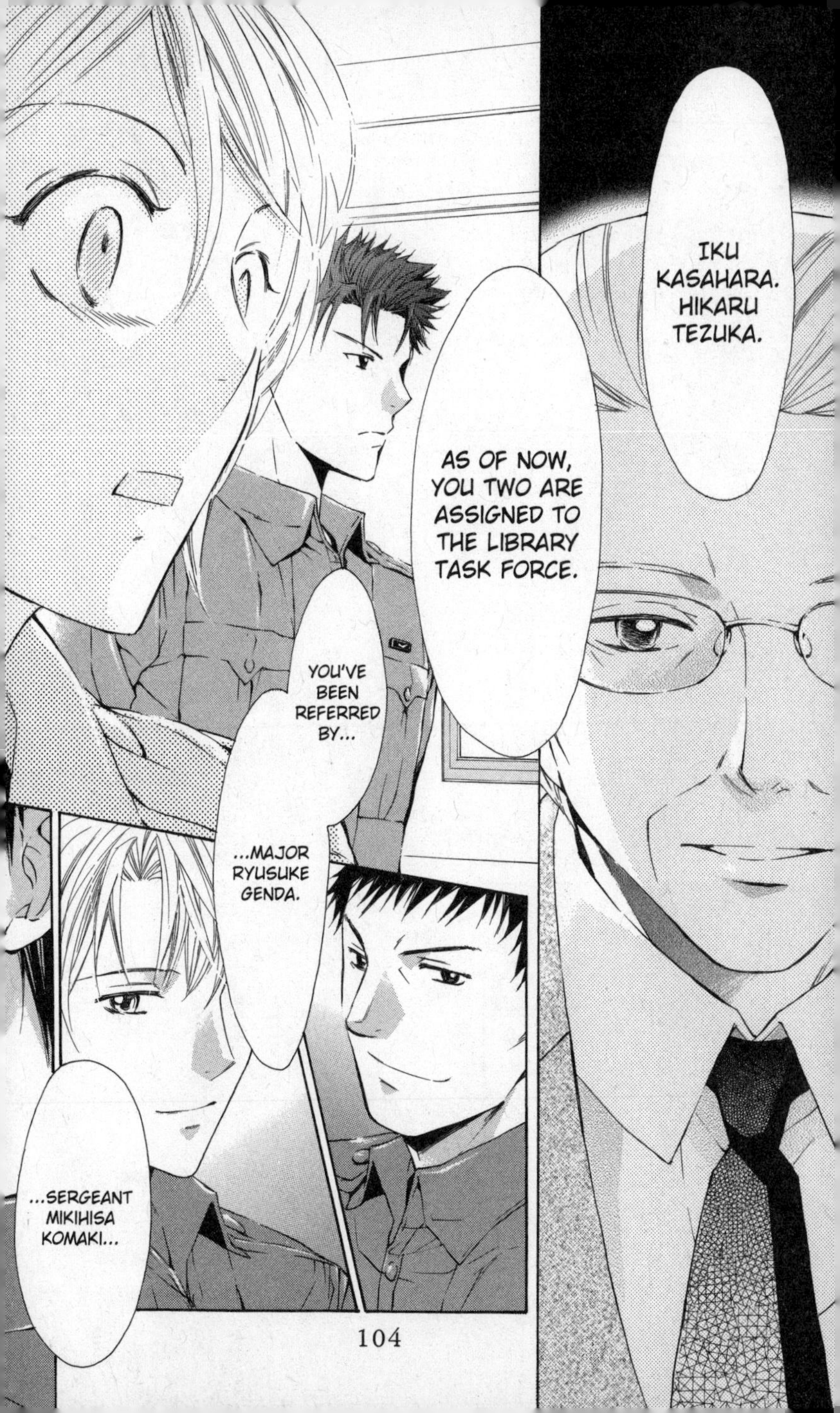
IKU KASAHARA. HIKARU TEZUKA.
AS OF NOW, YOU TWO ARE ASSIGNED TO THE LIBRARY TASK FORCE.
YOU'VE BEEN REFERRED BY...
...MAJOR RYUSUKE GENDA.
...SERGEANT MIKIHISA KOMAKI...

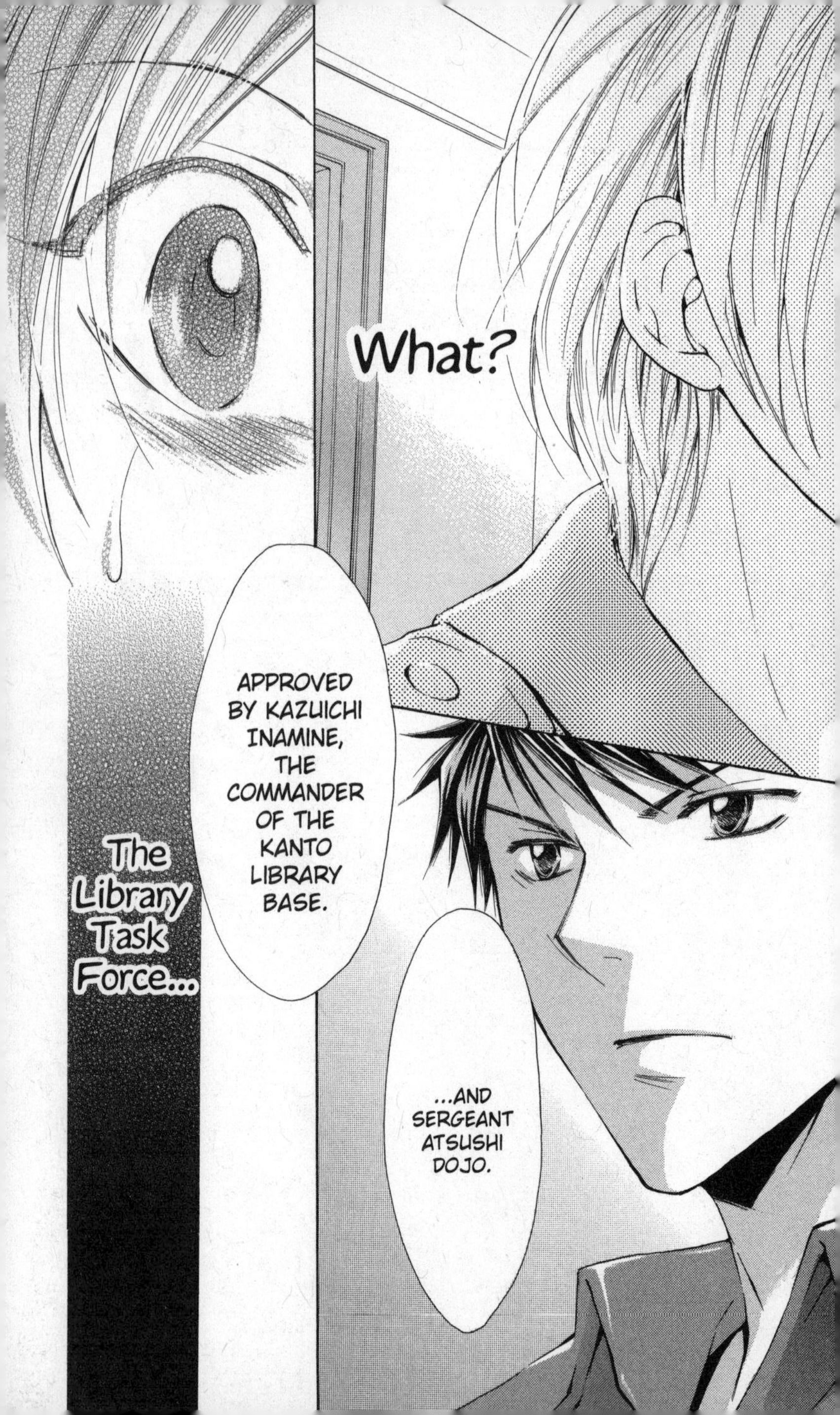

What?
APPROVED BY KAZUICHI INAMINE, THE COMMANDER OF THE KANTO LIBRARY BASE.
...AND SERGEANT ATSUSHI DOJO.
The Library Task Force...

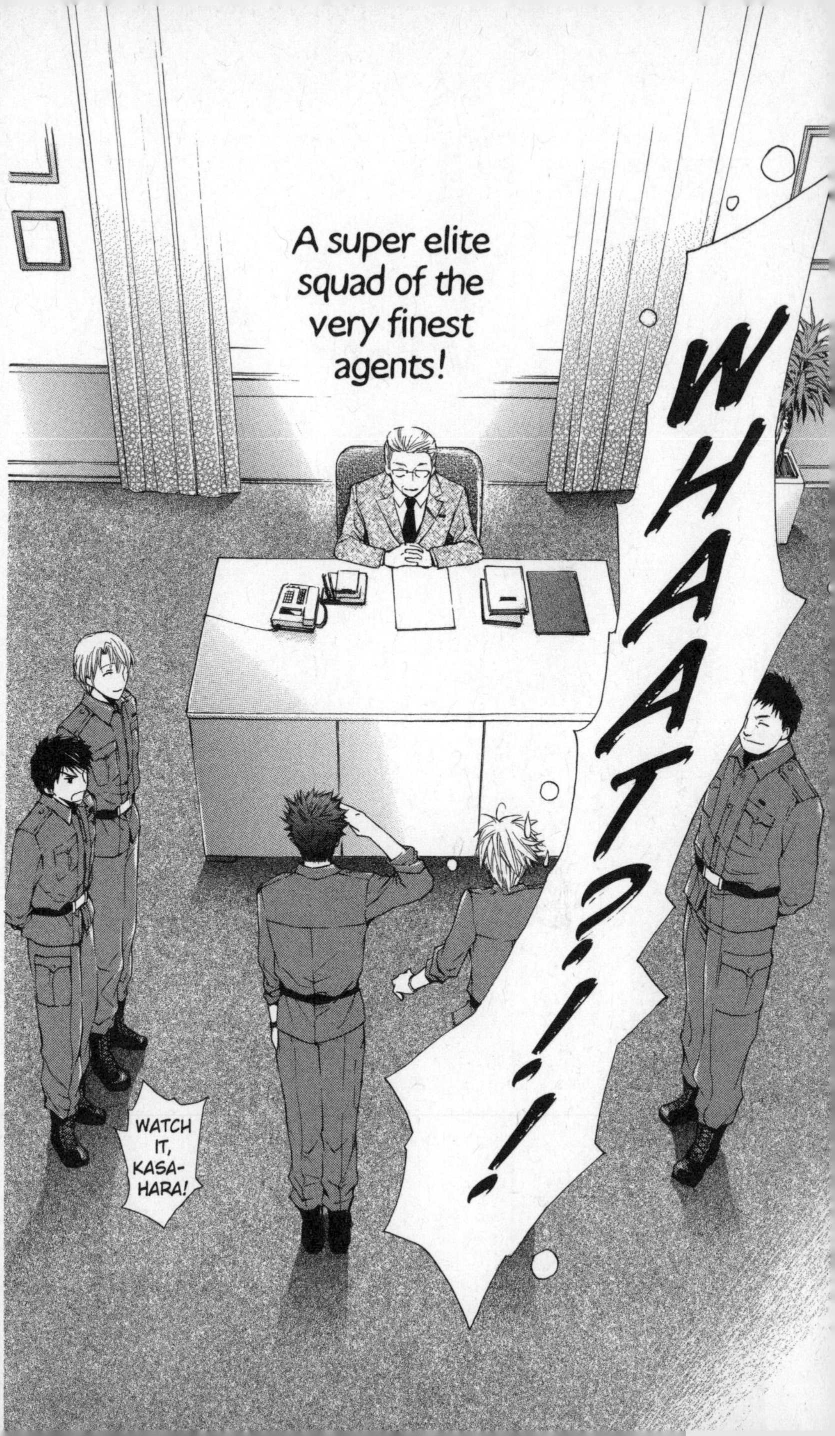
A super elite squad of the very finest agents!
WHAT?!!!
WATCH IT, KASA-HARA!

CHAPTER 3

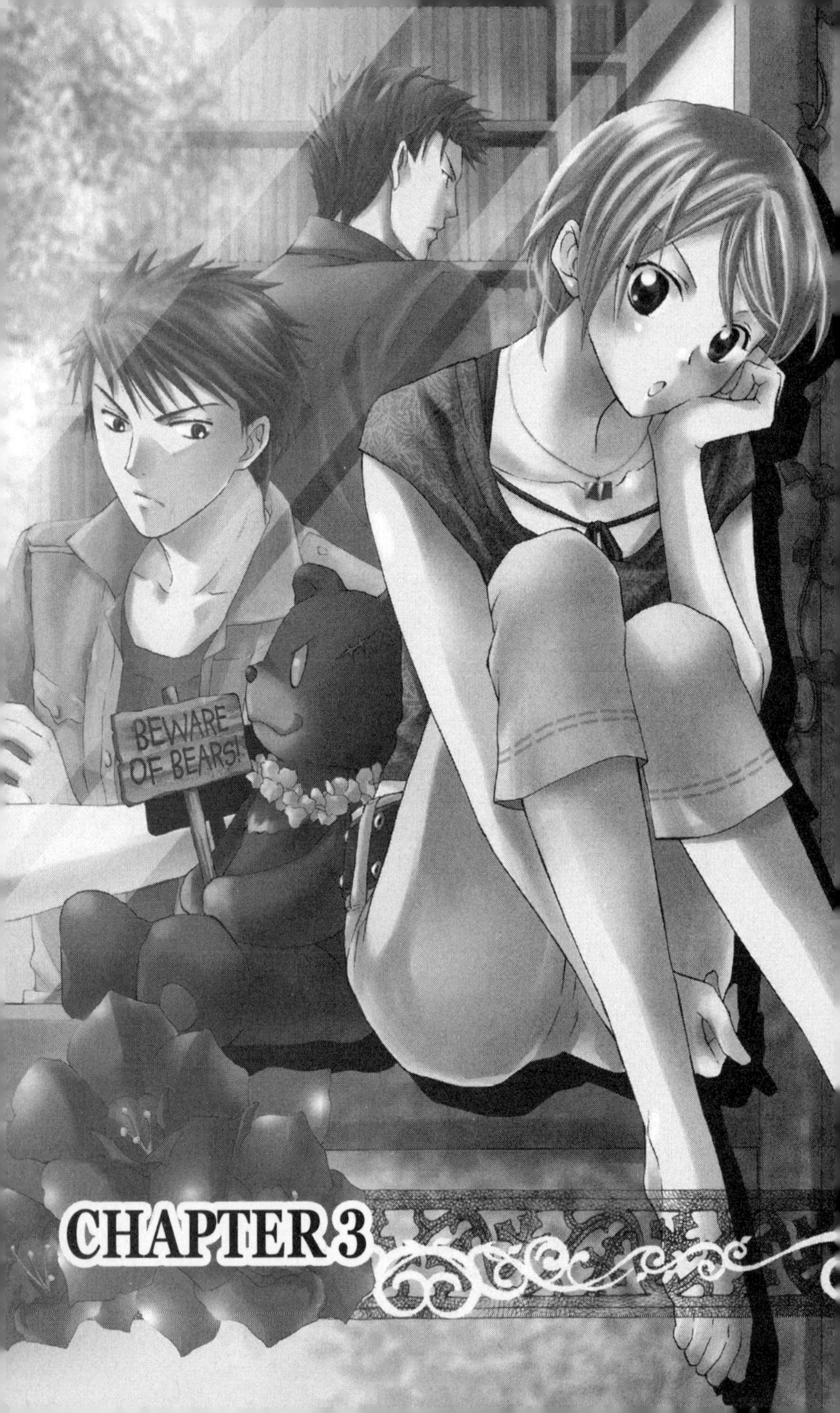
BEWARE OF BEARS!

Shibazaki & the Friend Who Puts Up with Her

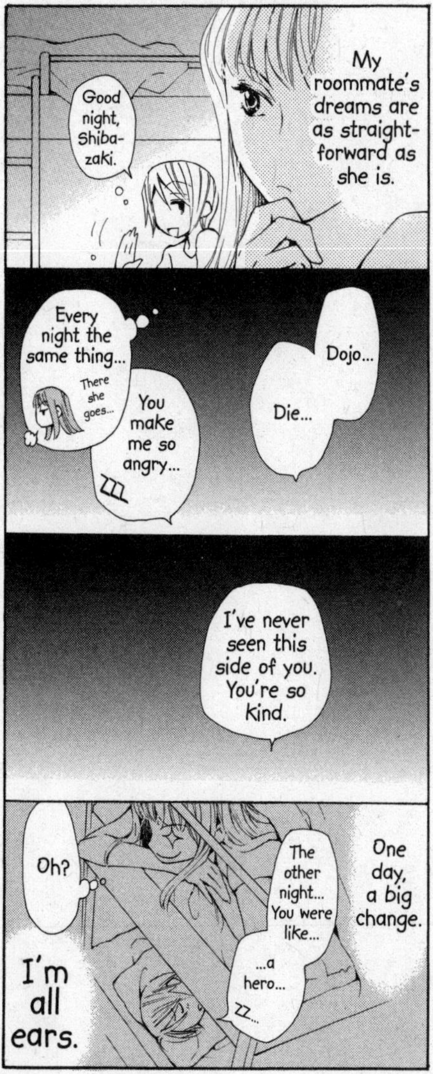
My roommate's dreams are as straightforward as she is.
Good night, Shibazaki.
Dojo...
Die...
Every night the same thing...
There she goes...
You make me so angry...
ZZZ
I've never seen this side of you. You're so kind.
One day, a big change.
The other night... You were like...
...a hero...
ZZ...
Oh?
I'm all ears.

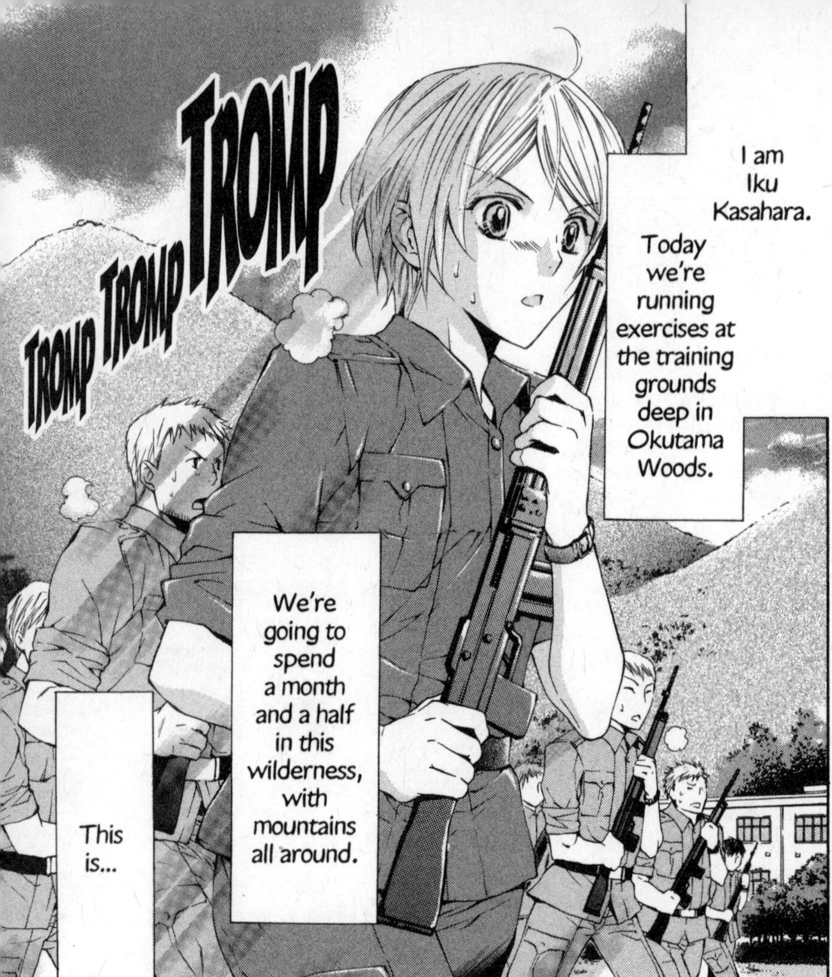
I am Iku Kasahara.
Today we're running exercises at the training grounds deep in Okutama Woods.
TROMP TROMP TROMP
We're going to spend a month and a half in this wilderness, with mountains all around.
This is...

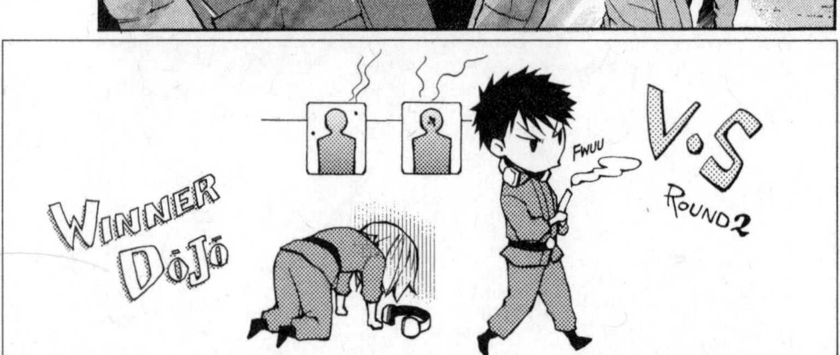
V.S
ROUND 2
FWUU
WINNER DōJō

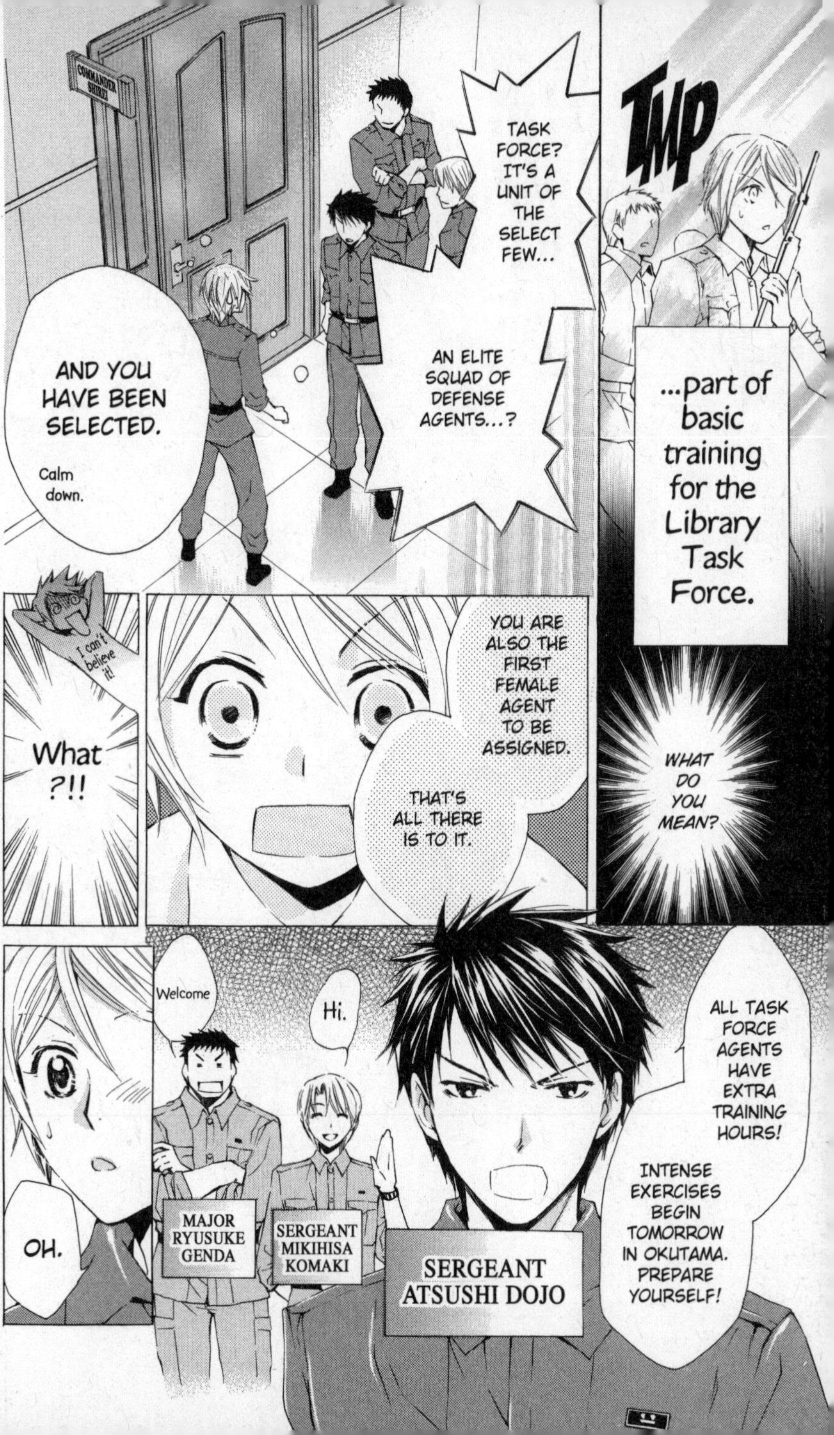
TMP
...part of basic training for the Library Task Force.
WHAT DO YOU MEAN?
TASK FORCE? IT'S A UNIT OF THE SELECT FEW...
AN ELITE SQUAD OF DEFENSE AGENTS...?
AND YOU HAVE BEEN SELECTED.
Calm down.
YOU ARE ALSO THE FIRST FEMALE AGENT TO BE ASSIGNED.
THAT'S ALL THERE IS TO IT.
I can't believe it!
What ?!!
ALL TASK FORCE AGENTS HAVE EXTRA TRAINING HOURS!
INTENSE EXERCISES BEGIN TOMORROW IN OKUTAMA. PREPARE YOURSELF!
SERGEANT ATSUSHI DOJO
Hi.
SERGEANT MIKIHISA KOMAKI
Welcome
MAJOR RYUSUKE GENDA
OH.

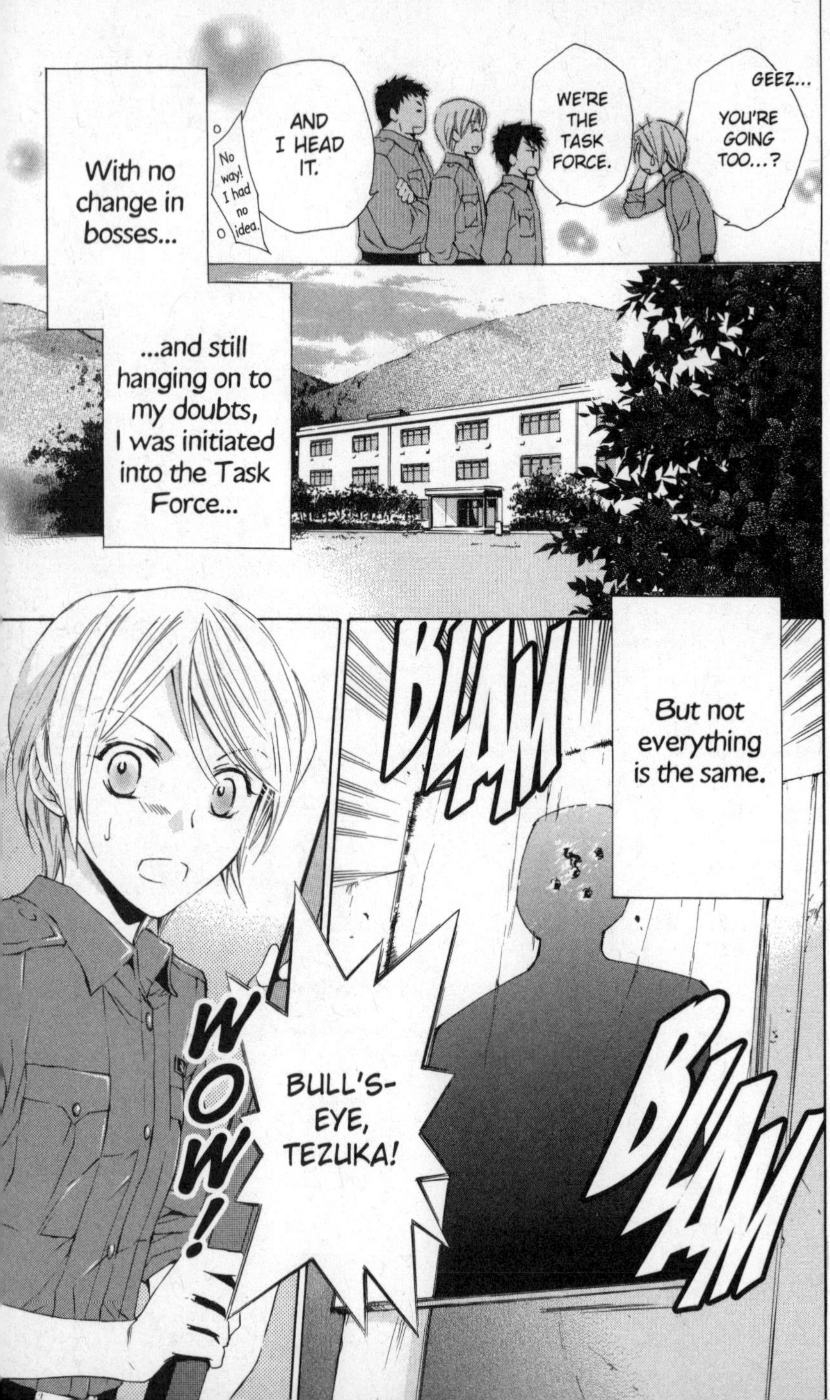
GEEZ...
YOU'RE GOING TOO...?
WE'RE THE TASK FORCE.
AND I HEAD IT.
No way! I had no idea.
With no change in bosses...
...and still hanging on to my doubts, I was initiated into the Task Force...
But not everything is the same.
BLAM
BLAM
BULL'S-EYE, TEZUKA!
WOW!

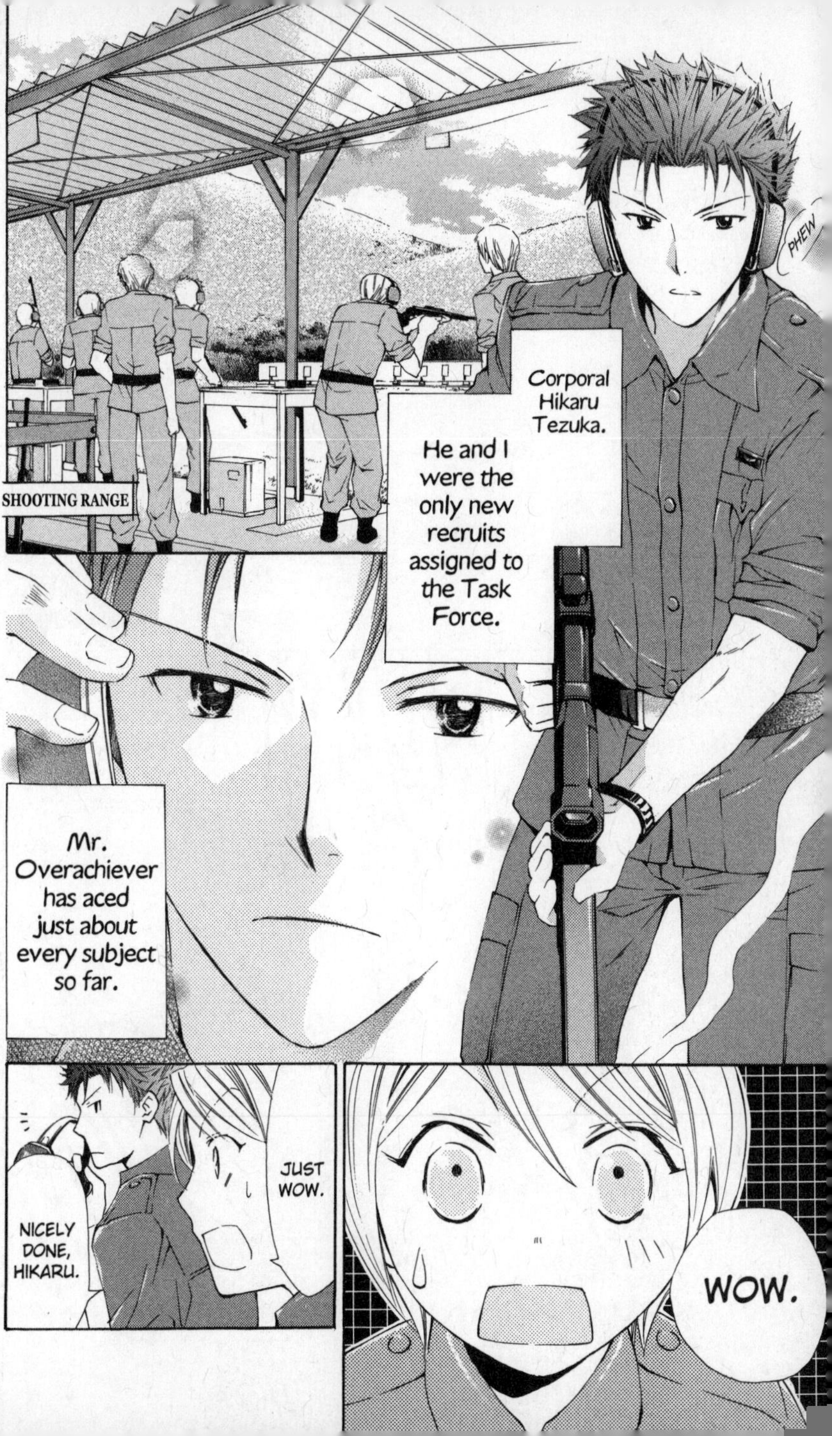
PHEW
Corporal Hikaru Tezuka.
He and I were the only new recruits assigned to the Task Force.
SHOOTING RANGE
Mr. Overachiever has aced just about every subject so far.
WOW.
JUST WOW.
NICELY DONE, HIKARU.

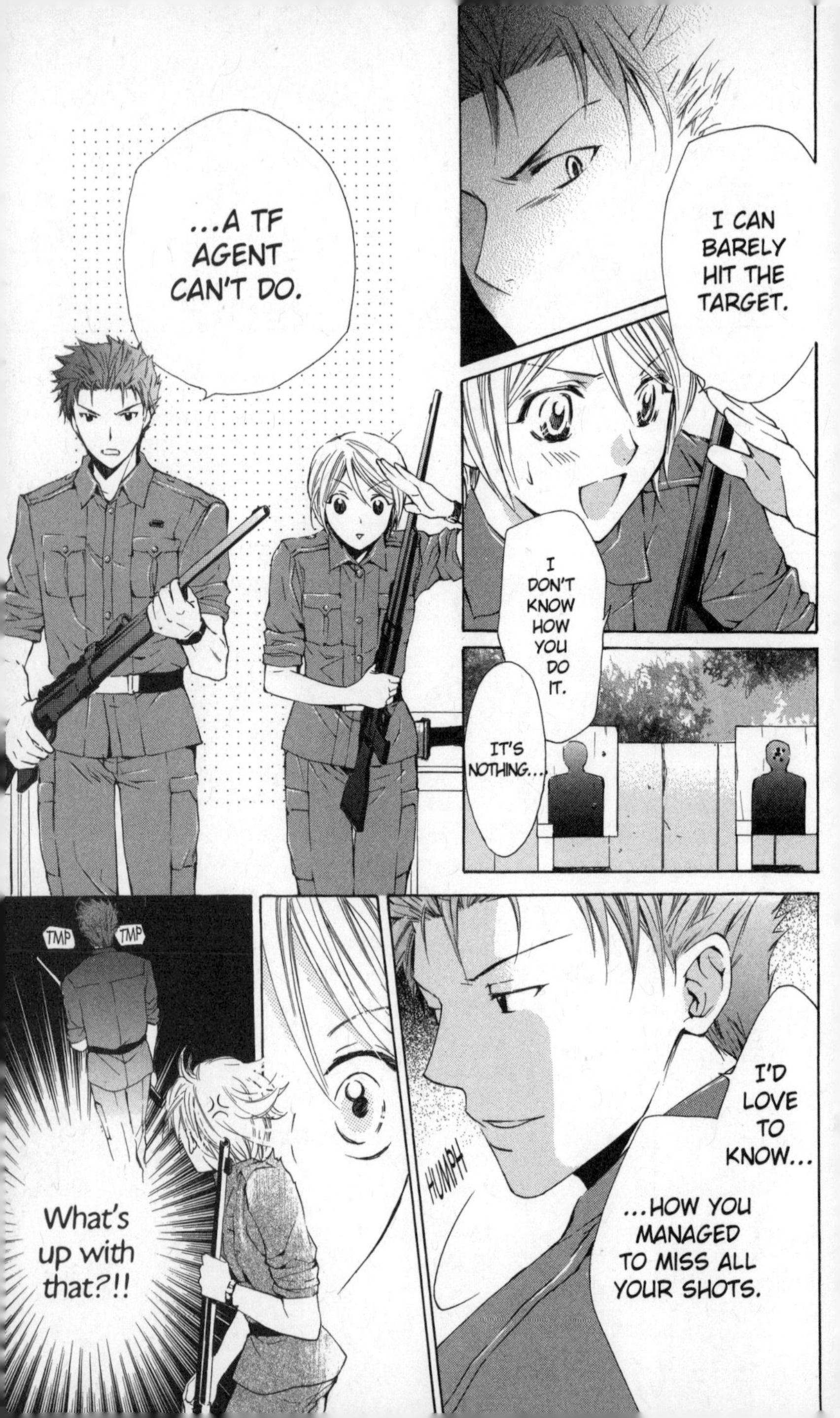
I CAN BARELY HIT THE TARGET.
I DON'T KNOW HOW YOU DO IT.
IT'S NOTHING...
...A TF AGENT CAN'T DO.
HUMPH
I'D LOVE TO KNOW...
...HOW YOU MANAGED TO MISS ALL YOUR SHOTS.
TMP
TMP
What's up with that?!!

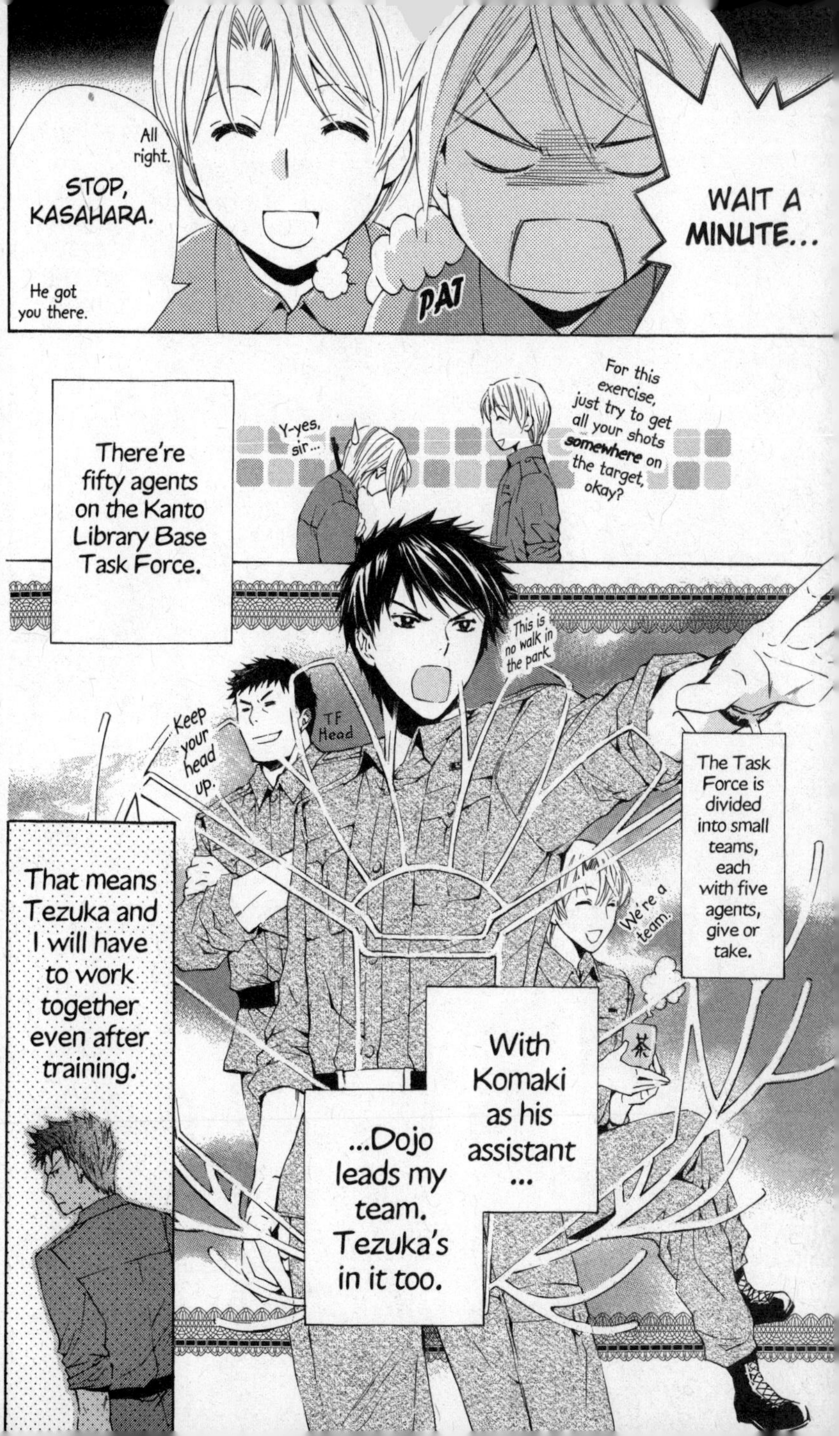
WAIT A MINUTE...
PAT
All right.
STOP, KASAHARA.
He got you there.
For this exercise, just try to get all your shots **somewhere** on the target, okay?
Y-yes, sir...
There're fifty agents on the Kanto Library Base Task Force.
This is no walk in the park.
The Task Force is divided into small teams, each with five agents, give or take.
TF Head
Keep your head up.
We're a team.
With Komaki as his assistant...
...Dojo leads my team. Tezuka's in it too.
That means Tezuka and I will have to work together even after training.

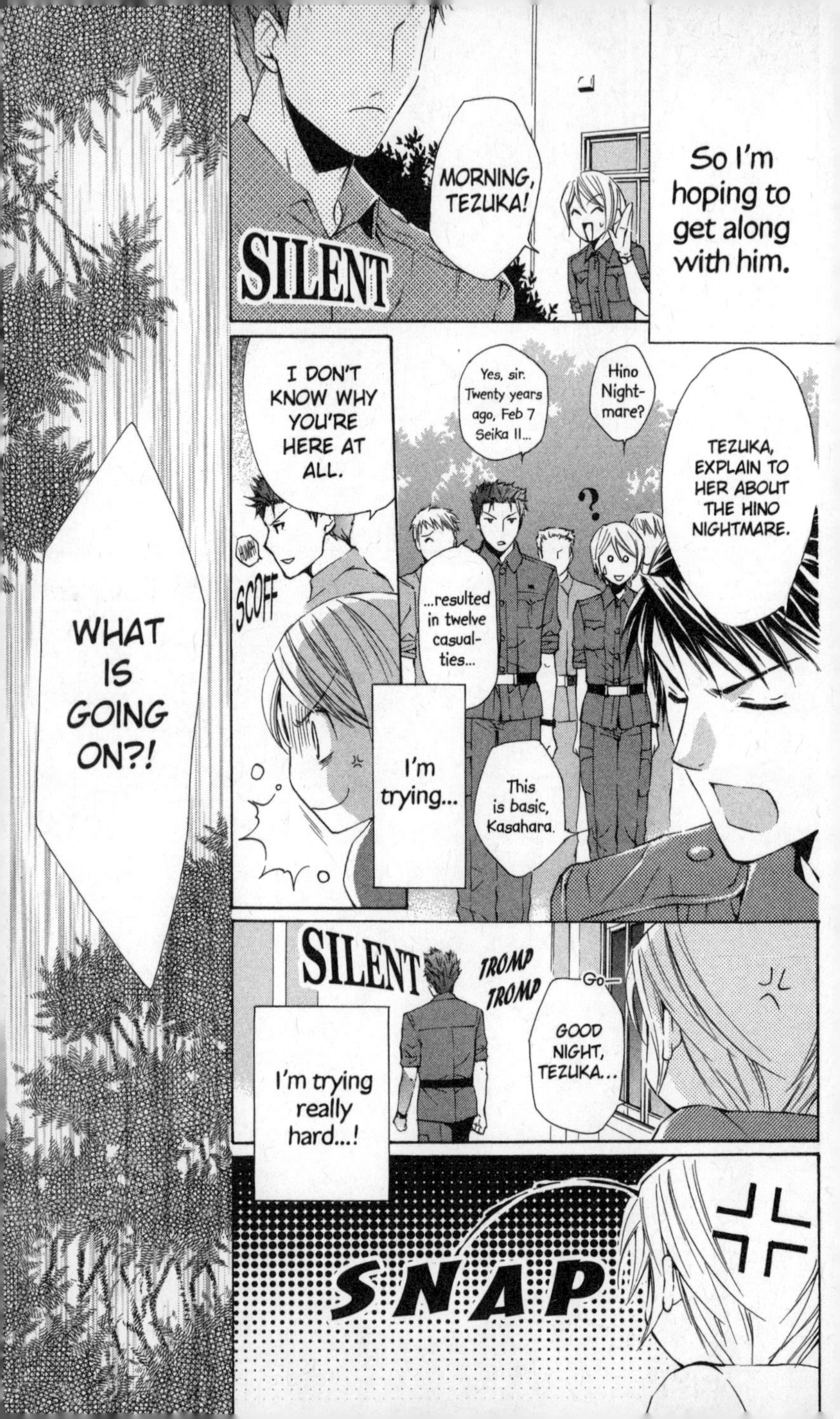
So I'm hoping to get along with him.
MORNING, TEZUKA!
SILENT
TEZUKA, EXPLAIN TO HER ABOUT THE HINO NIGHTMARE.
Hino Night-mare?
Yes, sir. Twenty years ago, Feb 7 Seika 11...
...resulted in twelve casual-ties...
This is basic, Kasahara.
I'm trying...
I DON'T KNOW WHY YOU'RE HERE AT ALL.
HUMPH
SCOFF
Go—
GOOD NIGHT, TEZUKA...
TROMP TROMP
SILENT
I'm trying really hard...!
SNAP
WHAT IS GOING ON?!

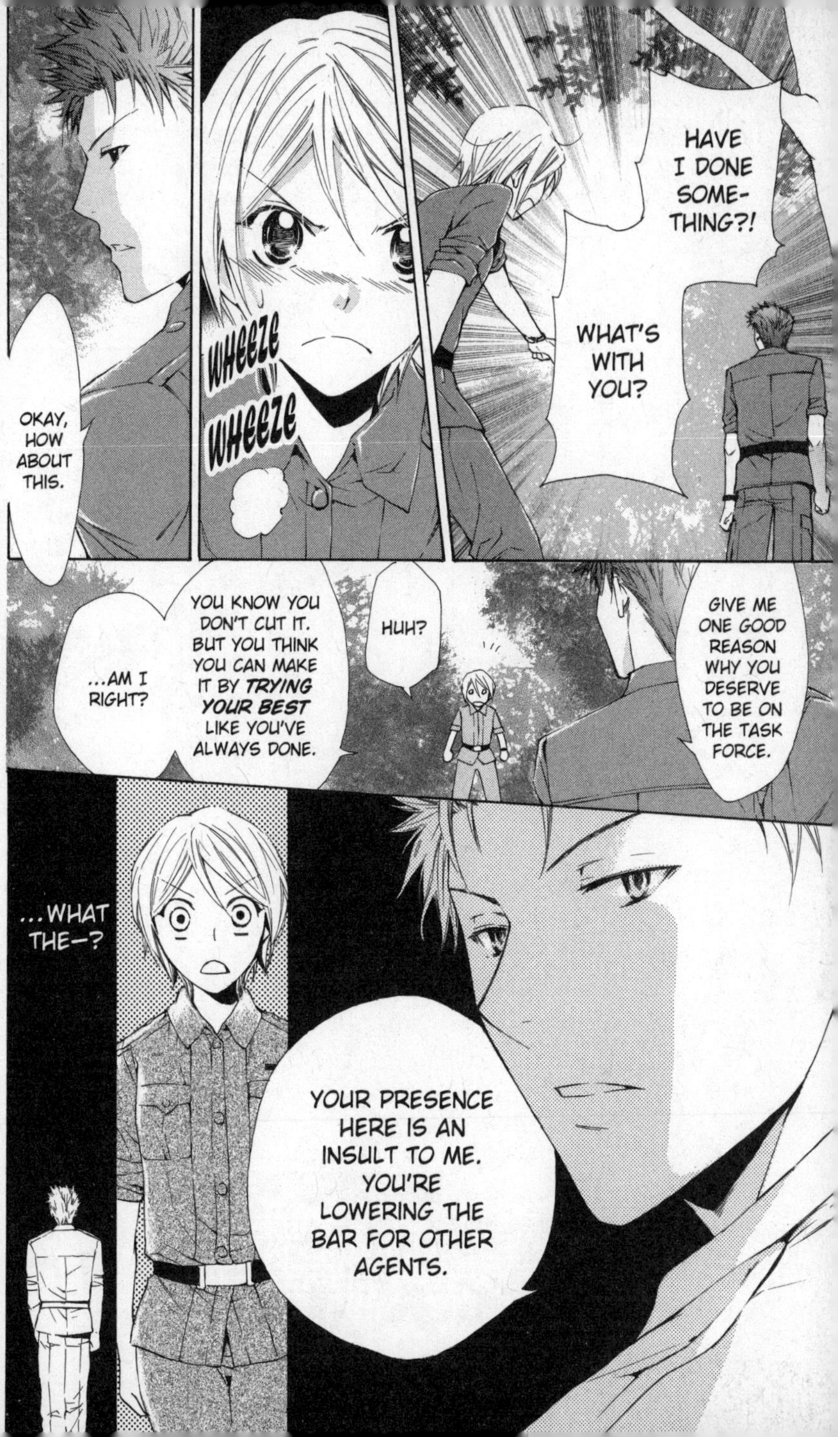
HAVE I DONE SOMETHING?!
WHAT'S WITH YOU?
WHEEZE
WHEEZE
OKAY, HOW ABOUT THIS.
GIVE ME ONE GOOD REASON WHY YOU DESERVE TO BE ON THE TASK FORCE.
HUH?
YOU KNOW YOU DON'T CUT IT. BUT YOU THINK YOU CAN MAKE IT BY *TRYING YOUR BEST* LIKE YOU'VE ALWAYS DONE.
...AM I RIGHT?
YOUR PRESENCE HERE IS AN INSULT TO ME. YOU'RE LOWERING THE BAR FOR OTHER AGENTS.
...WHAT THE—?

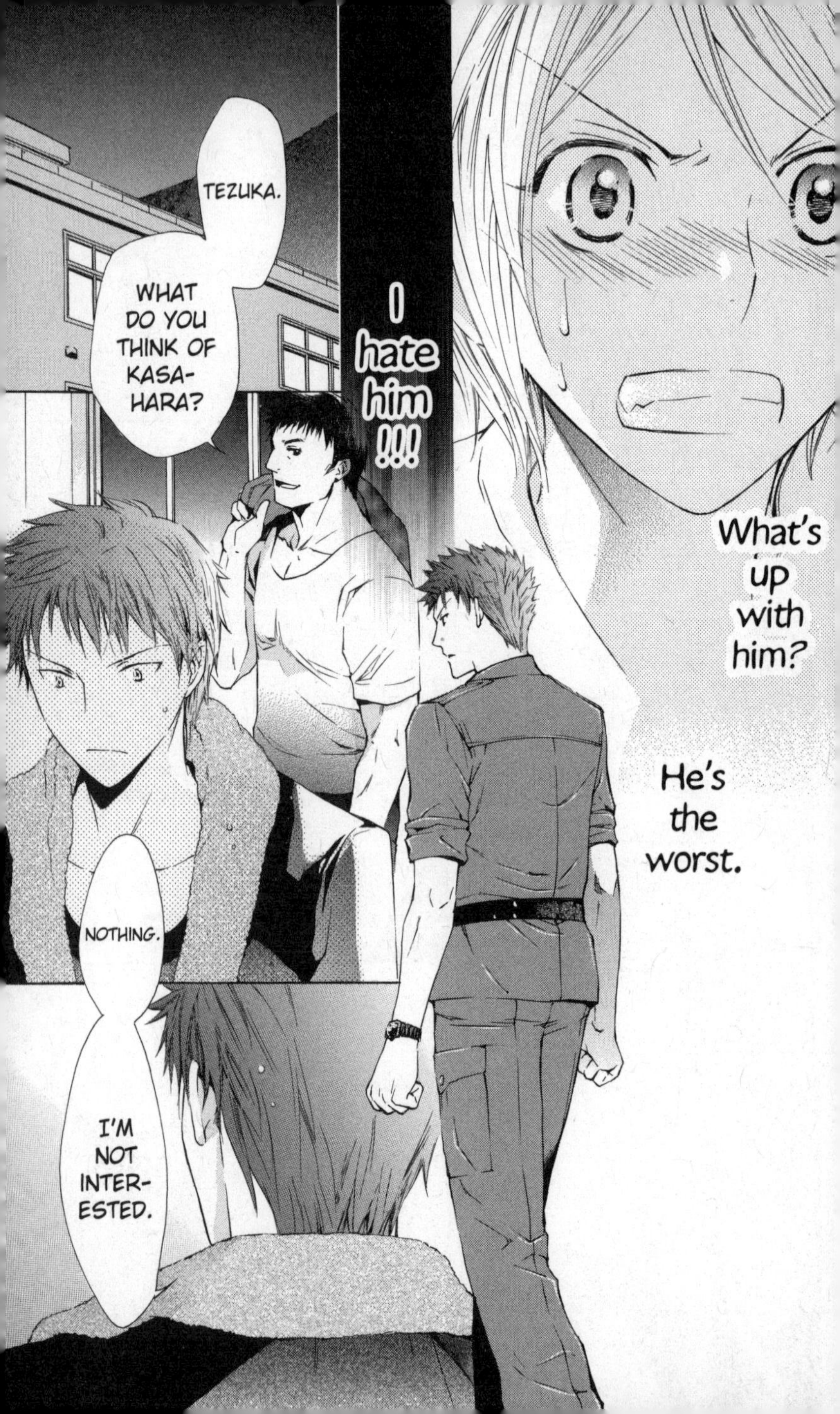
What's up with him?
He's the worst.
I hate him!!!
TEZUKA.
WHAT DO YOU THINK OF KASA-HARA?
NOTHING.
I'M NOT INTER-ESTED.

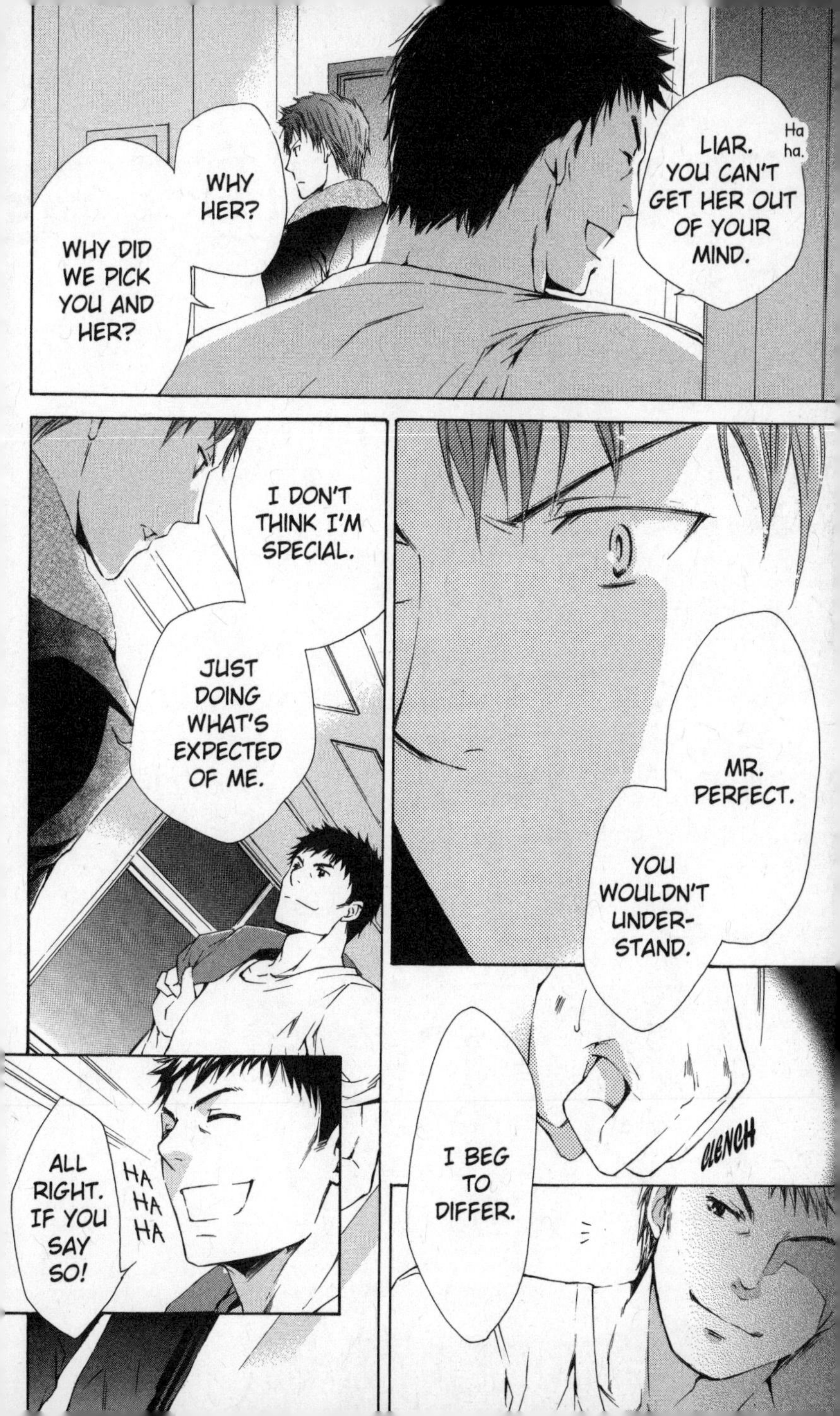
Ha ha.
LIAR. YOU CAN'T GET HER OUT OF YOUR MIND.
WHY HER?
WHY DID WE PICK YOU AND HER?
MR. PERFECT.
YOU WOULDN'T UNDER-STAND.
CLENCH
I BEG TO DIFFER.
I DON'T THINK I'M SPECIAL.
JUST DOING WHAT'S EXPECTED OF ME.
HA HA HA
ALL RIGHT. IF YOU SAY SO!

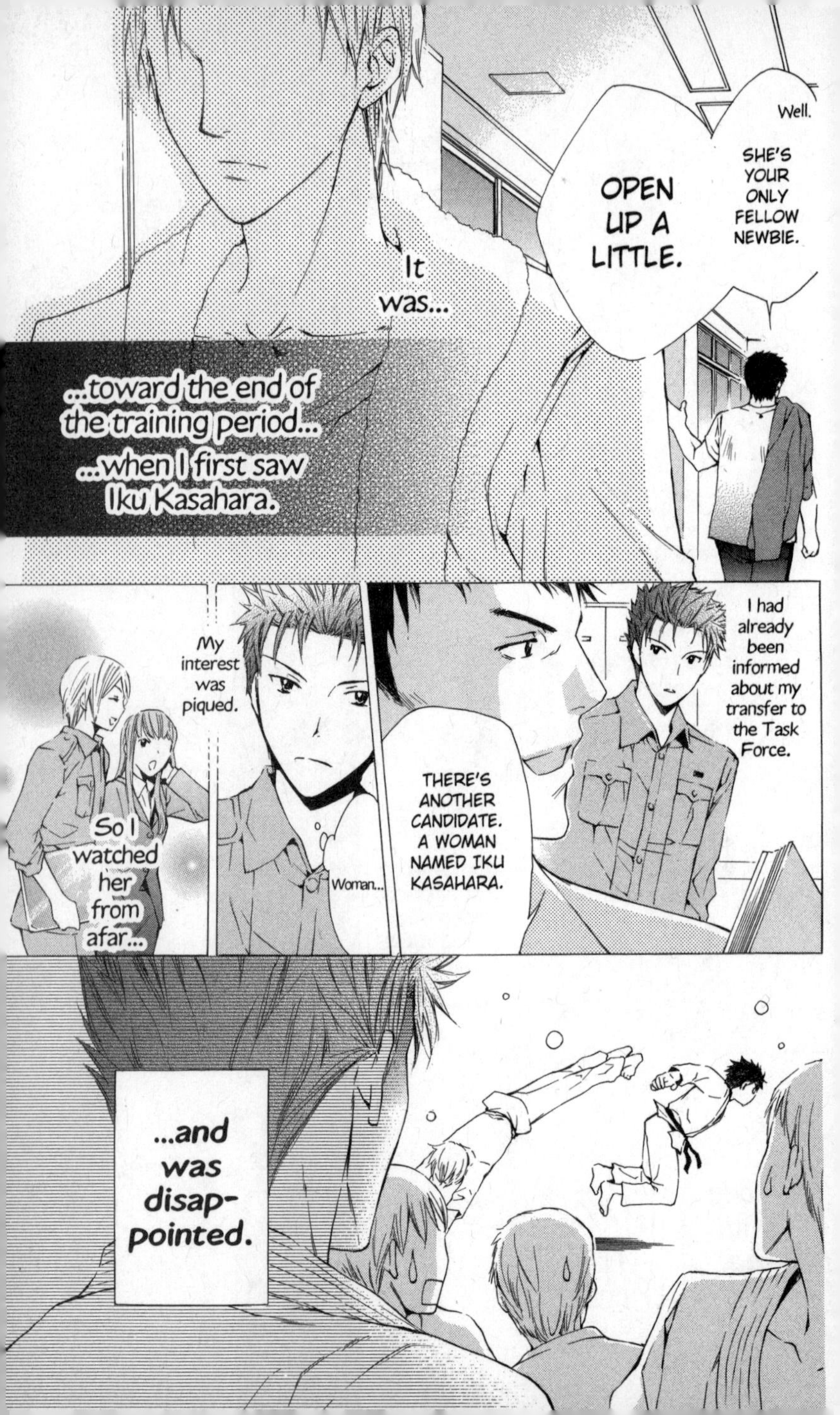

Well.
SHE'S YOUR ONLY FELLOW NEWBIE.
OPEN UP A LITTLE.
It was...
...toward the end of the training period...
...when I first saw Iku Kasahara.
I had already been informed about my transfer to the Task Force.
THERE'S ANOTHER CANDIDATE. A WOMAN NAMED IKU KASAHARA.
Woman...
My interest was piqued.
So I watched her from afar...
...and was disap-pointed.

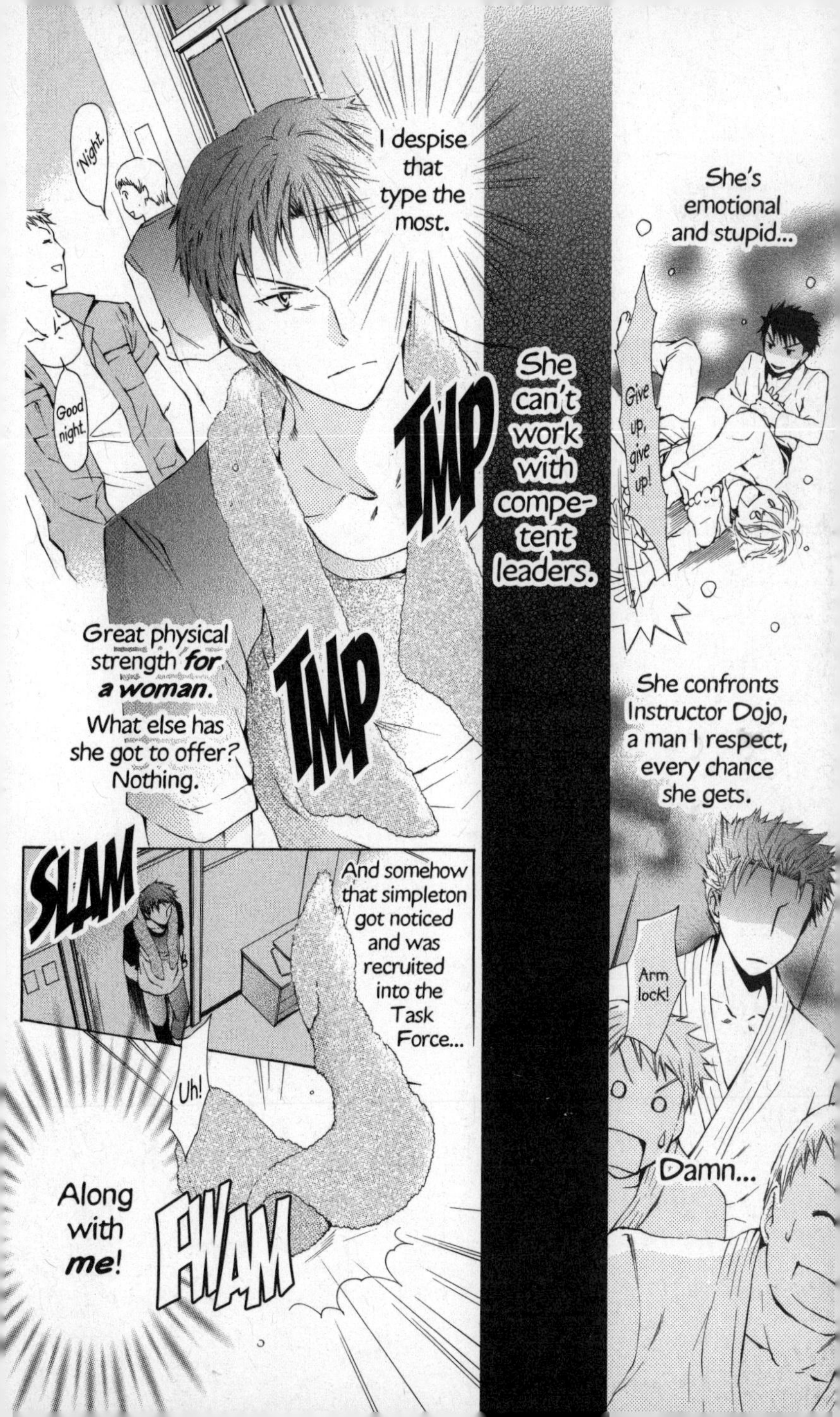
She's emotional and stupid...
Give up, give up!
She confronts Instructor Dojo, a man I respect, every chance she gets.
Arm lock!
Damn...
She can't work with compe-tent leaders.
I despise that type the most.
'Night.
Good night.
TMP
TMP
Great physical strength *for a woman*. What else has she got to offer? Nothing.
And somehow that simpleton got noticed and was recruited into the Task Force...
SLAM
Uh!
FWAM
Along with *me*!

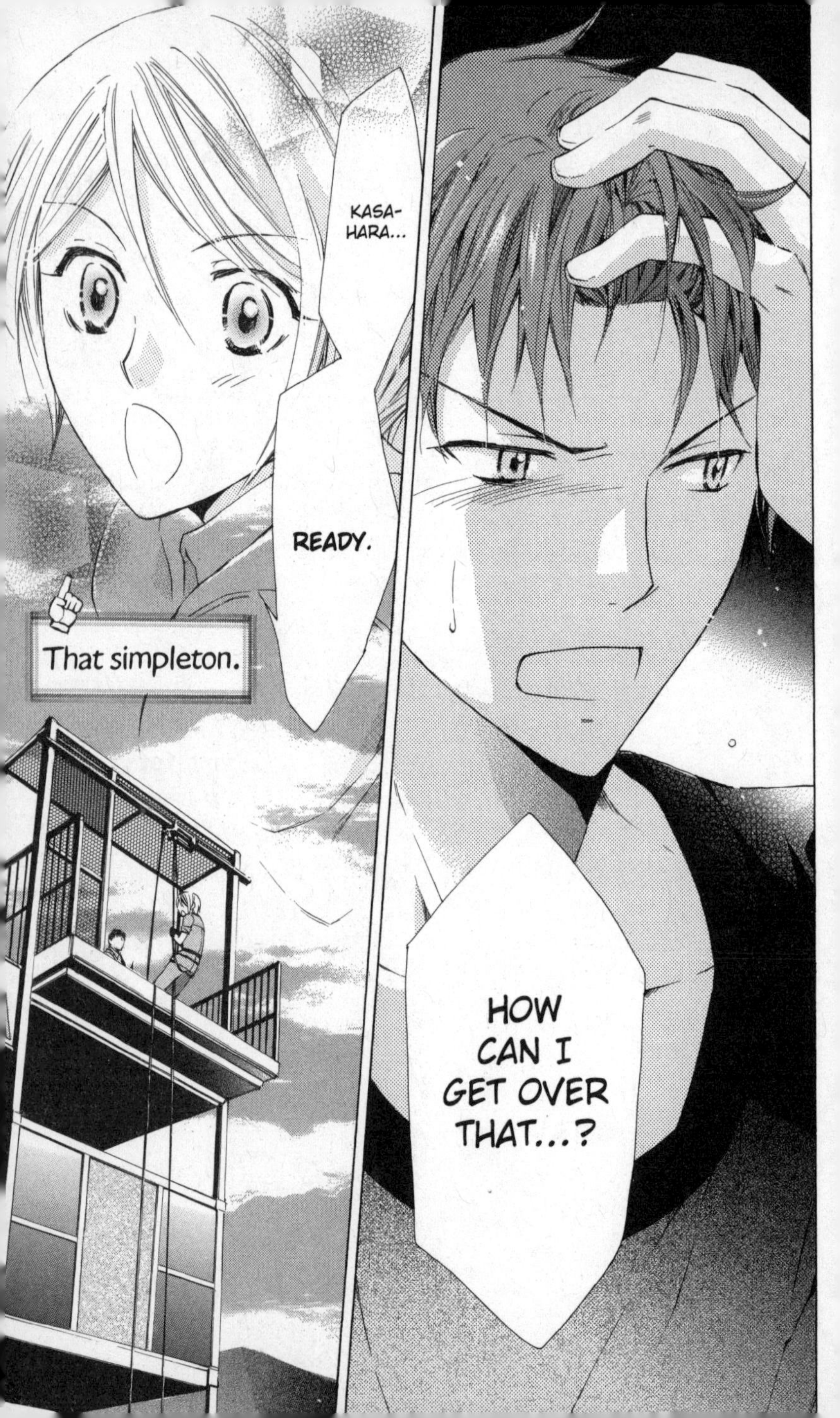
HOW CAN I GET OVER THAT...?
KASA-HARA...
READY.
That simpleton.

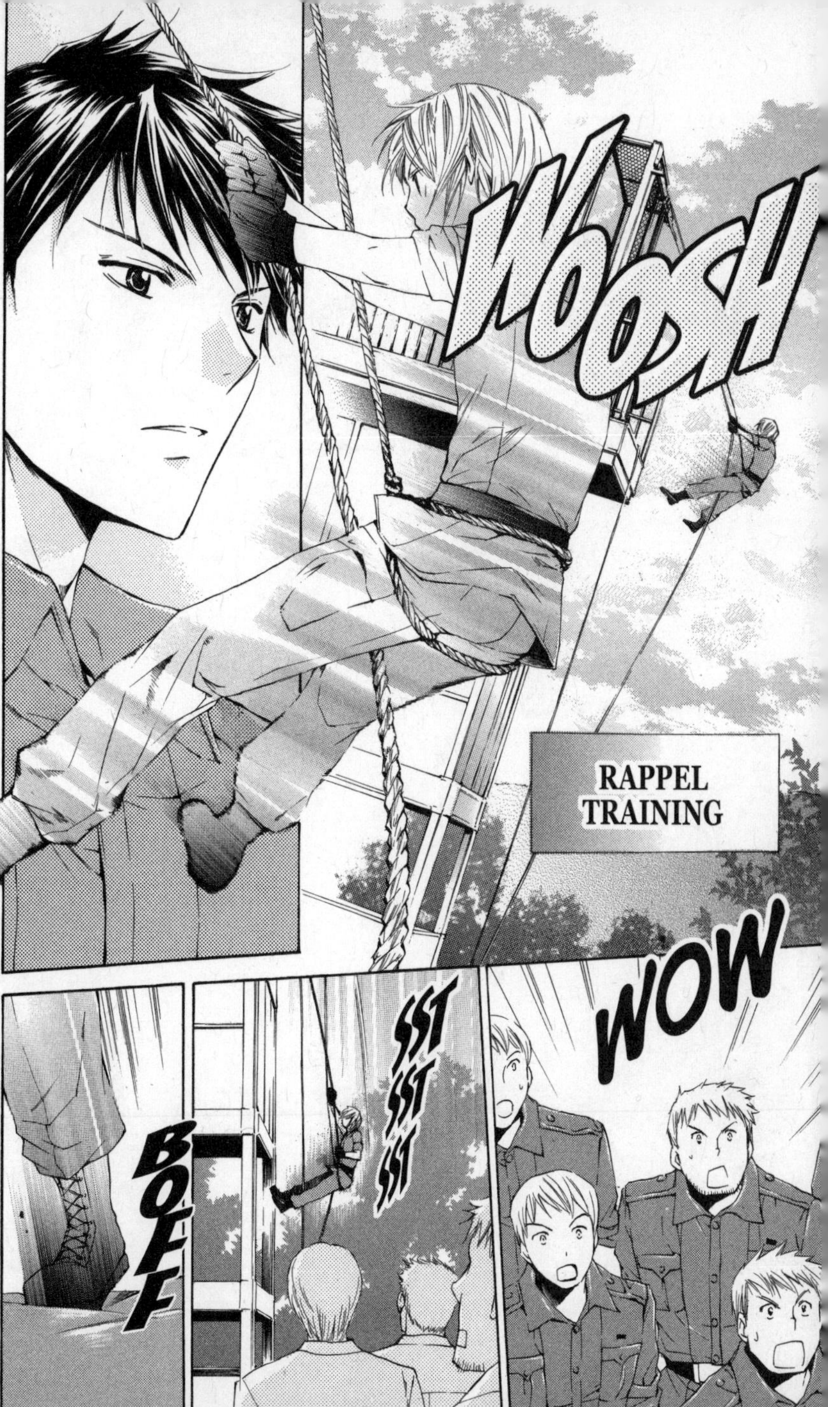
WOOSH
RAPPEL TRAINING
WOW
SST SST SST
BOFF

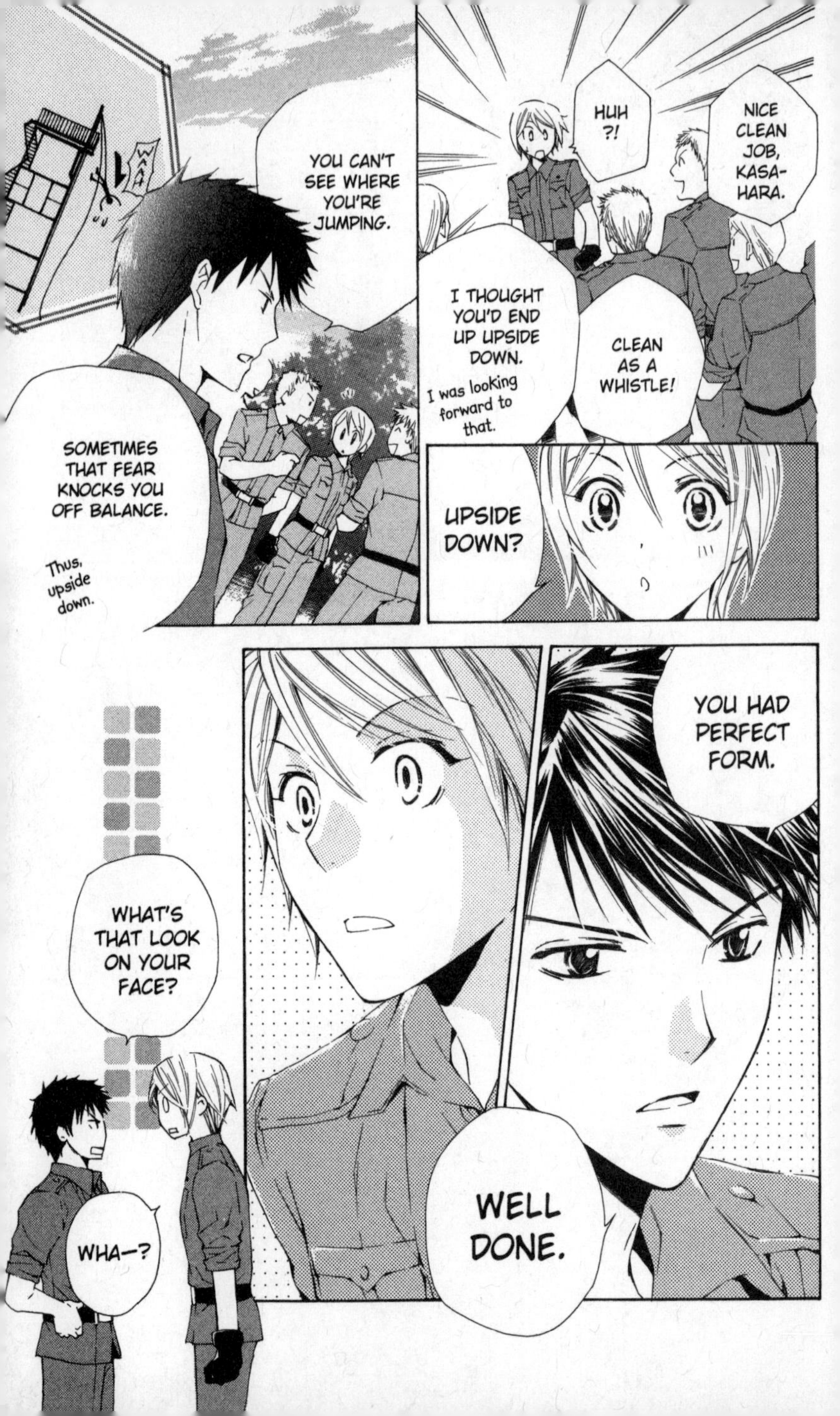
NICE CLEAN JOB, KASA-HARA.
HUH ?!
CLEAN AS A WHISTLE!
I THOUGHT YOU'D END UP UPSIDE DOWN.
I was looking forward to that.
UPSIDE DOWN?
YOU CAN'T SEE WHERE YOU'RE JUMPING.
SOMETIMES THAT FEAR KNOCKS YOU OFF BALANCE.
Thus, upside down.
YOU HAD PERFECT FORM.
WELL DONE.
WHAT'S THAT LOOK ON YOUR FACE?
WHA--?

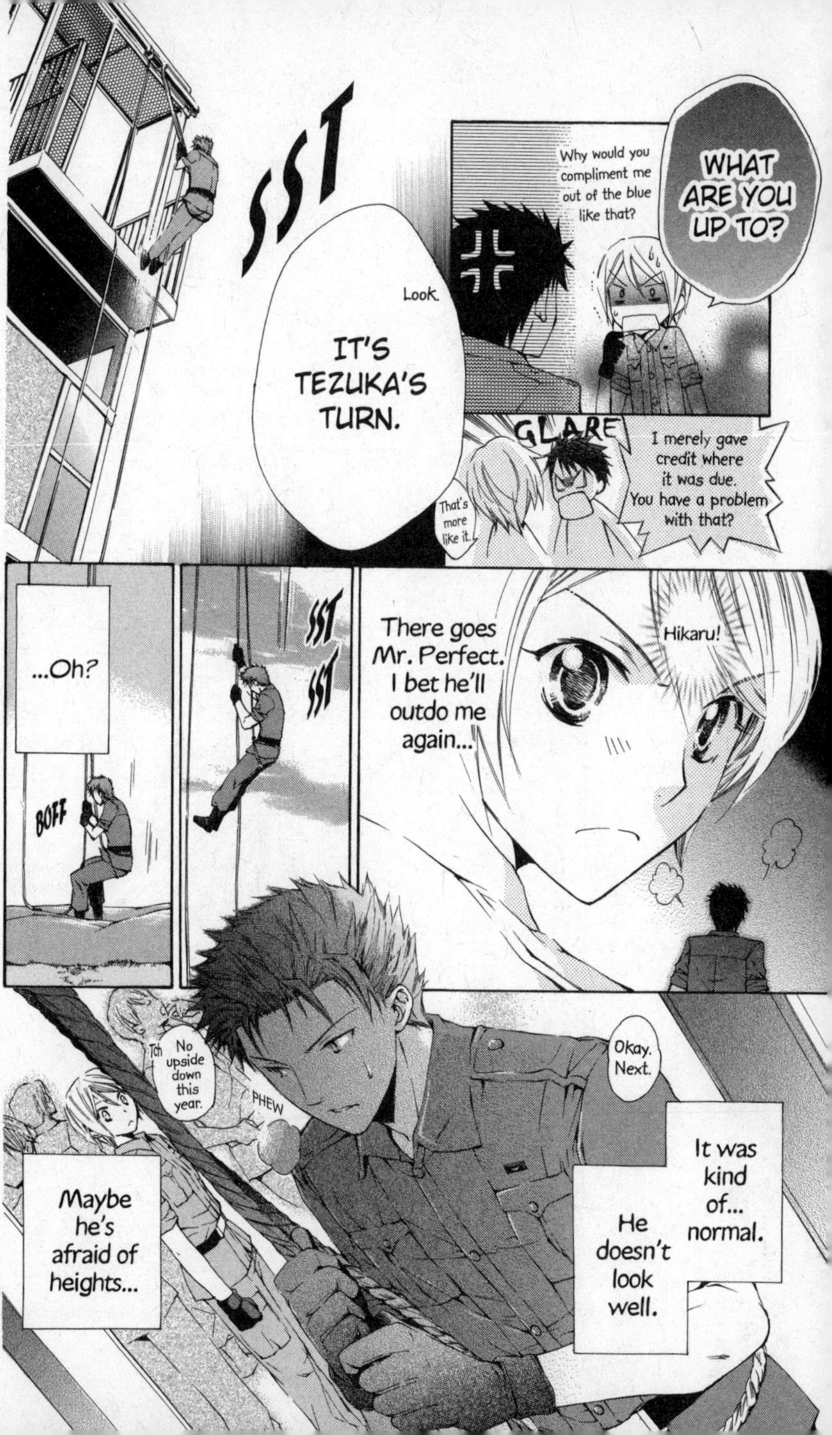
WHAT ARE YOU UP TO?
Why would you compliment me out of the blue like that?
GLARE
I merely gave credit where it was due. You have a problem with that?
That's more like it.
SST
Look.
IT'S TEZUKA'S TURN.
Hikaru!
There goes Mr. Perfect. I bet he'll outdo me again...
SST
SST
...Oh?
BOFF
Okay. Next.
It was kind of... normal.
He doesn't look well.
PHEW
No upside down this year.
Tch
Maybe he's afraid of heights...

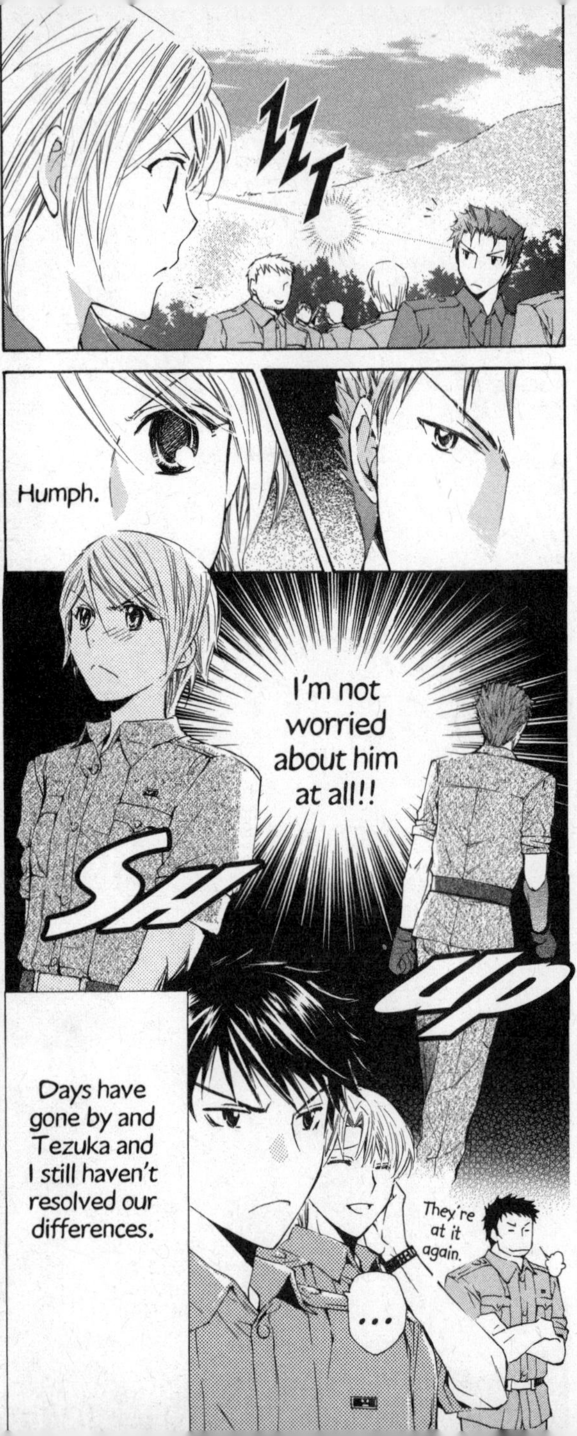
ZZT
Humph.
I'm not worried about him at all!!
SH
UP
Days have gone by and Tezuka and I still haven't resolved our differences.
They're at it again.
...

3

*

Sometimes my artwork is hard to look at. I am kind of disappointed with myself. I feel pretty confident when I'm doing it... Why...?!

I've been an assistant for nearly a decade and the opportunity to draw humans is an amazing experience for me (characters from my favorite series at that!) It seems excitement doesn't necessarily coincide with good performance. Hopefully I can draw people much better...!

It's almost my life goal.

*

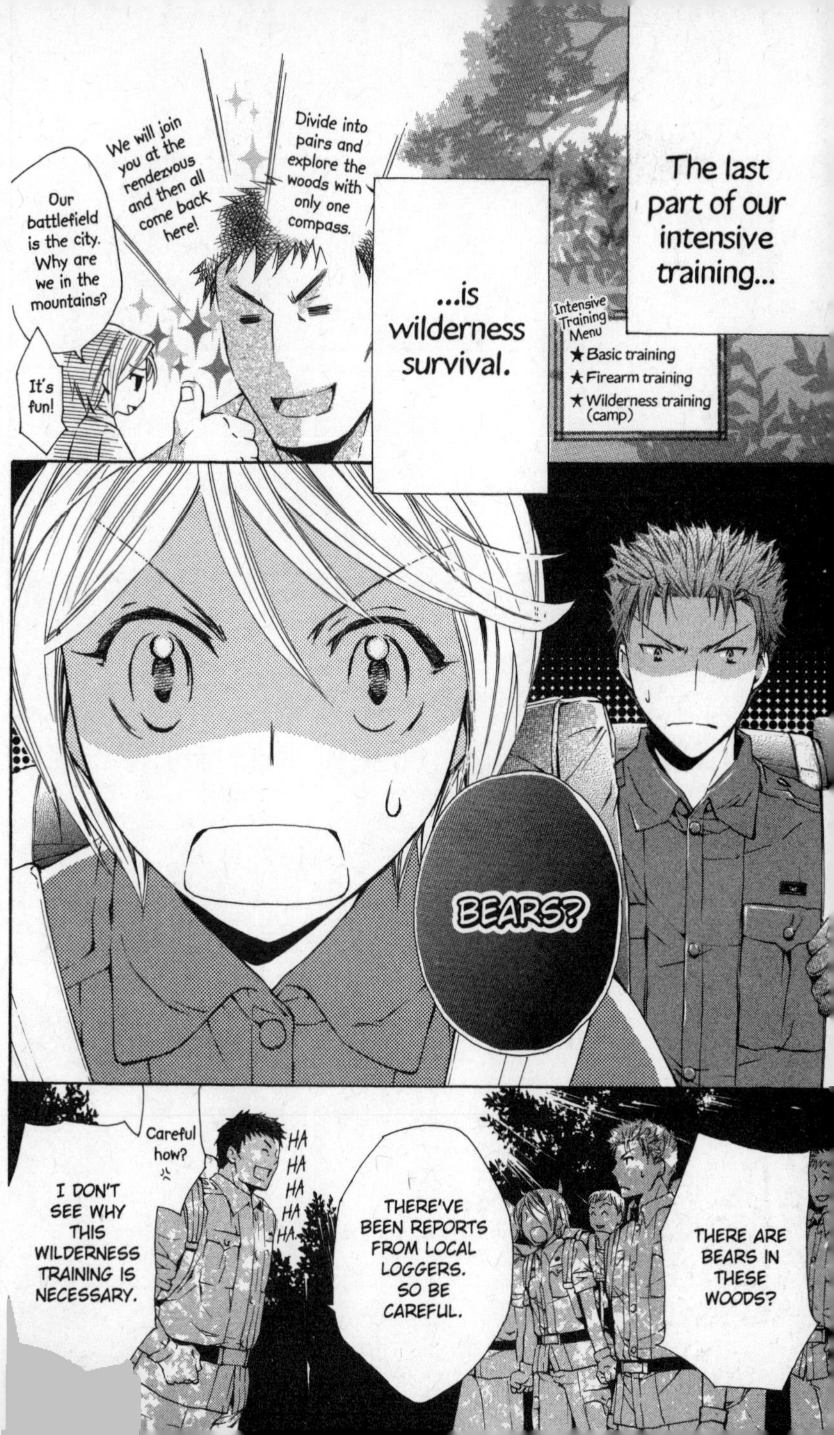
The last part of our intensive training...
Intensive Training Menu
★Basic training
★Firearm training
★Wilderness training (camp)
...is wilderness survival.
Divide into pairs and explore the woods with only one compass.
We will join you at the rendezvous and then all come back here!
Our battlefield is the city. Why are we in the mountains?
It's fun!
BEARS?
THERE ARE BEARS IN THESE WOODS?
THERE'VE BEEN REPORTS FROM LOCAL LOGGERS. SO BE CAREFUL.
HA HA HA HA HA.
Careful how?
I DON'T SEE WHY THIS WILDERNESS TRAINING IS NECESSARY.

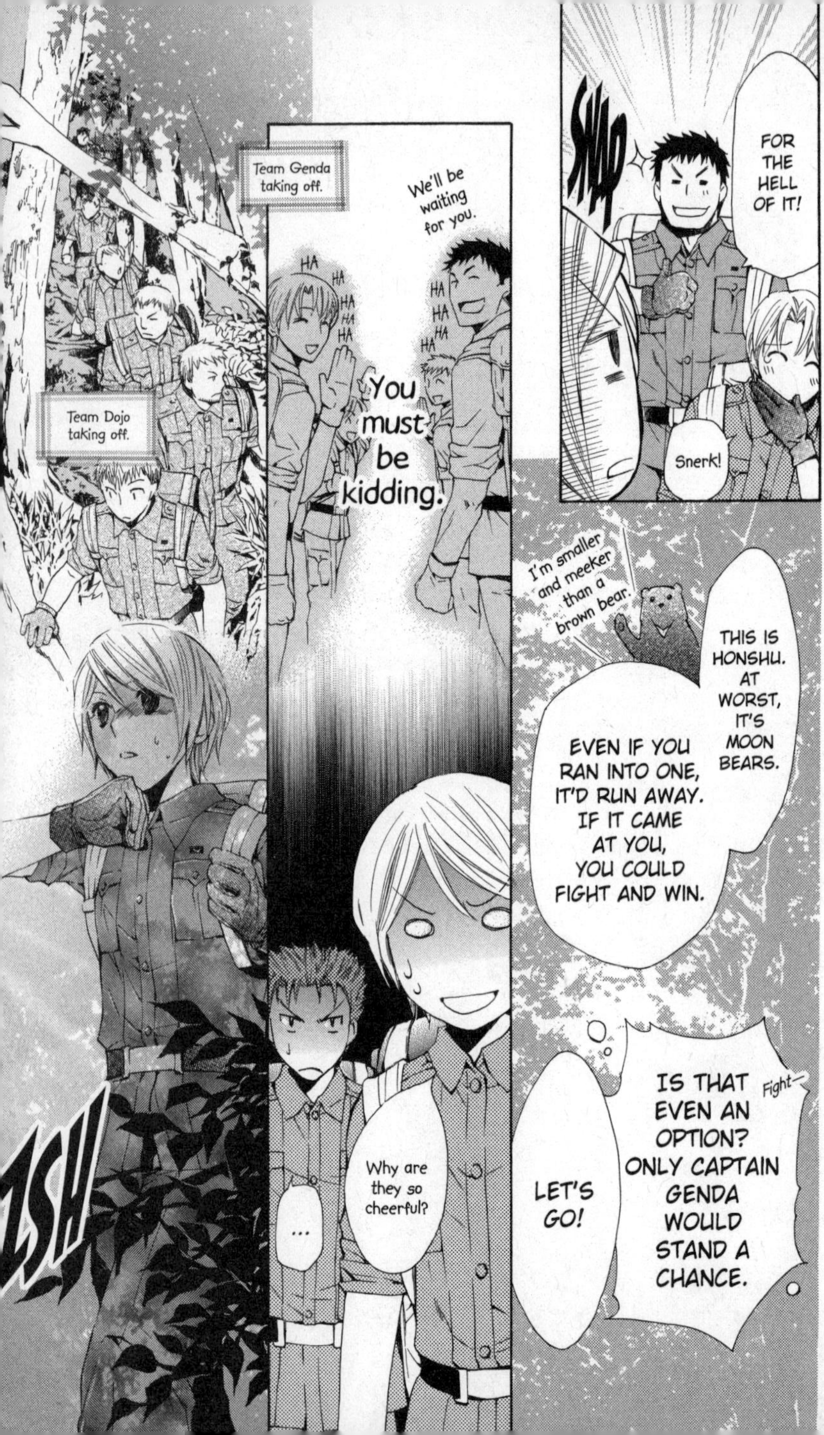
SNAP
FOR THE HELL OF IT!
Snerk!
THIS IS HONSHU. AT WORST, IT'S MOON BEARS.
I'm smaller and meeker than a brown bear.
EVEN IF YOU RAN INTO ONE, IT'D RUN AWAY. IF IT CAME AT YOU, YOU COULD FIGHT AND WIN.
Fight—
IS THAT EVEN AN OPTION? ONLY CAPTAIN GENDA WOULD STAND A CHANCE.
LET'S GO!
Team Genda taking off.
We'll be waiting for you.
HA HA HA HA HA
HA HA HA HA
You must be kidding.
Why are they so cheerful?
...
Team Dojo taking off.
ISH

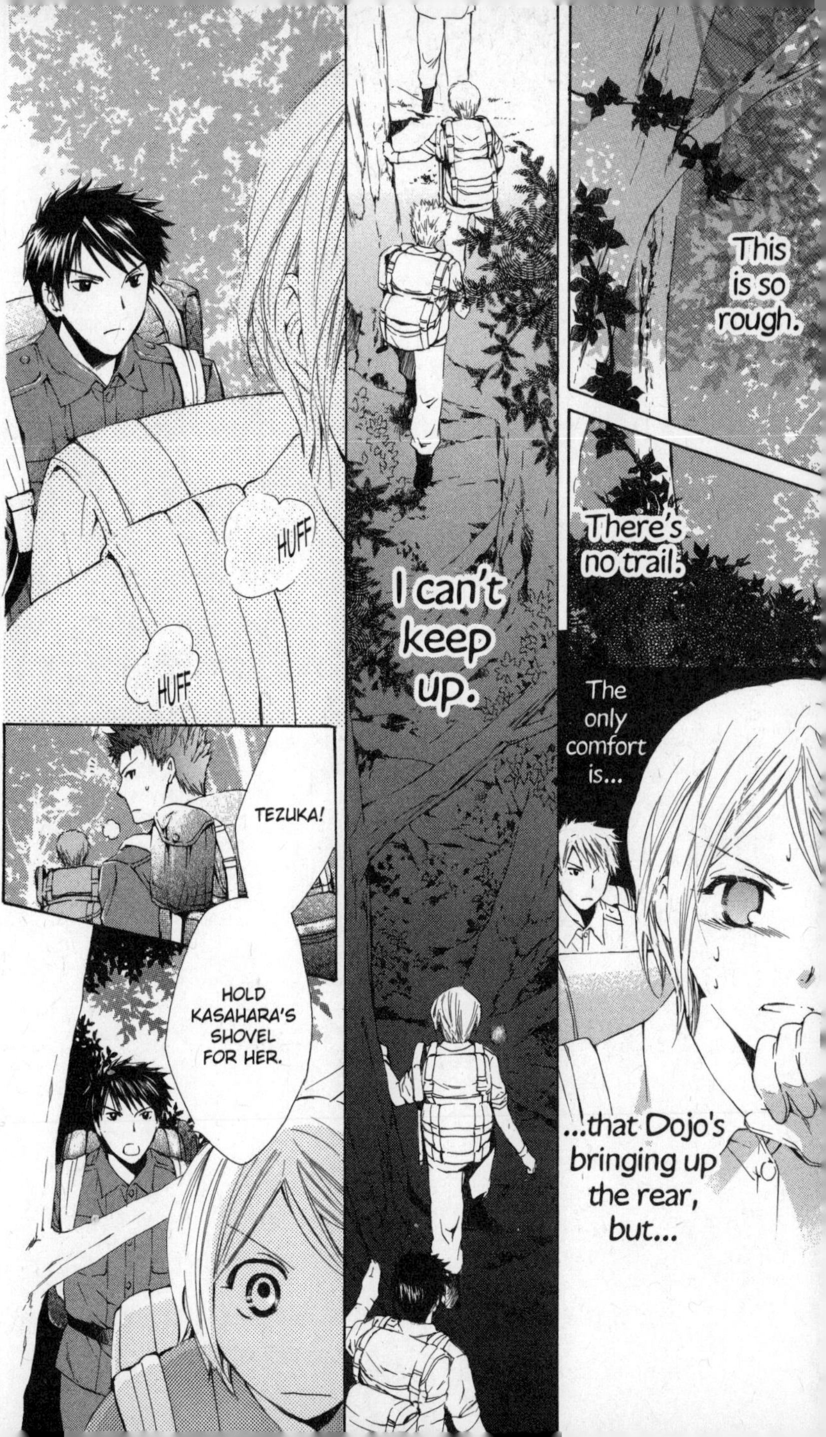
This is so rough.
There's no trail.
The only comfort is...
...that Dojo's bringing up the rear, but...
I can't keep up.
HUFF
HUFF
TEZUKA!
HOLD KASAHARA'S SHOVEL FOR HER.

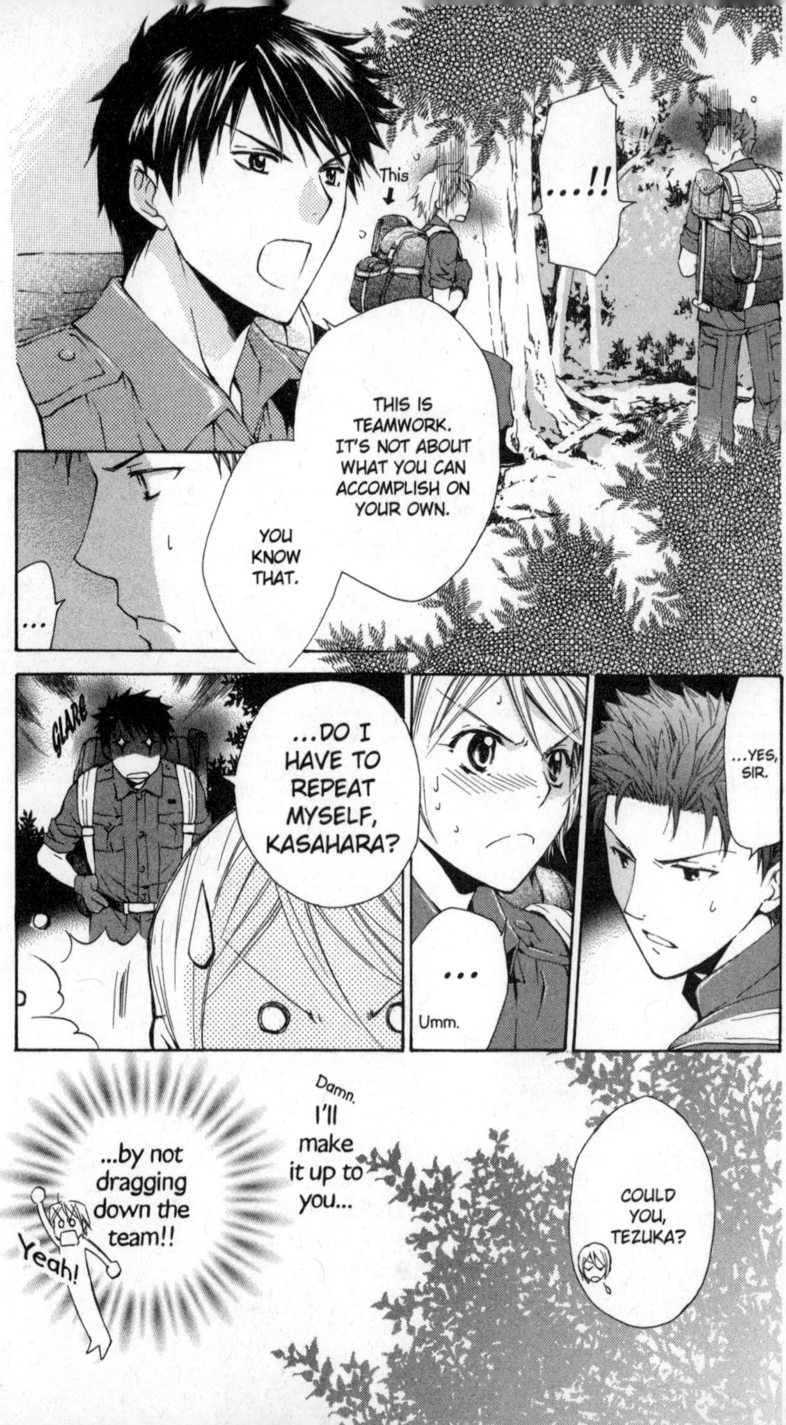
...!!
This
THIS IS TEAMWORK. IT'S NOT ABOUT WHAT YOU CAN ACCOMPLISH ON YOUR OWN.
YOU KNOW THAT.
...
...YES, SIR.
...
Umm.
...DO I HAVE TO REPEAT MYSELF, KASAHARA?
GLARE
COULD YOU, TEZUKA?
Damn.
I'll make it up to you...
...by not dragging down the team!!
Yeah!

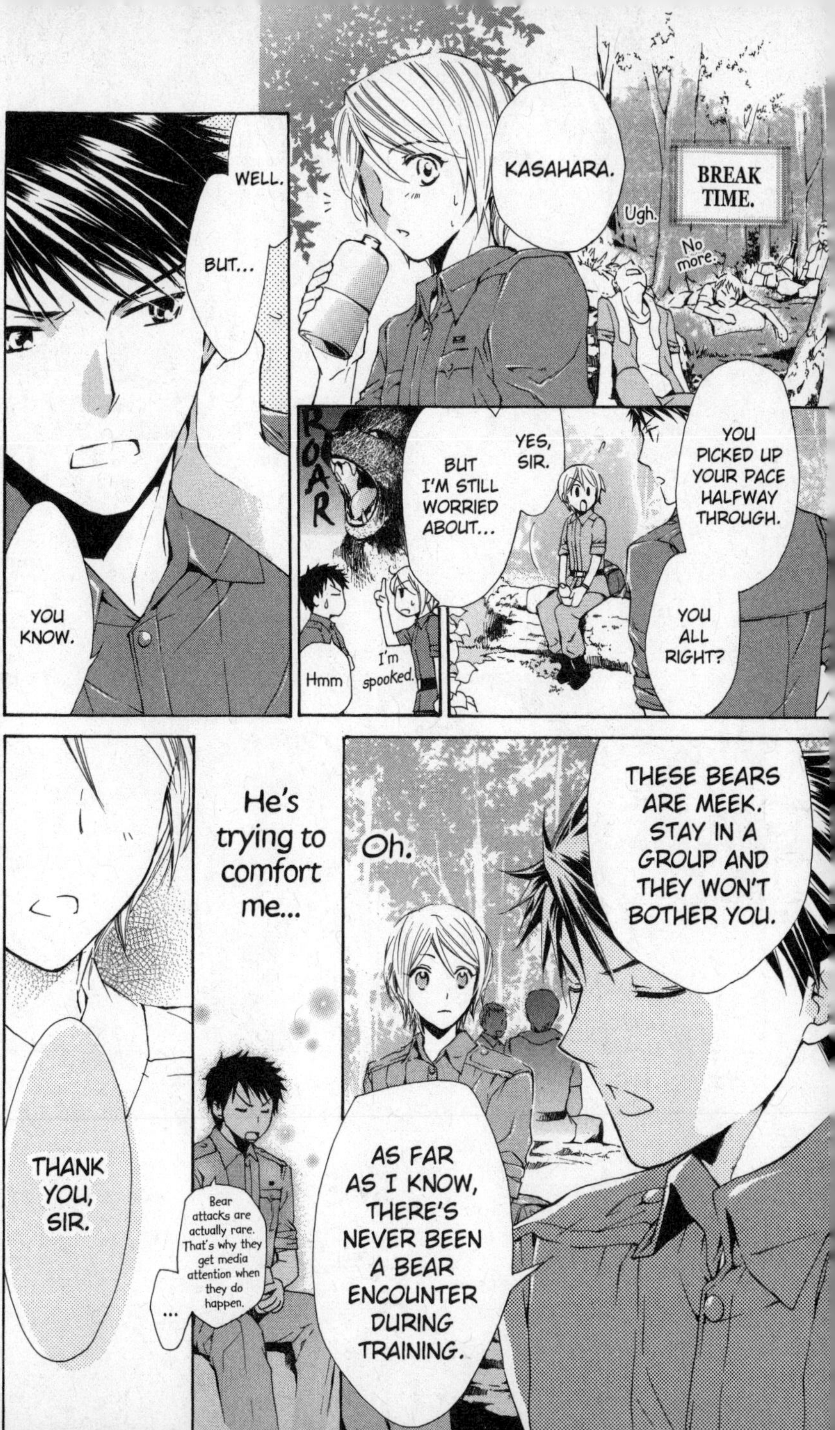
BREAK TIME.
KASAHARA.
Ugh.
No more.
YOU PICKED UP YOUR PACE HALFWAY THROUGH.
YOU ALL RIGHT?
YES, SIR.
BUT I'M STILL WORRIED ABOUT...
ROAR
I'm spooked.
Hmm
WELL.
BUT...
YOU KNOW.
THESE BEARS ARE MEEK. STAY IN A GROUP AND THEY WON'T BOTHER YOU.
Oh.
AS FAR AS I KNOW, THERE'S NEVER BEEN A BEAR ENCOUNTER DURING TRAINING.
Bear attacks are actually rare. That's why they get media attention when they do happen.
...
He's trying to comfort me...
THANK YOU, SIR.

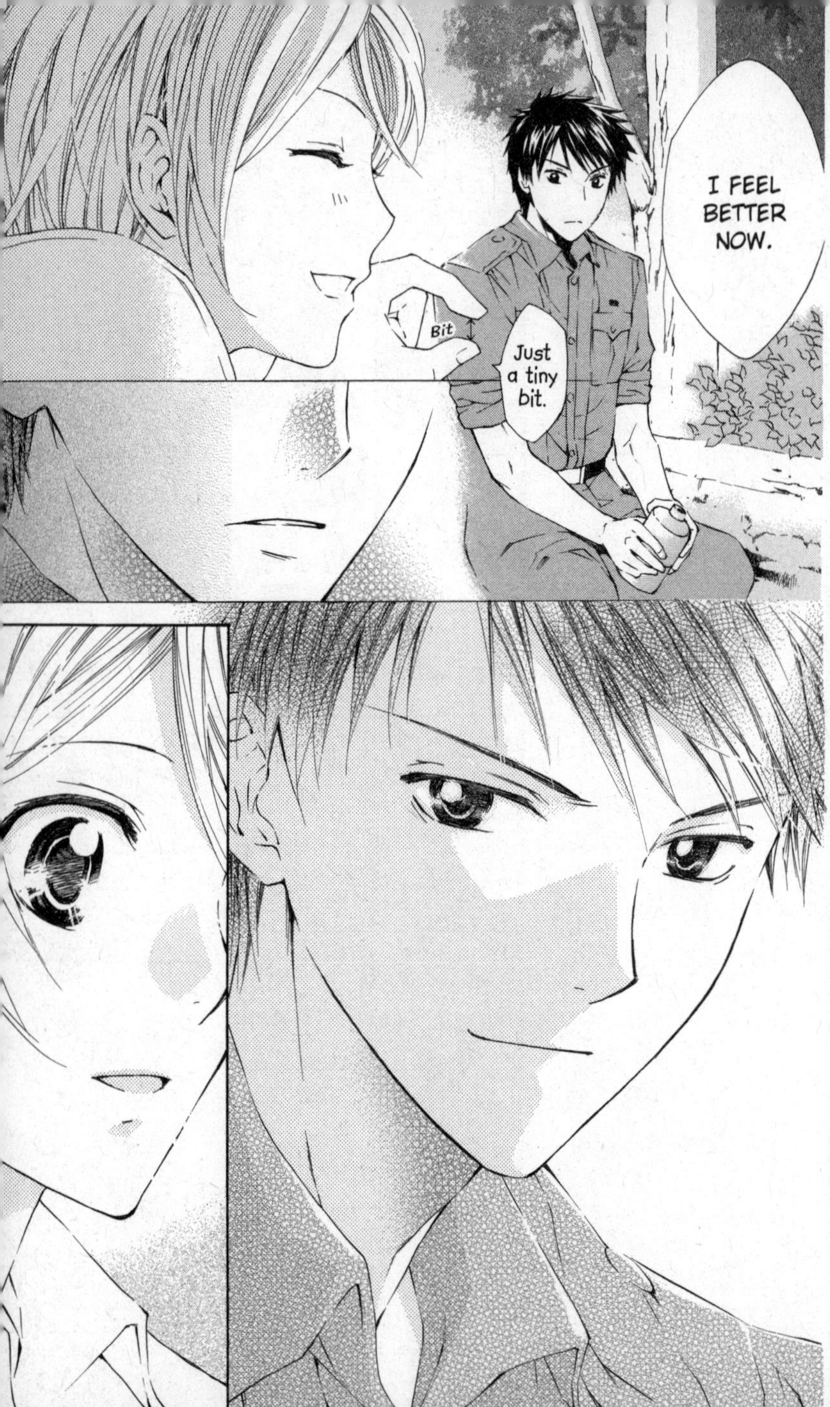
I FEEL BETTER NOW.
Just a tiny bit.
Bit

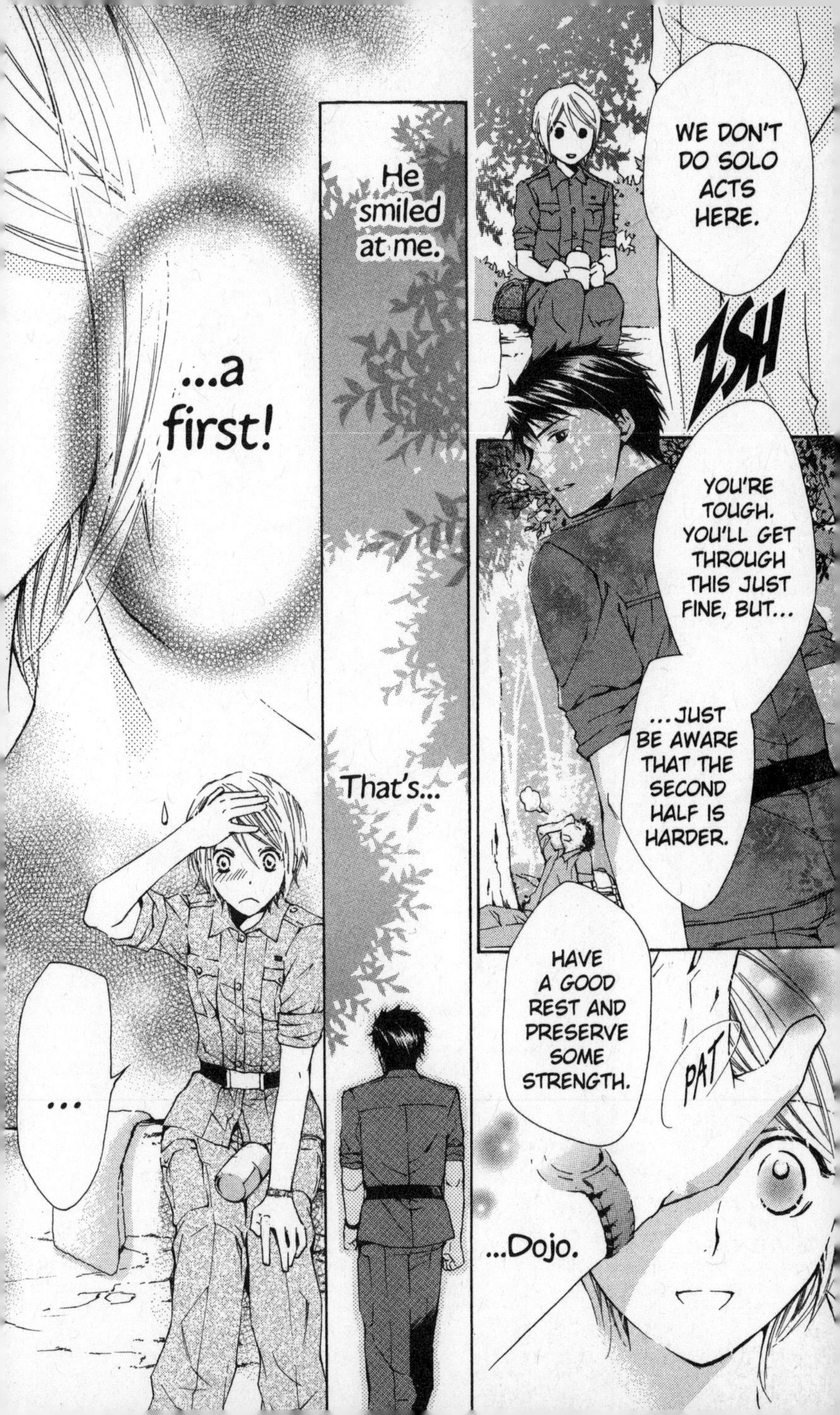
WE DON'T DO SOLO ACTS HERE.
ZSH
YOU'RE TOUGH. YOU'LL GET THROUGH THIS JUST FINE, BUT...
...JUST BE AWARE THAT THE SECOND HALF IS HARDER.
HAVE A GOOD REST AND PRESERVE SOME STRENGTH.
PAT
...Dojo.
He smiled at me.
That's...
...a first!
...

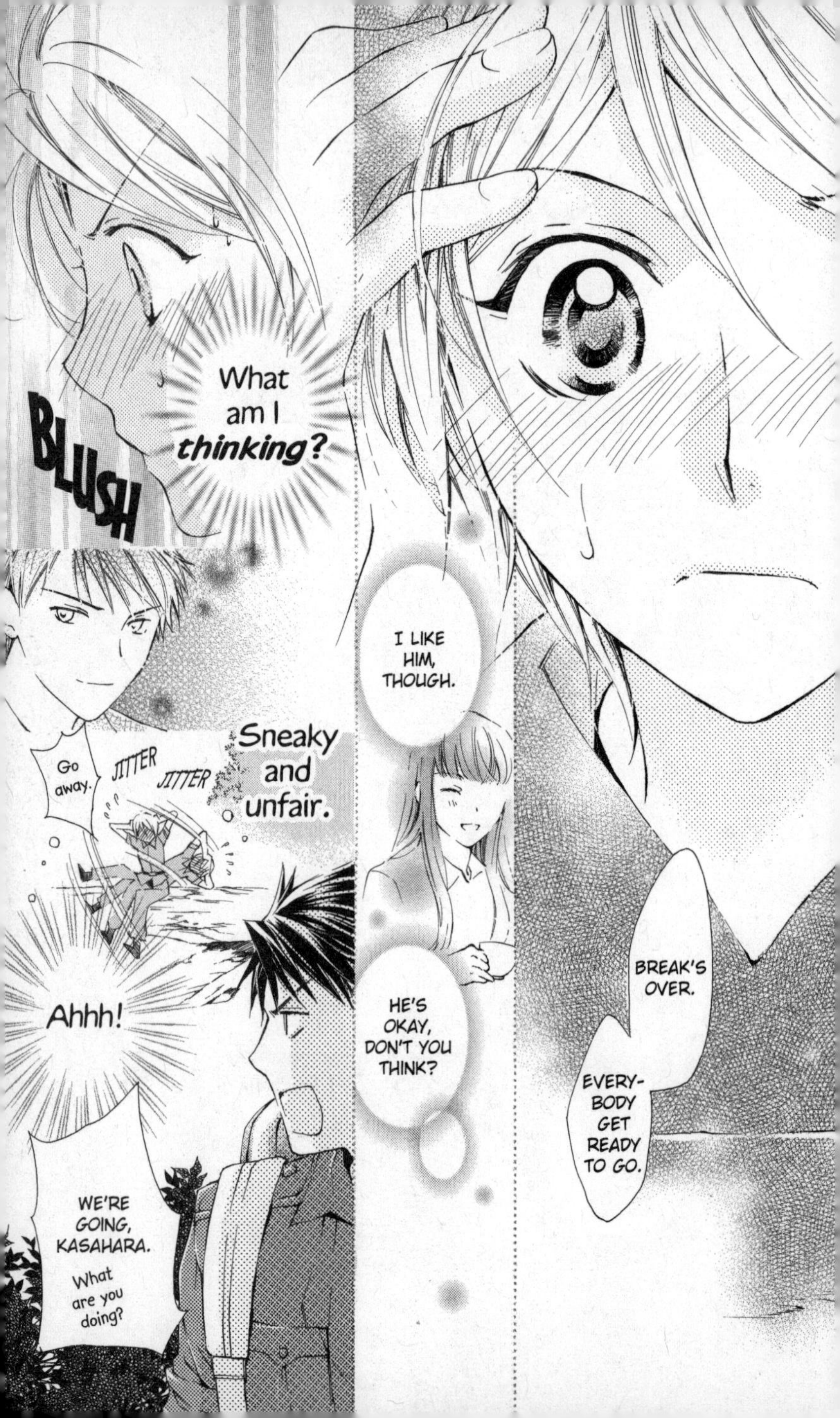
BREAK'S OVER.
EVERY-BODY GET READY TO GO.
I LIKE HIM, THOUGH.
HE'S OKAY, DON'T YOU THINK?
BLUSH
What am I *thinking?*
Sneaky and unfair.
Go away.
JITTER
JITTER
Ahhh!
WE'RE GOING, KASAHARA.
What are you doing?

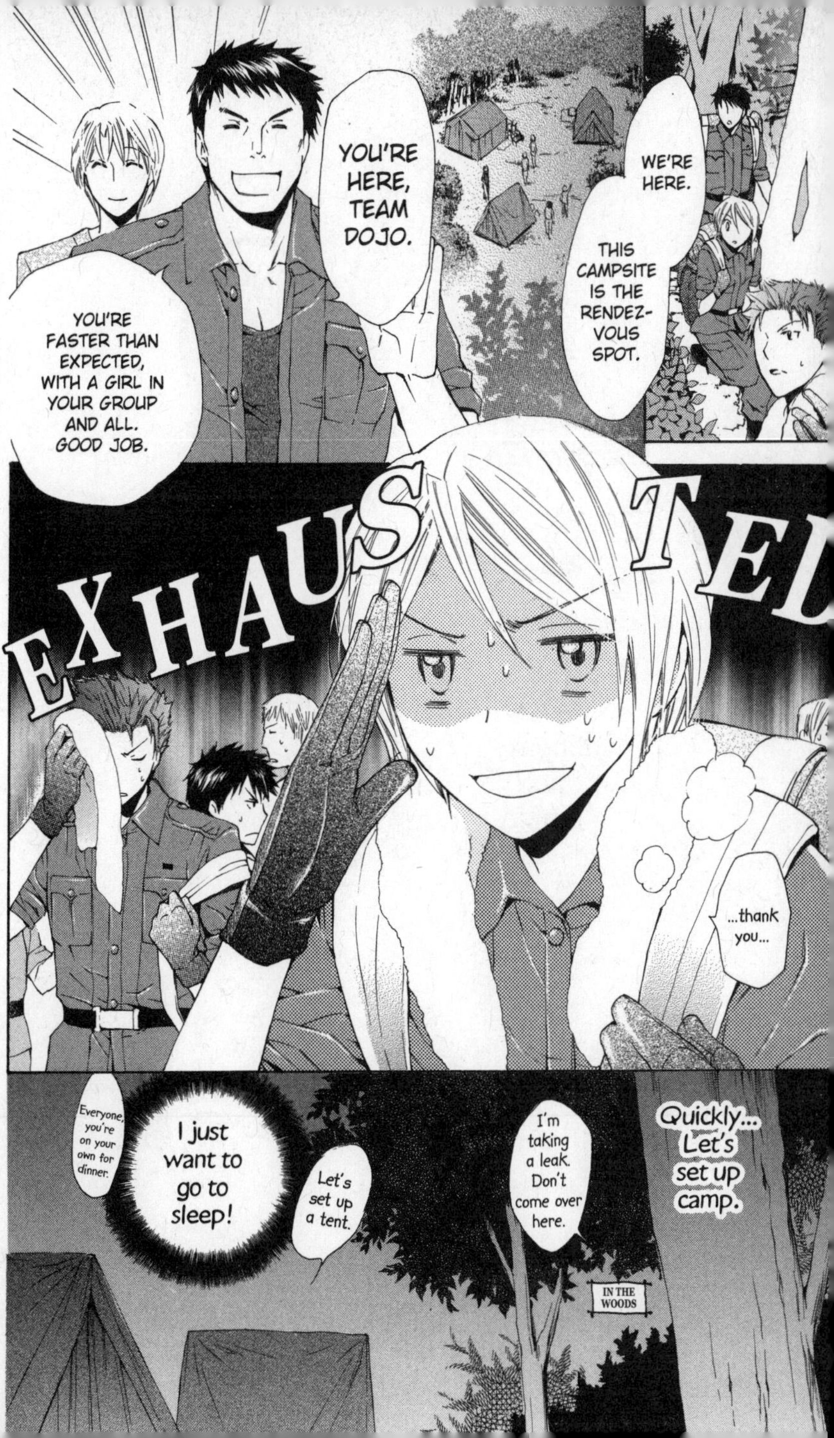
WE'RE HERE.
THIS CAMPSITE IS THE RENDEZ-VOUS SPOT.
YOU'RE HERE, TEAM DOJO.
YOU'RE FASTER THAN EXPECTED, WITH A GIRL IN YOUR GROUP AND ALL. GOOD JOB.
EXHAUSTED
...thank you...
Quickly... Let's set up camp.
I'm taking a leak. Don't come over here.
IN THE WOODS
Let's set up a tent.
I just want to go to sleep!
Everyone, you're on your own for dinner.

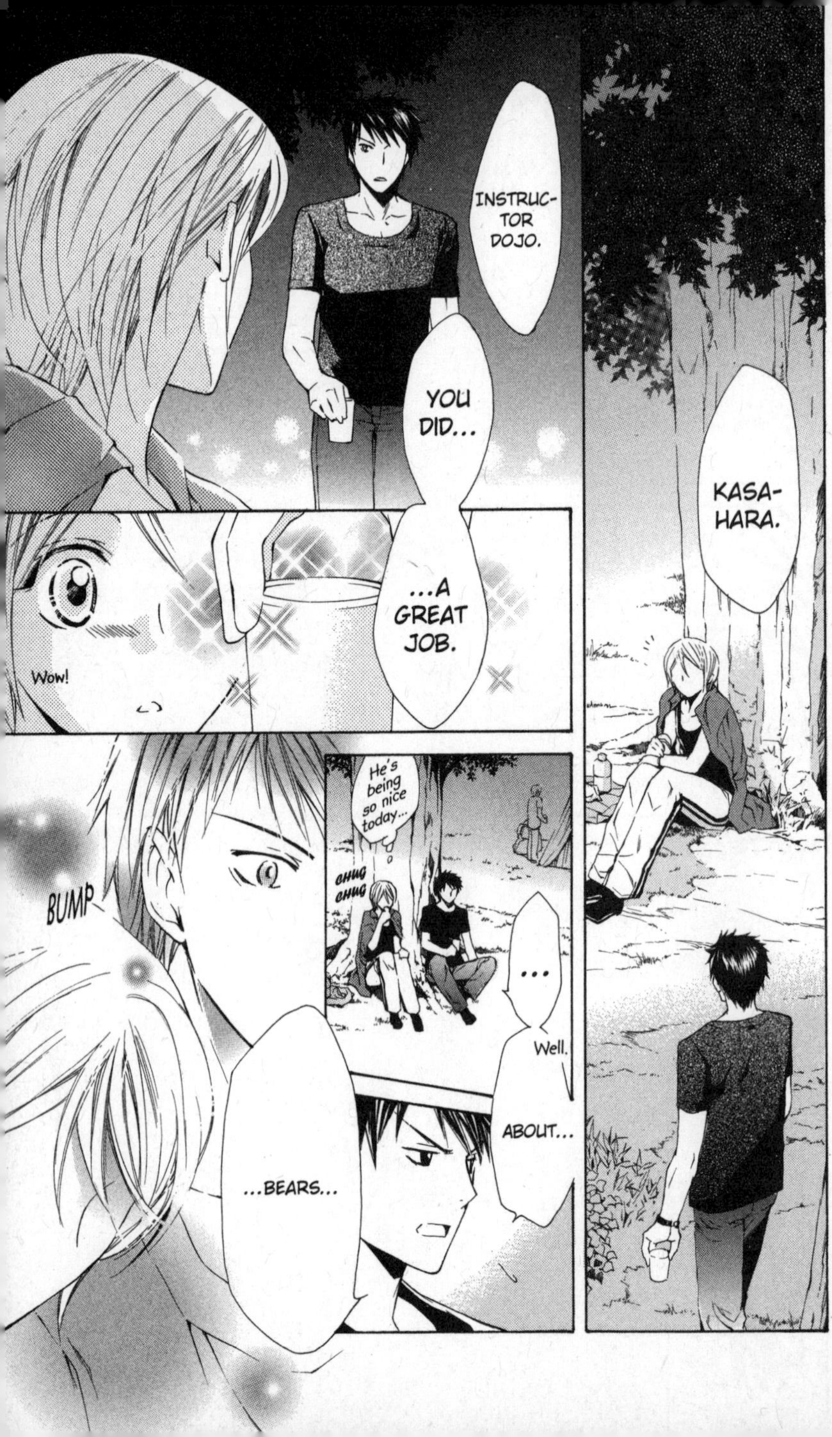
KASA-HARA.
INSTRUC-TOR DOJO.
YOU DID...
...A GREAT JOB.
Wow!
He's being so nice today...
CHUG CHUG
...
Well.
ABOUT...
...BEARS...
BUMP

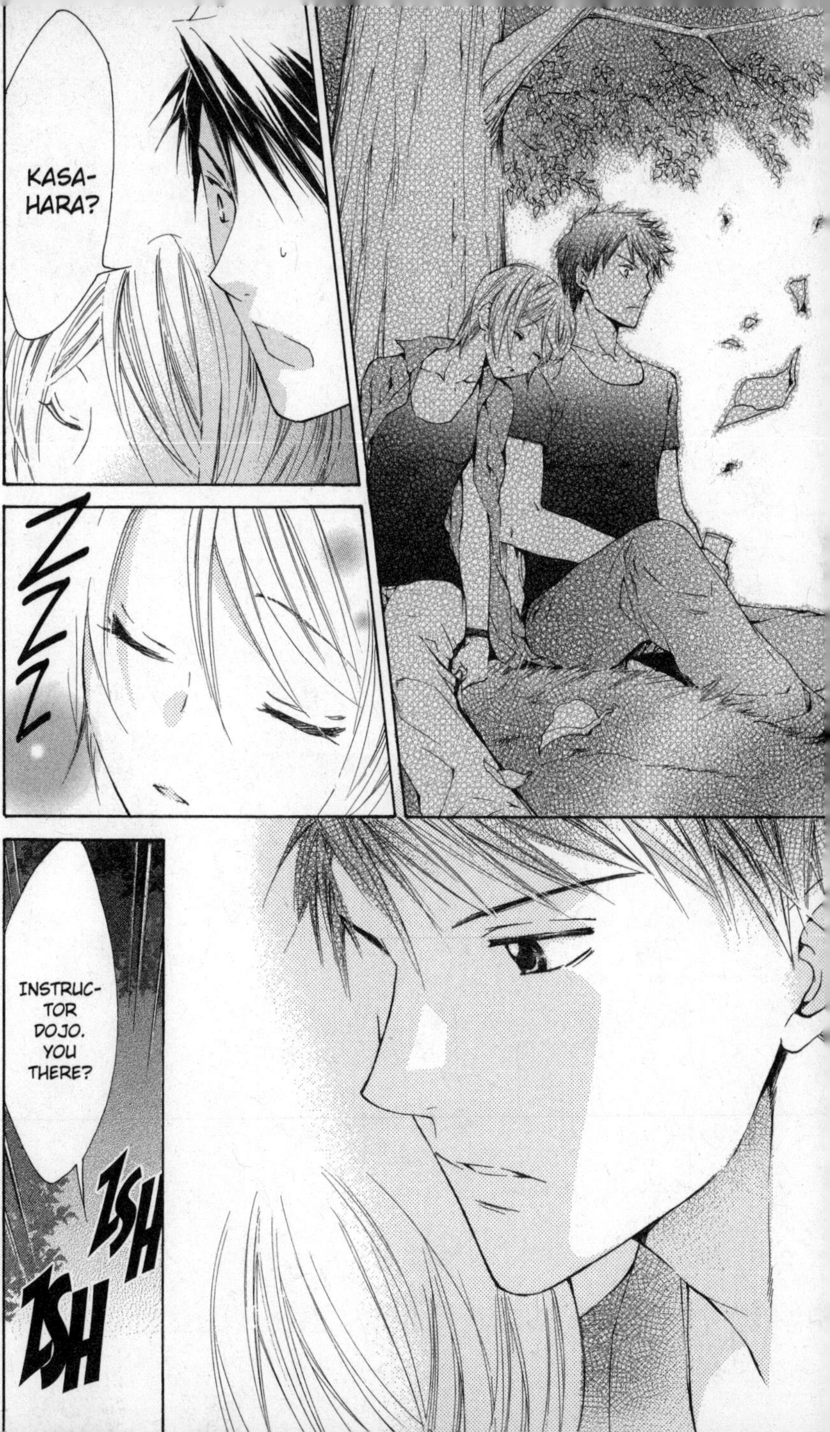
KASA-
HARA?
ZZZZ
INSTRUC-
TOR
DOJO.
YOU
THERE?
ZSH
ZSH

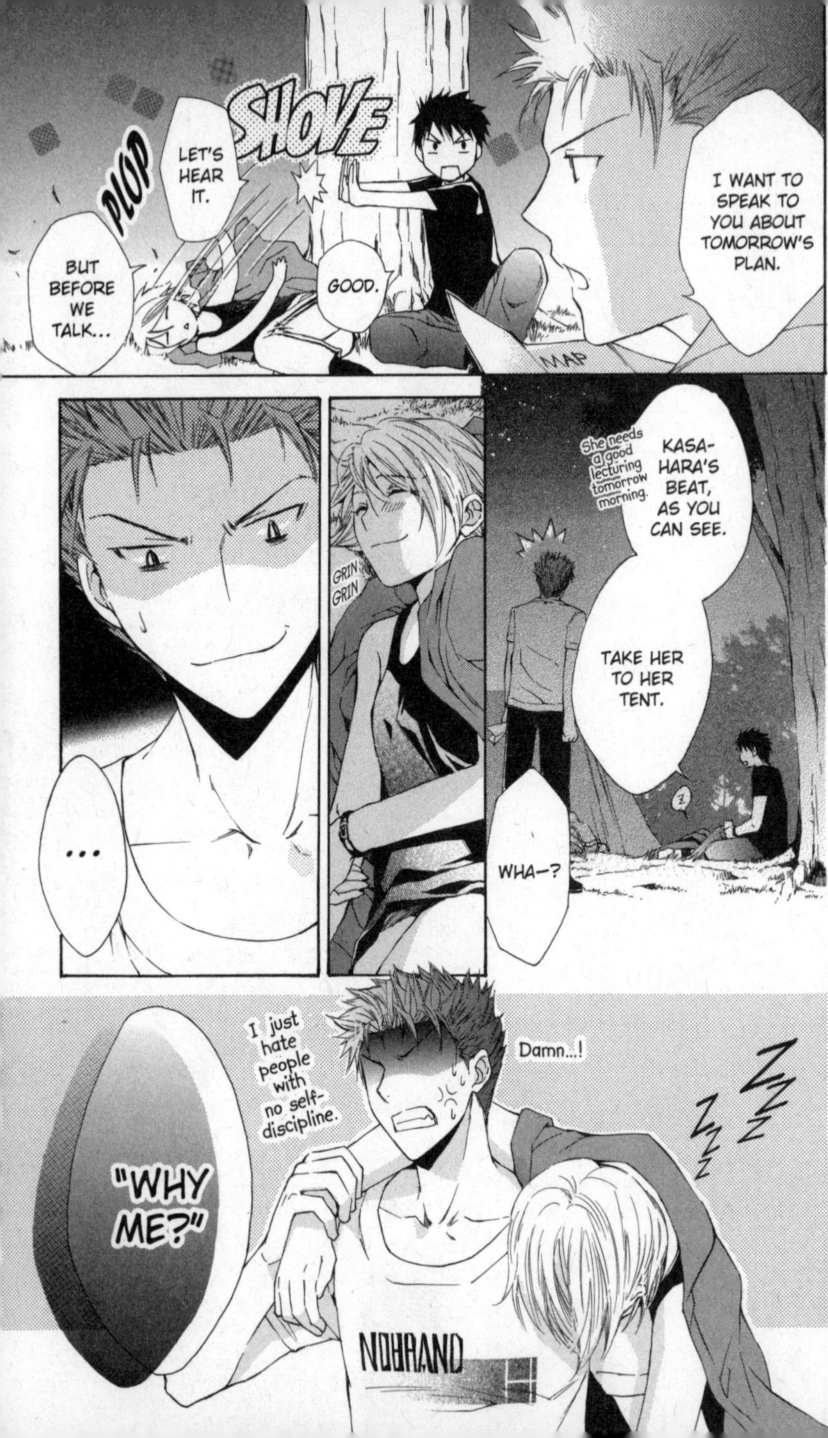
I WANT TO SPEAK TO YOU ABOUT TOMORROW'S PLAN.
MAP
GOOD.
SHOVE
LET'S HEAR IT.
PLOP
BUT BEFORE WE TALK...
KASA-HARA'S BEAT, AS YOU CAN SEE.
She needs a good lecturing tomorrow morning.
TAKE HER TO HER TENT.
WHA-?
GRIN GRIN
...
ZZZ
Damn...!
I just hate people with no self-discipline.
"WHY ME?"

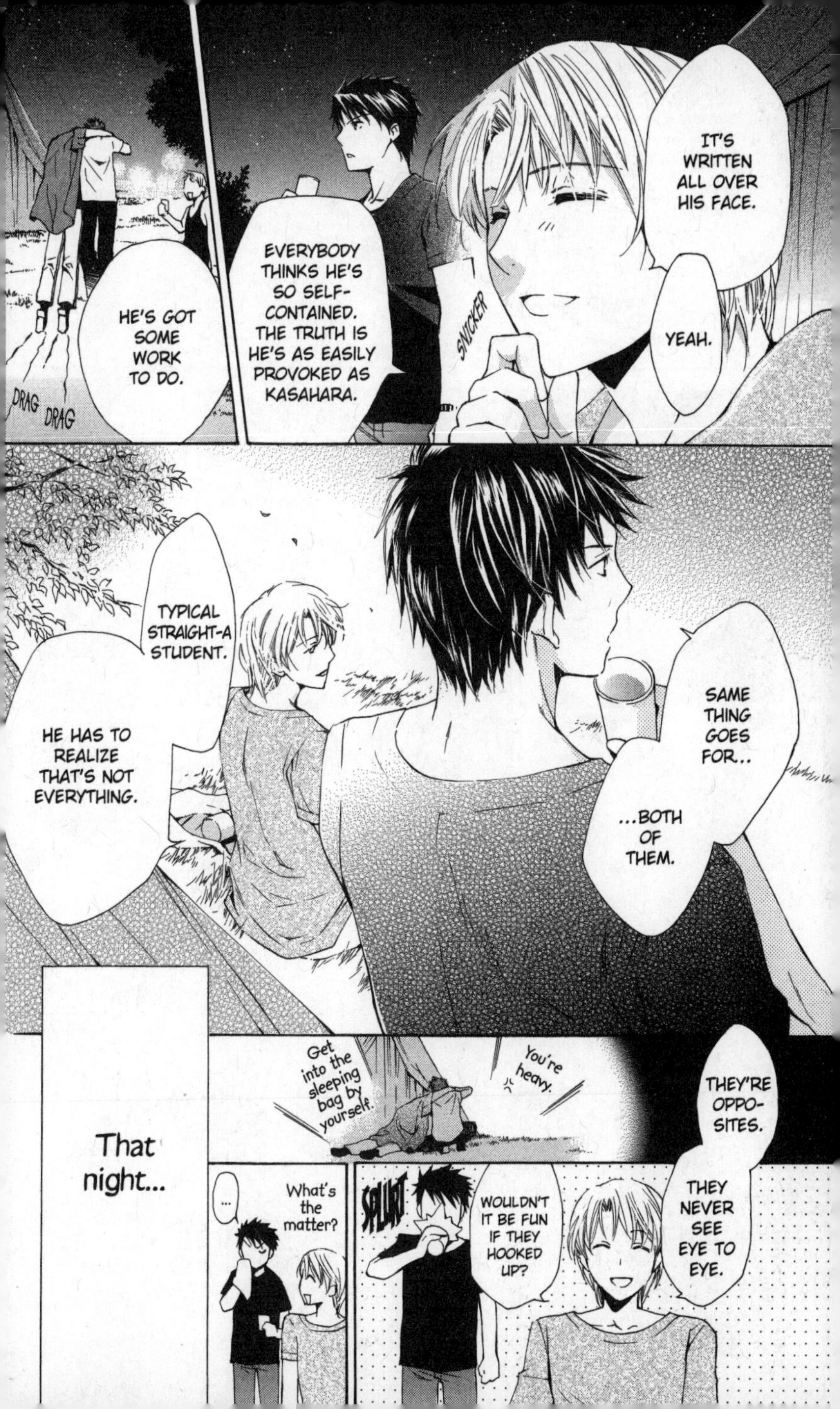

IT'S WRITTEN ALL OVER HIS FACE.
YEAH.
SNICKER
EVERYBODY THINKS HE'S SO SELF-CONTAINED. THE TRUTH IS HE'S AS EASILY PROVOKED AS KASAHARA.
HE'S GOT SOME WORK TO DO.
DRAG DRAG
SAME THING GOES FOR...
...BOTH OF THEM.
TYPICAL STRAIGHT-A STUDENT.
HE HAS TO REALIZE THAT'S NOT EVERYTHING.
THEY'RE OPPOSITES.
You're heavy.
Get into the sleeping bag by yourself.
THEY NEVER SEE EYE TO EYE.
WOULDN'T IT BE FUN IF THEY HOOKED UP?
SPLURT
...
What's the matter?
That night...

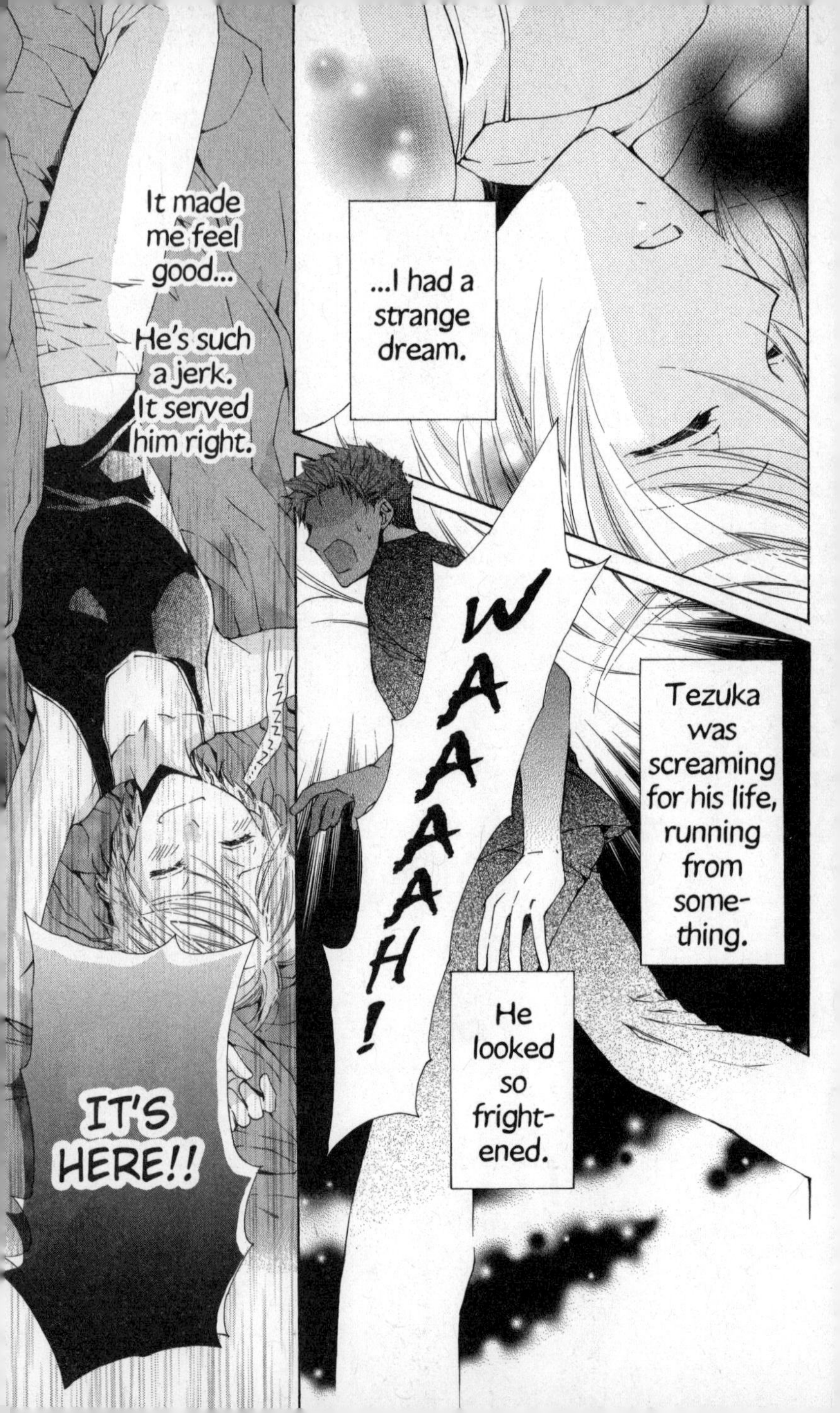
...I had a strange dream.
Tezuka was screaming for his life, running from something.
WAAAAAH!
He looked so frightened.
It made me feel good...
He's such a jerk. It served him right.
IT'S HERE!!

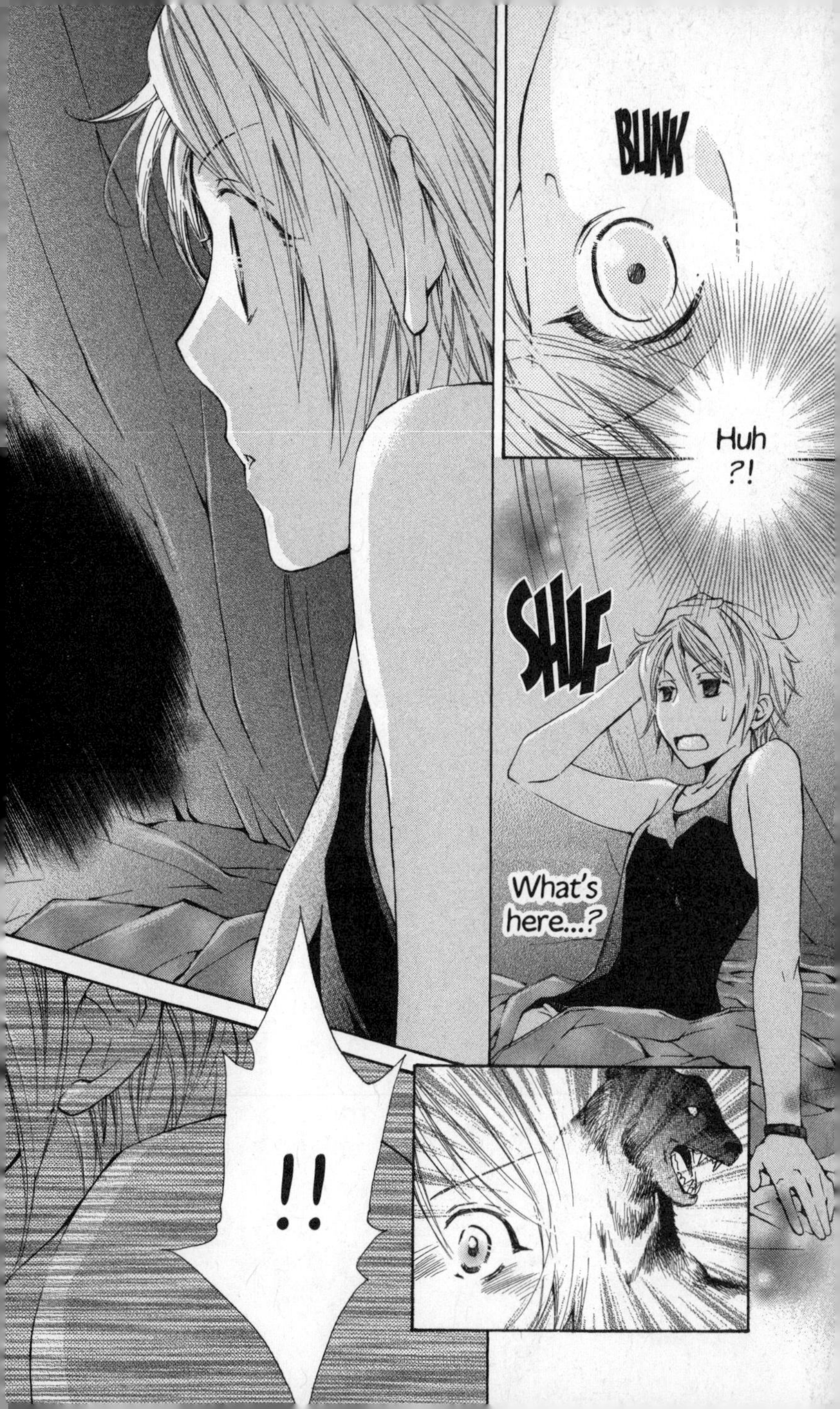
BLINK
Huh ?!
SHUF
What's here...?
!!

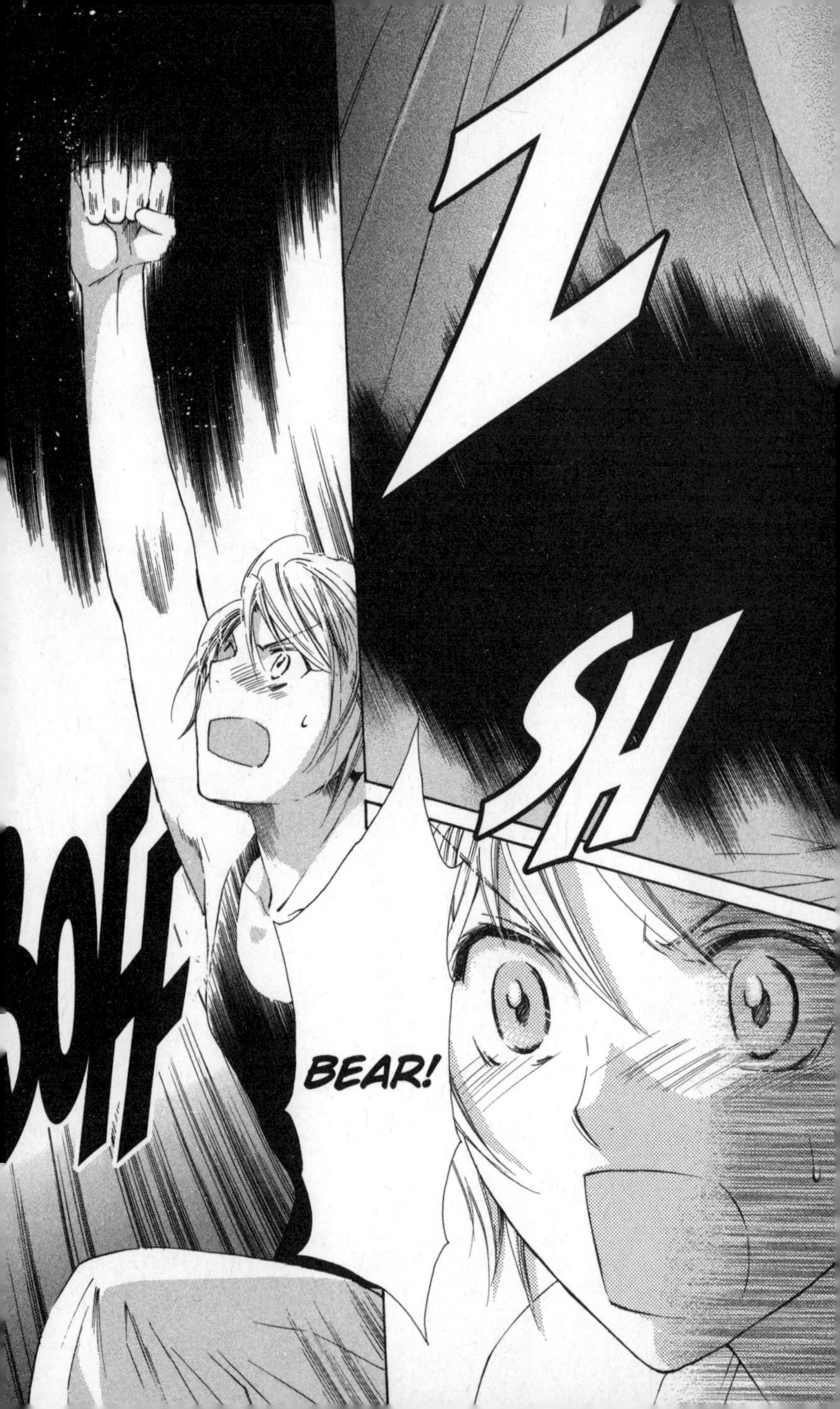
Z
SH
BEAR!

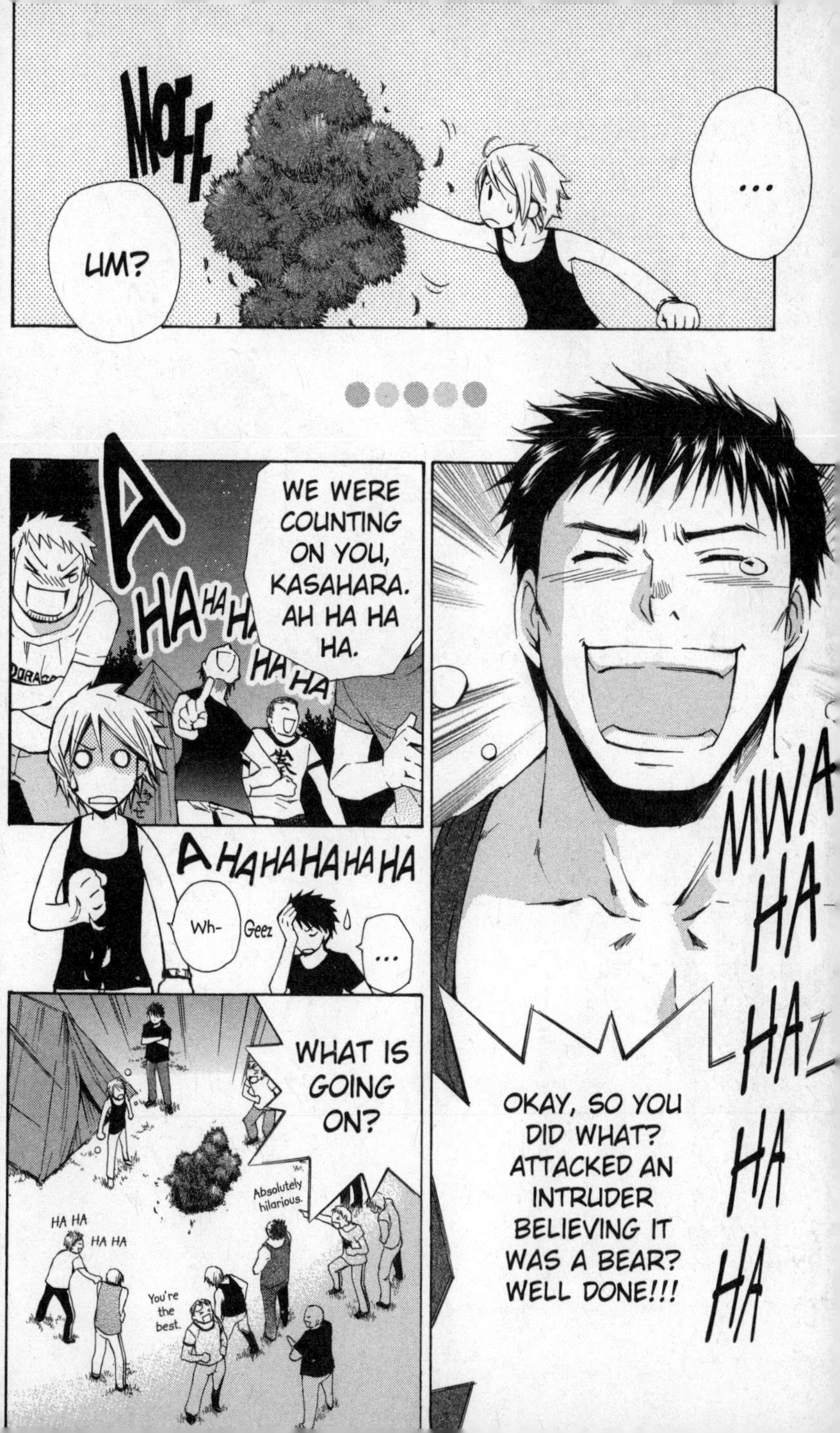
...
MOFF
UM?
MWA HA HA HA HA HA HA
OKAY, SO YOU DID WHAT? ATTACKED AN INTRUDER BELIEVING IT WAS A BEAR? WELL DONE!!!
WE WERE COUNTING ON YOU, KASAHARA. AH HA HA HA.
A HA HA HA HA HA
AHAHAHAHAHAHA
...
Geez
Wh-
WHAT IS GOING ON?
Absolutely hilarious.
HA HA
HA HA
You're the best.

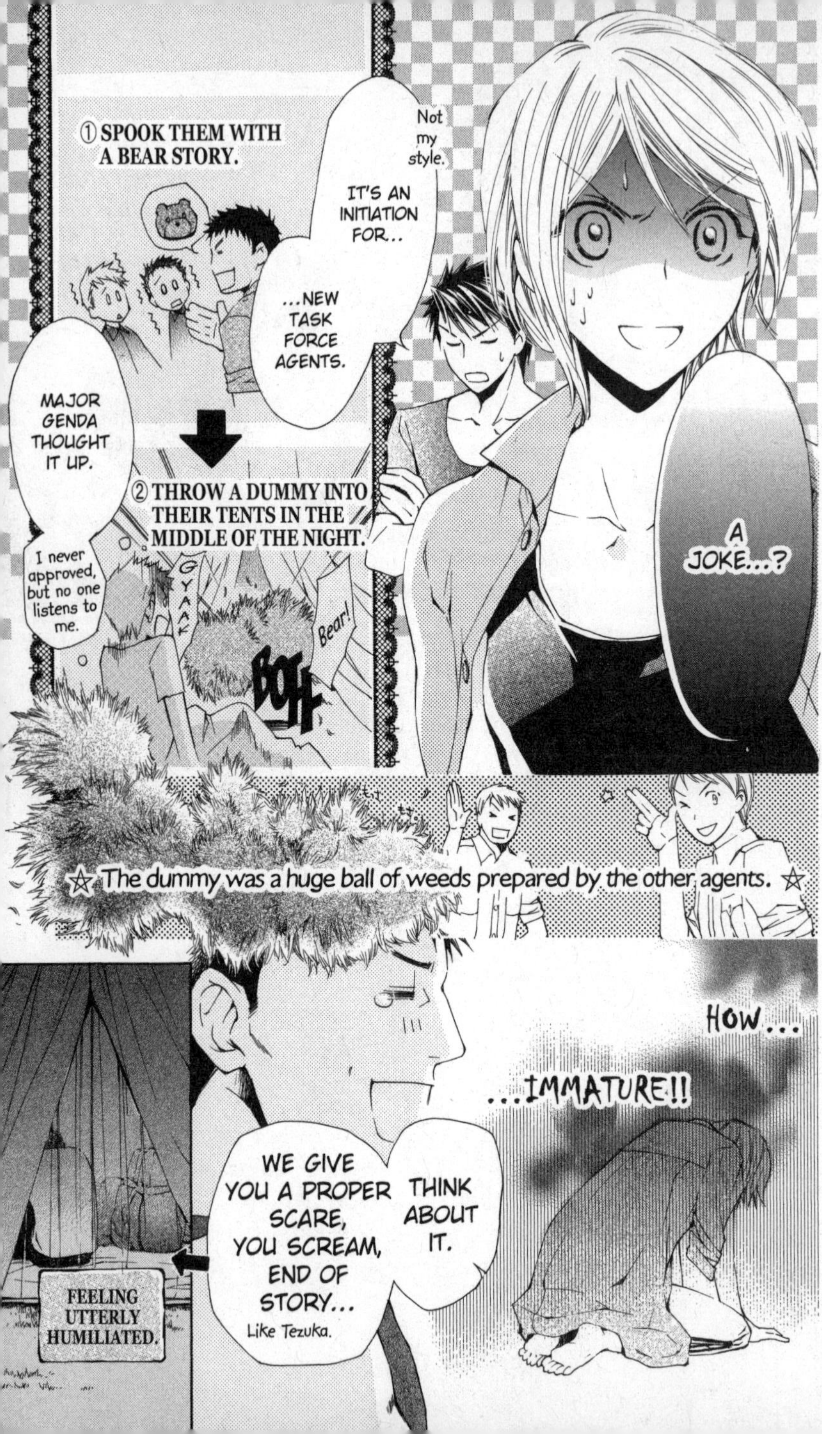

IT'S AN INITIATION FOR...
...NEW TASK FORCE AGENTS.
Not my style.
A JOKE...?
MAJOR GENDA THOUGHT IT UP.
① SPOOK THEM WITH A BEAR STORY.
② THROW A DUMMY INTO THEIR TENTS IN THE MIDDLE OF THE NIGHT.
I never approved, but no one listens to me.
GYAAAK
Bear!
BOFF
☆ The dummy was a huge ball of weeds prepared by the other agents. ☆
HOW...
...IMMATURE!!
THINK ABOUT IT.
WE GIVE YOU A PROPER SCARE, YOU SCREAM, END OF STORY...
Like Tezuka.
FEELING UTTERLY HUMILIATED.

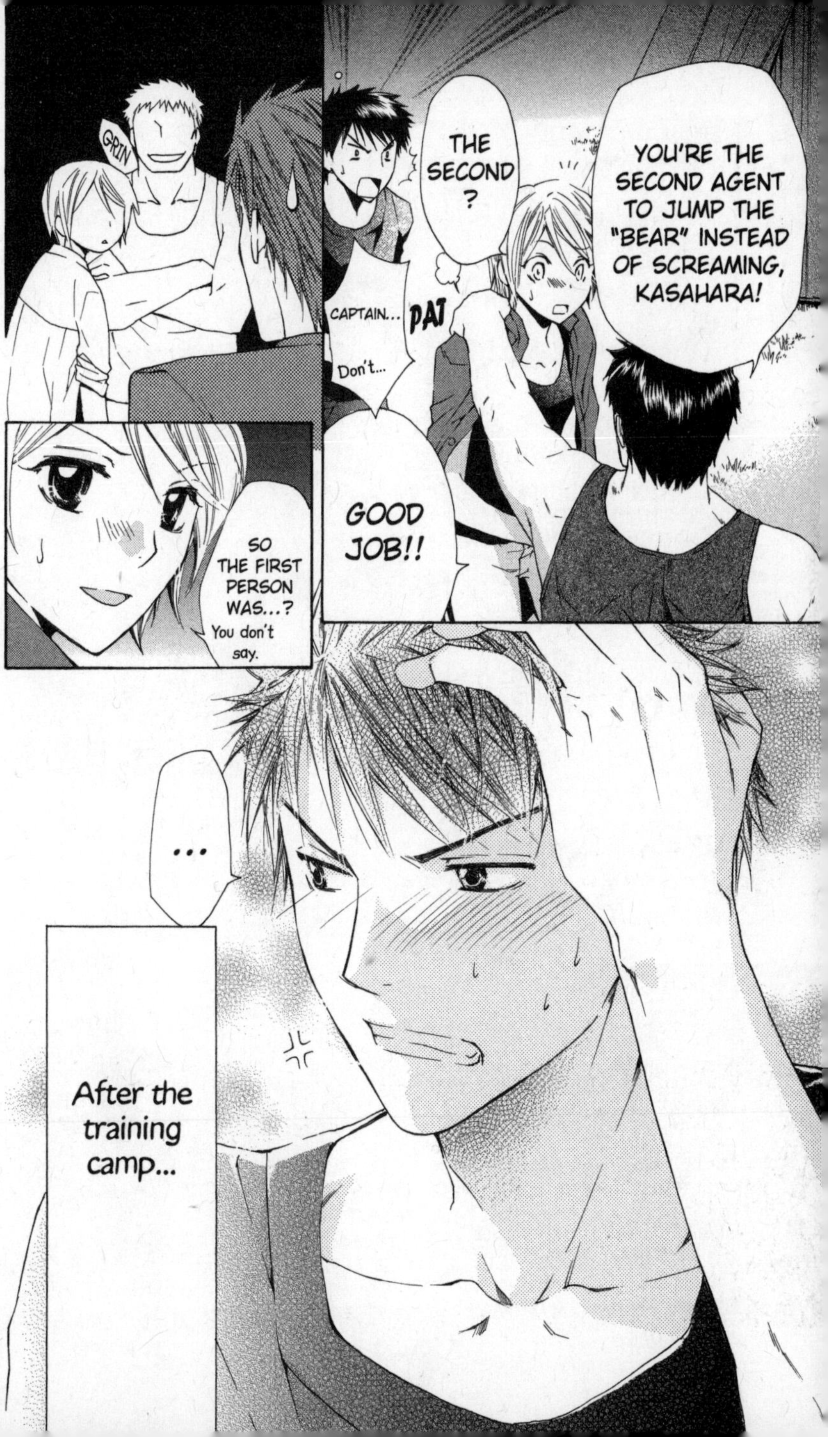
YOU'RE THE SECOND AGENT TO JUMP THE "BEAR" INSTEAD OF SCREAMING, KASAHARA!
THE SECOND?
PAT
CAPTAIN...
Don't...
GOOD JOB!!
GRIN
SO THE FIRST PERSON WAS...?
You don't say.
...
After the training camp...

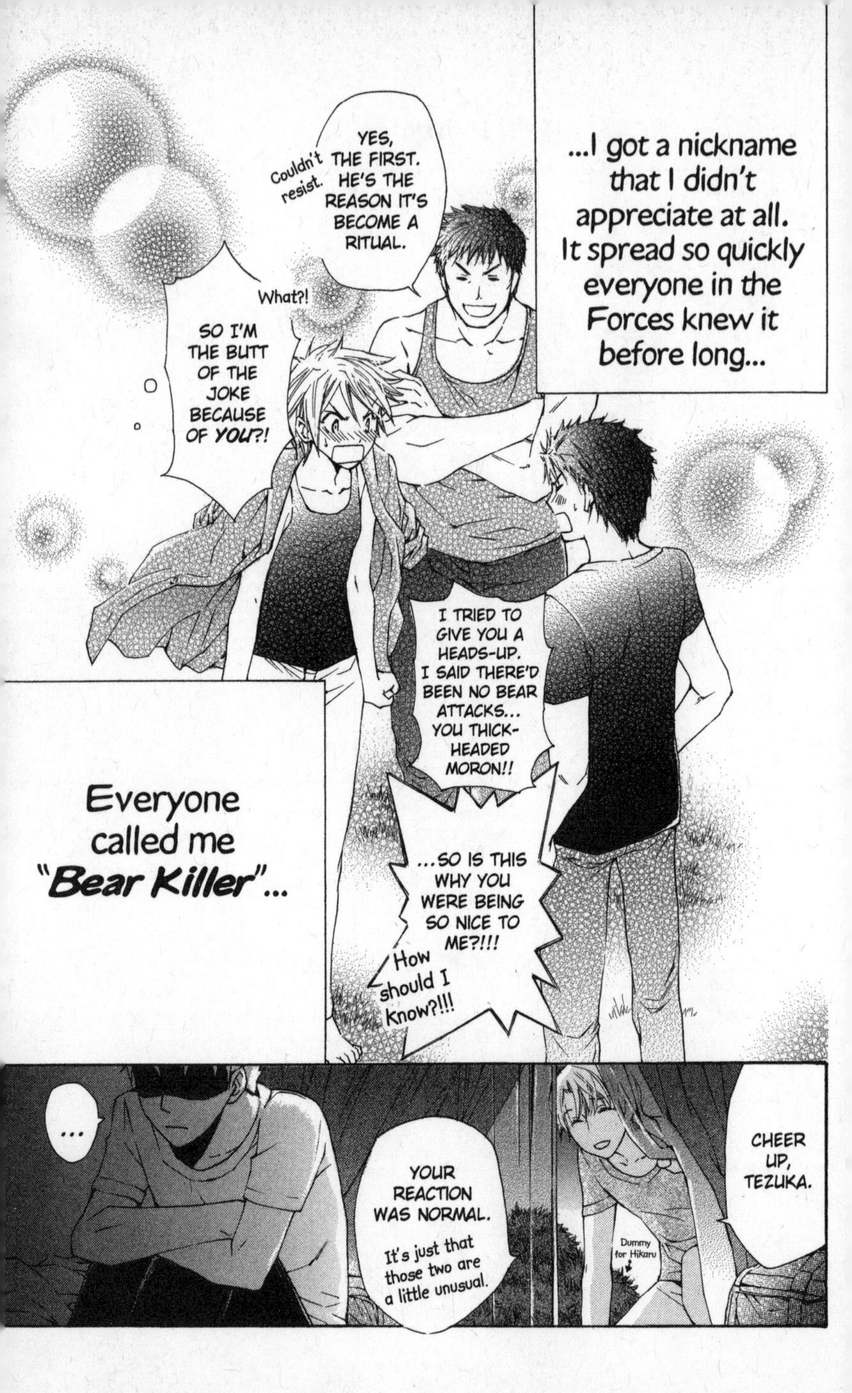
...I got a nickname that I didn't appreciate at all. It spread so quickly everyone in the Forces knew it before long...
YES, THE FIRST. HE'S THE REASON IT'S BECOME A RITUAL.
Couldn't resist.
What?!
SO I'M THE BUTT OF THE JOKE BECAUSE OF *YOU*?!
I TRIED TO GIVE YOU A HEADS-UP. I SAID THERE'D BEEN NO BEAR ATTACKS... YOU THICK-HEADED MORON!!
...SO IS THIS WHY YOU WERE BEING SO NICE TO ME?!!!
How should I know?!!!
Everyone called me "***Bear Killer***"...
CHEER UP, TEZUKA.
Dummy for Hikaru
YOUR REACTION WAS NORMAL.
It's just that those two are a little unusual.
...

BEAR SURPRISE AND DOJO

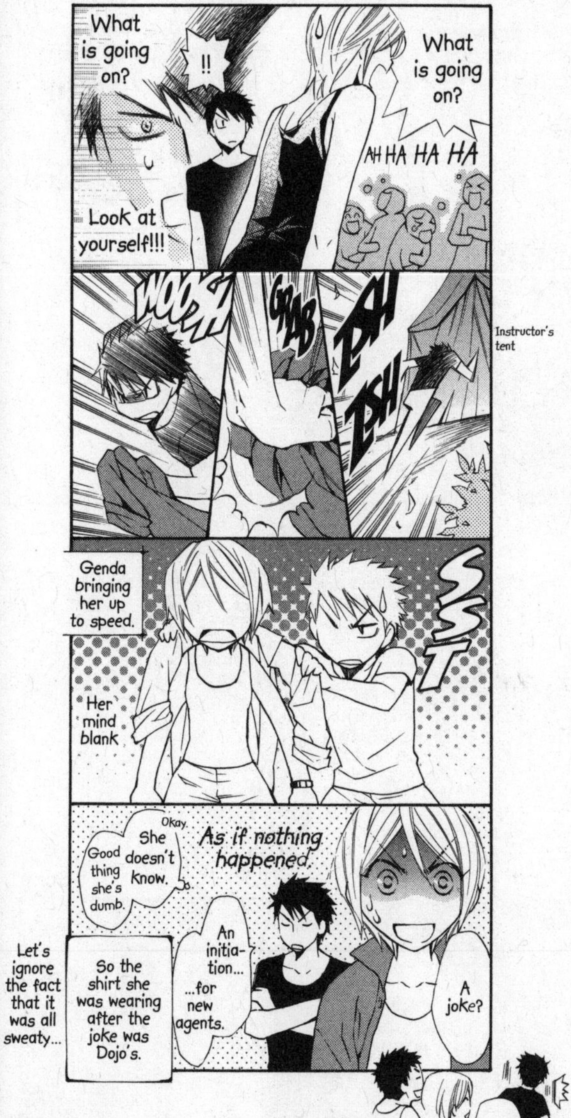
What is going on?
AH HA HA HA
!!
What is going on?
Look at yourself!!!
Instructor's tent
ZSH
ZSH
GRAB
WOOSH
SSST
Genda bringing her up to speed.
Her mind blank
A joke?
An initiation...
...for new agents.
As if nothing happened.
Okay.
She doesn't know.
Good thing she's dumb.
So the shirt she was wearing after the joke was Dojo's.
Let's ignore the fact that it was all sweaty...
Gent.
* Komaki and Genda saw it.

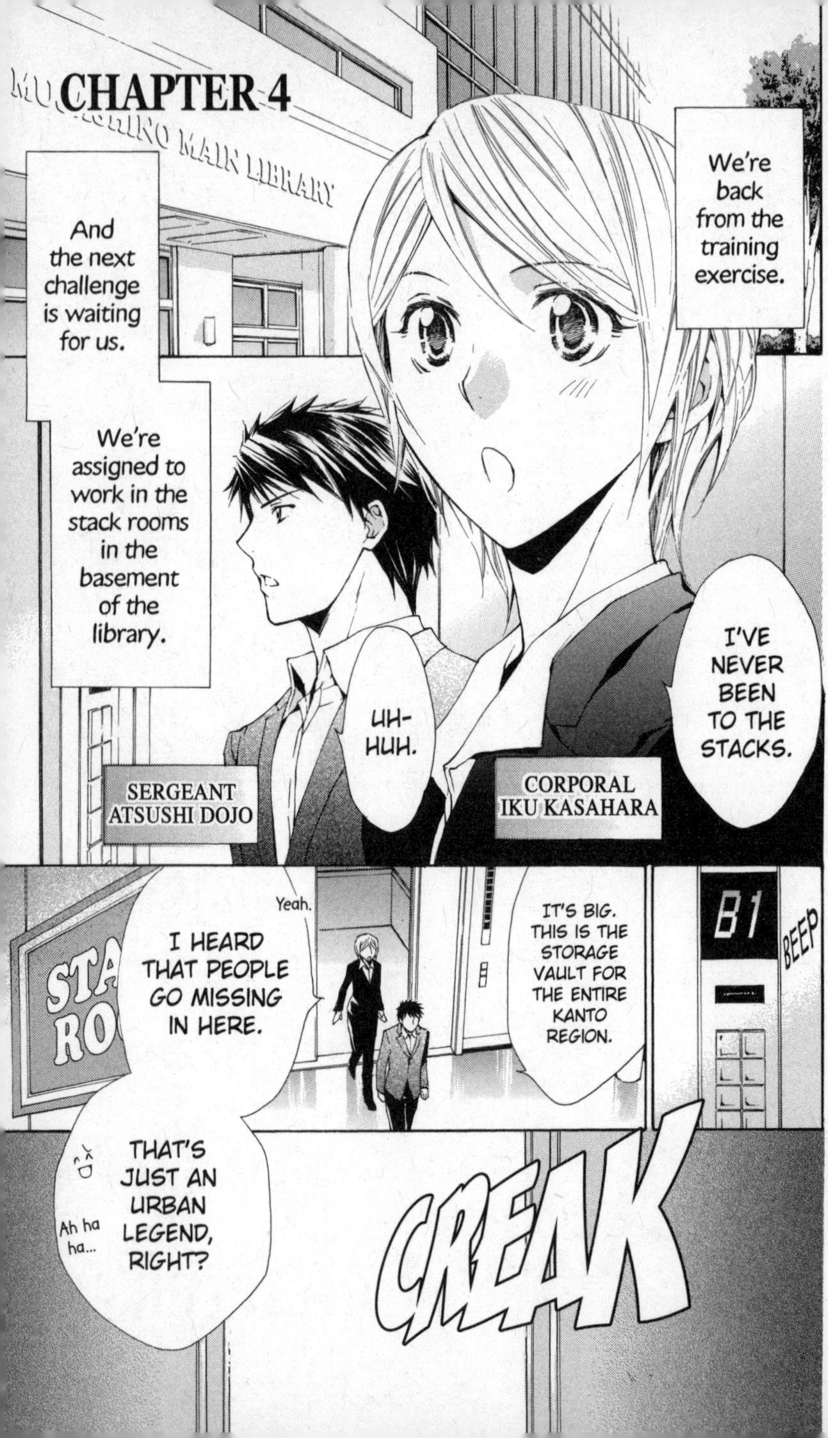
CHAPTER 4
MAIN LIBRARY
We're back from the training exercise.
And the next challenge is waiting for us.
We're assigned to work in the stack rooms in the basement of the library.
I'VE NEVER BEEN TO THE STACKS.
UH-HUH.
CORPORAL IKU KASAHARA
SERGEANT ATSUSHI DOJO
B1
BEEP
IT'S BIG. THIS IS THE STORAGE VAULT FOR THE ENTIRE KANTO REGION.
Yeah.
I HEARD THAT PEOPLE GO MISSING IN HERE.
CREAK
THAT'S JUST AN URBAN LEGEND, RIGHT?
Ah ha ha...

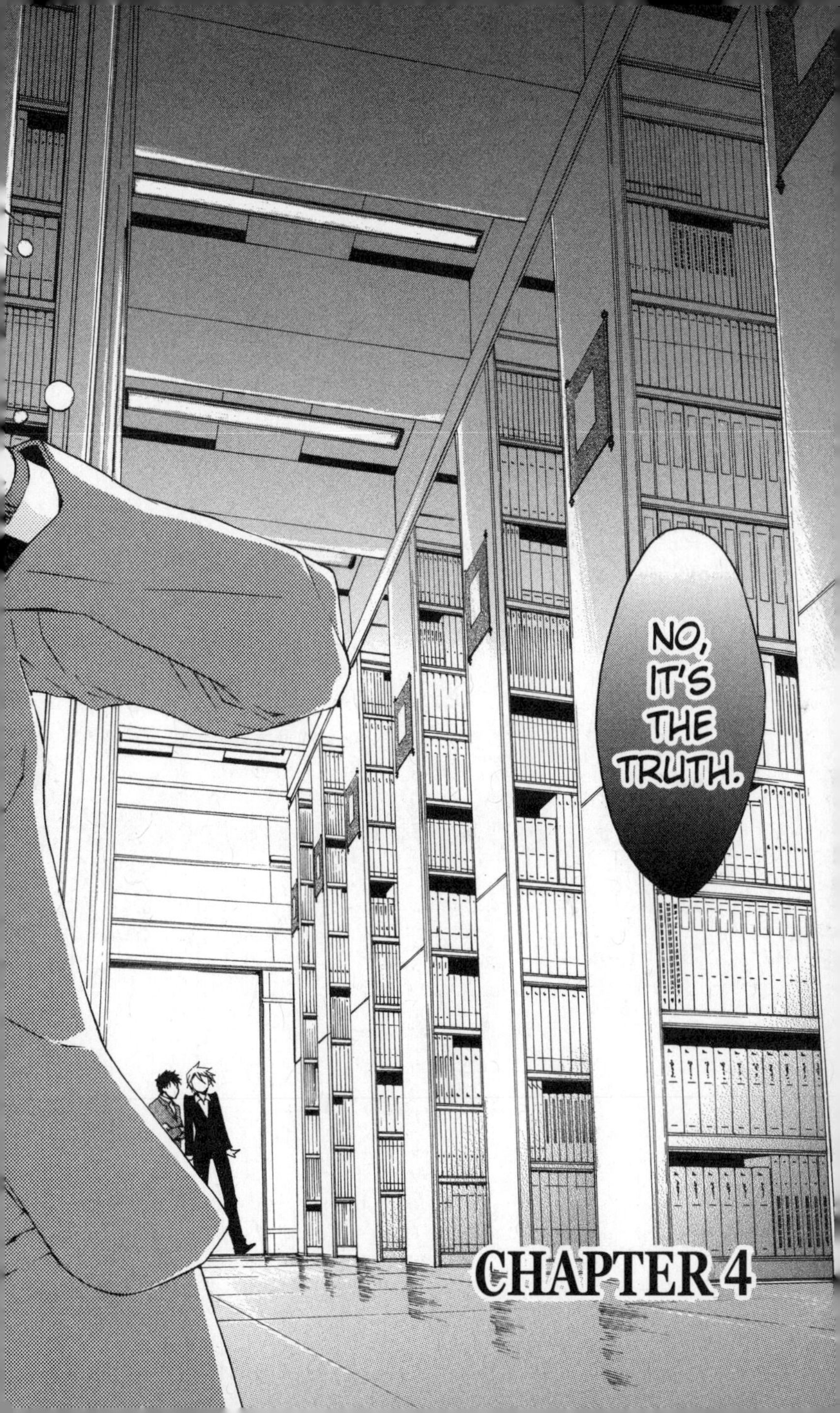
NO, IT'S THE TRUTH.
CHAPTER 4

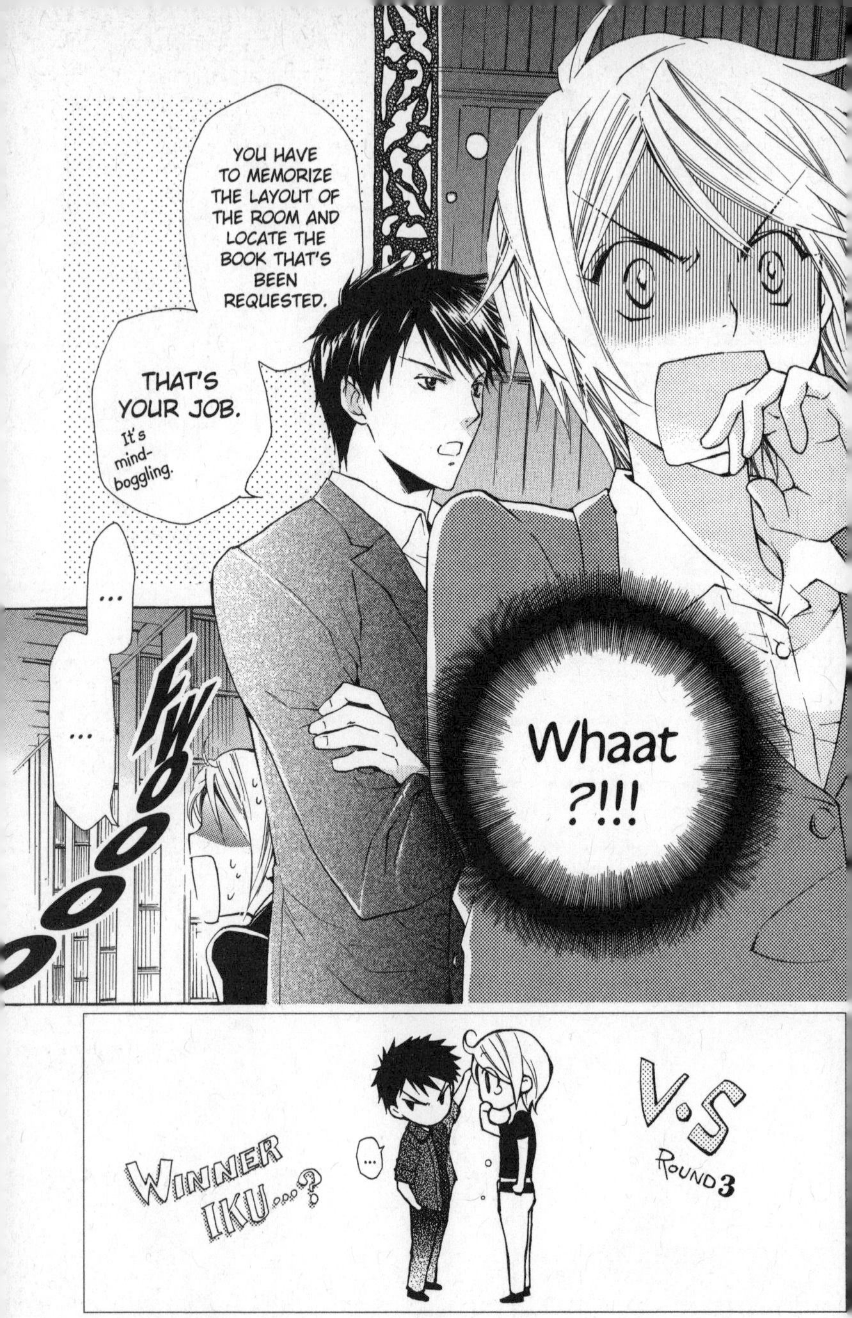
YOU HAVE TO MEMORIZE THE LAYOUT OF THE ROOM AND LOCATE THE BOOK THAT'S BEEN REQUESTED.
THAT'S YOUR JOB.
It's mind-boggling.
Whaat ?!!!
...
...
V.S ROUND 3
...
WINNER IKU...?

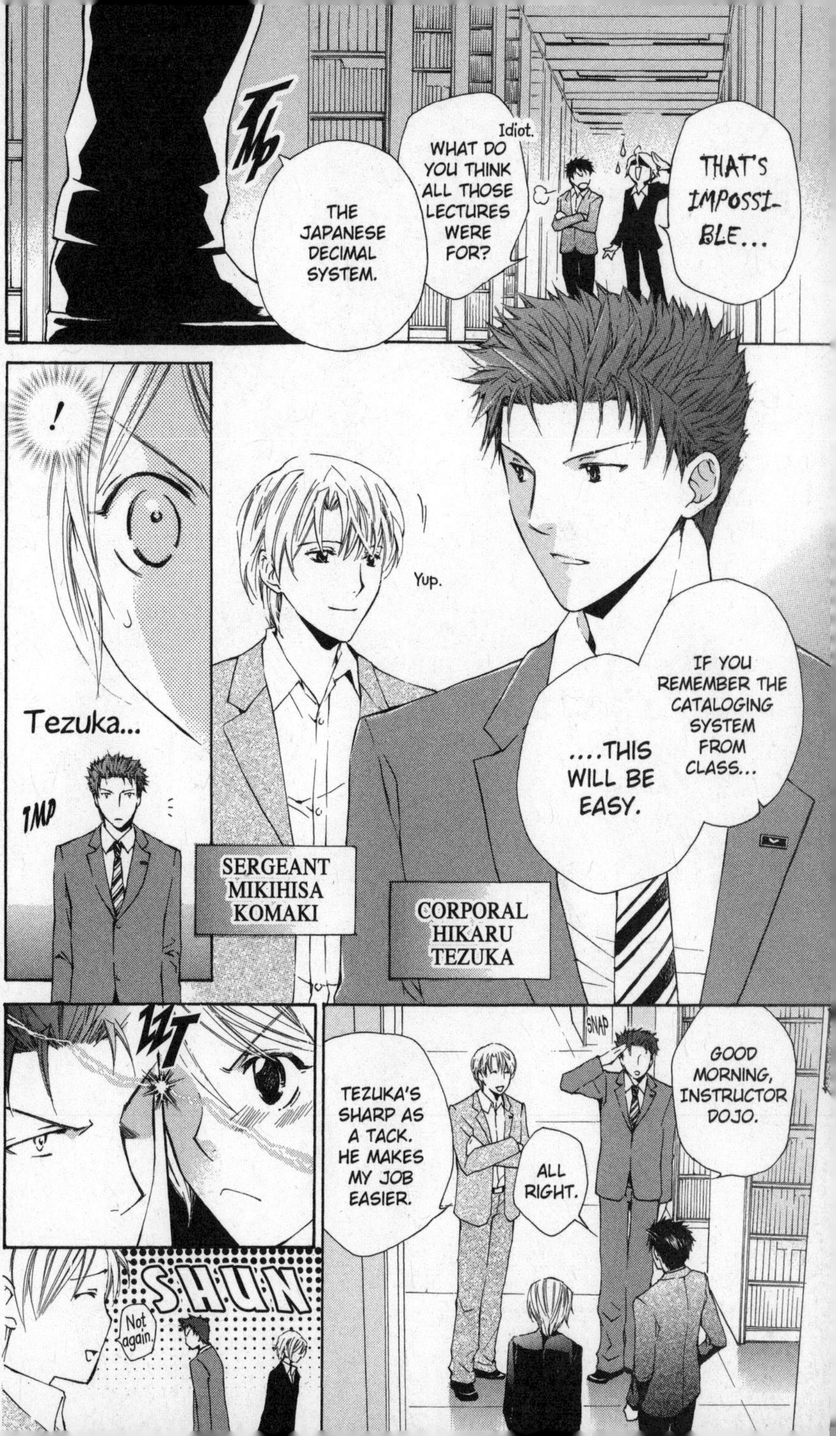
THAT'S IMPOSSI-BLE...
Idiot.
WHAT DO YOU THINK ALL THOSE LECTURES WERE FOR?
THE JAPANESE DECIMAL SYSTEM.
TMP
IF YOU REMEMBER THE CATALOGING SYSTEM FROM CLASS...
....THIS WILL BE EASY.
Yup.
CORPORAL HIKARU TEZUKA
SERGEANT MIKIHISA KOMAKI
!
Tezuka...
TMP
SNAP
GOOD MORNING, INSTRUCTOR DOJO.
ALL RIGHT.
TEZUKA'S SHARP AS A TACK. HE MAKES MY JOB EASIER.
ZZT
SHUN
Not again.

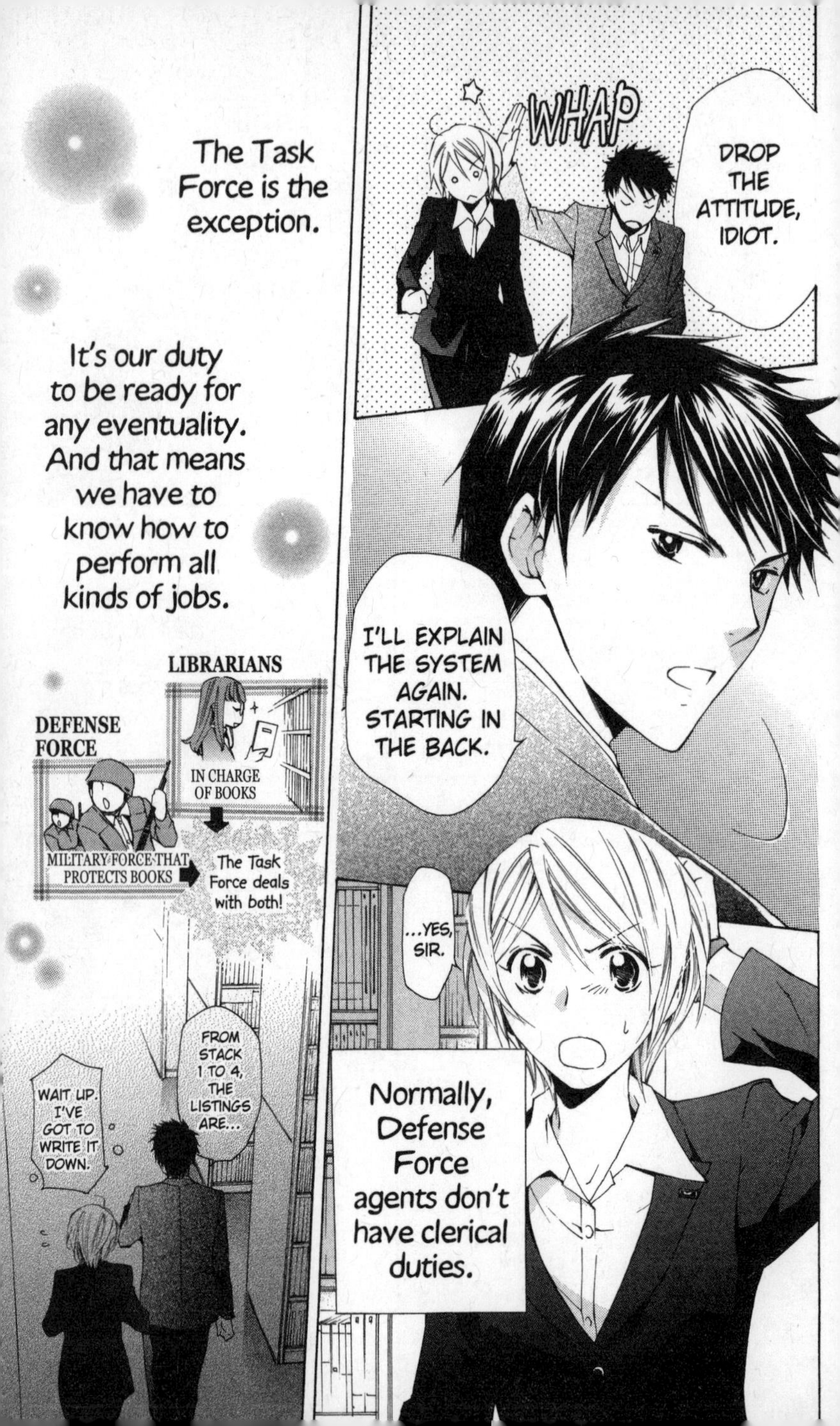
WHAP
DROP THE ATTITUDE, IDIOT.
I'LL EXPLAIN THE SYSTEM AGAIN. STARTING IN THE BACK.
...YES, SIR.
Normally, Defense Force agents don't have clerical duties.
The Task Force is the exception.
It's our duty to be ready for any eventuality. And that means we have to know how to perform all kinds of jobs.
LIBRARIANS
IN CHARGE OF BOOKS
DEFENSE FORCE
MILITARY FORCE THAT PROTECTS BOOKS
The Task Force deals with both!
FROM STACK 1 TO 4, THE LISTINGS ARE...
WAIT UP. I'VE GOT TO WRITE IT DOWN.

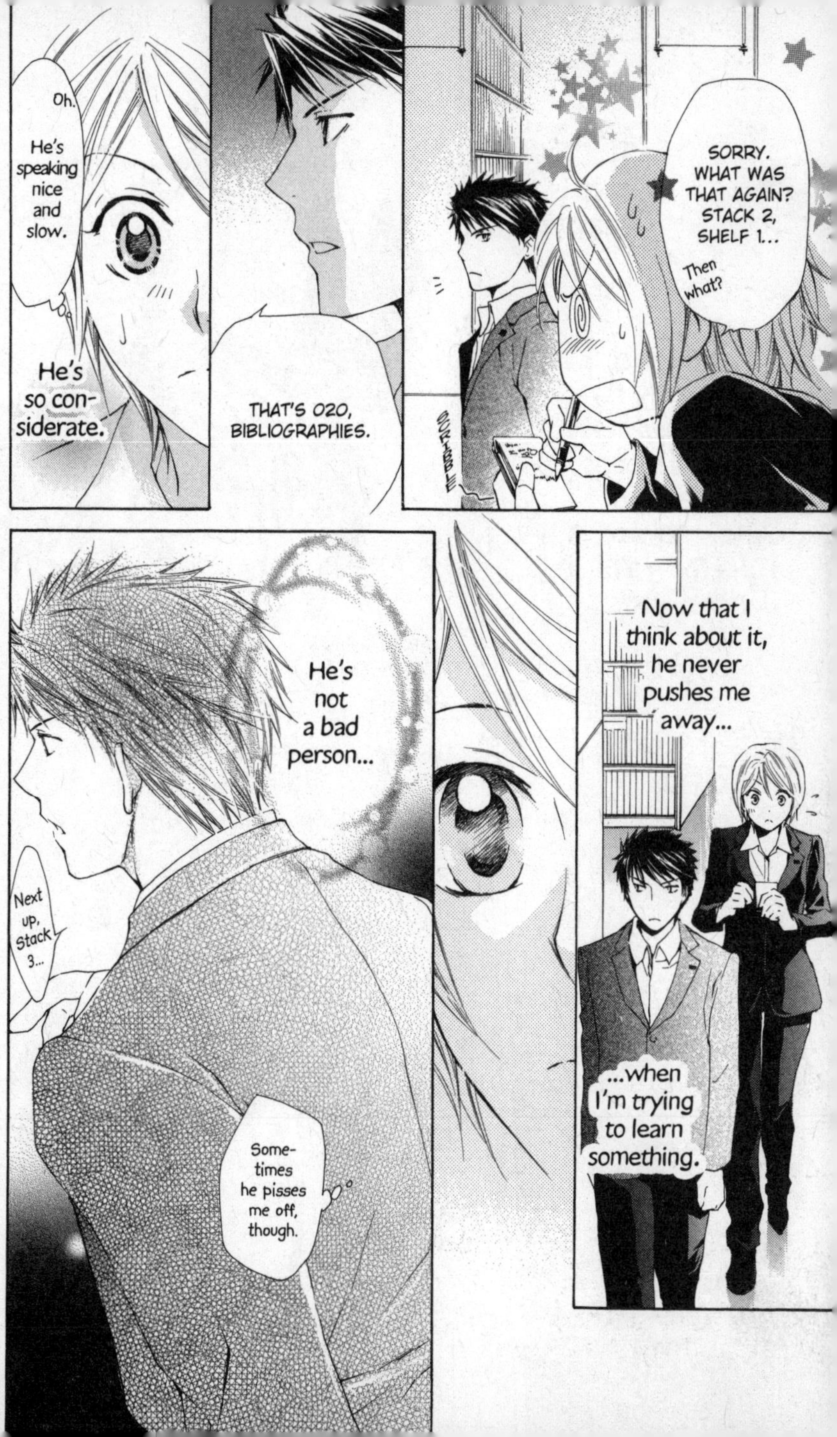
SORRY. WHAT WAS THAT AGAIN? STACK 2, SHELF 1...
Then what?
SCRIBBLE
THAT'S 020, BIBLIOGRAPHIES.
Oh.
He's speaking nice and slow.
He's so considerate.
Now that I think about it, he never pushes me away...
...when I'm trying to learn something.
He's not a bad person...
Next up, Stack 3...
Sometimes he pisses me off, though.

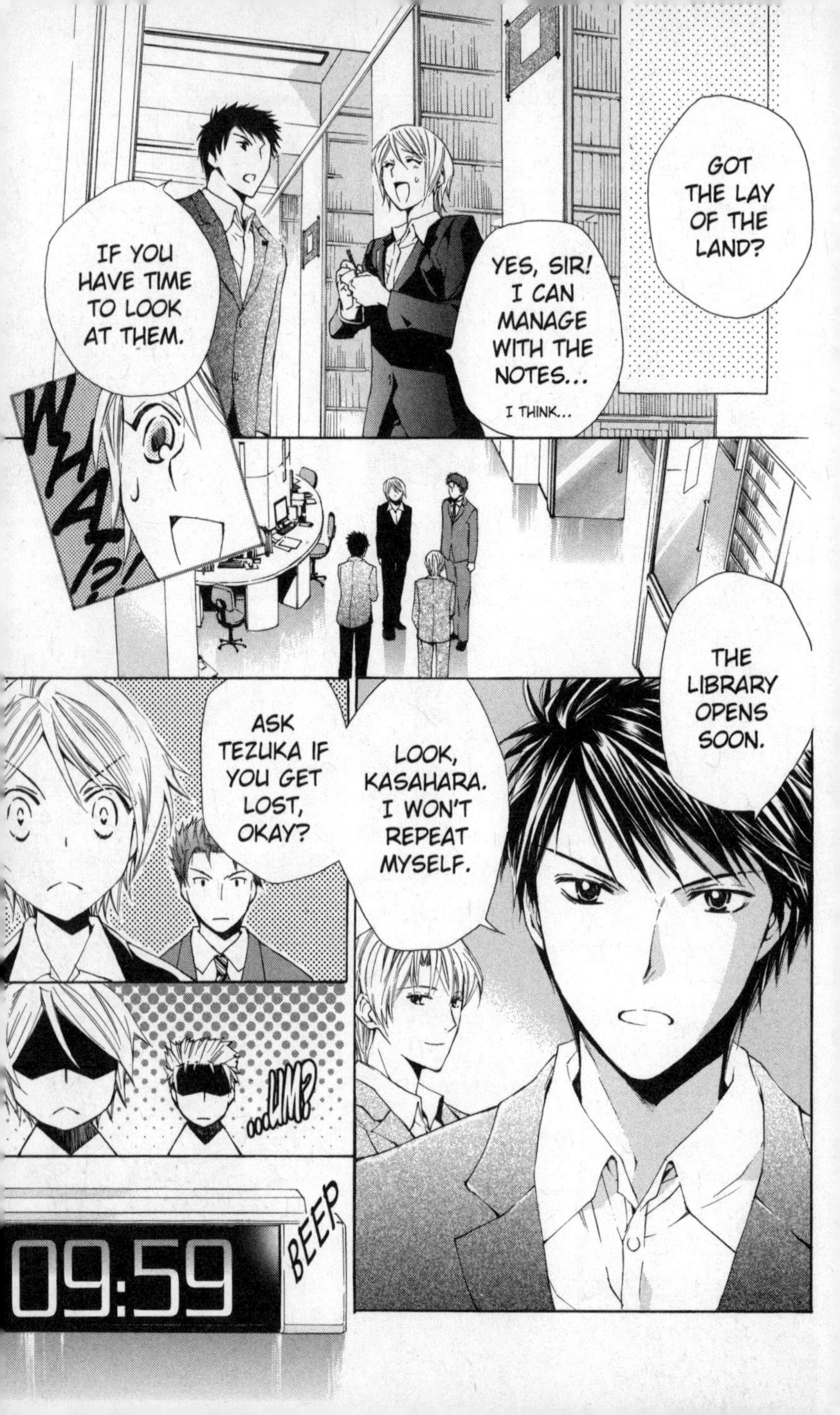
GOT THE LAY OF THE LAND?
YES, SIR! I CAN MANAGE WITH THE NOTES...
I THINK...
IF YOU HAVE TIME TO LOOK AT THEM.
WHAT?!
THE LIBRARY OPENS SOON.
LOOK, KASAHARA. I WON'T REPEAT MYSELF.
ASK TEZUKA IF YOU GET LOST, OKAY?
BEEP
09:59

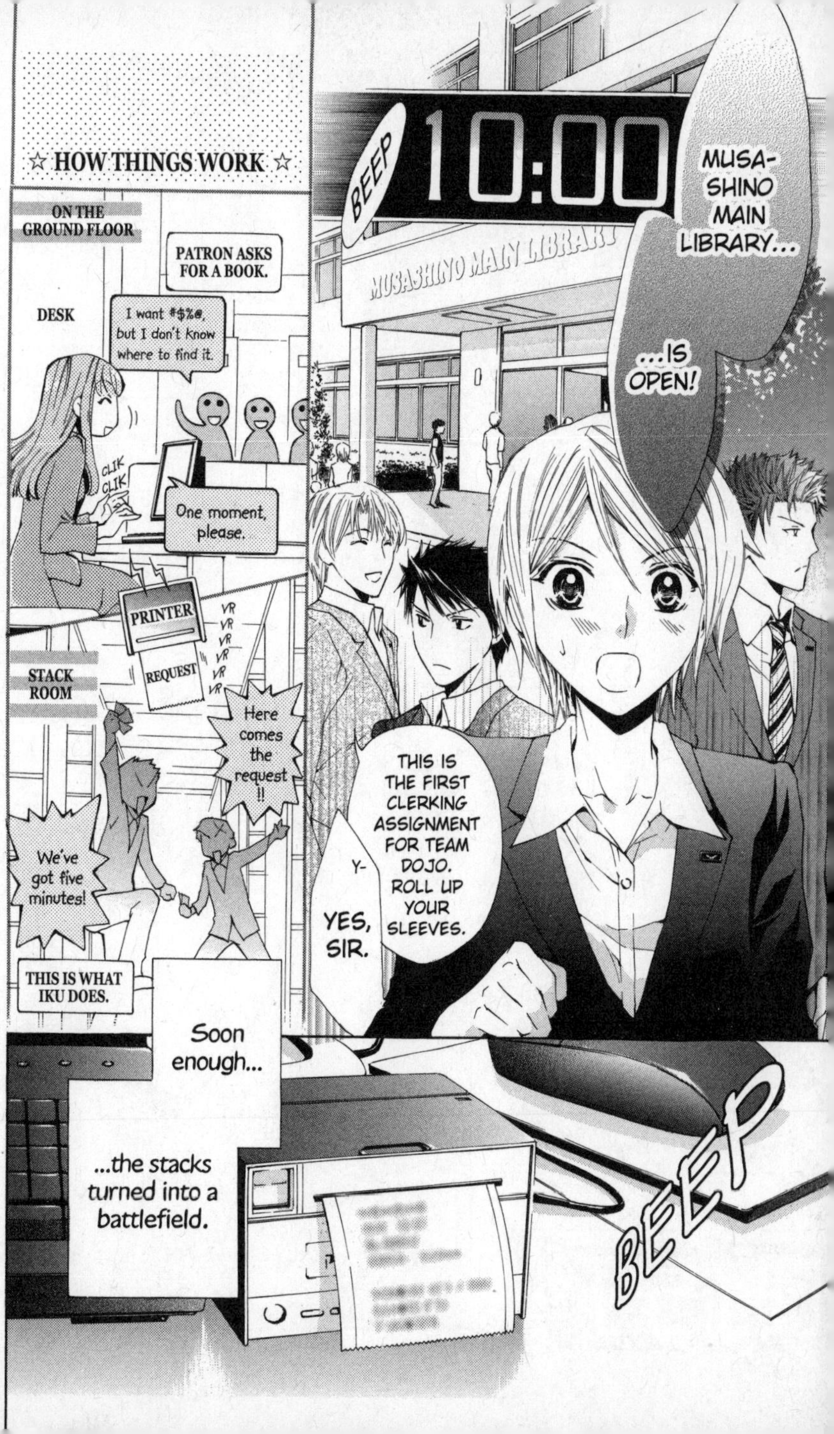
BEEP
10:00
MUSASHINO MAIN LIBRARY
MUSA-SHINO MAIN LIBRARY...
...IS OPEN!
THIS IS THE FIRST CLERKING ASSIGNMENT FOR TEAM DOJO. ROLL UP YOUR SLEEVES.
Y-
YES, SIR.
☆ HOW THINGS WORK ☆
ON THE GROUND FLOOR
PATRON ASKS FOR A BOOK.
DESK
I want #$%@, but I don't know where to find it.
CLIK CLIK
One moment, please.
PRINTER
REQUEST
VR VR VR VR VR VR
STACK ROOM
Here comes the request !!
We've got five minutes!
THIS IS WHAT IKU DOES.
Soon enough...
...the stacks turned into a battlefield.
BEEP

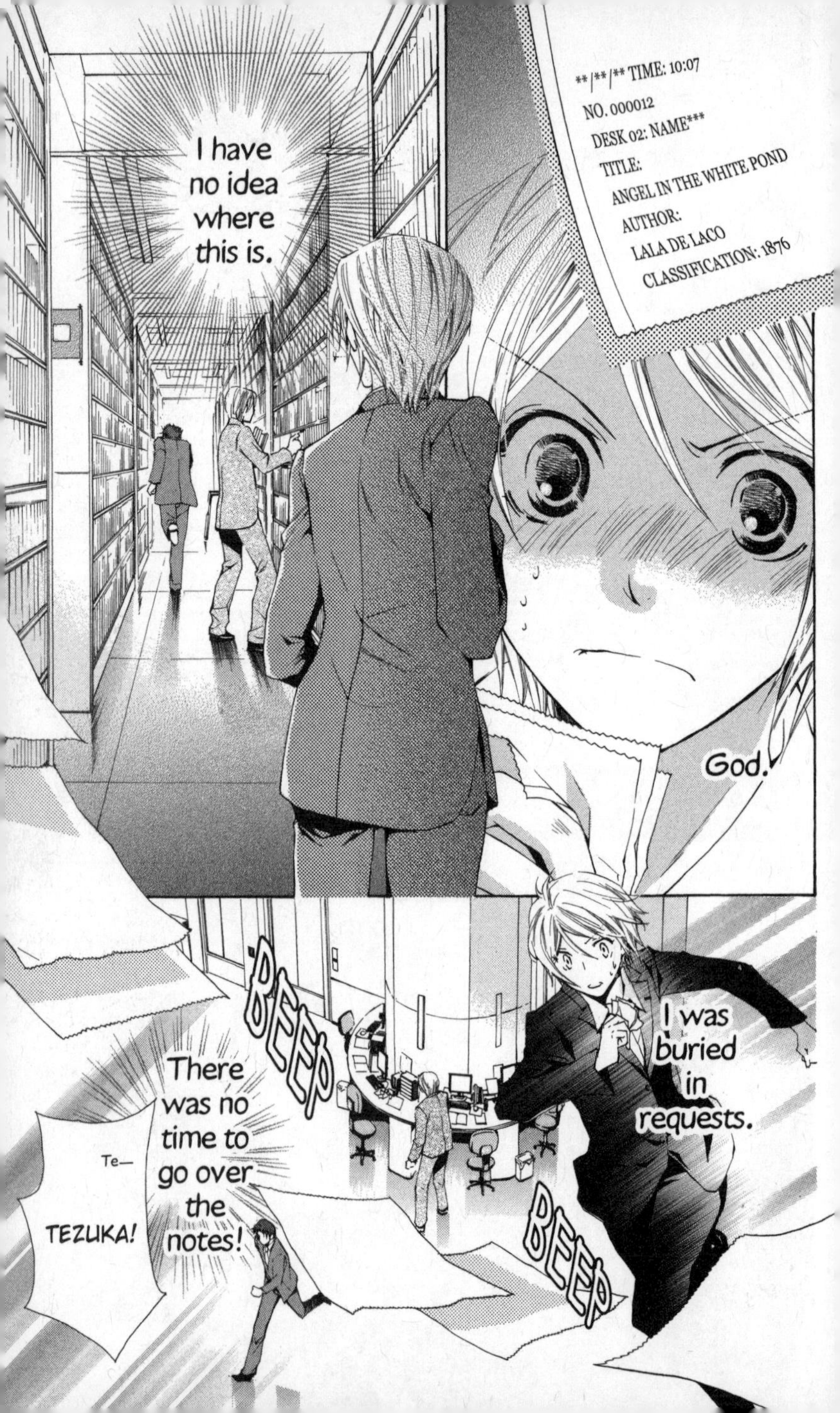
//** TIME: 10:07
NO. 000012
DESK 02: NAME***
TITLE:
ANGEL IN THE WHITE POND
AUTHOR:
LALA DE LACO
CLASSIFICATION: 1876
God.
I have no idea where this is.
I was buried in requests.
BEEP
BEEP
There was no time to go over the notes!
Te—
TEZUKA!

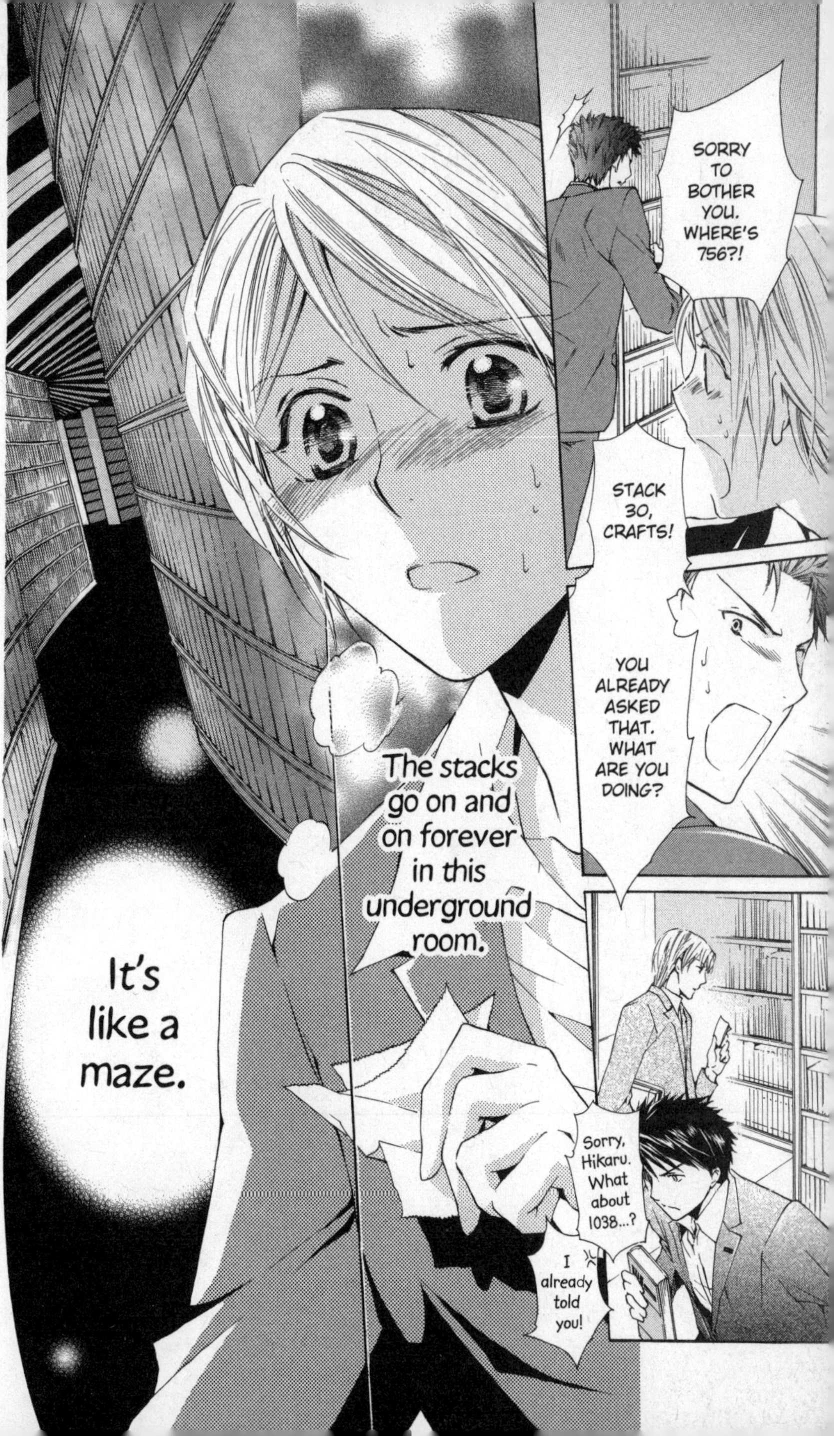
SORRY TO BOTHER YOU. WHERE'S 756?!
STACK 30, CRAFTS!
YOU ALREADY ASKED THAT. WHAT ARE YOU DOING?
Sorry, Hikaru. What about 1038...?
I already told you!
The stacks go on and on forever in this underground room.
It's like a maze.

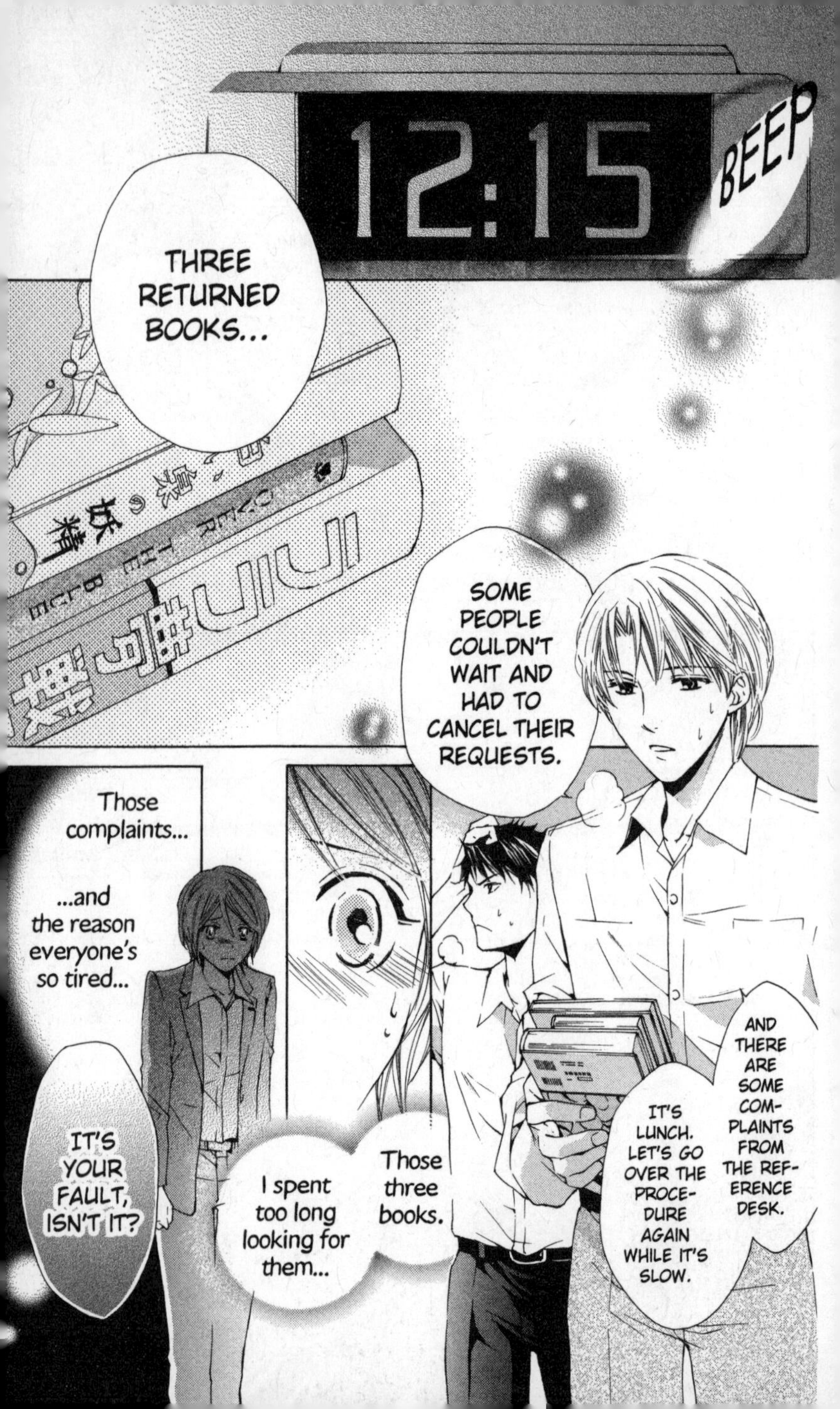
12:15
BEEP
THREE RETURNED BOOKS...
OVER THE BLUE
SOME PEOPLE COULDN'T WAIT AND HAD TO CANCEL THEIR REQUESTS.
AND THERE ARE SOME COM-PLAINTS FROM THE REF-ERENCE DESK.
IT'S LUNCH. LET'S GO OVER THE PROCE-DURE AGAIN WHILE IT'S SLOW.
Those three books.
I spent too long looking for them...
Those complaints...
...and the reason everyone's so tired...
IT'S YOUR FAULT, ISN'T IT?

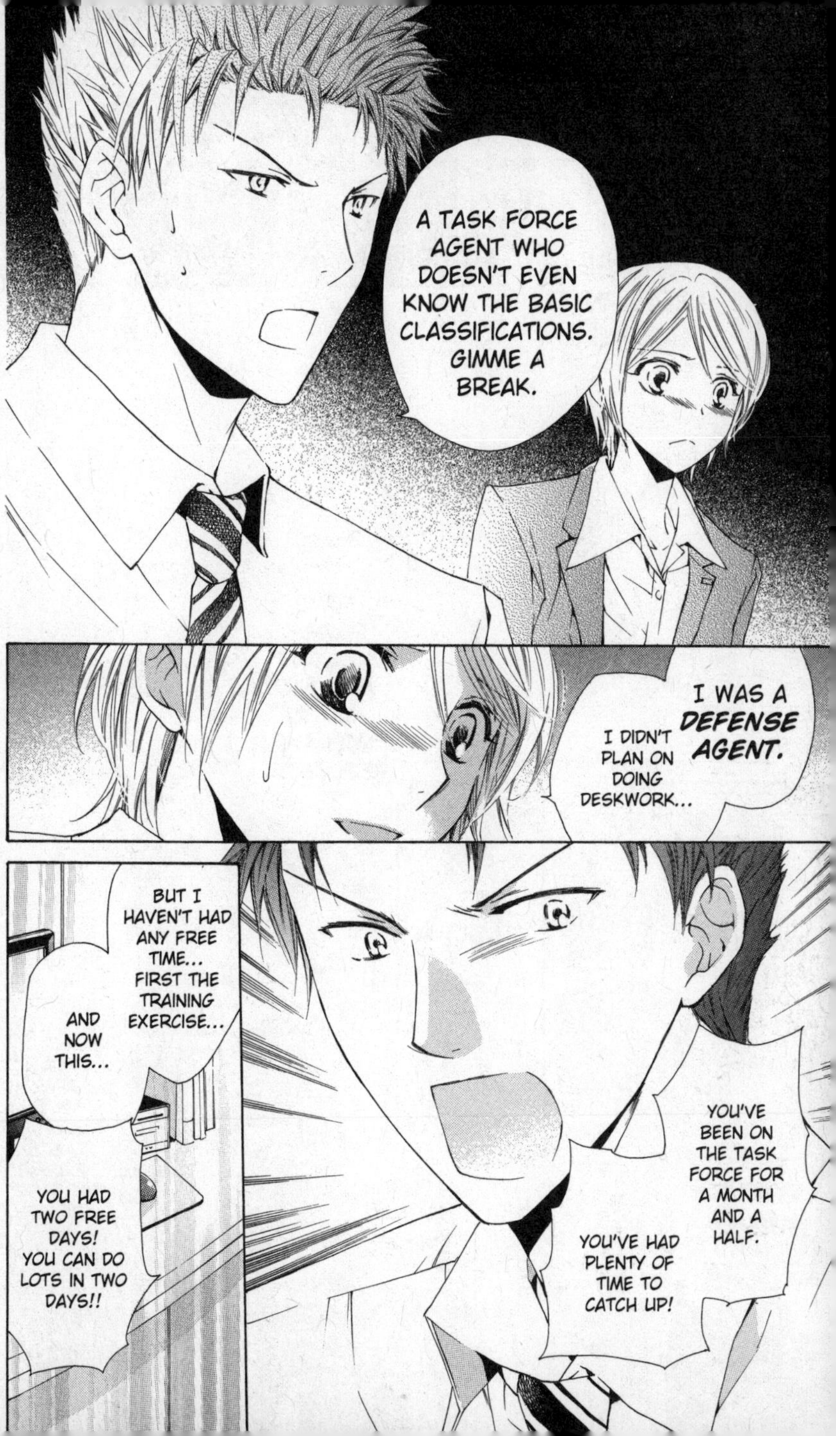
A TASK FORCE AGENT WHO DOESN'T EVEN KNOW THE BASIC CLASSIFICATIONS. GIMME A BREAK.
I WAS A ***DEFENSE AGENT.***
I DIDN'T PLAN ON DOING DESKWORK...
BUT I HAVEN'T HAD ANY FREE TIME... FIRST THE TRAINING EXERCISE...
AND NOW THIS...
YOU'VE BEEN ON THE TASK FORCE FOR A MONTH AND A HALF.
YOU'VE HAD PLENTY OF TIME TO CATCH UP!
YOU HAD TWO FREE DAYS! YOU CAN DO LOTS IN TWO DAYS!!

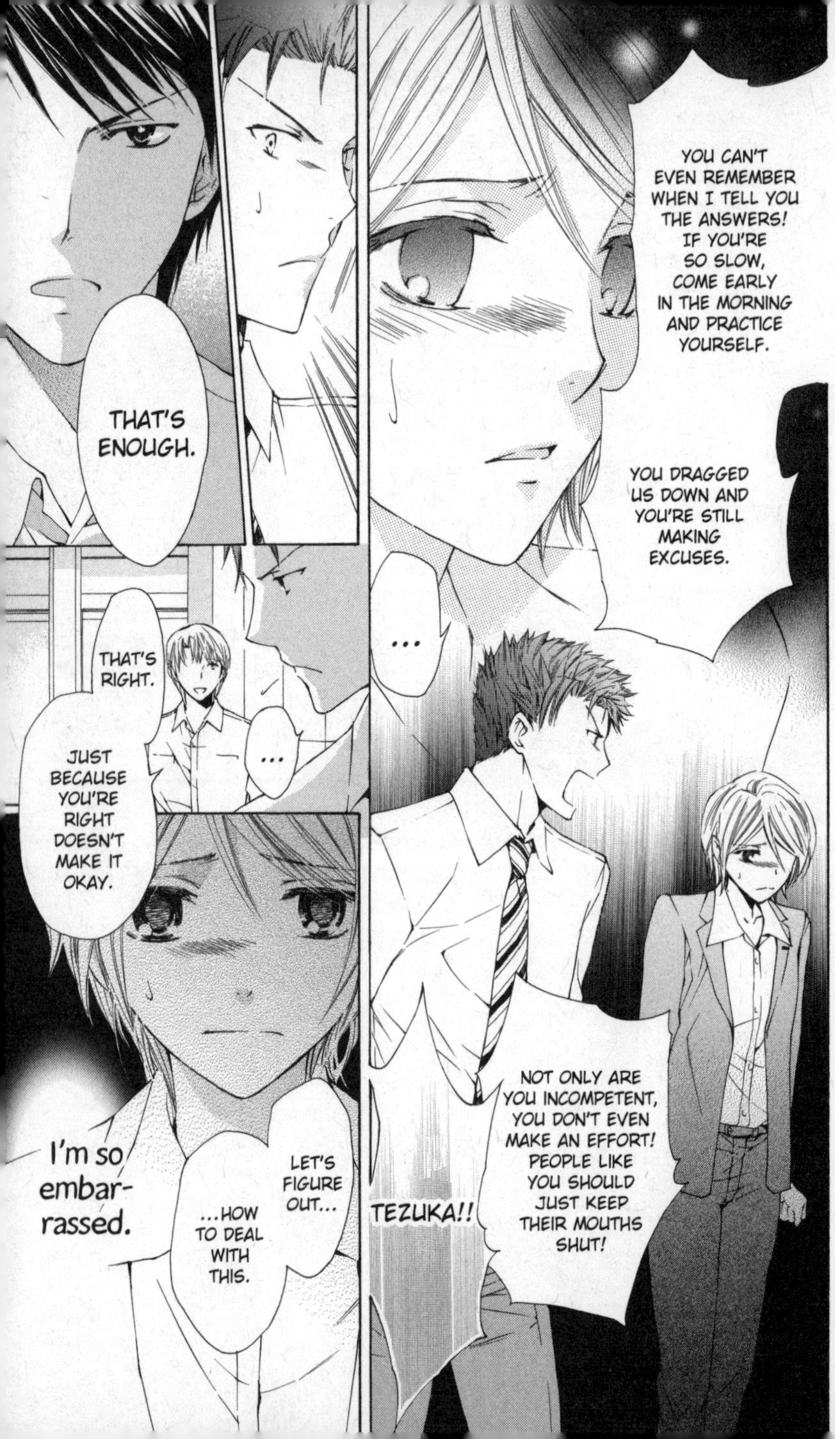
YOU CAN'T EVEN REMEMBER WHEN I TELL YOU THE ANSWERS! IF YOU'RE SO SLOW, COME EARLY IN THE MORNING AND PRACTICE YOURSELF.
YOU DRAGGED US DOWN AND YOU'RE STILL MAKING EXCUSES.
...
NOT ONLY ARE YOU INCOMPETENT, YOU DON'T EVEN MAKE AN EFFORT! PEOPLE LIKE YOU SHOULD JUST KEEP THEIR MOUTHS SHUT!
TEZUKA!!
THAT'S ENOUGH.
THAT'S RIGHT.
...
JUST BECAUSE YOU'RE RIGHT DOESN'T MAKE IT OKAY.
LET'S FIGURE OUT...
...HOW TO DEAL WITH THIS.
I'm so embar-rassed.

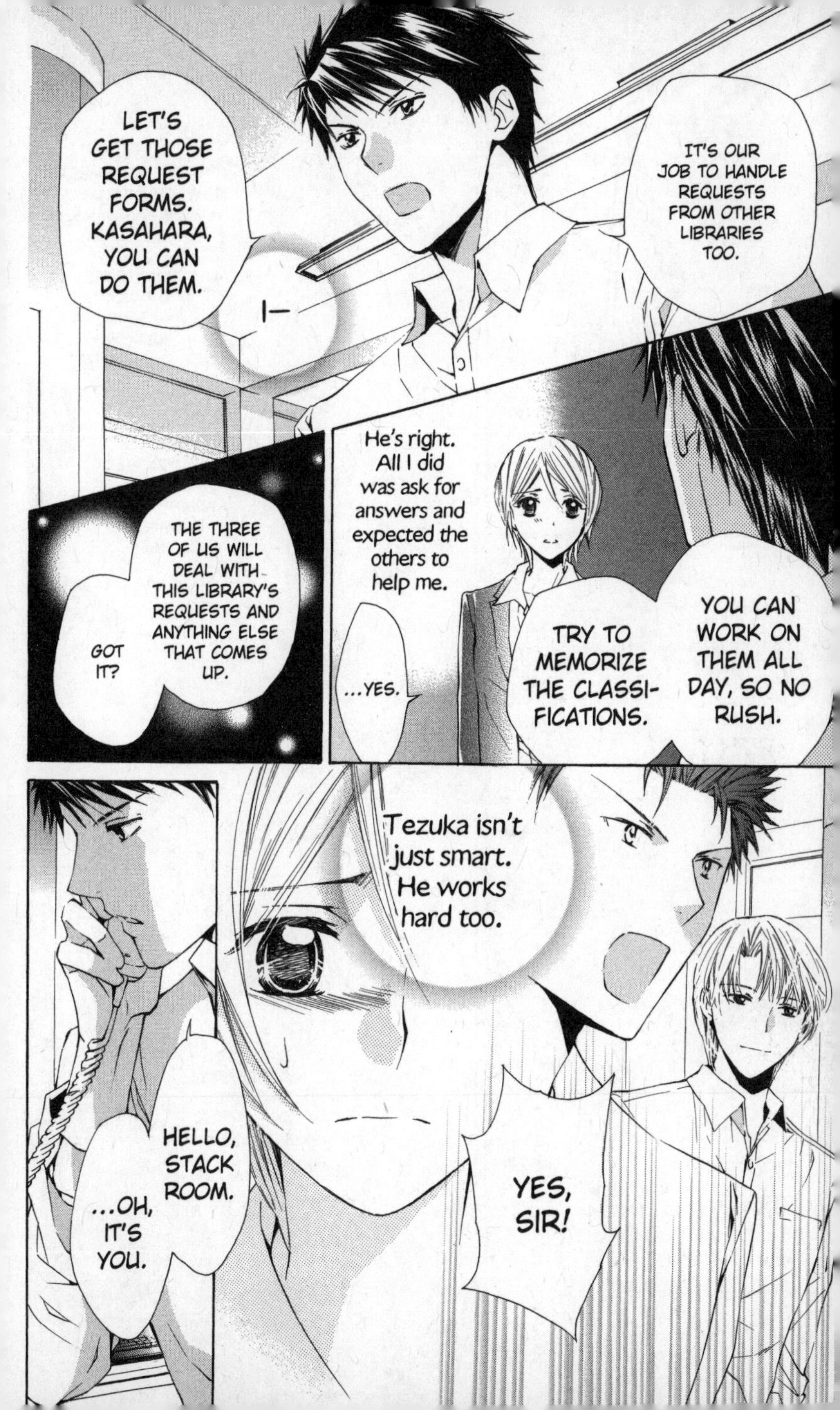
IT'S OUR JOB TO HANDLE REQUESTS FROM OTHER LIBRARIES TOO.
LET'S GET THOSE REQUEST FORMS. KASAHARA, YOU CAN DO THEM.
I—
YOU CAN WORK ON THEM ALL DAY, SO NO RUSH.
TRY TO MEMORIZE THE CLASSIFICATIONS.
He's right. All I did was ask for answers and expected the others to help me.
...YES.
THE THREE OF US WILL DEAL WITH THIS LIBRARY'S REQUESTS AND ANYTHING ELSE THAT COMES UP.
GOT IT?
Tezuka isn't just smart. He works hard too.
YES, SIR!
HELLO, STACK ROOM.
...OH, IT'S YOU.

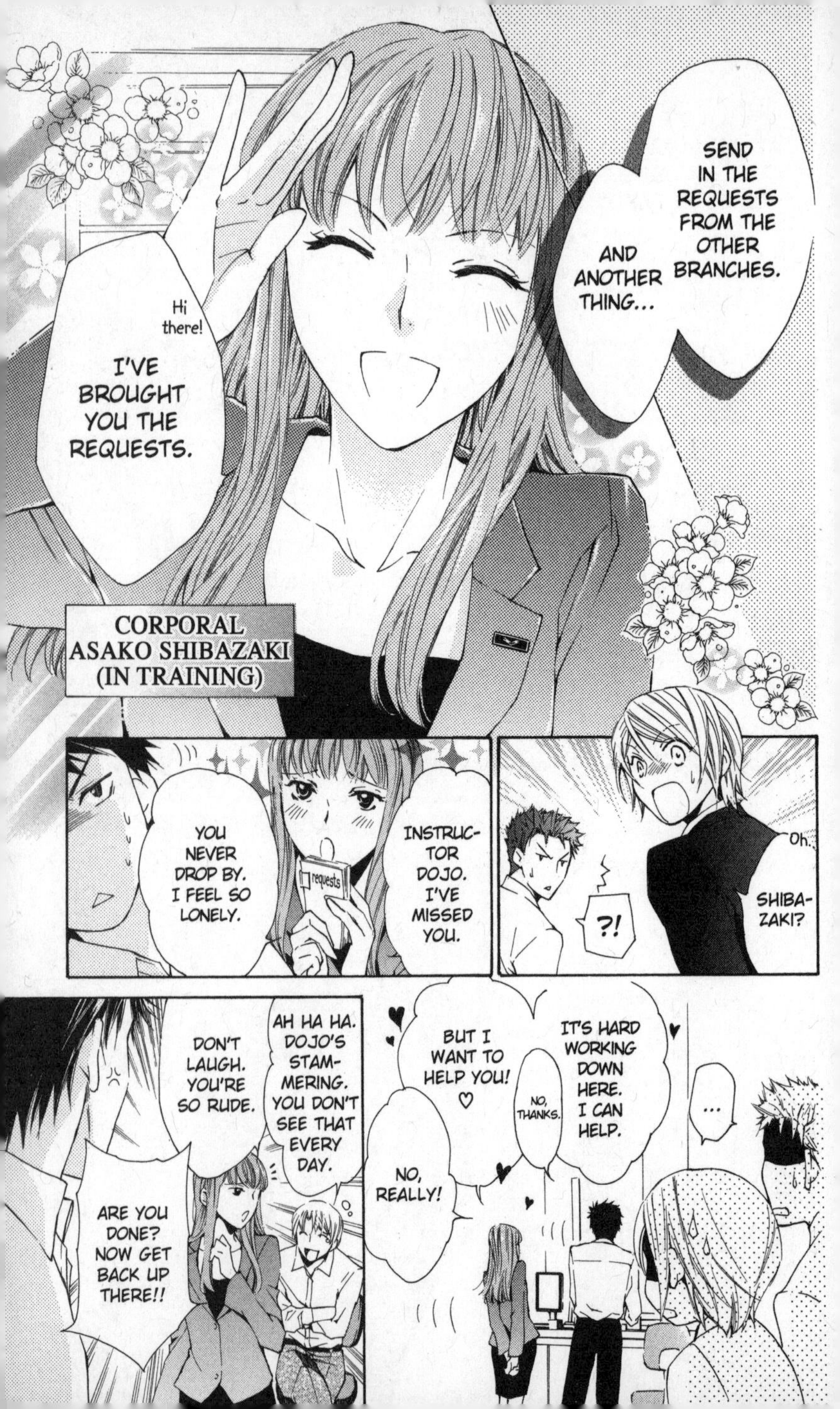
SEND IN THE REQUESTS FROM THE OTHER BRANCHES.
AND ANOTHER THING...
Hi there!
I'VE BROUGHT YOU THE REQUESTS.
CORPORAL ASAKO SHIBAZAKI (IN TRAINING)
Oh.
SHIBA-ZAKI?
?!
INSTRUC-TOR DOJO. I'VE MISSED YOU.
requests
YOU NEVER DROP BY. I FEEL SO LONELY.
...
IT'S HARD WORKING DOWN HERE. I CAN HELP.
NO, THANKS.
BUT I WANT TO HELP YOU! ♡
NO, REALLY!
AH HA HA. DOJO'S STAM-MERING. YOU DON'T SEE THAT EVERY DAY.
DON'T LAUGH. YOU'RE SO RUDE.
ARE YOU DONE? NOW GET BACK UP THERE!!

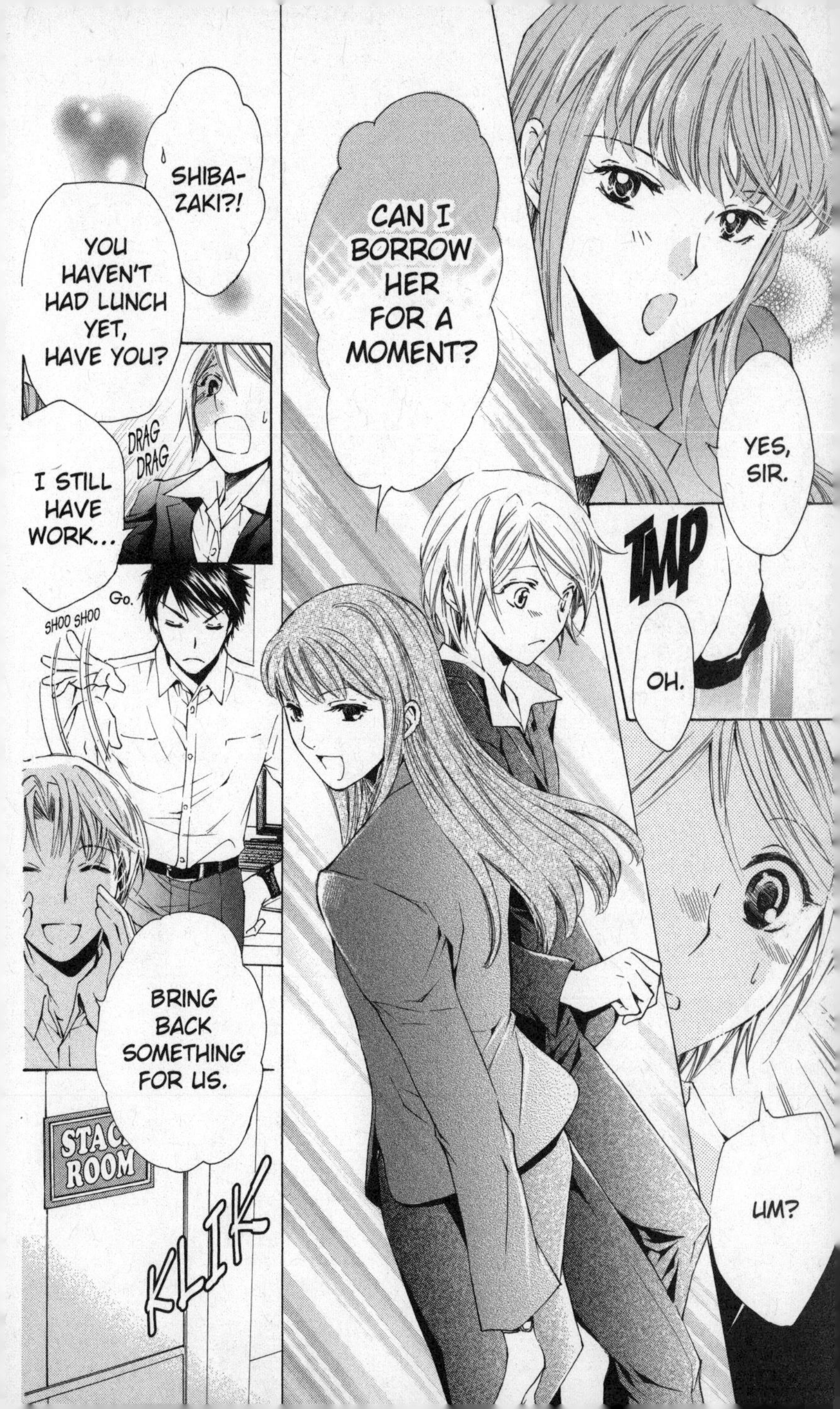
YES, SIR.
TMP
OH.
UM?
CAN I BORROW HER FOR A MOMENT?
SHIBA-ZAKI?!
YOU HAVEN'T HAD LUNCH YET, HAVE YOU?
DRAG DRAG
I STILL HAVE WORK...
Go.
SHOO SHOO
BRING BACK SOMETHING FOR US.
STAC ROOM
KLIK

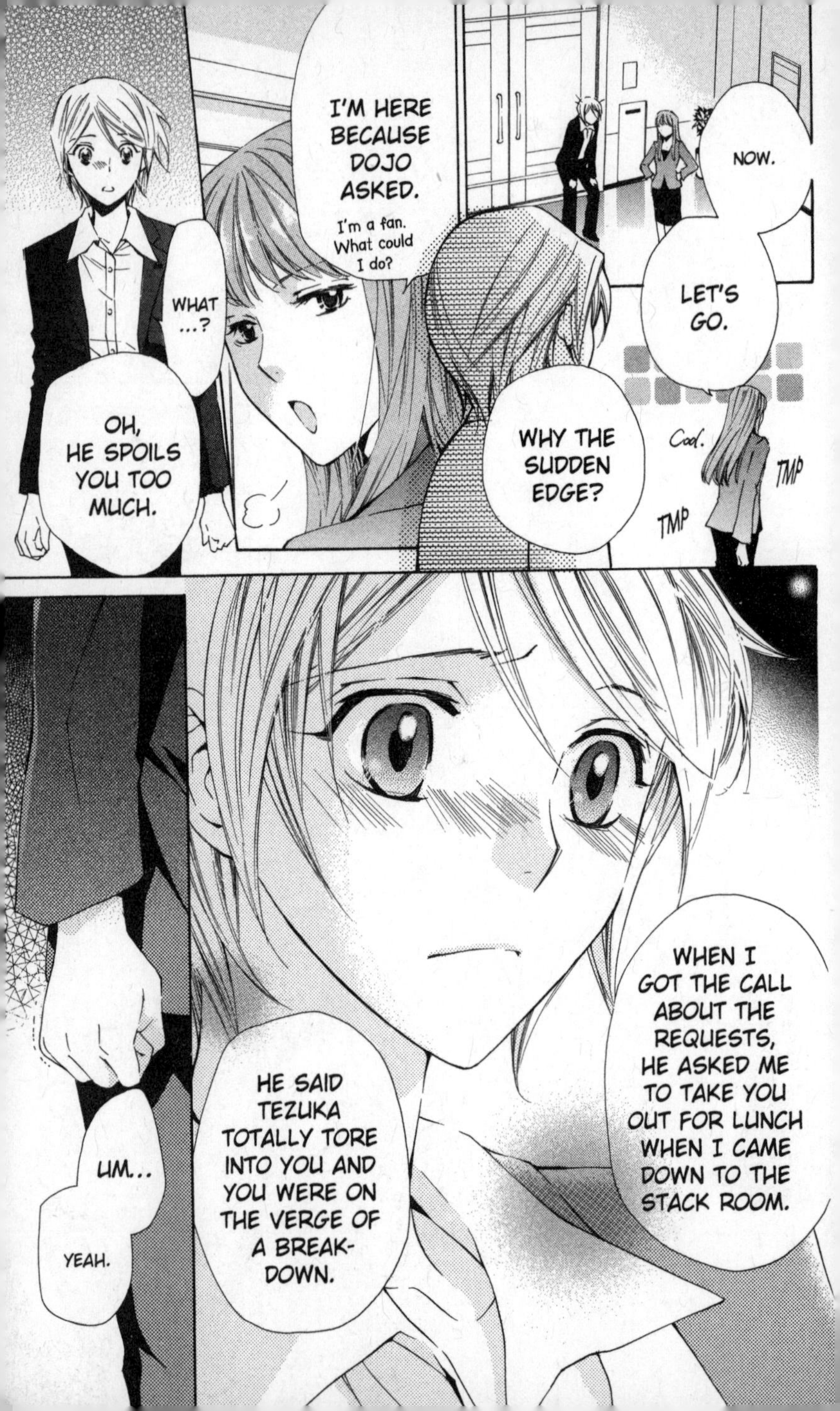
NOW.
LET'S GO.
Cool.
TMP
TMP
I'M HERE BECAUSE DOJO ASKED.
I'm a fan. What could I do?
WHY THE SUDDEN EDGE?
WHAT ...?
OH, HE SPOILS YOU TOO MUCH.
WHEN I GOT THE CALL ABOUT THE REQUESTS, HE ASKED ME TO TAKE YOU OUT FOR LUNCH WHEN I CAME DOWN TO THE STACK ROOM.
HE SAID TEZUKA TOTALLY TORE INTO YOU AND YOU WERE ON THE VERGE OF A BREAK-DOWN.
UM...
YEAH.

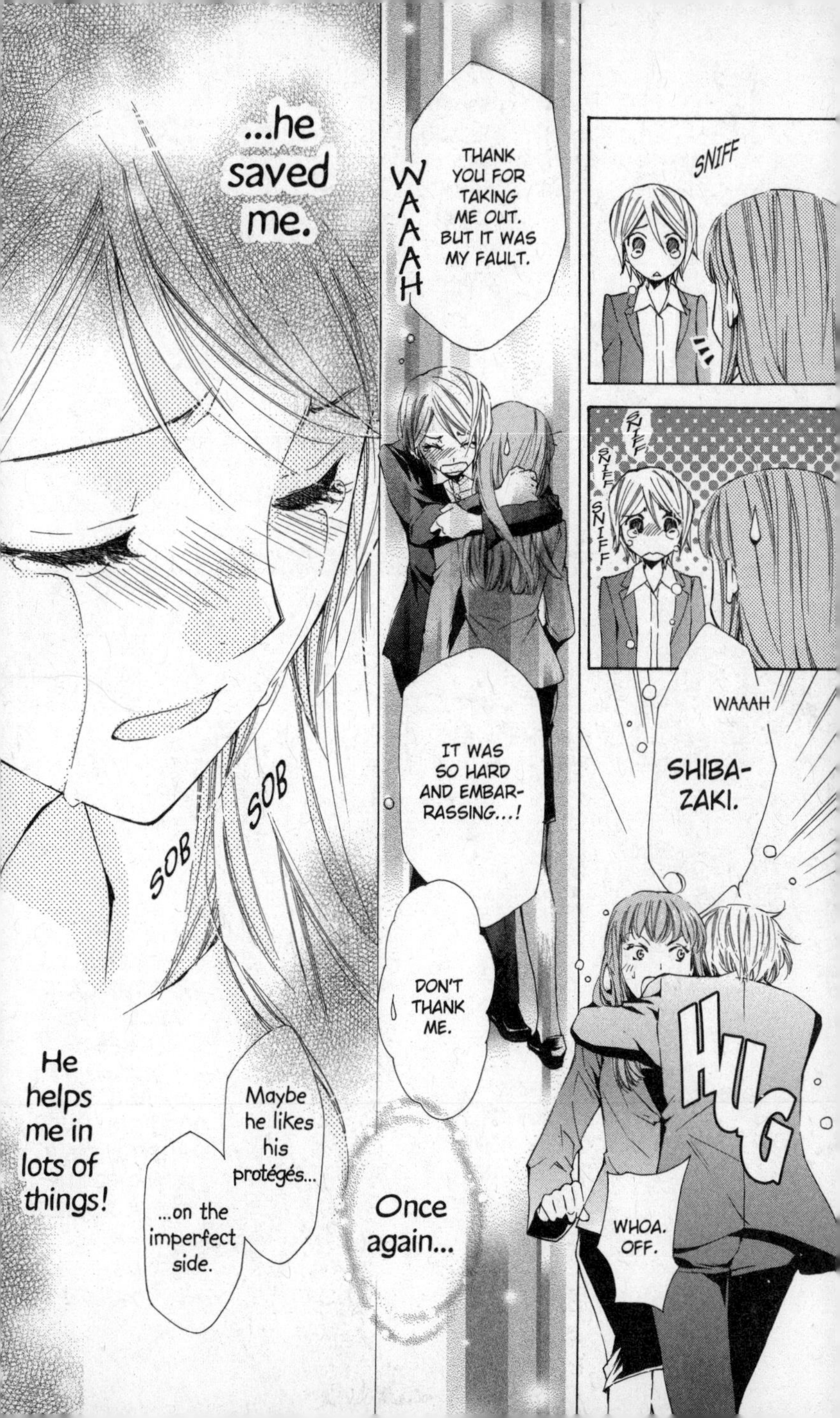
SNIFF
SNIFF
SNIFF
SNIFF
WAAAH
SHIBA-ZAKI.
HUG
WHOA. OFF.
WAAAH
THANK YOU FOR TAKING ME OUT. BUT IT WAS MY FAULT.
IT WAS SO HARD AND EMBAR-RASSING...!
DON'T THANK ME.
Once again...
...he saved me.
SOB
SOB
Maybe he likes his protégés...
...on the imperfect side.
He helps me in lots of things!

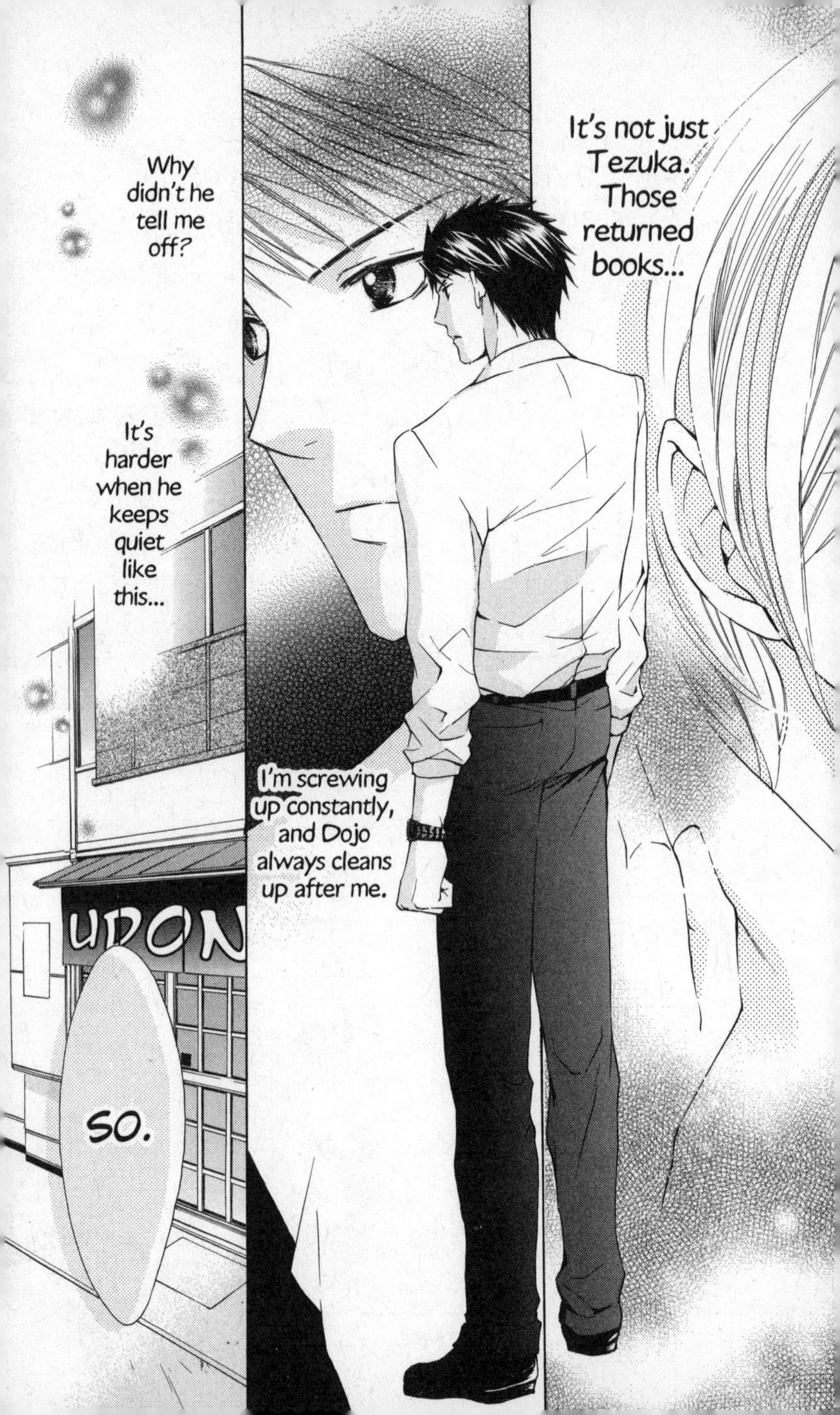
It's not just Tezuka. Those returned books...
I'm screwing up constantly, and Dojo always cleans up after me.
Why didn't he tell me off?
It's harder when he keeps quiet like this...
UDON
SO.

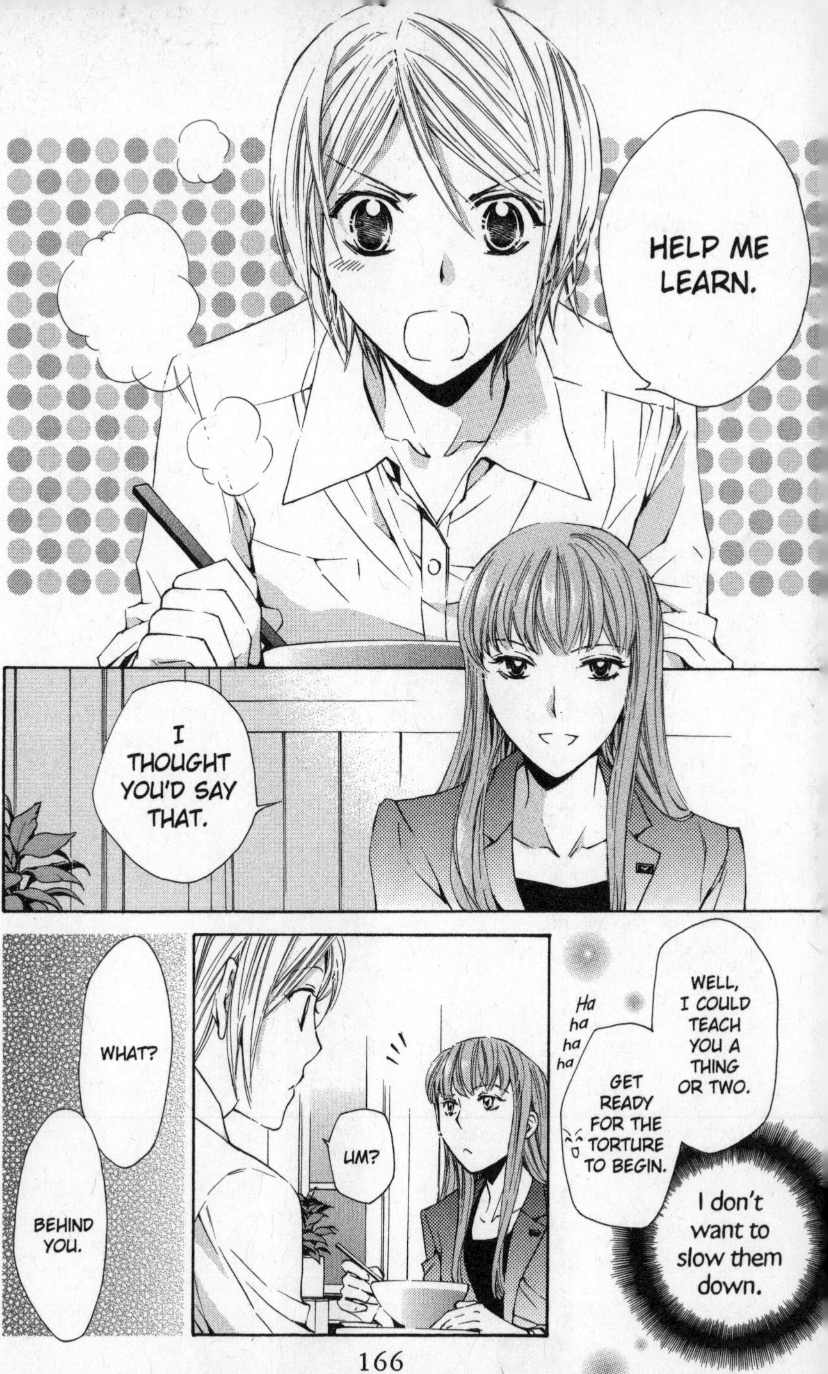
HELP ME LEARN.
I THOUGHT YOU'D SAY THAT.
WELL, I COULD TEACH YOU A THING OR TWO.
Ha ha ha ha
GET READY FOR THE TORTURE TO BEGIN.
I don't want to slow them down.
UM?
WHAT?
BEHIND YOU.

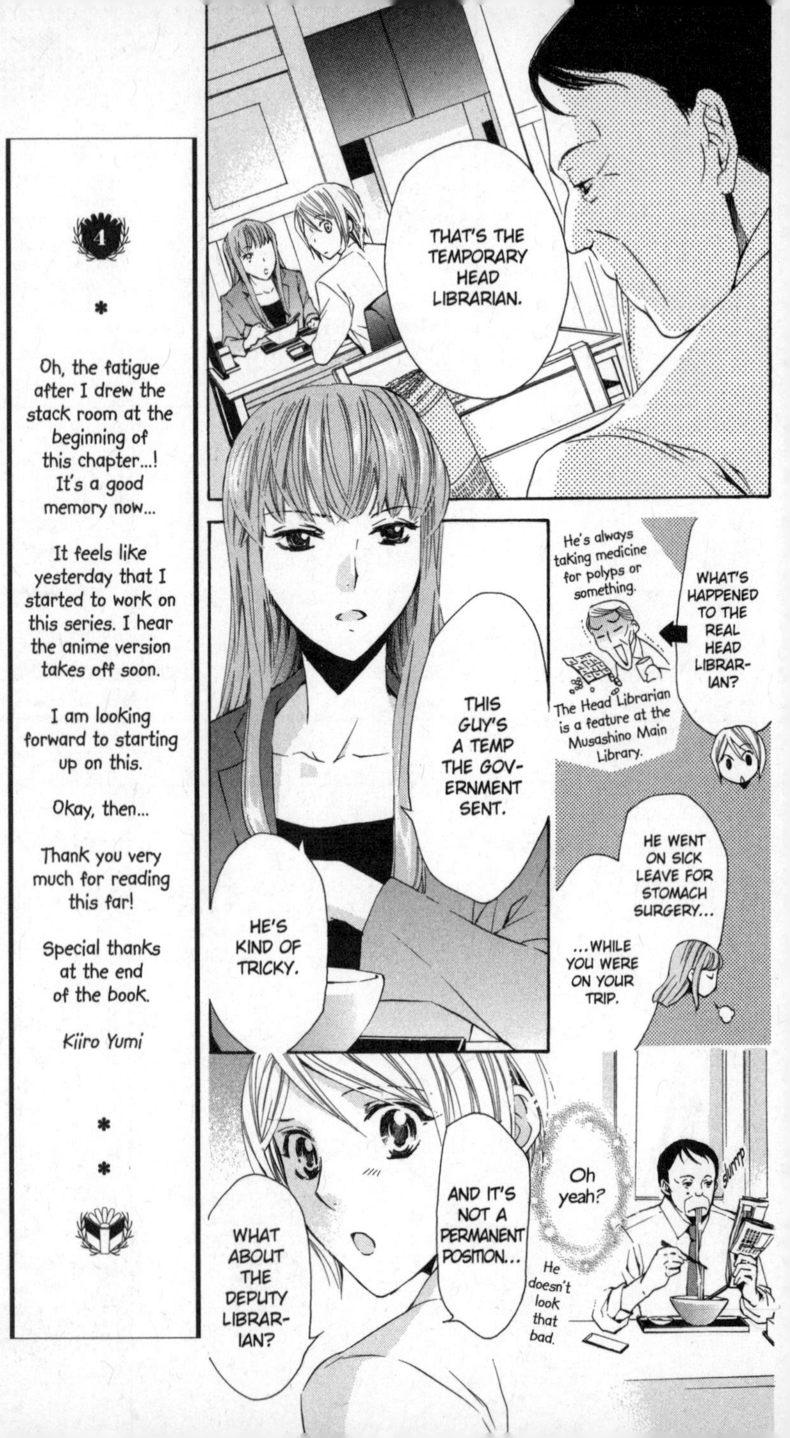
THAT'S THE TEMPORARY HEAD LIBRARIAN.
WHAT'S HAPPENED TO THE REAL HEAD LIBRARIAN?
He's always taking medicine for polyps or something.
The Head Librarian is a feature at the Musashino Main Library.
HE WENT ON SICK LEAVE FOR STOMACH SURGERY...
...WHILE YOU WERE ON YOUR TRIP.
THIS GUY'S A TEMP THE GOV-ERNMENT SENT.
HE'S KIND OF TRICKY.
Oh yeah?
He doesn't look that bad.
slurrrp
AND IT'S NOT A PERMANENT POSITION...
WHAT ABOUT THE DEPUTY LIBRAR-IAN?

4

*

Oh, the fatigue after I drew the stack room at the beginning of this chapter...! It's a good memory now...

It feels like yesterday that I started to work on this series. I hear the anime version takes off soon.

I am looking forward to starting up on this.

Okay, then...

Thank you very much for reading this far!

Special thanks at the end of the book.

Kiiro Yumi

*

*

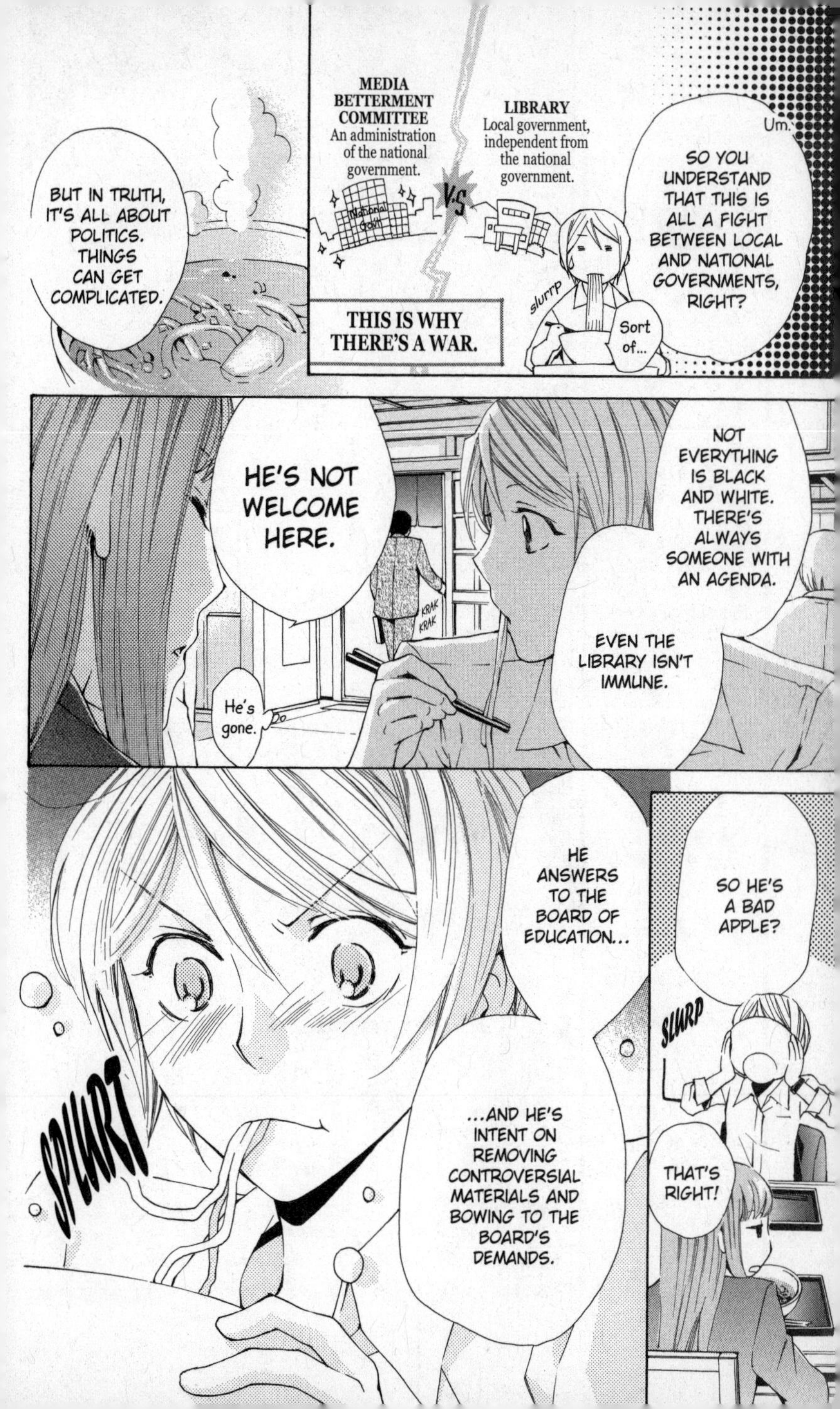

Um.
SO YOU UNDERSTAND THAT THIS IS ALL A FIGHT BETWEEN LOCAL AND NATIONAL GOVERNMENTS, RIGHT?
MEDIA BETTERMENT COMMITTEE
An administration of the national government.
National Gov't
VS
LIBRARY
Local government, independent from the national government.
slurrp
Sort of...
THIS IS WHY THERE'S A WAR.
BUT IN TRUTH, IT'S ALL ABOUT POLITICS. THINGS CAN GET COMPLICATED.
NOT EVERYTHING IS BLACK AND WHITE. THERE'S ALWAYS SOMEONE WITH AN AGENDA.
EVEN THE LIBRARY ISN'T IMMUNE.
HE'S NOT WELCOME HERE.
KRAK KRAK
He's gone.
SO HE'S A BAD APPLE?
SLURP
THAT'S RIGHT!
HE ANSWERS TO THE BOARD OF EDUCATION...
...AND HE'S INTENT ON REMOVING CONTROVERSIAL MATERIALS AND BOWING TO THE BOARD'S DEMANDS.
SPLURT

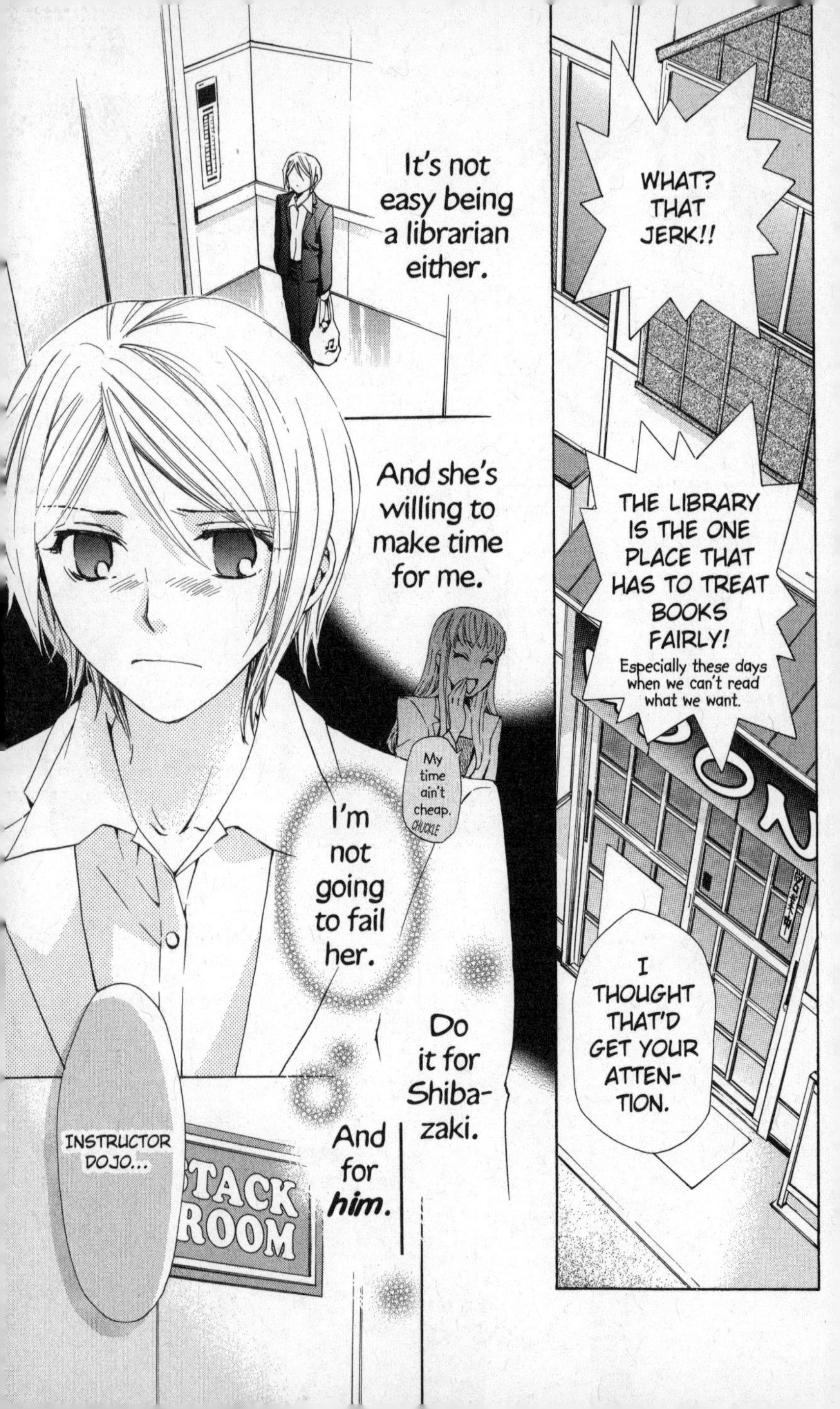
WHAT? THAT JERK!!
THE LIBRARY IS THE ONE PLACE THAT HAS TO TREAT BOOKS FAIRLY!
Especially these days when we can't read what we want.
I THOUGHT THAT'D GET YOUR ATTEN-TION.
It's not easy being a librarian either.
And she's willing to make time for me.
My time ain't cheap.
CHUCKLE
I'm not going to fail her.
Do it for Shiba-zaki.
And for *him*.
INSTRUCTOR DOJO...
STACK ROOM

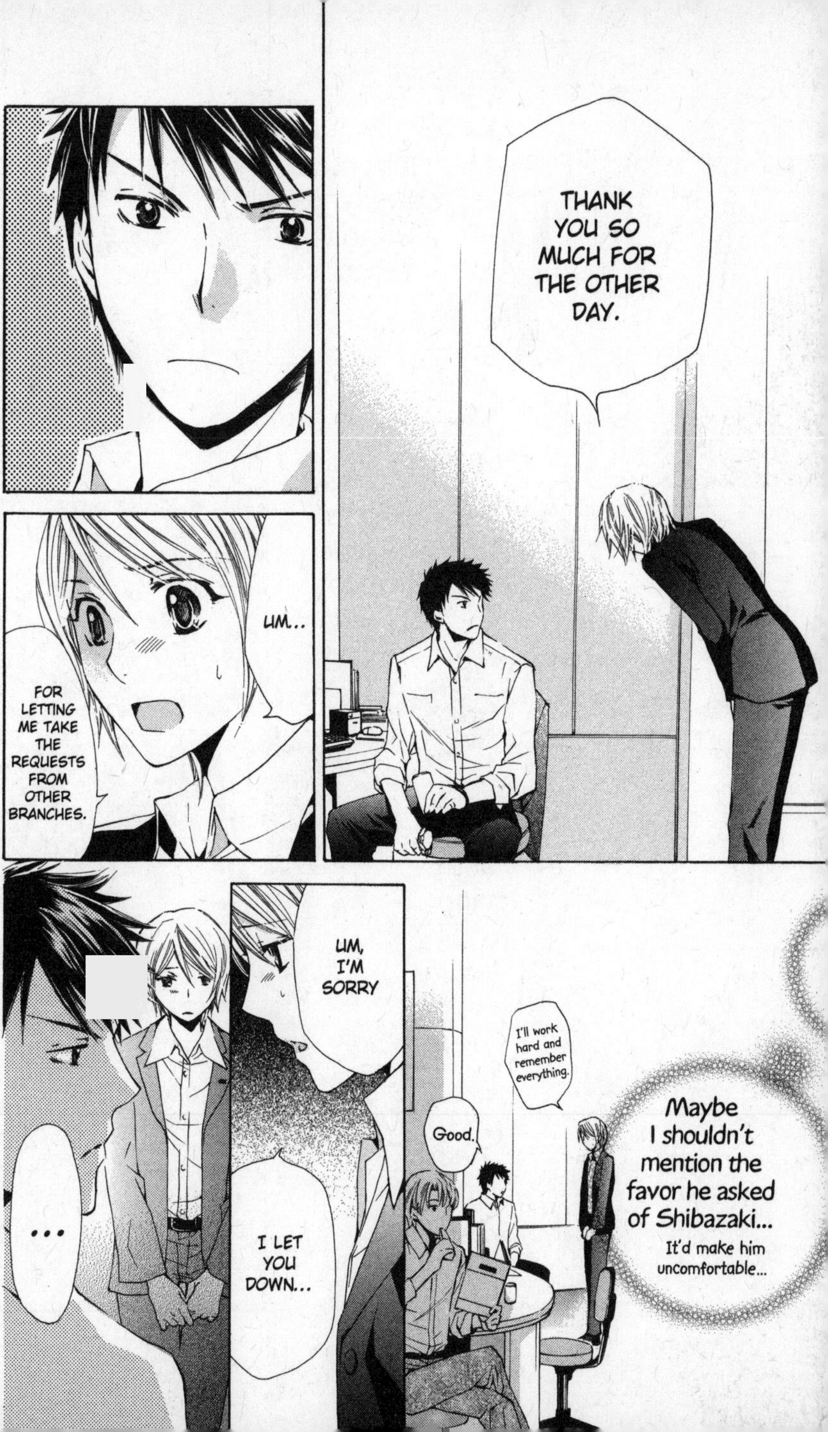
THANK YOU SO MUCH FOR THE OTHER DAY.
UM...
FOR LETTING ME TAKE THE REQUESTS FROM OTHER BRANCHES.
Maybe I shouldn't mention the favor he asked of Shibazaki...
It'd make him uncomfortable...
I'll work hard and remember everything.
Good.
UM, I'M SORRY
I LET YOU DOWN...
...

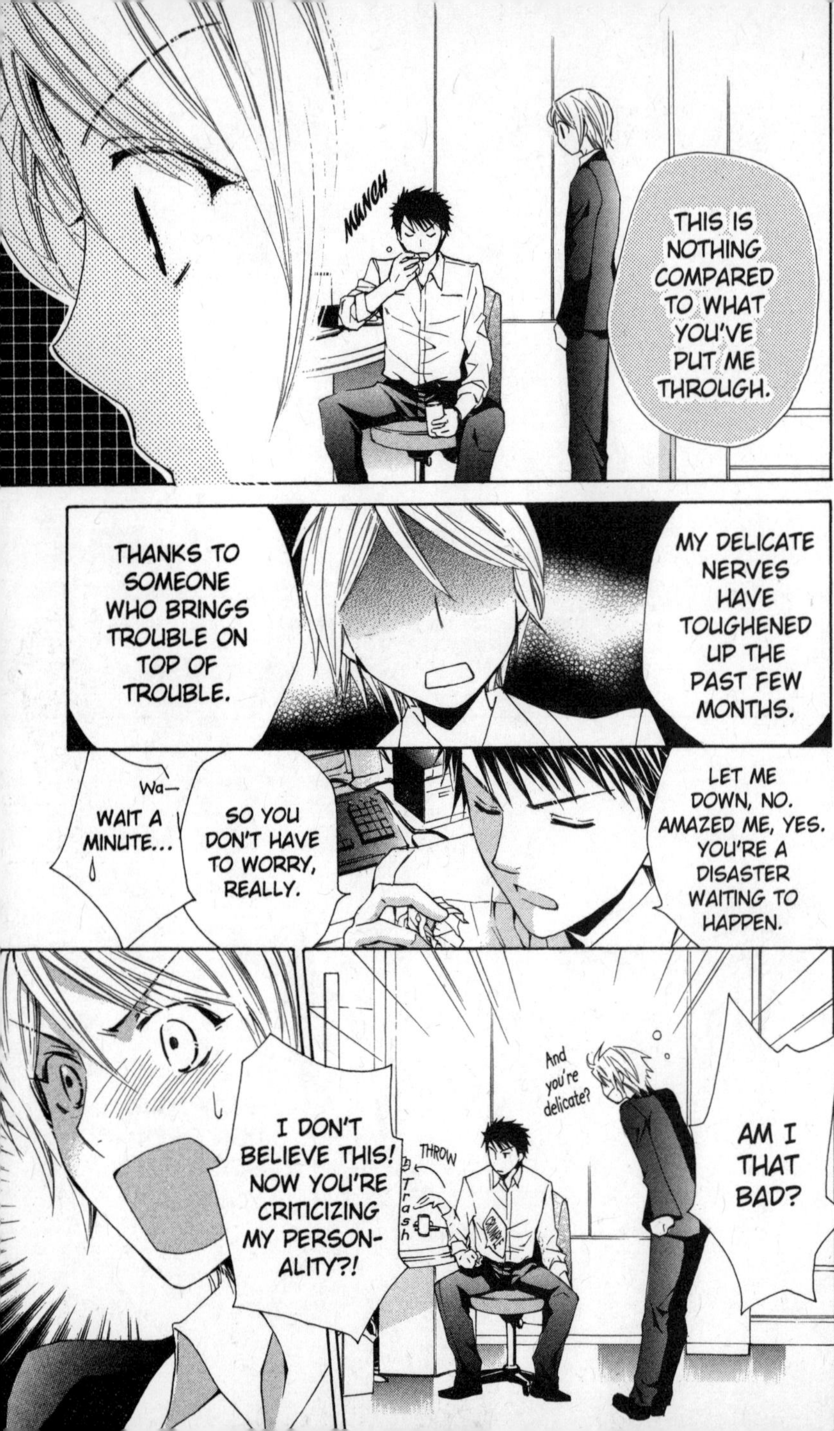
THIS IS NOTHING COMPARED TO WHAT YOU'VE PUT ME THROUGH.
MUNCH
MY DELICATE NERVES HAVE TOUGHENED UP THE PAST FEW MONTHS.
THANKS TO SOMEONE WHO BRINGS TROUBLE ON TOP OF TROUBLE.
LET ME DOWN, NO. AMAZED ME, YES. YOU'RE A DISASTER WAITING TO HAPPEN.
SO YOU DON'T HAVE TO WORRY, REALLY.
Wa—
WAIT A MINUTE...
AM I THAT BAD?
And you're delicate?
THROW
Trash
I DON'T BELIEVE THIS! NOW YOU'RE CRITICIZING MY PERSON-ALITY?!

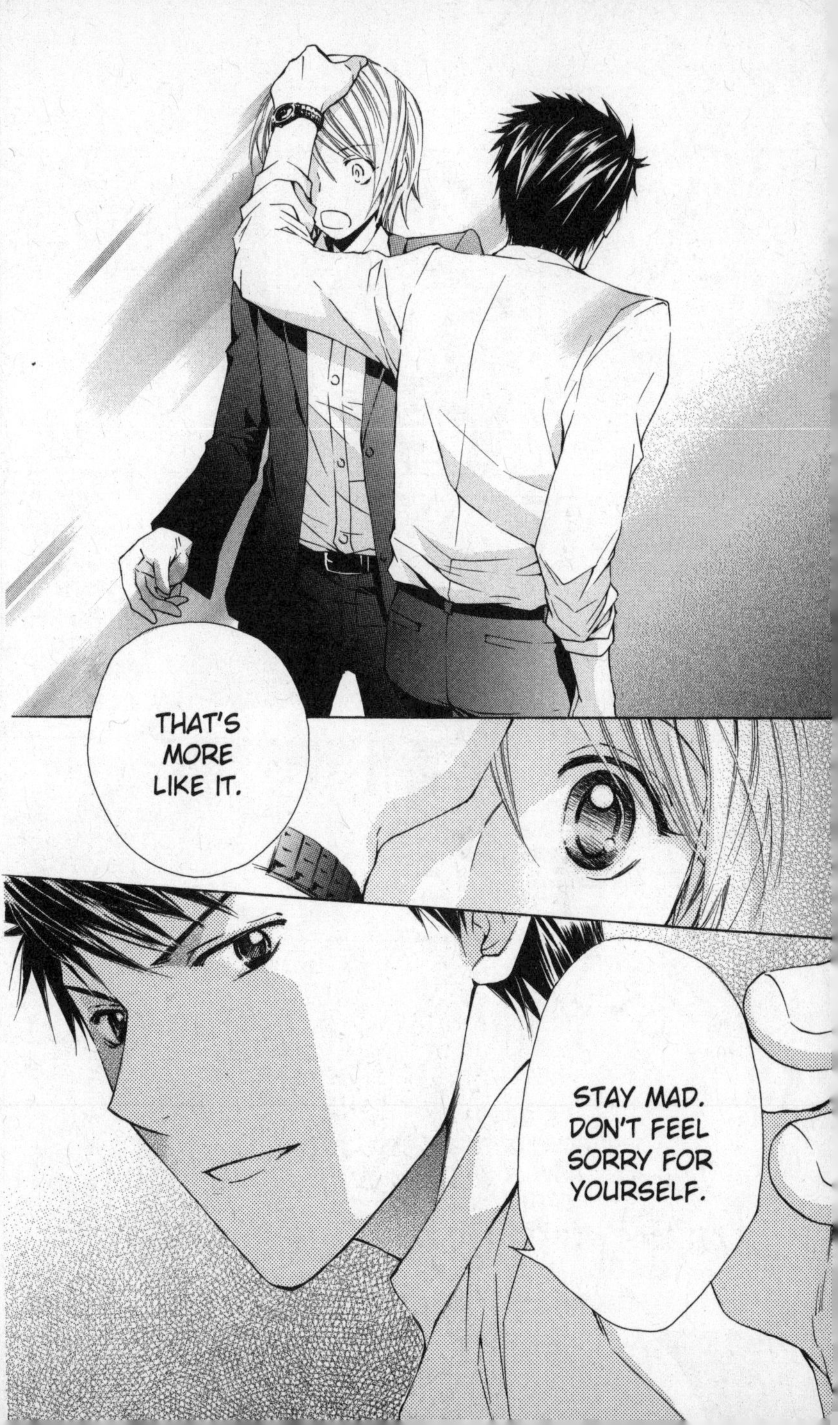
THAT'S MORE LIKE IT.
STAY MAD. DON'T FEEL SORRY FOR YOURSELF.

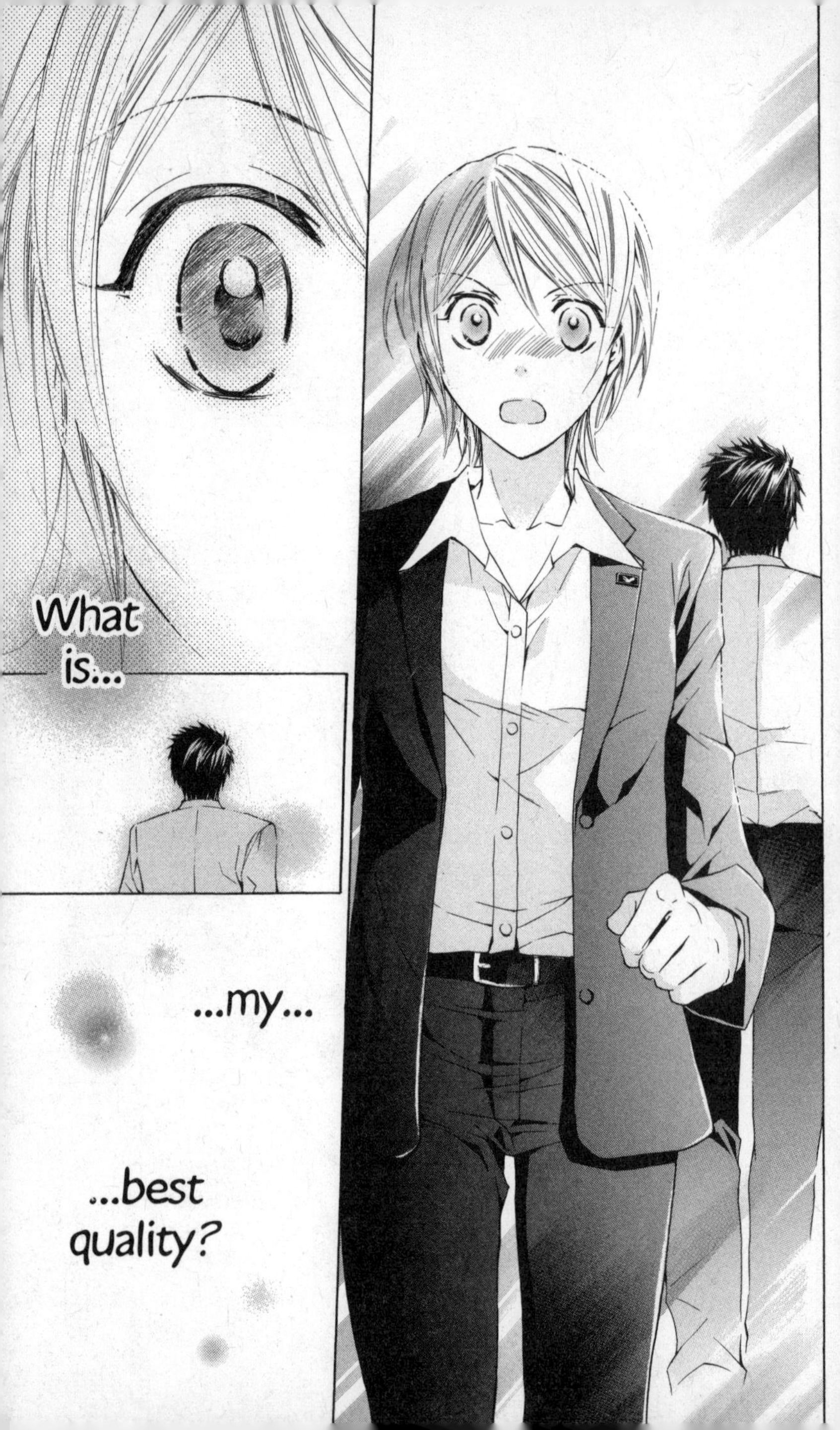
What is...
...my...
...best quality?

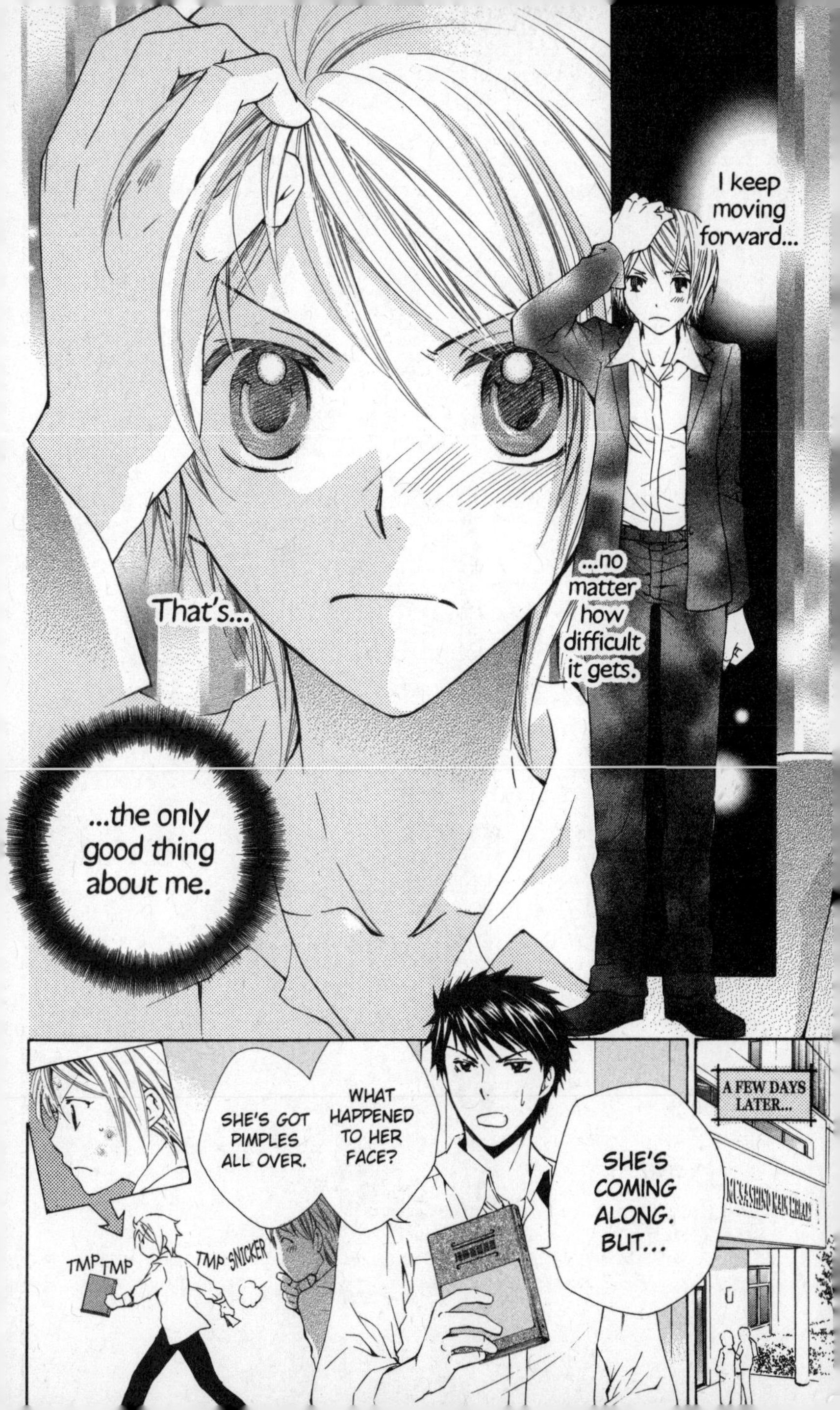
I keep moving forward...
...no matter how difficult it gets.
That's...
...the only good thing about me.
A FEW DAYS LATER...
SHE'S COMING ALONG. BUT...
WHAT HAPPENED TO HER FACE?
SHE'S GOT PIMPLES ALL OVER.
TMP TMP
TMP
SNICKER

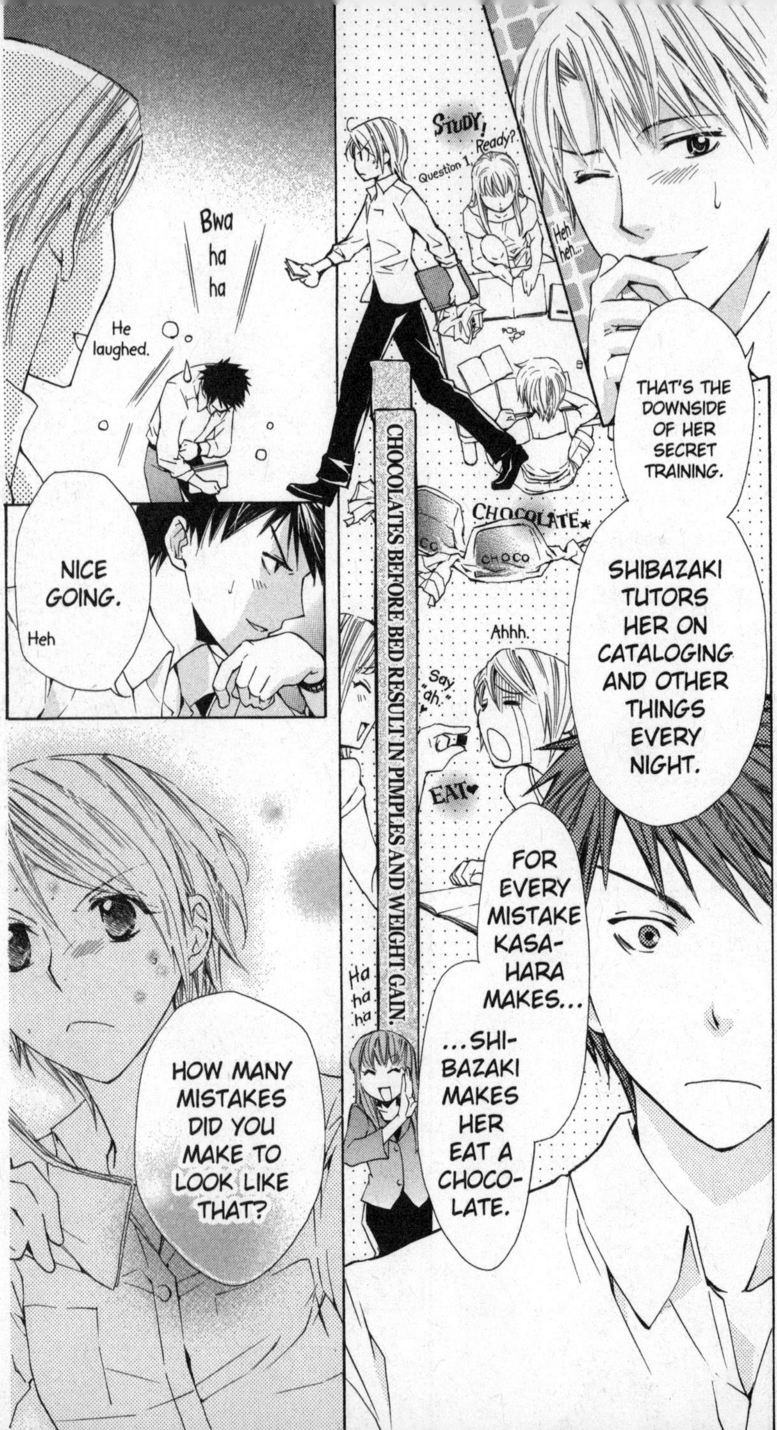
Heh heh...
THAT'S THE DOWNSIDE OF HER SECRET TRAINING.
STUDY!
Ready?
Question 1.
CHOCOLATE★
CHOCO
CO
SHIBAZAKI TUTORS HER ON CATALOGING AND OTHER THINGS EVERY NIGHT.
Ahhh.
Say "ah."
EAT♥
FOR EVERY MISTAKE KASAHARA MAKES...
...SHIBAZAKI MAKES HER EAT A CHOCOLATE.
Ha ha ha
CHOCOLATES BEFORE BED RESULT IN PIMPLES AND WEIGHT GAIN.
Bwa ha ha
He laughed.
NICE GOING.
Heh
HOW MANY MISTAKES DID YOU MAKE TO LOOK LIKE THAT?

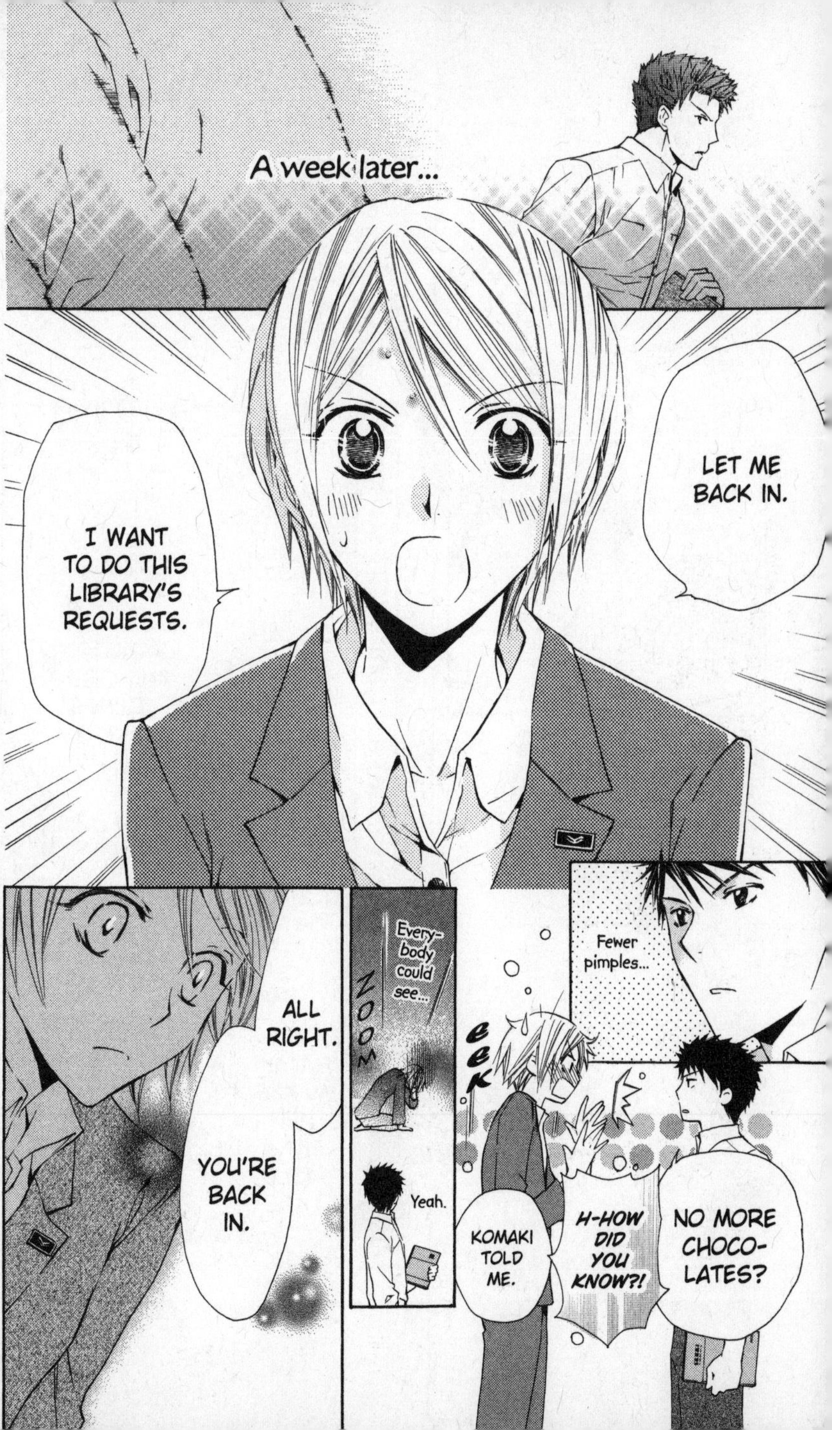
A week later...
LET ME BACK IN.
I WANT TO DO THIS LIBRARY'S REQUESTS.
Fewer pimples...
NO MORE CHOCO-LATES?
eek
H-HOW DID YOU KNOW?!
KOMAKI TOLD ME.
Every-body could see...
ZOOM
Yeah.
ALL RIGHT.
YOU'RE BACK IN.

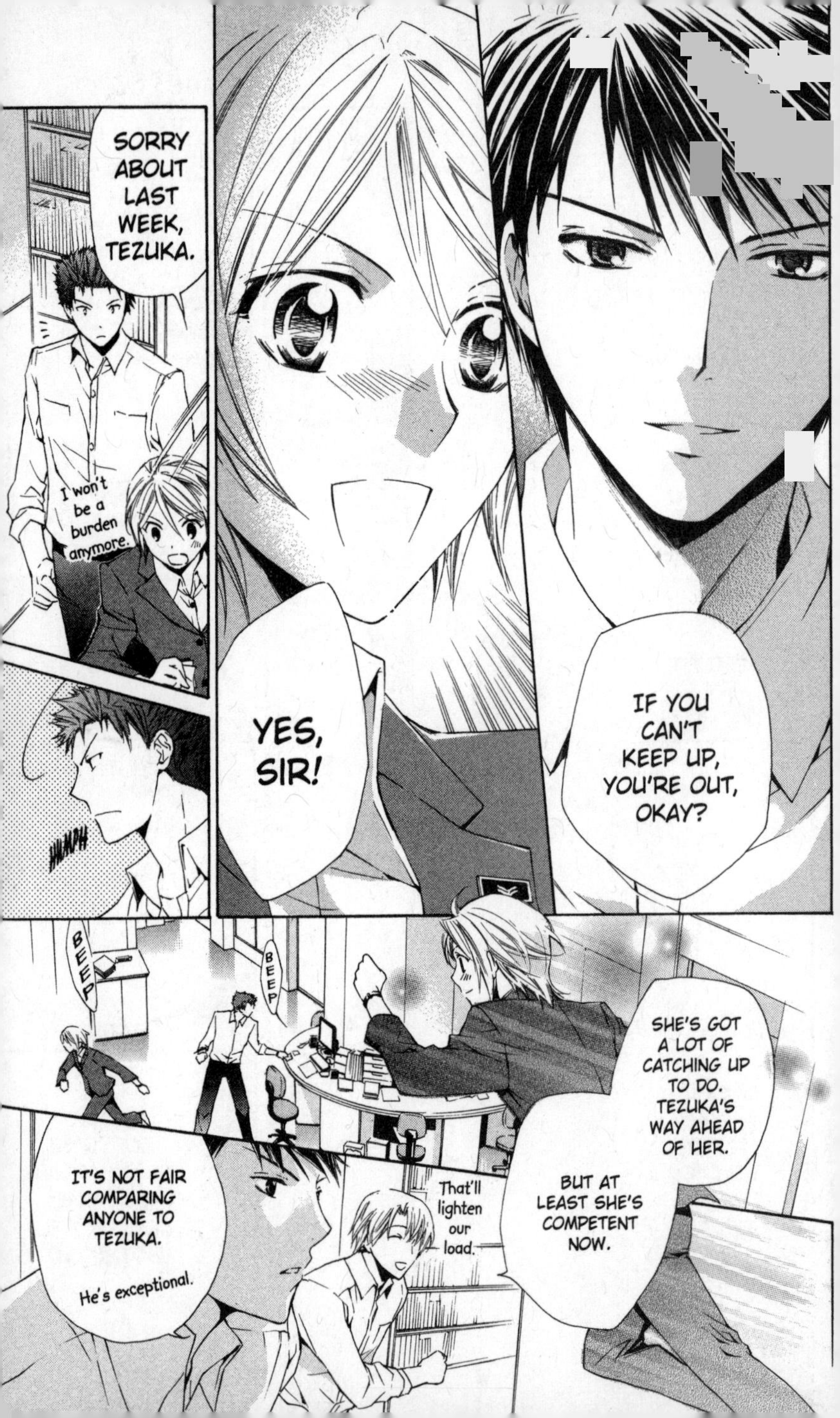
IF YOU CAN'T KEEP UP, YOU'RE OUT, OKAY?
YES, SIR!
SORRY ABOUT LAST WEEK, TEZUKA.
I won't be a burden anymore.
HUMPH
BEEP
BEEP
SHE'S GOT A LOT OF CATCHING UP TO DO. TEZUKA'S WAY AHEAD OF HER.
BUT AT LEAST SHE'S COMPETENT NOW.
That'll lighten our load.
IT'S NOT FAIR COMPARING ANYONE TO TEZUKA.
He's exceptional.

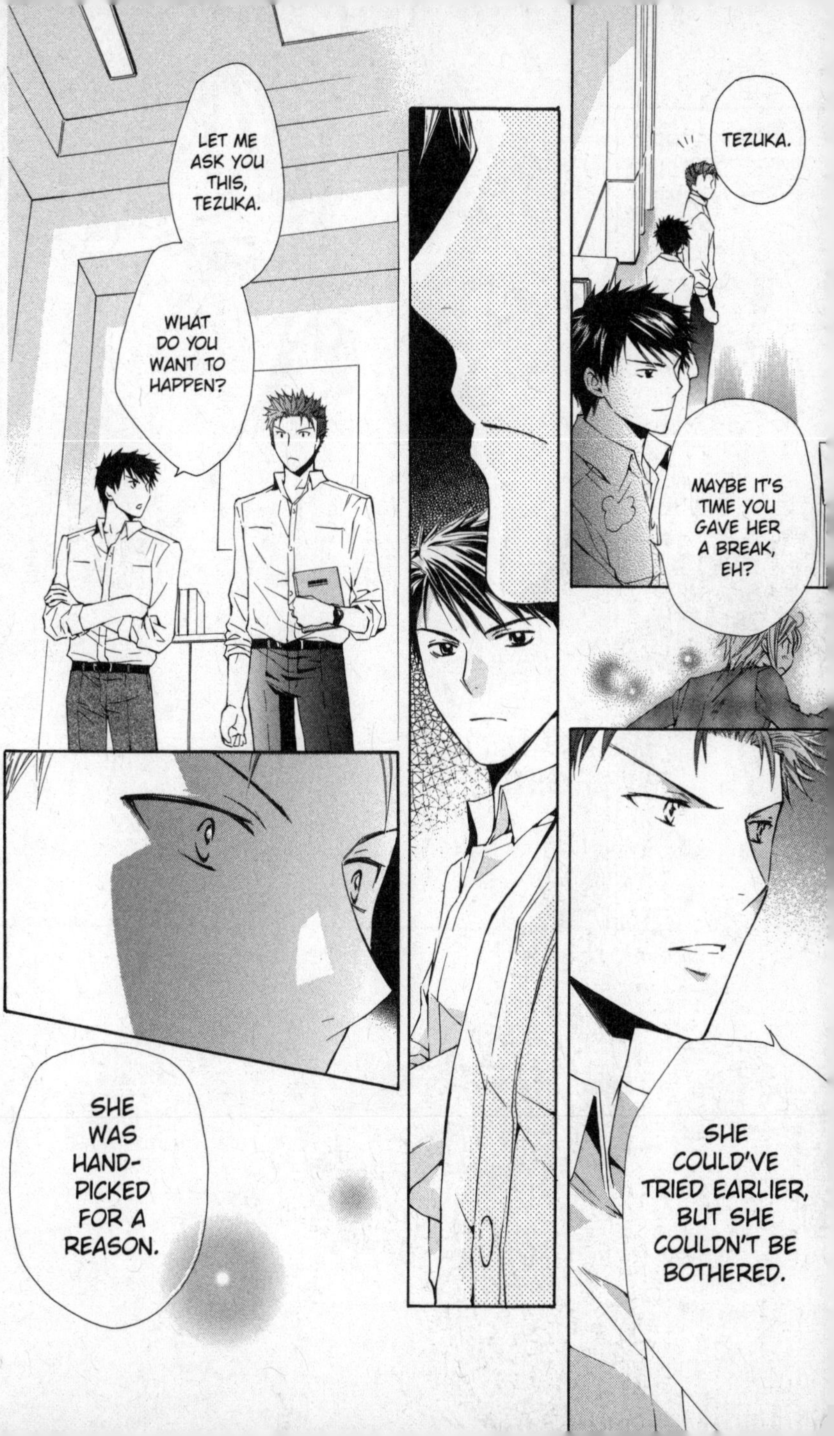
TEZUKA.
MAYBE IT'S TIME YOU GAVE HER A BREAK, EH?
SHE COULD'VE TRIED EARLIER, BUT SHE COULDN'T BE BOTHERED.
LET ME ASK YOU THIS, TEZUKA.
WHAT DO YOU WANT TO HAPPEN?
SHE WAS HAND-PICKED FOR A REASON.

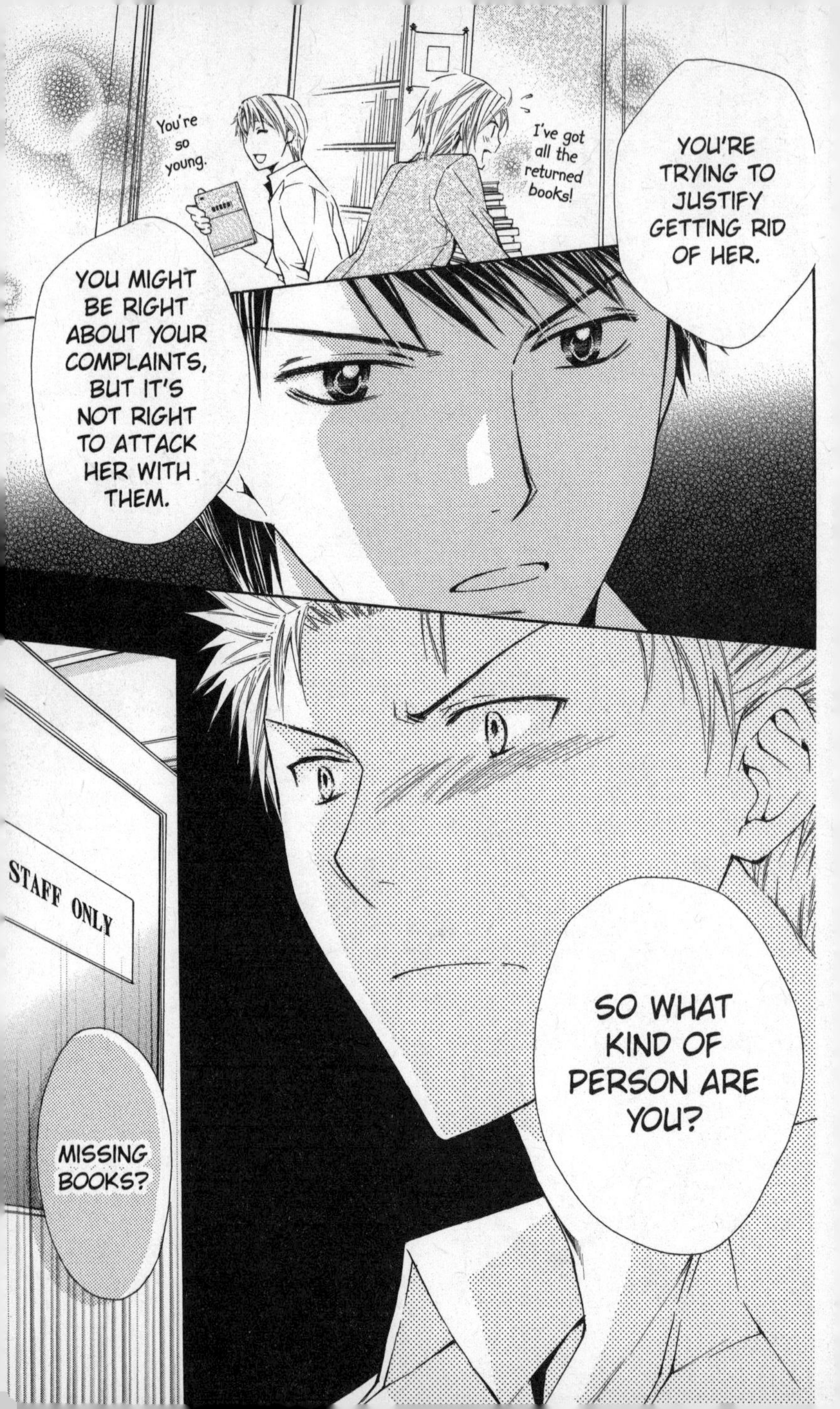
YOU'RE TRYING TO JUSTIFY GETTING RID OF HER.
I've got all the returned books!
You're so young.
YOU MIGHT BE RIGHT ABOUT YOUR COMPLAINTS, BUT IT'S NOT RIGHT TO ATTACK HER WITH THEM.
SO WHAT KIND OF PERSON ARE YOU?
STAFF ONLY
MISSING BOOKS?

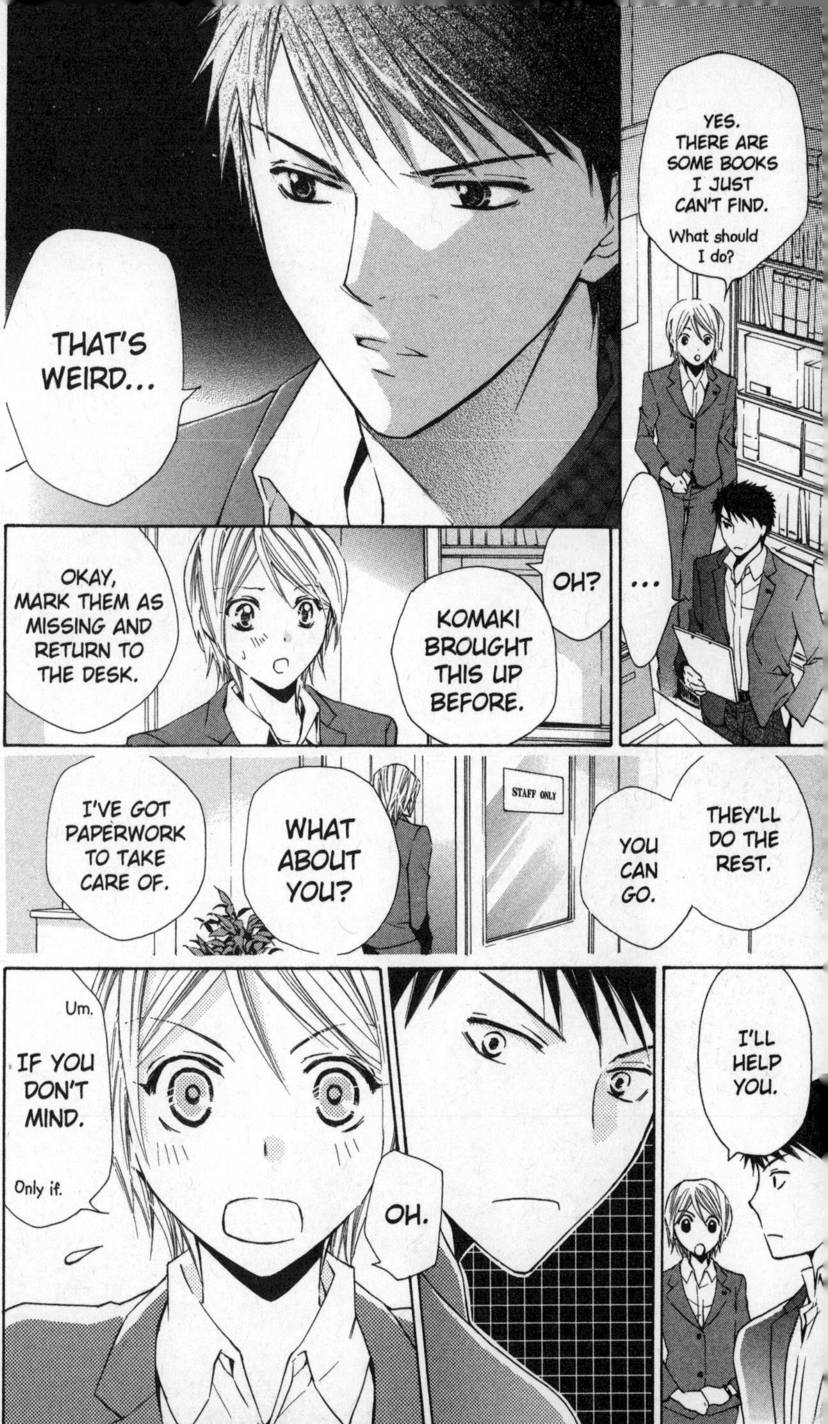
YES. THERE ARE SOME BOOKS I JUST CAN'T FIND.
What should I do?
...
THAT'S WEIRD...
OH?
KOMAKI BROUGHT THIS UP BEFORE.
OKAY, MARK THEM AS MISSING AND RETURN TO THE DESK.
THEY'LL DO THE REST.
YOU CAN GO.
STAFF ONLY
WHAT ABOUT YOU?
I'VE GOT PAPERWORK TO TAKE CARE OF.
I'LL HELP YOU.
OH.
Um.
IF YOU DON'T MIND.
Only if.

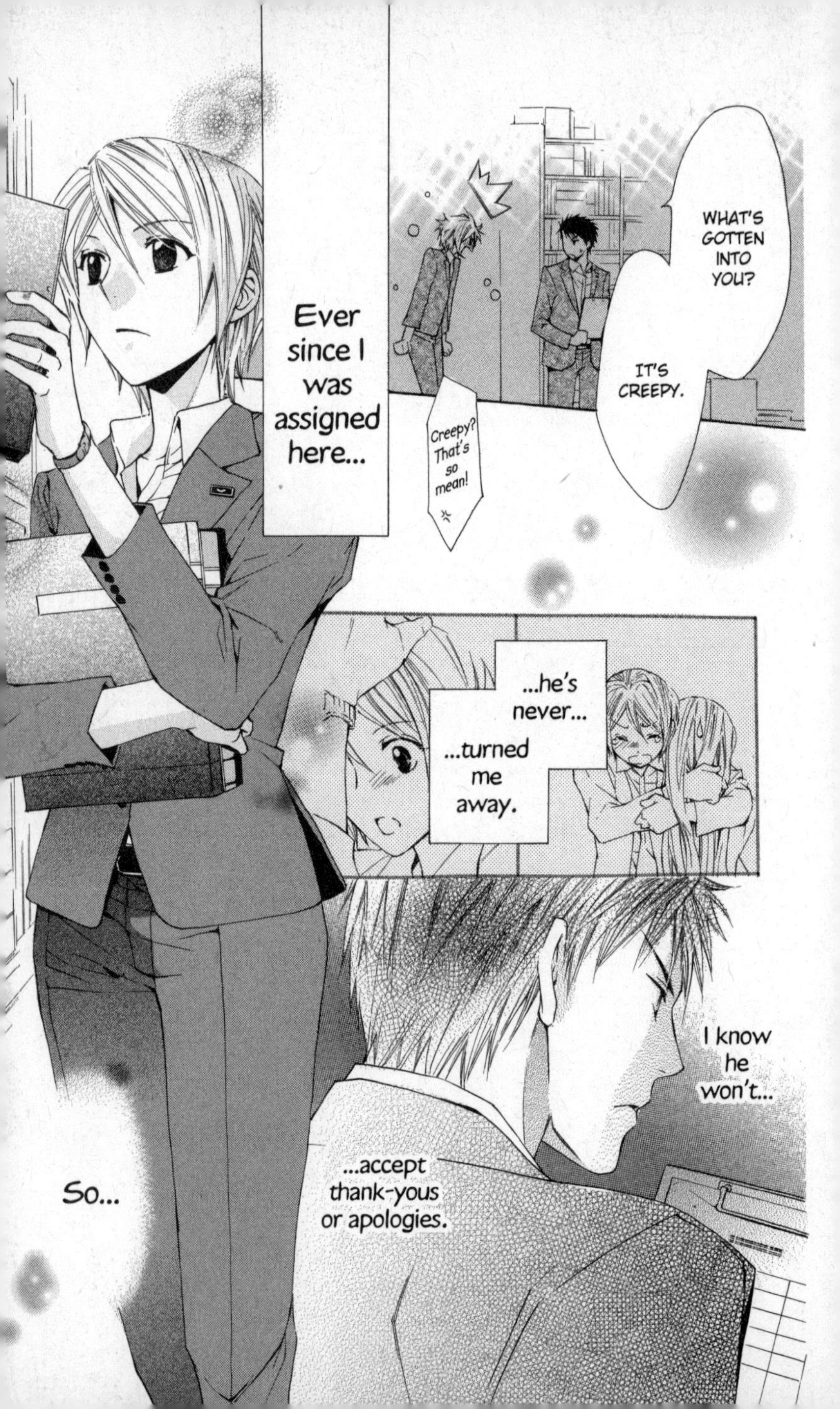

WHAT'S GOTTEN INTO YOU?
IT'S CREEPY.
Creepy? That's so mean!
Ever since I was assigned here...
...he's never...
...turned me away.
I know he won't...
...accept thank-yous or apologies.
So...

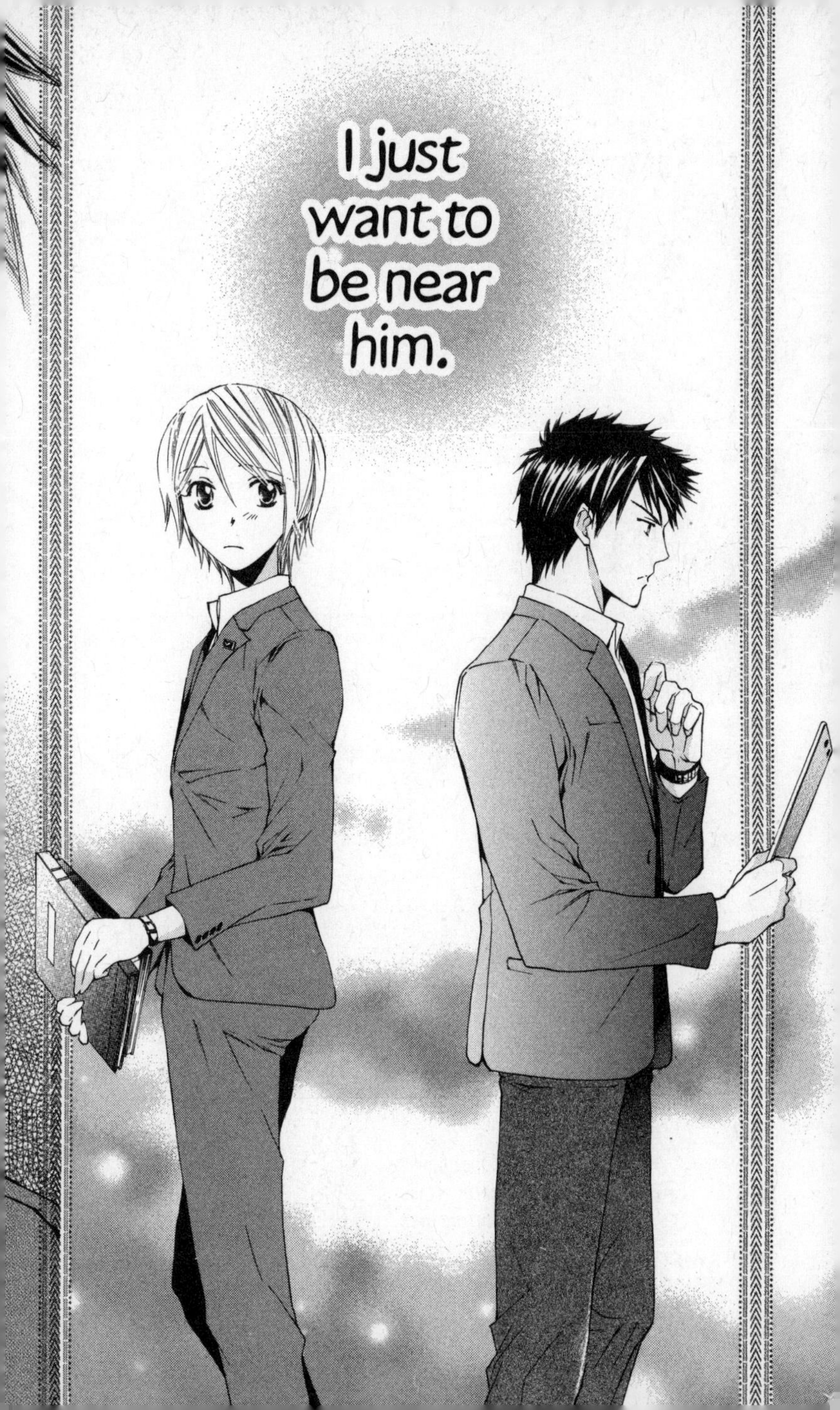
I just want to be near him.

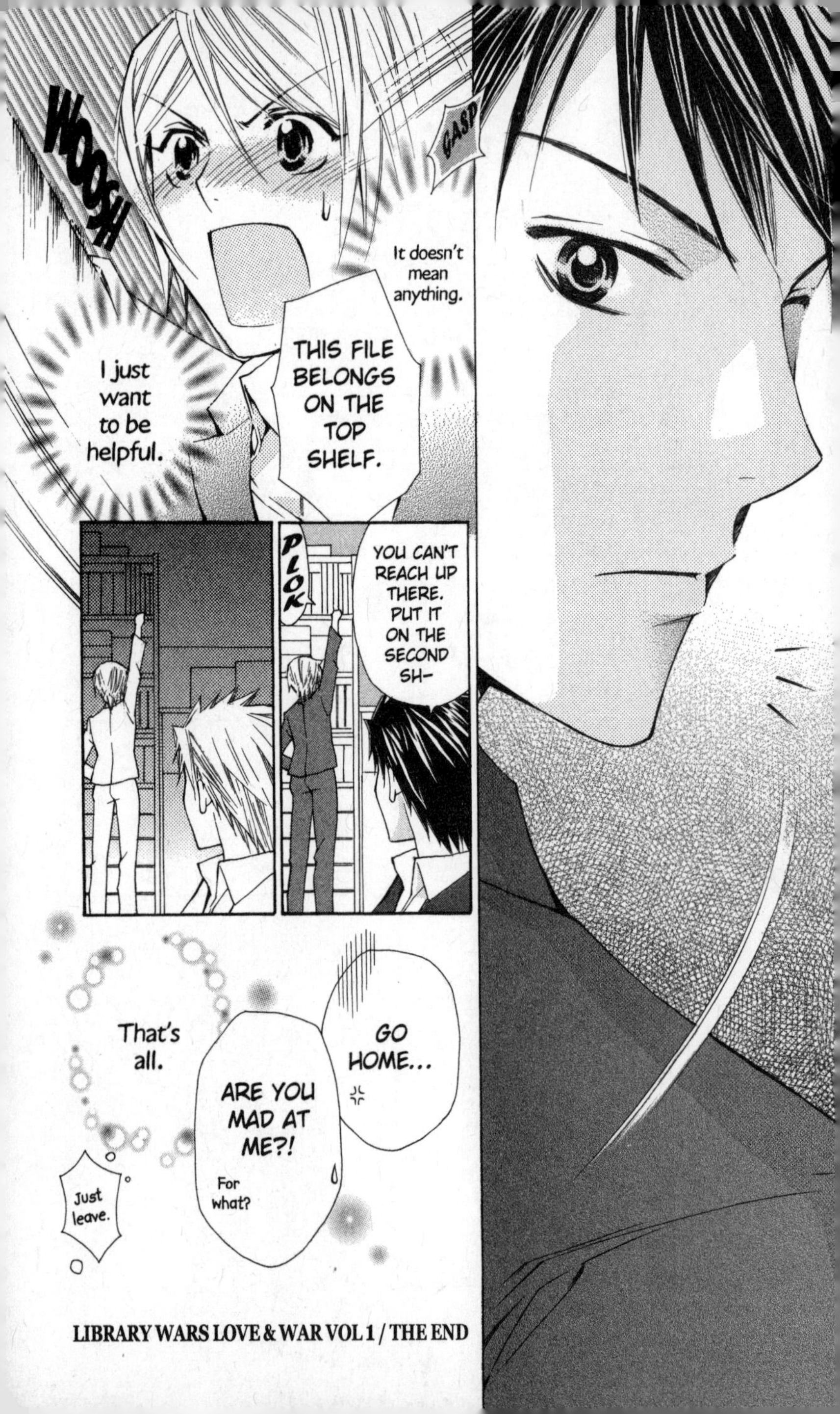
GASP
WOOSH
It doesn't mean anything.
THIS FILE BELONGS ON THE TOP SHELF.
I just want to be helpful.
PLOK
YOU CAN'T REACH UP THERE. PUT IT ON THE SECOND SH-
GO HOME...
ARE YOU MAD AT ME?!
For what?
That's all.
Just leave.

LIBRARY WARS LOVE & WAR VOL 1 / THE END

☆ BONUS MANGA ☆

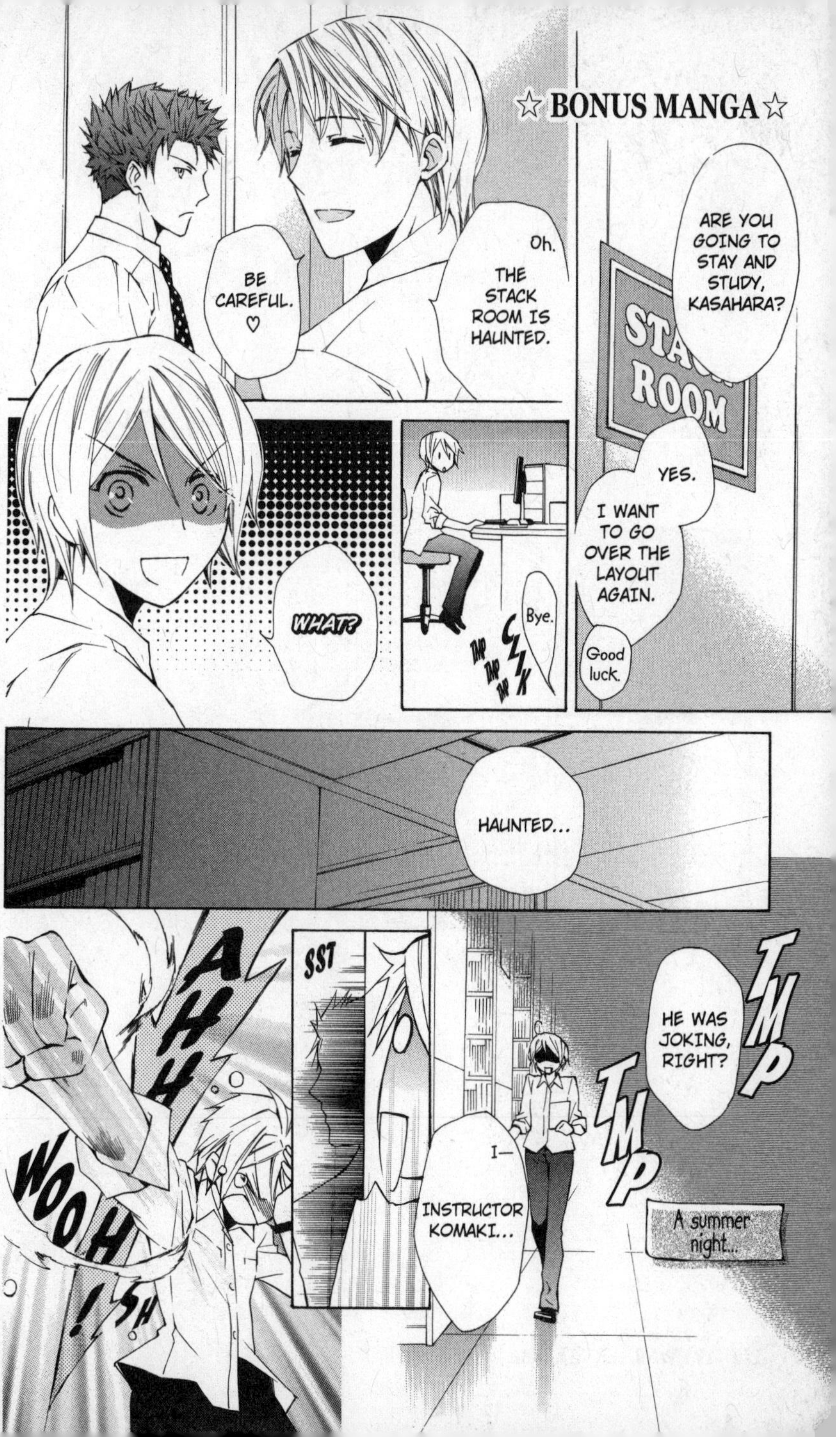
ARE YOU GOING TO STAY AND STUDY, KASAHARA?
STACK ROOM
YES.
I WANT TO GO OVER THE LAYOUT AGAIN.
Good luck.
Oh.
THE STACK ROOM IS HAUNTED.
BE CAREFUL. ♡
Bye.
CLIK
TAP TAP TAP
WHAT?
HAUNTED...
A summer night...
HE WAS JOKING, RIGHT?
TMP
TMP
I—
INSTRUCTOR KOMAKI...
SST
AHHH
WOOH!
SH

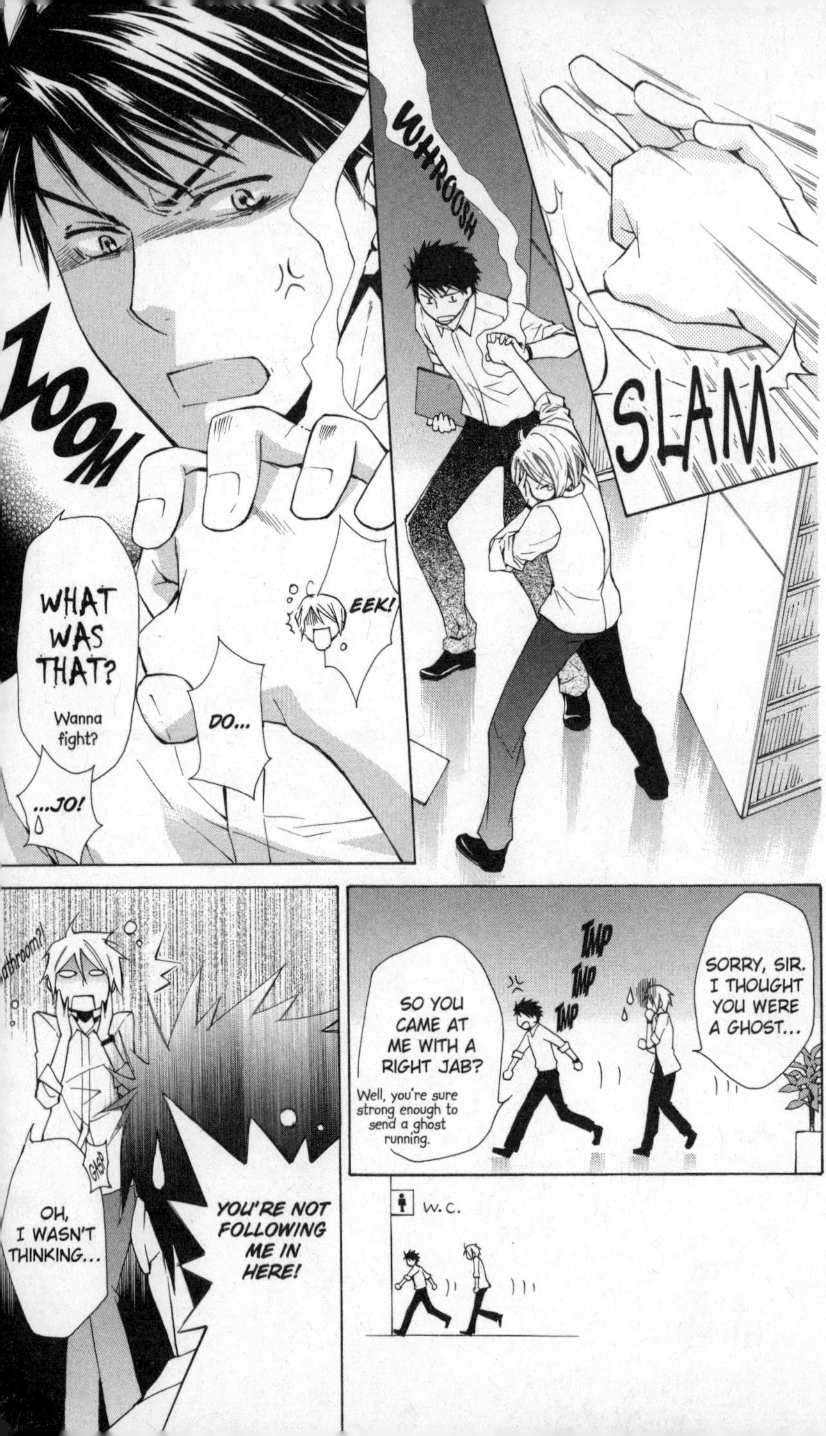

SLAM
WHROOSH
EEK!
DO...
WHAT WAS THAT?
Wanna fight?
ZOOM
...JO!
SORRY, SIR. I THOUGHT YOU WERE A GHOST...
TMP TMP TMP
SO YOU CAME AT ME WITH A RIGHT JAB?
Well, you're sure strong enough to send a ghost running.
W.C.
YOU'RE NOT FOLLOWING ME IN HERE!
GASP
OH, I WASN'T THINKING...

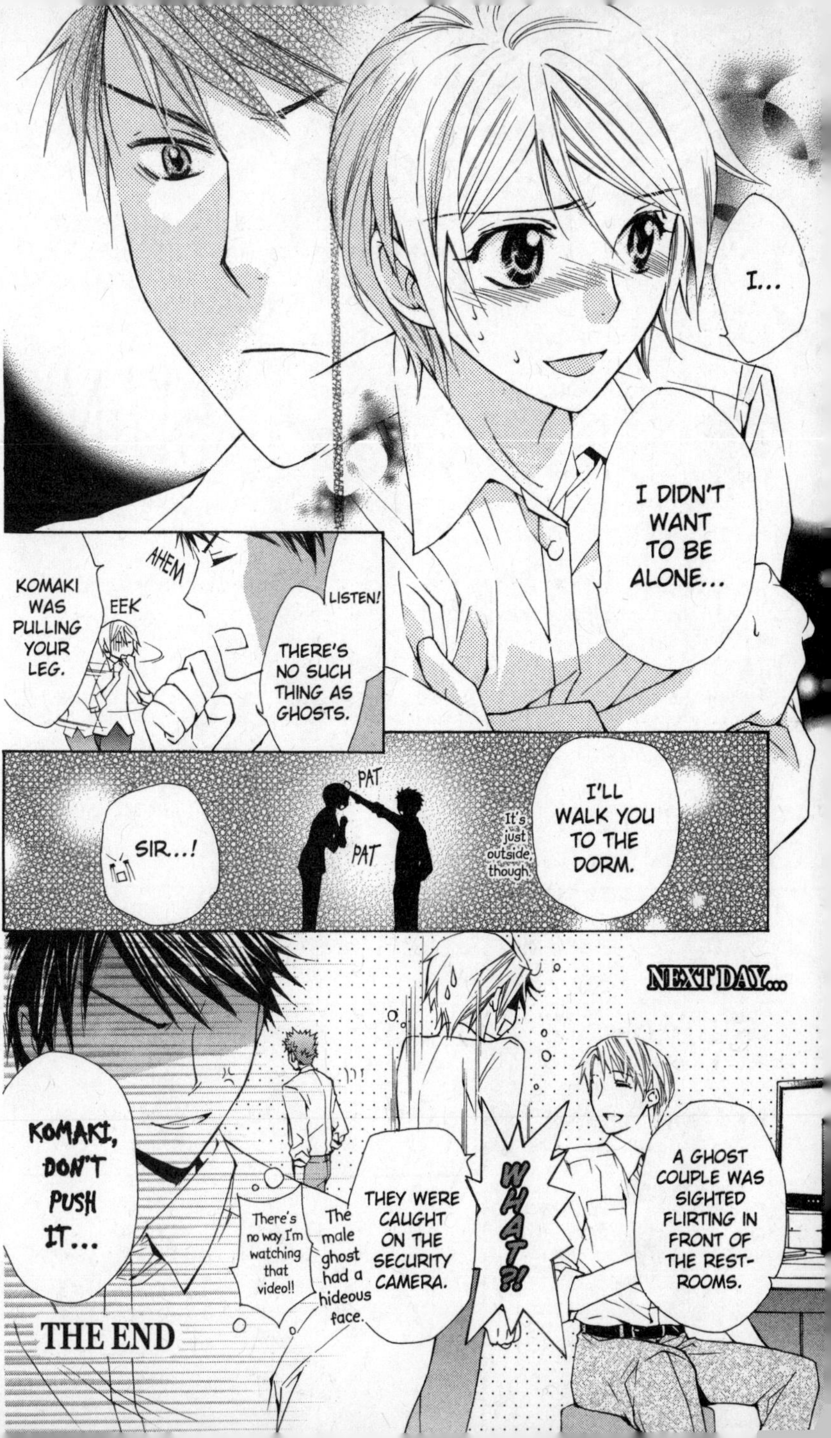
I...
I DIDN'T WANT TO BE ALONE...
AHEM
LISTEN!
THERE'S NO SUCH THING AS GHOSTS.
EEK
KOMAKI WAS PULLING YOUR LEG.
I'LL WALK YOU TO THE DORM.
It's just outside, though.
PAT
PAT
SIR...!
NEXT DAY...
A GHOST COUPLE WAS SIGHTED FLIRTING IN FRONT OF THE REST-ROOMS.
WHAT?!
THEY WERE CAUGHT ON THE SECURITY CAMERA.
The male ghost had a hideous face.
There's no way I'm watching that video!!
KOMAKI, DON'T PUSH IT...
THE END

Message from Hiro Arikawa

When we first saw Ms. Yumi's artwork, we instantly knew we had the right artist. She captured the right essence for every character. The manga is based on the original novels, but she brought a fresh perspective to it. I mean, my editor and I should be the ones most familiar with the series, but I was surprised by a lot of things.

I got to enjoy the first volume before anyone else, even the readers. Ms. Yumi reorganized the whole plot after thoroughly reading all the novels. So her version is really exciting for me to read. As the original author, I know where the story is going, but Ms. Yumi keeps it fresh and unpredictable. Sometimes she's bold, but the story never loses its consistency, which requires a perfect grasp of the plot.

I wondered how she did it, and then I heard she liked watching movies. I see a lot of movies, old and new. So I know that writing a novel is very close to building tension in a movie. Manga artists know this too.

Keiichi Shigusawa from Mediaworks bought the *LaLa* issue with the first chapter. He said he loved every minute of it! Even though it wasn't my work, I was so thrilled to hear that.

Mr. Shigusawa said, "I like Dojo's duality. He's harsh to Iku but actually cares about her."

"Really? You don't mean Iku?! She's like that too."

"It's Dojo! I'm going to subscribe to *Lala* for Dojo! There're several other manga series I want to follow too."

So he added *Lala* to his reading list. I'm sure he keeps up with *Library Wars: Love & War*.

Ms. Yumi. I am looking forward to seeing how you're going to surprise me!

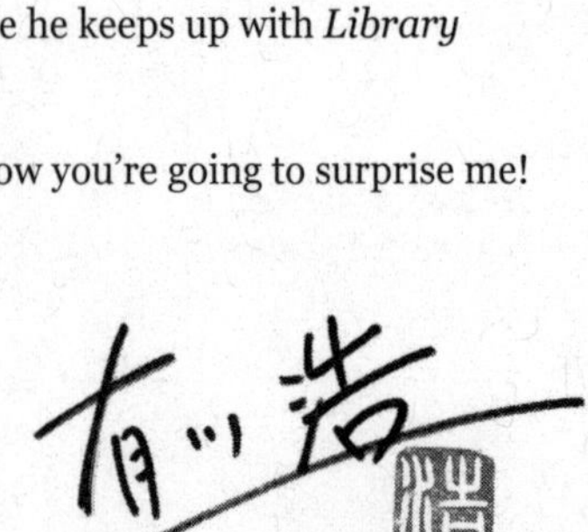

Hiroshi Arikawa

Special Thanks!!!

Ms. Arikawa.
Ms. Arikawa's Editors (Mediaworks)

★

Mamada, Murakami

★

Ootsuka, Ogata, Saito,
Tanaka, Nonaka,
Hariyama, Masuko

★

My family

★

My editor

★
★
★

Readers
I cannot thank you enough.

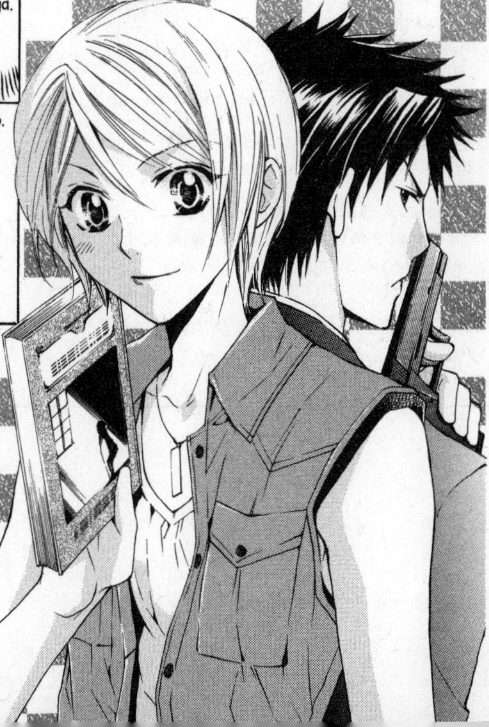

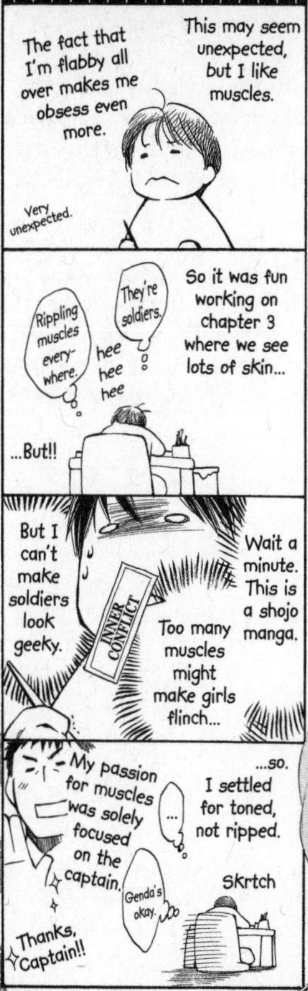
This may seem unexpected, but I like muscles.
The fact that I'm flabby all over makes me obsess even more.
Very unexpected.
So it was fun working on chapter 3 where we see lots of skin...
They're soldiers.
Rippling muscles everywhere.
hee hee hee
...But!!
Wait a minute. This is a shojo manga.
Too many muscles might make girls flinch...
INNER CONFLICT
But I can't make soldiers look geeky.
...so. I settled for toned, not ripped.
...
Skrtch
Genda's okay.
My passion for muscles was solely focused on the captain.
Thanks, Captain!!

Hope to see you in the next volume.

Kiiro Yumi きいろ.

End notes

Page 10, panel 1: Seika 31
In Japan, years are often identified by eras
rather than the Western calendar. For example,
2010 is Heisei 22, or the 22nd year of the
reign of the emperor Akihito. Seika is a
fictional era name placed in the near future.

Page 10, panel 1: Kanto
A region of Japan that includes Tokyo.

Page 15, panel 1: Musashino
A suburb of Tokyo.

Page 17, panel 2: Army
The armed forces of Japan are actually called
the SDF, or Self-Defense Forces, and until
recently were only active in Japan and not
deployed abroad.

Page 24, panel 1: Ude Hishigi
The most powerful armlock in various martial
arts, including judo.

Page 127, panel 2: Honshu, moon bear
Honshu is the largest and main Japanese
island. Black Asiatic bears (*Ursus thibetanus*)
are also called "moon bears" because of the
white crescent-shaped marking on their chests.

Page 150, panel 1: Japanese Decimal System
The Nippon Decimal System or Nippon
Decimal Classification is based on the
Dewey Decimal System.

Page 184, panel 6: A summer night
Summer is a popular time for ghost stories
in Japan.

Kiiro Yumi won the 42nd *LaLa* Manga Grand Prix Fresh Debut award for her manga *Billy Bocchan no Yuutsu* (Little Billy's Depression). Her latest series is *Toshokan Senso Love&War* (*Library Wars: Love & War*), which runs in *LaLa* magazine in Japan and is published in English by VIZ Media.

Hiro Arikawa won the 10th Dengeki Novel Prize for her work *Shio no Machi: Wish on My Precious* in 2003, and debuted with the same novel in 2004. Of her many works, Arikawa is best known for the *Library Wars* series and her *Jieitai Sanbusaku* trilogy which consists of *Sora no Naka* (In the Sky), *Umi no Soko* (The Bottom of the Sea), and *Shio no Machi* (City of Salt).